DICTIONARY OF
CHEMISTRY

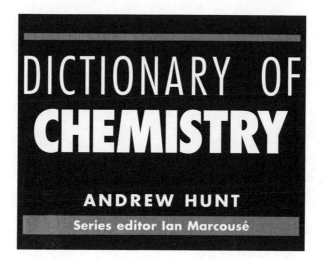

DICTIONARY OF
CHEMISTRY

ANDREW HUNT

Series editor Ian Marcousé

FITZROY DEARBORN PUBLISHERS
LONDON · CHICAGO

Copyright © 1998, 1999 Andrew Hunt

This edition based on *The Complete A-Z Chemistry Handbook*, first published in the United Kingdom by Hodder and Stoughton Educational, 1998

Published in the United States of America by
Fitzroy Dearborn Publishers
919 North Michigan Avenue
Chicago, Illinois 60611
USA

A Cataloging-in-Publication Record is available from the Library of Congress

ISBN 1-57958-140-4

First published in the USA 1999

Typeset by GreenGate Publishing Services, Tonbridge, England and Alacrity, Banwell Castle, Weston-super-Mare, England

Printed in the UK by Antony Rowe Ltd., Chippenham, UK

PREFACE

The *Dictionary of Chemistry* is an alphabetical text designed for ease of use. Entries begin with one-sentence definitions that explain why the terms are important. These are followed by fuller explanations and examples, together with diagrams, tables and equations. Words in italics are cross-references to other entries in the book.

This concise, alphabetical book makes it easy for you to find the explanations, information and examples that you need when studying a new topic. Worked examples show you how to tackle the calculations.

Entries include many aspects of practical and applied chemistry, including both analytical chemistry and organic preparations. Furthermore, the book explains some of the terms in more specialist areas so it will help you to get started on topics such as spectroscopy, environmental chemistry and biochemistry.

Some entries give you an overview of important topics and help you to link ideas. Key terms such as inorganic chemistry, organic chemistry, physical chemistry, the chemical industry and qualitative analysis tell you about the main features of important aspects of chemistry, with cross-references leading to related terms in each field. Other overview entries give a historical perspective, showing in outline how important themes of chemistry have developed. Examples are atomic theory, biochemistry, environmental chemistry and polymer chemistry. There is a tradition in chemistry of naming theories, processes and reactions after the scientists who developed them. Here you find out some of the background to the names you are likely to meet.

Andrew Hunt

ACKNOWLEDGMENTS

First I thank Geoffrey Barraclough who read and checked the whole book.

Secondly I thank Ian Marcousé, the series editor, and three experienced chemistry teachers: Rod Clough, Jeffrey Hancock and Ted Lister, who read early drafts. Their wise comments helped me to develop the content and style of this book.

Thirdly I thank Tim Gregson-Williams of Hodder & Stoughton, London, David Mackin of GreenGate Publishing Services and all the people who work with them. Their skill and determination made it possible for this book to be produced in less than a year.

Finally I thank all the people I have worked with while contributing to the Nuffield Advanced Chemistry, SATIS 16–19, Salters Advanced Chemistry and Nuffield Science in Practice projects. Writing and editing for these projects has clarified my understanding of chemical ideas and taught me much about the importance of chemistry in our lives.

The publishers would like to thank the following for permission to reproduce illustrations in this book:

(page 74) from *Science for Understanding Tomorrow's World: Global Change for Education*, with permission of the International Council for Science, 51, Bd. de Montmorency, 75016 Paris, France.

(page 78, bottom) from *Salters' Advanced Chemistry, Chemical Storylines* by Salters, with permission of Heinemann Educational Publishers, a division of Reed Educational & Professional Publishing Ltd.

While every effort has been made to contact copyright holders, any omissions brought to our attention will be remedied in future printings.

A_r *A_r* is the symbol for *relative atomic mass*.

absolute zero (0 K) is the temperature at which atoms and molecules in crystals are effectively motionless. It is the lowest temperature on the absolute or *kelvin* temperature scale. A plot of the *volume* of a sample of gas against temperature at constant pressure is a straight line that on extrapolation cuts the temperature axis at $-273.15°C$.

Gases appear to behave as if they would have zero volume at absolute zero. This would be true of a nonexistent *ideal gas* but in practice real gases turn to liquids and solids and occupy a definite volume before absolute zero is reached.

Absolute zero is now defined precisely by setting the *triple point* of water at 273.16 K.

absorbance shows how strongly a sample absorbs radiation. Absorbance measures the extent of absorption of *electromagnetic radiation* by a sample in a spectrometer or by *colorimetry*.

Absorbance, A is defined by this relationship: $A = \lg \dfrac{I_0}{I_S}$

where lg is the *logarithm* to base 10. I_0 is the intensity of the radiation beam after passing through the reference, which is typically the solvent used to dissolve the material being examined. I_S is the intensity of the beam after passing through the sample.

The advantage of this definition of absorbance is that it is proportional to the concentration of the absorbing molecule or ion in a solution.

absorption of liquids and gases happens when a *fluid* soaks into the pores of a material, like water soaking into a sponge. Absorption should be carefully distinguished from *adsorption*.

absorption of radiation: when *electromagnetic radiation* passes through a material some or all of the wavelengths of the radiation may be absorbed. When white light passes through a red filter, for example, all the wavelengths are absorbed except for red, which passes through – so it looks red.

The gases in the *atmosphere* absorb most of the radiation reaching the Earth from the Sun.

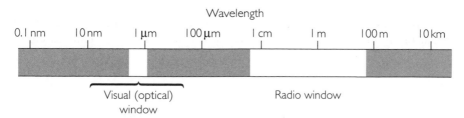

The bands of wavelengths in the electromagnetic spectrum of sunlight that can pass through the Earth's atmosphere to reach the surface of the Earth. It is as if there are two "windows" letting through bands of radiation while all other wavelengths are shut out (by absorption).

Ozone in the upper atmosphere helps to protect living things by absorbing harmful *ultraviolet radiation*. Chemists use *spectroscopy* to study the absorption of radiation. From an *absorption spectrum* they can make deductions about the composition and structure of the sample.

absorption spectrum: a plot showing how strongly a sample absorbs radiation over a range of frequencies. Absorption spectra from *infrared spectroscopy* and *ultraviolet spectroscopy* give chemists valuable information about the composition and structure of chemicals.

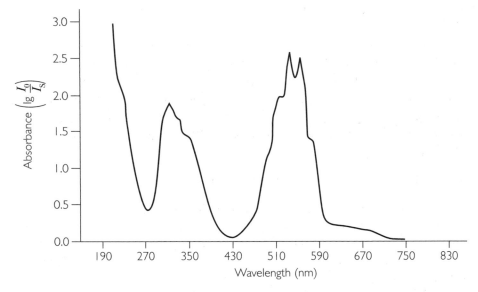

Absorption spectrum of potassium manganate(VII) in the ultraviolet and visible regions

accuracy of data is determined by the agreement between a measured quantity and the correct value. In chemical analysis the correct value is often not known and so chemists need to estimate the *errors of measurement* that may have affected their results and set *confidence limits* on the values they quote.

acid anhydrides are related to *carboxylic acids*. The *functional group* in an anhydride is formed by eliminating a molecule of water from two carboxylic acid groups. Sometimes this happens simply on heating the acid but generally anhydrides are made in other ways.

Acid anhydrides are acylating agents that react in a similar way as *acyl chlorides* with water, alcohols and amines. Anhydrides are less reactive than acyl chlorides and so

$$CH_3-C \overset{O}{\underset{O}{\diagdown}} \quad \xrightarrow[\text{water}]{+H_2O} \quad 2CH_3CO_2H$$
$$CH_3-C \underset{O}{\diagup} \qquad\qquad \text{ethanoic acid}$$

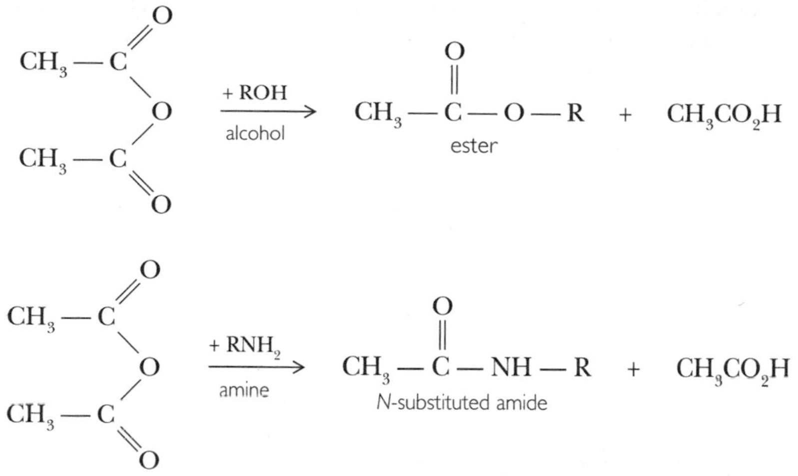

Reactions of ethanoic anhydride

are often preferred for laboratory and industrial syntheses. Their reactions may require heating under reflux (see *reflux condenser*).

acid–base equilibria are equilibrium systems involving *acid–base reactions.* Acid–base reactions are *reversible.* This is illustrated by a solution of an *ammonium salt* in water.

$$\underset{\text{acid 1}}{NH_4^+(aq)} + \underset{\text{base 2}}{H_2O(l)} \rightleftharpoons \underset{\text{base 1}}{NH_3(aq)} + \underset{\text{acid 2}}{H_3O^+(aq)}$$

There is competition for *protons* (hydrogen ions) between ammonia molecules and water molecules. On the left-hand side of the equation the protons are held by *lone pairs of electrons* on the ammonia molecules. On the right-hand side they are held by lone pairs on water molecules.

The *equilibrium law* applies. The position of equilibrium is determined by the value of the equilibrium constant for the reaction. For the example in the equation, the relevant equilibrium constant is the *acid dissociation constant* for the ammonium ion.

The equilibrium involves two conjugate acid–base pairs:

- NH_4^+ and NH_3
- H_3O^+ and H_2O.

An acid turns into its conjugate base when it loses a proton. A base turns into its conjugate acid when it gains a proton.

acid–base indicators are used to show up changes in pH of solutions. Indicators are *weak acids* or *weak bases* that change color when they lose or gain hydrogen ions. When added to a solution an indicator gains or loses protons depending on the *pH* of the solution. It is conventional to represent a weak acid indicator as HIn where In is a shorthand for the rest of the molecule. In water:

$$\underset{\substack{\text{un-ionized}\\\text{indicator}\\\text{color 1}}}{HIn(aq)} + H_2O(l) \rightleftharpoons H_3O^+(aq) + \underset{\substack{\text{indicator after}\\\text{losing a proton}\\\text{color 2}}}{In^-(aq)}$$

Indicators such as phenolphthalein, methyl orange and bromothymol blue change color over a range of pH values and are used to detect the *end point* in *acid–base titrations*.

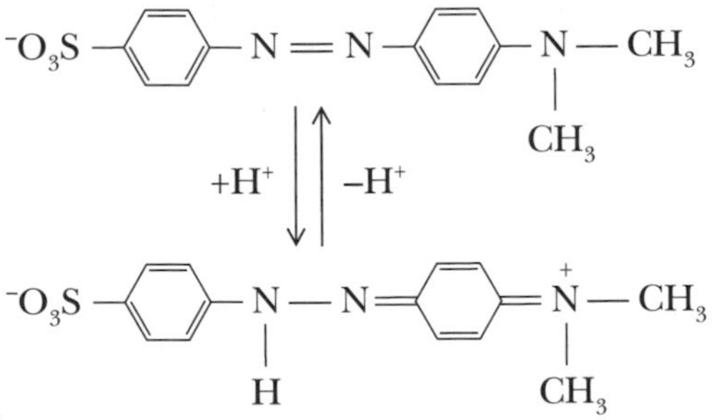

The structures of methyl orange in acid and alkaline solutions. In acid solution the added hydrogen ion (proton) localizes two electrons to form a covalent bond. In alkaline solution the removal of the hydrogen ion allows the two electrons to join the other delocalized electrons. The change in the number of delocalized electrons causes a shift in the peak of the wavelengths of light absorbed, so the color changes and the molecule acts as an indicator.

The pH range over which an indicator changes color is determined by its strength as an acid (or base). Typically the range is given roughly by $pK_a \pm 1$ (see the *Henderson–Hasselbalch equation* for an explanation).

Indicator	pK_a	color change HIn/In⁻	pH range over which color change occurs
methyl orange	3.6	red/yellow	3.2–4.2
methyl red	5.0	yellow/red	4.2–6.3
bromothymol blue	7.1	yellow/blue	6.0–7.6
phenolphthalein	9.4	colorless/red	8.2–10.0

acid–base reactions, according to the *Brønsted–Lowry theory*, are reactions involving the transfer of protons from an *acid* to a *base*.

acid–base titration: a practical technique used to determine the *concentration* of an *acid* or an *alkali*. A *titration* measures the volume of a *standard solution* of alkali or acid needed to react exactly with a measured volume of the unknown solution. The procedure for an acid–base titration is the same as for any other titration but the method for finding the end point is distinctive: the analyst either adds an *acid–base indicator* or uses a pH meter.

Worked example:

Limewater is a saturated solution of calcium hydroxide in water. 25.0 cm³ of 0.04 mol dm⁻³ hydrochloric acid from a burette neutralized 20.0 cm³ of limewater. What was the concentration of the limewater?

Notes on the method

Always start by writing the equation for the reaction. See *titration* for a general method for the calculations.

Remember to convert volumes in cm^3 to volumes in dm^3 by dividing by 1000.

In any titration there is one unknown – in this case the concentration of the limewater, c_A.

Answer

The equation for the reaction is:

$$Ca(OH)_2(aq) + 2HCl(aq) \longrightarrow CaCl_2(aq) + 2H_2O(l)$$

The volume of calcium hydroxide in the flask, $V_A = \dfrac{20.0}{1000}$ dm^3

Let the concentration of calcium hydroxide be c_A.

The volume of hydrochloric acid added from the burette, $V_B = \dfrac{25.0}{1000}$ dm^3

The concentration of hydrochloric acid, $c_B = 0.04$ mol dm^{-3}

$$\frac{V_A \times c_A}{V_B \times c_B} = \frac{n_A}{n_B}$$

$$\frac{^{20.0}\!/_{1000} \times c_A}{^{25.0}\!/_{1000} \times c_B} = \frac{1}{2}$$

Therefore $c_A = \dfrac{25.0 \times 0.04}{2 \times 20.0} = 0.025$ mol dm^{-3}

The concentration of the limewater was 0.025 mol dm^{-3}.

---

acid catalysis: any reaction speeded up by an acid *catalyst*. One example is the acid-catalyzed *hydrolysis* of *esters* to give a *carboxylic acid* and an *alcohol*. All the chemicals are in the same solution so this is an example of *homogeneous catalysis*.

acid dissociation constants measure the strength of acids. They show the extent to which acids dissociate into ions in solution. Acid dissociation constants are used to compare the strengths of relatively *weak acids*, which are only partly ionized in solution.

For a weak acid represented by the formula HA:

$$HA(aq) + H_2O(l) \rightleftharpoons H_3O^+(aq) + A^-(aq)$$

According to the *equilibrium law*, the equilibrium constant,

$$K_c = \frac{[H_3O^+(aq)][A^-(aq)]}{[HA(aq)][H_2O(l)]}$$

In dilute solution the concentration of water is effectively constant, so the expression can be written in this form:

$$K_a = \frac{[H_3O^+(aq)][A^-(aq)]}{[HA(aq)]}, \text{ where } K_a \text{ is the acid dissociation constant}$$

Acid	K_a/mol dm^{-3}	
nitric(III) acid (nitrous acid), HNO$_2$	4.7×10^{-4}	stronger
methanoic acid, HCO$_2$H	1.6×10^{-4}	
ethanoic acid, CH$_3$CO$_2$H	1.7×10^{-5}	
chloric(I) acid, HOCl	3.7×10^{-8}	
phenol, C$_6$H$_5$OH	1.3×10^{-10}	weaker

Worked example:

Calculate the hydrogen ion concentration and the pH of a 0.01 mol dm^{-3} solution of ethanoic acid. K_a for the acid is 1.7×10^{-5} mol dm^{-3}.

Notes on the method

Two approximations simplify the calculation.

1. The first assumption is that $[H_3O^+(aq)] = [A^-(aq)]$. In this example A$^-$ is the ethanoate ion $CH_3CO_2^-$. This assumption seems obvious from the equation for the ionization of a weak acid but it ignores the hydrogen ions from the ionization of water. Water produces far fewer hydrogen ions than most weak acids so its ionization can be ignored.

2. The second assumption is that so little of the ethanoic acid ionizes in water that $[HA(aq)] \approx 0.01$ mol dm^{-3}. Here HA represents ethanoic acid. This is a riskier assumption that has to be checked because in very dilute solutions the degree of ionization may become quite large relative to the amount of acid in the solution.

Answer

$$K_a = \frac{[H_3O^+(aq)][A^-(aq)]}{[HA(aq)]} = \frac{[H_3O^+(aq)]^2}{0.01 \text{ mol dm}^{-3}} = 1.7 \times 10^{-5} \text{ mol dm}^{-3}$$

Therefore $[H_3O^+(aq)]^2 = 1.7 \times 10^{-7}$ mol^2 dm^{-6}

So $[H_3O^+(aq)] = 4.12 \times 10^{-4}$ mol dm^{-3}

pH $= -\lg [H_3O^+(aq)] = -\lg [4.12 \times 10^{-4}] = 3.39$

Check the second assumption: in this case about 0.0004 mol dm^{-3} of the 0.0100 mol dm^{-3} of acid (4%) has ionized. In this instance the degree of ionization is just about small enough to justify the assumption that $[HA(aq)] \approx$ the concentration of un-ionized acid.

---

acidic oxide: an oxide of a *nonmetal* that reacts with water to form an *acid*. Some acidic oxides are insoluble but they can be recognized because they react directly with *basic oxides* to form *salts*. Note that acidic oxides are not themselves *acids* as defined by the Brønsted–Lowry theory because they do not contain ionizable hydrogen atoms, so they cannot act as proton donors.

Oxide	Acid formed with water
carbon dioxide, CO_2	carbonic acid, H_2CO_3
sulfur dioxide, SO_2	sulfurous acid, H_2SO_3 [sulfuric(IV) acid]
sulfur trioxide, SO_3	sulfuric acid, H_2SO_4 [sulfuric(VI) acid]
phosphorus(V) oxide, P_2O_5	phosphoric acid, H_3PO_4

Silica or silicon dioxide (SiO_2) is an acidic oxide that is insoluble in water. Silica reacts with basic metal oxides at high temperatures in furnaces during glassmaking and in steelmaking. Calcium oxide (quicklime) is added to a *blast furnace* to remove silica and other impurities. The calcium silicate is a liquid at the temperature of the furnace; it runs toward the bottom where it floats on top of the molten iron as a slag that can be tapped off separately.

$$CaO(s) + SiO_2(s) \longrightarrow CaSiO_3(l)$$

acid rain is a type of pollution produced when burning fuels or industrial processes release *acidic oxides* into the air. Sulfur dioxide (SO_2) and *nitrogen oxides* (NO_x) form when fuels burn in engines, furnaces and power stations. These primary pollutants are converted to secondary pollutants by chemical reactions in the air. Among the secondary pollutants are sulfuric acid, nitric acid and ammonium sulfate. The pollutants cause acidification by being deposited in the environment as gases or particles (dry deposition) or in the form of rain or mist (wet deposition).

acids are compounds with characteristic properties. Acids:

- form solutions in water with a *pH* below 7
- change the colors of *acid–base indicators*
- react with *metals* such as magnesium to produce hydrogen gas

$$Mg(s) + 2HCl(aq) \longrightarrow MgCl_2(aq) + H_2(g)$$

- react with carbonates such as calcium carbonate to form carbon dioxide gas and water

$$CaCO_3(s) + 2HCl(aq) \longrightarrow CaCl_2(aq) + CO_2(g) + H_2O(g)$$

- react with *basic oxides* to form salts and water

$$CuO(s) + H_2SO_4(aq) \longrightarrow CuSO_4(aq) + H_2O(g)$$

Pure acids may be solids (such as citric and tartaric acids), liquids (such as *sulfuric, nitric* and *ethanoic* acids) or gases (such as hydrogen chloride, which becomes *hydrochloric acid* when it dissolves in water).

Definitions of acids are based on the theories used to explain why they have similar properties. Chemists use different theories in different contexts. When considering acids in solution in water they still sometimes refer to the theory suggested by the Swedish chemist Svante Arrhenius (1859–1927). He explained the behavior of acids in terms of hydrogen ions. What acids have in common, according to this theory, is that they produce hydrogen ions when they dissolve in water.

$$HCl(g) \longrightarrow H^+(aq) + Cl^-(aq)$$

The definition of an acid generally used today is based on the *Brønsted–Lowry theory*, which defines an acid as a molecule or ion that can give away a hydrogen ion to something else. Acids are hydrogen ion (*proton*) donors. This definition is more general than the Arrhenius theory because it covers reactions that happen without water. According to this theory hydrogen chloride molecules give hydrogen ions to water molecules when they dissolve in water, producing hydrated hydrogen ions called *oxonium ions*. The water is acting as a *base*.

$$HCl(g) \quad + \quad H_2O(l) \rightleftharpoons H_3O^+(aq) \quad + \quad Cl^-(aq)$$

An example of an *acid–base reaction* in the absence of water is the formation of a white smoke of ammonium chloride when *ammonia* gas mixes with hydrogen chloride gas.

$$NH_3(g) \quad + \quad HCl(g) \rightleftharpoons NH_4^+Cl^-(s)$$

Lewis put forward an even more general theory defining *Lewis acids and bases* including changes that are not covered by the Brønsted–Lowry theory, such as the reaction of an *acidic oxide* with a *basic oxide.*

acid salt: a compound formed by partly neutralizing *acids* such as *sulfuric acid,* H_2SO_4, or *phosphoric acid,* H_3PO_4. These are acids with two or three ionizable hydrogen atoms. Sodium hydrogensulfate, $NaHSO_4$, and sodium dihydrogenphosphate, NaH_2PO_4, are examples of acid salts.

The negative ion in an acid salt can act either as an acid by giving away a further proton, or as a *base* by accepting a proton. The pH of an *aqueous solution* of an acid salt depends on the acid strength of the parent acid.

A solution of sodium hydrogensulfate, a salt of a *strong acid,* is acidic with a pH below 7 because the hydrogensulfate ion is also an acid, giving protons to water molecules:

$$HSO_4^- + H_2O \rightleftharpoons SO_4^{2-} + H_3O^+$$

A solution of sodium hydrogencarbonate, a salt of the *weak acid* called carbonic acid, is alkaline with a pH above 7 because the hydrogencarbonate ion is a base, taking protons (H^+) from water molecules:

$$HCO_3^- + H_2O \rightleftharpoons H_2CO_3 + OH^-$$

acid strength: see *strong acid, weak acid* and *acid dissociation constant.*

acid strength of organic hydroxy compounds: the order of acid strength for organic compounds with — OH groups is:

carboxylic acids > phenols > water > alcohols.

Carboxylic acids are *weak acids* that ionize to a significant extent by giving protons to water, forming a solution with pH 3–4. *Phenol* is acid enough to lower the pH of a solution in water to 5–6 but it ionizes significantly only when mixed with a stronger base such as the hydroxide ions in a solution of sodium hydroxide. Ethanol and other *alcohols* are such weak acids that they do not ionize to a significant extent in water or in a solution of a strong alkali.

actinides (or actinoids) are the *f-block elements* in period 7 of the *periodic table.* They are the 14 elements from thorium to lawrencium that lie between actinium (element 89) and element 104, unnilquadium.

activated complex: a combination of reacting atoms, molecules or ions at that point during a chemical reaction when they are at the top of the *activation energy* barrier between reactants and products. An activated complex is a combination of reacting particles at a higher energy because chemical bonds are stretched. The activated complex is the *transition state* for the reaction step.

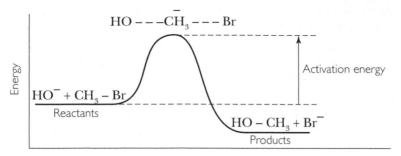

Progress of reaction

Activated complex formed in the course of a substitution reaction

activation energy: the minimum energy needed in a collision between molecules if they are to react. The activation energy is the height of the energy barrier separating reactants and products during a chemical reaction. (See *activated complex*.)

Activation energy is an important idea in the *collision theory* of reaction rates. It accounts for the fact that reactions go much more slowly than would be expected if every collision between atoms and molecules led to a reaction. Only a very small proportion of collisions bring about chemical change. Molecules react only if they collide with enough energy between them to overcome the energy barrier. At around room temperature only a small proportion of molecules have enough energy to react.

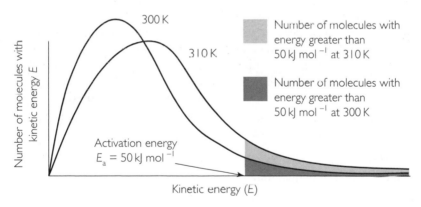

Maxwell–Boltzman distribution curve for the kinetic energies of molecules at about room temperature, 300 K and 310 K. The shaded area shows the proportion of molecules having at least the activation energy for a reaction. This area is bigger at a higher temperature.

Activation energies account for the way in which reaction rates vary with temperature, T. At a higher temperature there are more molecules with enough energy to react when they collide.

The activation energies for many reactions in biochemical systems are around 50 kJ mol^{-1} and for these reactions the rate of reaction doubles for each 10 K rise in temperature.

It is possible to determine the activation energy for a reaction by measuring its rate over a range of temperatures and then using the *Arrhenius equation.*

active site: the part of a *catalyst* that is responsible for its catalytic activity. *Zeolites* are examples of inorganic catalysts, for example, which owe their catalytic activity to active sites in the crystal structure that can adsorb specific molecules so that they can react to produce the required products.

Enzymes are biological catalysts. An enzyme molecule consists of a coiled *protein* chain. The coiling gives rise to an active site with a precise three-dimensional shape. The enzyme can act only on molecules with the right shape to fit into the active site. This accounts for the specificity of enzymes.

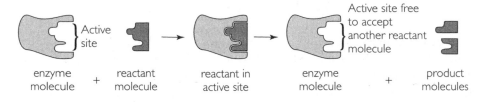

$$\text{enzyme molecule} \quad + \quad \text{reactant molecule} \quad \rightarrow \quad \text{reactant in active site} \quad \rightarrow \quad \text{enzyme molecule} \quad + \quad \text{product molecules}$$

A model illustrating an enzyme with an active site splitting a molecule into two smaller molecules

activity series: a series that compares the reactivities of elements. The activity series for metals is a list of *metals* in order of reactivity. Metal reactivities are compared by watching reactions of samples of the metals with a range of substances such as air, water and acids. The disadvantage of a series defined in this way is that it confuses rates (*reaction kinetics*) and equilibria (*thermochemistry*). *Aluminum*, for example, is a reactive metal as measured by thermochemical quantities but it is covered by a layer of *oxide* that acts as a barrier, slowing down or stopping reactions that might otherwise be expected to be fast. The metal reacts as fast as expected if the oxide film is removed.

It is better to compare the reactivities of elements and compounds with the help of an *electrochemical series* based on *standard electrode potentials.*

acyl chlorides are made from *carboxylic acids* by replacing the hydroxyl group with a chlorine atom.

$$CH_3 - CO_2H + SOCl_2 \longrightarrow CH_3 - \overset{\overset{\displaystyle O}{\|}}{C} - Cl + HCl + SO_2$$

sulfur dichloride oxide

$$CH_3 - CO_2H + PCl_5 \longrightarrow CH_3 - \overset{\overset{\displaystyle O}{\|}}{C} - Cl + POCl_3 + HCl$$

phosphorus pentachloride

Formation of ethanoyl chloride from ethanoic acid

Acyl chlorides are very reactive. They are powerful acylating agents. Most are quickly hydrolyzed back to the parent acid by cold water. Acyl chlorides react rapidly with *alcohols* and *phenols* to form *esters*.

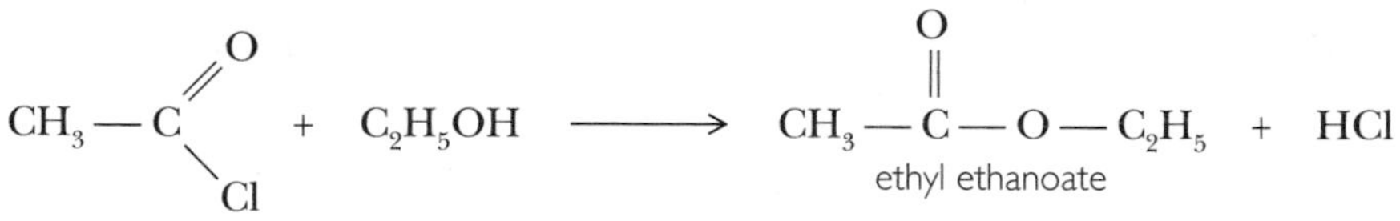

$$CH_3-C{\overset{O}{\underset{Cl}{\diagup}}} + C_2H_5OH \longrightarrow CH_3-\overset{\overset{O}{\|}}{C}-O-C_2H_5 + HCl$$

ethyl ethanoate

Formation of an ester

Acyl chlorides react with *ammonia* and *amines* to form *amides*.

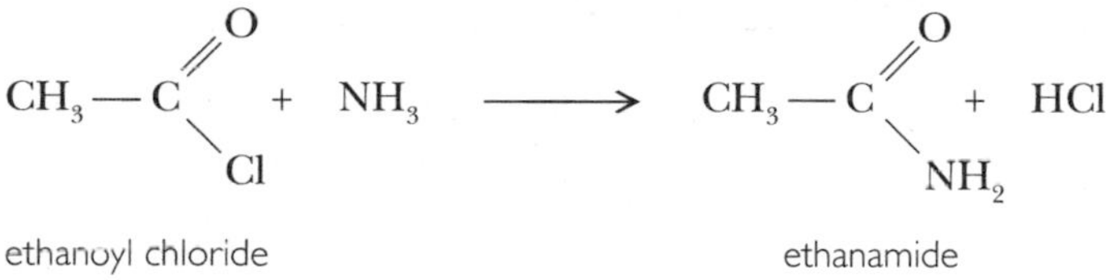

$$CH_3-C{\overset{O}{\underset{Cl}{\diagup}}} + NH_3 \longrightarrow CH_3-C{\overset{O}{\underset{NH_2}{\diagup}}} + HCl$$

ethanoyl chloride   ethanamide

Formation of an amide

Acyl chlorides can also acylate *benzene* by the *Friedel–Crafts reaction*.

acylation is a reaction that substitutes an acyl group for a hydrogen atom. The H atom may be part of an — OH group, an — NH₂ group or a *benzene* ring. Acylating agents are either *acyl chlorides* or *acid anhydrides*.

$$CH_3-C{\overset{O}{\diagup}}$$

The ethanoyl group – an acyl group

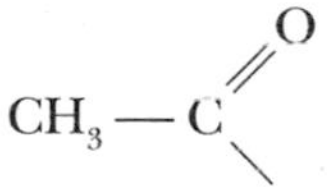

Acylation is the reaction that converts 2-hydroxybenzoic acid to *aspirin*.

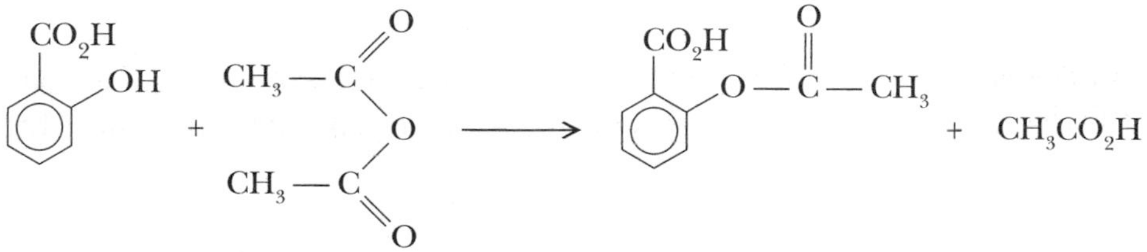

Formation of aspirin by acylation of 2-hydroxybenzoic acid with ethanoic anhydride

Acylation of benzene is an example of the *Friedel–Crafts reaction*.

addition–elimination reactions take place when two molecules first add together and then immediately split off a small molecule such as water. They are often called *condensation reactions*.

Addition–elimination reactions of *carbonyl compounds* take place with compounds of the form X — NH₂.

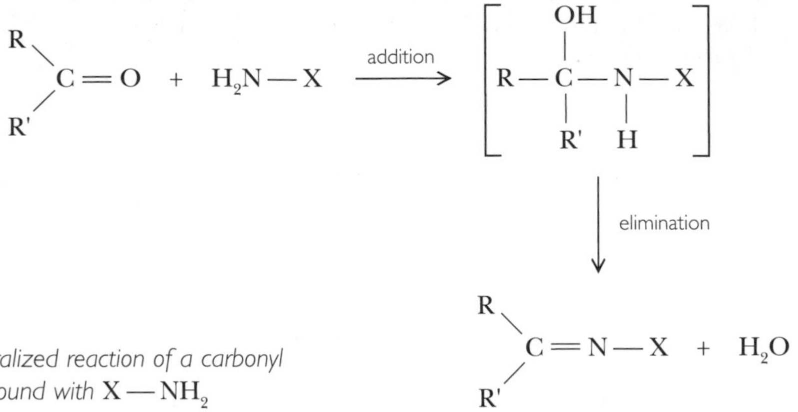

$$\underset{R'}{\overset{R}{\diagdown}}C = O \;+\; H_2N-X \;\xrightarrow{\text{addition}}\; \left[R-\underset{\underset{R'}{|}}{\overset{\overset{OH}{|}}{C}}-\underset{\underset{H}{|}}{N}-X \right]$$

↓ elimination

Generalized reaction of a carbonyl compound with $X-NH_2$

$$\underset{R'}{\overset{R}{\diagdown}}C = N-X \;+\; H_2O$$

Reagent	Product from reaction with a carbonyl compound, RCOR" (R and R" are both alkyl groups in ketones. R = H and R" is an alkyl group in an aldehyde.)
2,4-dinitrophenylhydrazine (Brady's reagent) 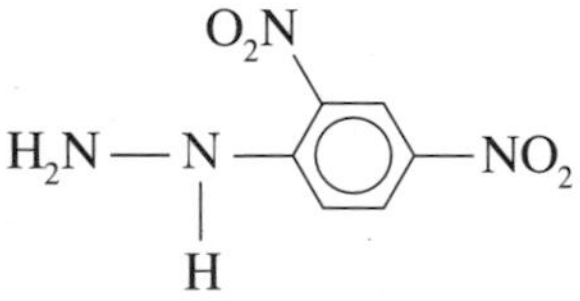	A 2,4-dinitrophenylhydrazone 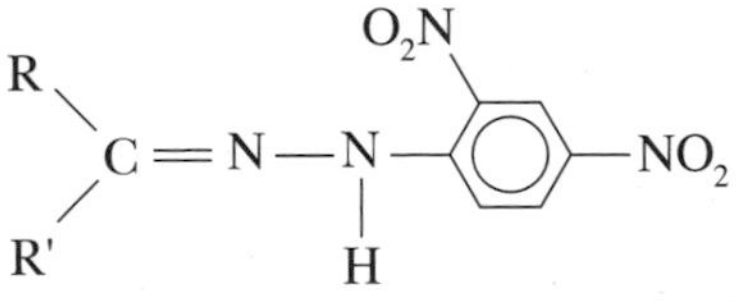

(See also *nucleophilic addition reaction*.)

addition polymerization is a process for making *polymers* from compounds containing *double bonds*. Many molecules of the *monomer* add together to form a long-chain polymer. Ethene, for example, polymerizes to form poly(ethene).

$$n CH_2 = CH_2 \;\longrightarrow\; \{CH_2-CH_2\}_n$$

(See the table on page 13.)

addition reaction: a reaction in which two molecules combine to form a single product. Bromine, for example, adds to ethene to form the addition product 1,2-dibromoethane.

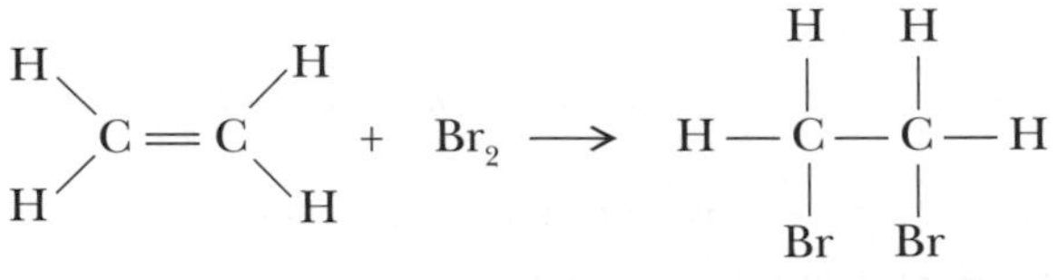

$$\underset{H}{\overset{H}{\diagdown}}C = C\underset{H}{\overset{H}{\diagup}} \;+\; Br_2 \;\longrightarrow\; H-\underset{\underset{Br}{|}}{\overset{\overset{H}{|}}{C}}-\underset{\underset{Br}{|}}{\overset{\overset{H}{|}}{C}}-H$$

Structure diagram to show addition of bromine to ethene

1,2-dibromoethane

Addition reactions are characteristic of *unsaturated compounds* such as the *alkenes* and *carbonyl compounds*.

Monomer	Polymer	Notes
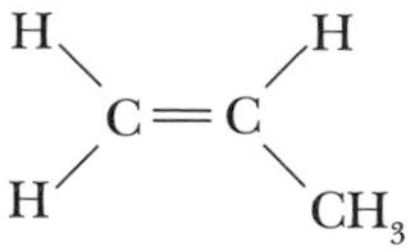 H—C=C—H with H and CH₃ propene	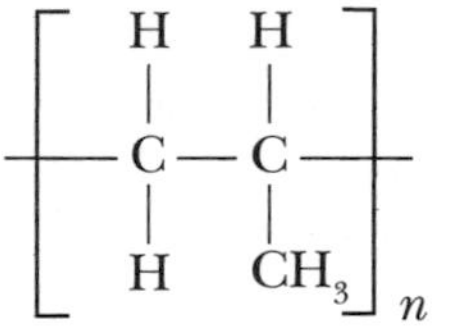 $\left[\begin{array}{c} \text{—C—C—} \\ \text{H H} \\ \text{H CH}_3 \end{array}\right]_n$ poly(propene) or polypropylene	A high-pressure, high-temperature process in the presence of a peroxide initiator produces low-density poly(ethene) with branched chains. A low-pressure, low-temperature process with a *Ziegler–Natta catalyst* produces high-density poly(ethene). The polymer chains pack closer because they have no side branches.
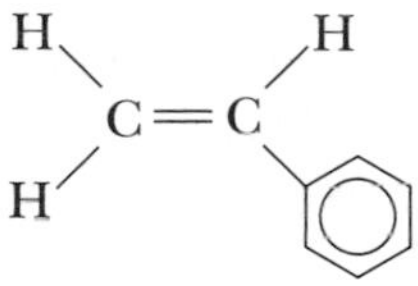 H—C=C—H with H and phenyl phenylethene	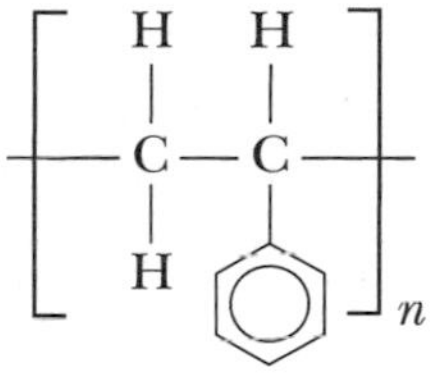 $\left[\begin{array}{c} \text{—C—C—} \\ \text{H H} \\ \text{H } C_6H_5 \end{array}\right]_n$ poly(phenylethene) or polystyrene	Expanded polystyrene has low density and is an excellent thermal insulator. It is used for packaging because it absorbs shocks.
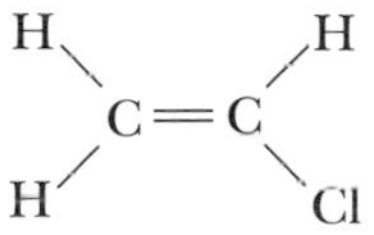 H—C=C—H with H and Cl chloroethene	$\left[\begin{array}{c} \text{—C—C—} \\ \text{H H} \\ \text{H Cl} \end{array}\right]_n$ poly(chloroethene) or polyvinylchloride (PVC)	Unplasticized uPVC is a rigid polymer suitable for guttering and window frames. Plasticized PVC is flexible and used for packaging, flooring and cable insulation.

Addition polymerization

adenine is one of the four nitrogenous bases found in *DNA*, so it represents one of the four "letters" in the genetic code. In the double-helix structure of DNA, adenine is always paired with thymine and the two are held together by a pair of *hydrogen bonds*.

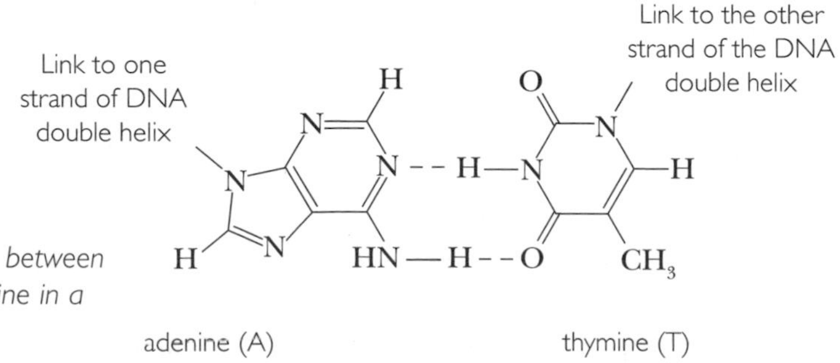

Link to one strand of DNA double helix

Link to the other strand of the DNA double helix

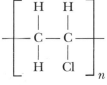

Hydrogen bonding between adenine and thymine in a DNA double helix

adenine (A)

thymine (T)

adsorption is a process in which atoms, molecules or ions are held on the surface of a solid. Adsorption processes are important in *heterogeneous catalysis* and in some types of *chromatography*. Adsorption should be carefully distinguished from *absorption*.

aerobic respiration: see *respiration.*

aerosols are *colloids* in which particles of a solid, or droplets of a liquid, are finely dispersed in a gas. Smoke is an aerosol in which the dispersed particles are solid. Examples of aerosols with liquid droplets are mist, clouds and insecticide or paint sprays.

agrochemicals include *pesticides* that destroy the organisms that damage crops such as insects (insecticides) and weeds (herbicides). Other agrochemicals include growth regulators that can stimulate or inhibit plant growth. The chemical industry distinguishes agrochemicals from *fertilizers*, which provide the chemicals needed for healthy plant growth.

air is a mixture of gases as shown in the table. The proportion of water *vapor* in the air varies widely according to the weather conditions. Air pollution adds other gases such as *nitrogen oxides*, sulfur dioxide, *ozone* and *hydrocarbons* (see also *acid rain* and *photochemical smog*).

gas	percentage by volume in dry air	boiling point/K
nitrogen	78.0	77
oxygen	21.0	90
argon	0.9	87
carbon dioxide (about 0.04%) and small traces of neon, helium and krypton	0.1	

The gases are separated on a large scale by *fractional distillation* of liquid air.

air condenser: a glass tube without a water jacket used for condensing *vapors* during *distillation* or refluxing (see *reflux condenser*). An air condenser is fitted when the temperature of the vapor is so high that the surrounding air is cool enough to condense the liquid. Normally this is when the boiling point of the liquid being distilled is above about 150°C.

alcohols are compounds with the formula R—OH where R represents an *alkyl group*. The hydroxy group —OH is the *functional group* that gives the compounds their characteristic reactions.

The chemical industry makes alcohols by the *hydration* of *alkenes* in the presence of an acid *catalyst*.

Equation for the industrial production of ethanol. Ethanol is also produced by fermentation.

Alcohols are named by changing the ending of the corresponding *alkane* to –ol. So ethane becomes ethanol.

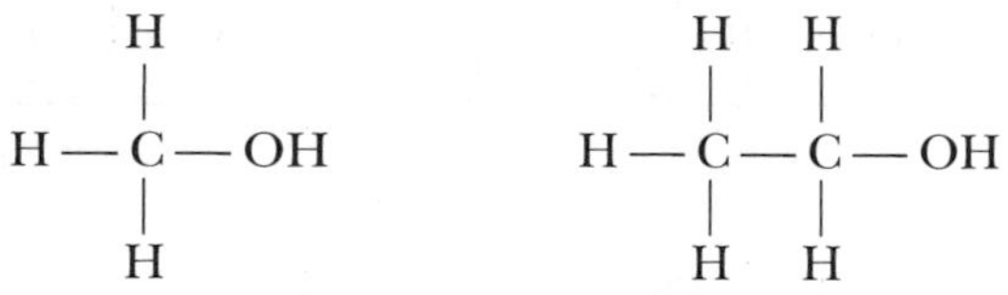

$$H - \underset{\underset{H}{|}}{\overset{\overset{H}{|}}{C}} - OH \qquad\qquad H - \underset{\underset{H}{|}}{\overset{\overset{H}{|}}{C}} - \underset{\underset{H}{|}}{\overset{\overset{H}{|}}{C}} - OH$$

methanol   ethanol

$$CH_3 - CH_2 - CH_2 - CH_2 - OH$$ butan-1-ol, a primary alcohol

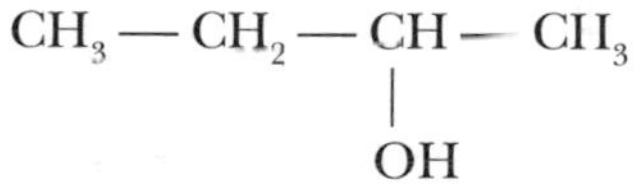

$$CH_3 - CH_2 - \underset{\underset{OH}{|}}{CH} - CH_3$$ butan-2-ol, a secondary alcohol

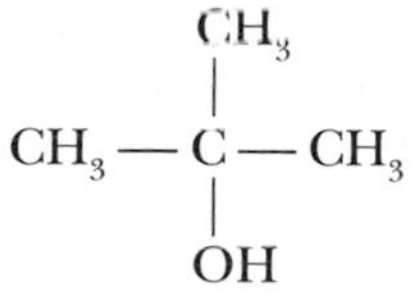

$$CH_3 - \underset{\underset{OH}{|}}{\overset{\overset{CH_3}{|}}{C}} - CH_3$$ 2-methylpropan-2-ol, a tertiary alcohol

Names and structures of alcohols

Even the simplest alcohols such as methanol and ethanol are liquids at room temperature because of *hydrogen bonding* between the hydroxy groups. For the same reason alcohols with relatively short hydrocarbon chains mix freely with water.

The reactions of ethanol are typical of the alcohols in general.

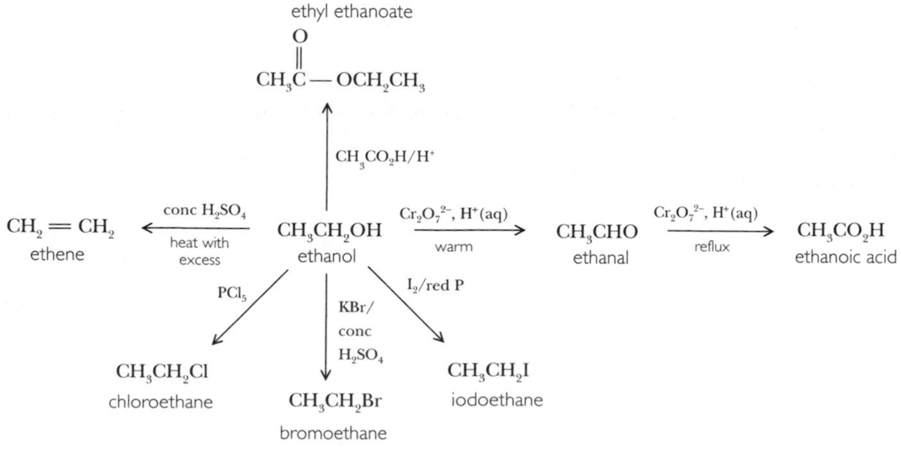

Reactions of ethanol

Oxidation reactions distinguish primary alcohols, secondary alcohols and tertiary alcohols (see *primary, secondary and tertiary organic compounds*).

primary alcohol $\xrightarrow[\text{warm}]{Cr_2O_7^{2-}, H^+(aq)}$ aldehyde $\xrightarrow[\text{reflux}]{\text{excess } Cr_2O_7^{2-}, H^+(aq)}$ carboxylic acid

secondary alcohol $\xrightarrow[\text{reflux}]{Cr_2O_7^{2-}, H^+(aq)}$ ketone

tertiary alcohol   no reaction

Use of oxidation with an acidified solution of dichromate(VI) ions to distinguish primary, secondary and tertiary alcohols

aldehydes are *carbonyl compounds* in which the carbonyl group is attached to two hydrogen atoms or an *alkyl group* and a hydrogen atom, so the carbonyl group is at the end of a carbon chain. The — CHO group is the *functional group* that gives aldehydes their characteristic reactions. They are named after the *alkane* with the same carbon skeleton by changing the ending -e to -al (so ethane becomes ethanal).

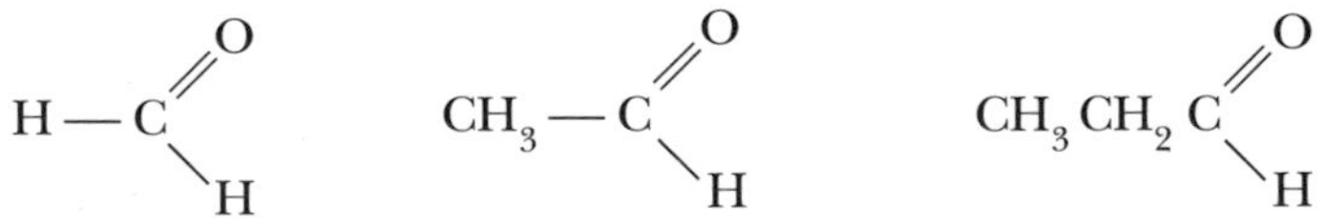

methanal   ethanal   propanal

Structures and names of aldehydes

Methanal is a gas at room temperature. Ethanal boils at 21°C so it may be a liquid or gas at room temperature depending on the conditions.

Aldehydes are formed by *oxidation* of primary *alcohols* on heating with a mixture of dilute sulfuric acid and potassium dichromate(VI) under conditions that allow the aldehyde to distill off as it forms. Unlike *ketones*, aldehydes can easily be oxidized further to *carboxylic acids* by longer heating with an excess of the reagent.

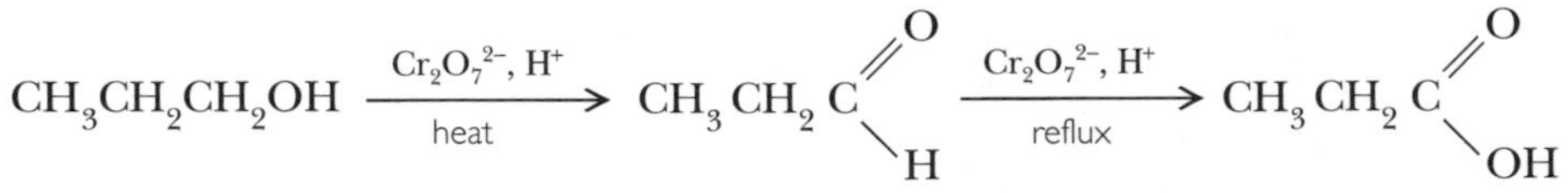

propan-1-ol   propanal   propanoic acid

Two-stage oxidation of propan-1-ol

Fehling's solution and *Tollens reagent* are mild oxidizing agents that are used to distinguish aldehydes from ketones.

Sodium tetrahydridoborate(III) (NaBH$_4$) reduces aldehydes to primary alcohols.

$$CH_3CH_2 - C \overset{O}{\underset{H}{\big\backslash\big/}} \xrightarrow{Na^+BH_4^-} CH_3\,CH_2\,CH_2OH$$

Reduction of propanal to propan-1-ol

Owing to the double bond in the carbonyl group, aldehydes (like ketones) undergo *addition reactions*. These are *nucleophilic addition reactions*.

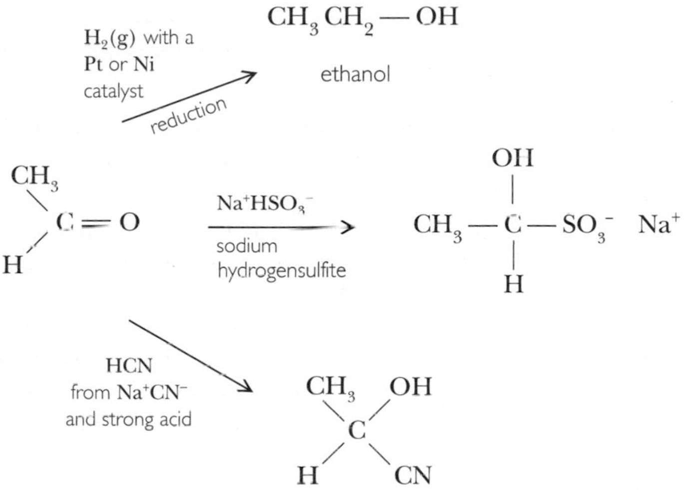

H$_2$(g) with a
Pt or Ni
catalyst

reduction

CH$_3$ CH$_2$ — OH

ethanol

$$\overset{CH_3}{\underset{H}{\big\backslash\big/}}C = O \xrightarrow[\text{sodium hydrogensulfite}]{Na^+HSO_3^-} CH_3 - \overset{OH}{\underset{H}{C}} - SO_3^- \ Na^+$$

HCN
from Na$^+$CN$^-$
and strong acid

$$\underset{H \qquad CN}{\overset{CH_3 \quad OH}{C}}$$

2-hydroxypropanenitrile
(acetaldehyde cyanohydrin)

Addition reactions of ethanal

In some reactions addition is immediately followed by elimination of water. These are *addition–elimination reactions*.

alicyclic hydrocarbons are *hydrocarbons* with rings of carbon atoms (but no *benzene* rings). Examples are cycloalkanes and cycloalkenes.

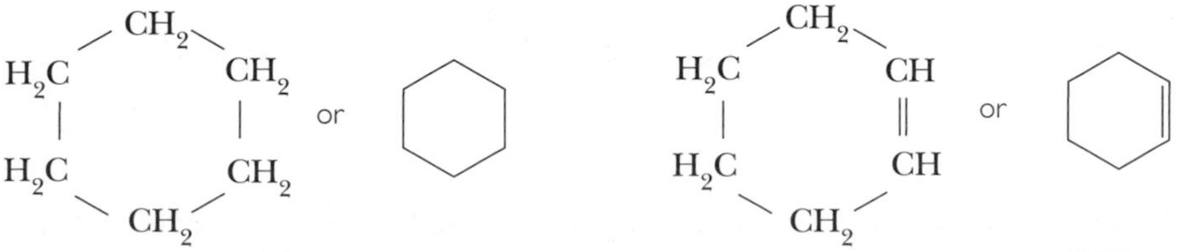

cyclohexane C$_6$H$_{12}$

cyclohexene C$_6$H$_{10}$

Structures of cyclohexane and cyclohexene

aliphatic hydrocarbons are *hydrocarbons* with no rings of carbon atoms. The chains of carbon atoms may be branched or unbranched. *Alkanes, alkenes* and *alkynes* are all aliphatic compounds.

aliquot: a measured volume taken from a liquid sample for analysis. Typically aliquots are taken by a pipette for *titration.*

alkali metals: the elements in *group 1* of the periodic table. All the elements react with water to form alkaline solutions of the metal hydroxide. Sodium, for example, reacts to form *sodium hydroxide.* It is important to remember that the hydroxides are alkaline because of the presence of OH$^-$ ions. Alkali metal ions themselves, such as sodium ions, Na$^+$, do *not* make solutions alkaline.

alkaline cell: an *electrochemical cell* in which the electrolyte is the alkali, potassium hydroxide. Alkaline cells last longer than zinc–carbon *dry cells;* they are less likely to leak and can supply a larger current. They are suitable for toys and cassette recorders with a motor drawing a heavy or continuous current.

alkaline earth metals: the elements in *group 2* of the periodic table. The alkaline earths are the *oxides* of these metals and are much less soluble in water than the corresponding group 1 oxides.

alkalis are *bases* that dissolve in water. The common laboratory alkalis are the hydroxides of sodium and potassium, calcium hydroxide (in limewater) and *ammonia.* Alkalis form solutions with a *pH* above 7 so they change the colors of *acid–base indicators.* What alkalis have in common is that they dissolve in water to produce hydroxide (OH$^-$) ions. Sodium hydroxide (Na$^+$OH$^-$) and potassium hydroxide (K$^+$OH$^-$) contain hydroxide ions in the solid as well as in solution. Ammonia produces hydroxide ions by reacting with water. Ammonia acting as a base takes *protons* from water molecules.

$$NH_3(g) \quad + \quad H_2O(g) \quad \rightleftharpoons \quad NH_4^+(aq) + OH^-(aq)$$

alkaloids are organic nitrogen compounds extracted from plants. Alkaloids can have a powerful effect on the human nervous system and can be very poisonous. Caffeine, the stimulant in tea and coffee, is an alkaloid. Other alkaloids are the *drugs* quinine, morphine and codeine.

Structure of caffeine

alkanes are the *hydrocarbons* that make up most of crude oil and natural gas. Alkanes are *saturated compounds* with the general formula C_nH_{2n+2}. The carbon atoms in alkane molecules may be in straight chains or branched chains but all the bonds are single bonds.

Name	Molecular formula	Structure
methane	CH_4	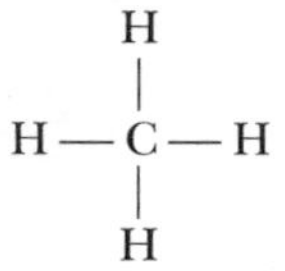
ethane	C_2H_6	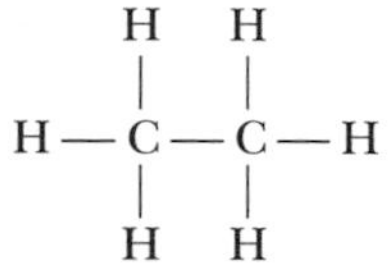
propane	C_3H_8	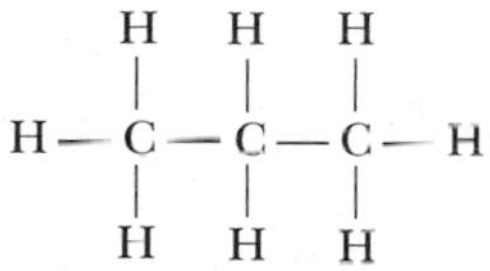

(methane structure)

$$\begin{array}{c} H \\ | \\ H-C-H \\ | \\ H \end{array}$$

(ethane structure)

$$\begin{array}{cc} H & H \\ | & | \\ H-C-C-H \\ | & | \\ H & H \end{array}$$

(propane structure)

$$\begin{array}{ccc} H & H & H \\ | & | & | \\ H-C-C-C-H \\ | & | & | \\ H & H & H \end{array}$$

The names of branched alkanes are based on the longest straight chain in the molecule with the positions of the side-chain alkyl groups identified by numbering the carbon atoms.

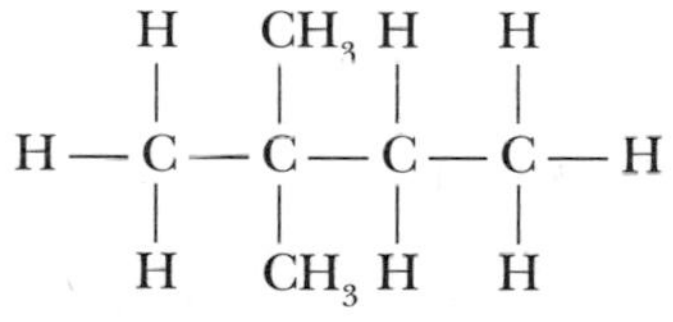

$$\begin{array}{cccc} H & CH_3 & H & H \\ | & | & | & | \\ H-C-C-C-C-H \\ | & | & | & | \\ H & CH_3 & H & H \end{array}$$

2,2-dimethylbutane

$$\begin{array}{cccc} H & CH_3 & CH_3 & H \\ | & | & | & | \\ H-C-C-C-C-H \\ | & | & | & | \\ H & H & H & H \end{array}$$

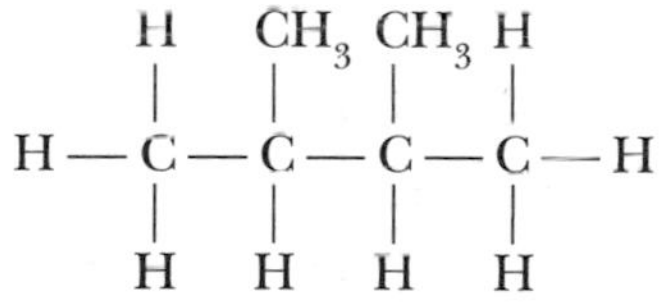

2,3-dimethylbutane

Names and structures of some branched alkanes

Alkane molecules are nonpolar so they do not mix with, or dissolve in, *polar solvents* such as water. The molecules are only held together by weak *intermolecular forces* (*van der Waals forces*). The longer the molecules, the greater the attraction between them. The boiling points rise as the number of carbon atoms per molecule increases. Alkanes in the range C_1 to C_4 are gases at room temperature and pressure. Under the same conditions, alkanes in the range C_5 to C_{17} are liquids while those with more than 17 carbon atoms per molecule are solids. Liquid alkanes with longer chain lengths are *viscous liquids* used as lubricants.

The *bond enthalpies* for C—C and C—H bonds are high so the bonds are relatively hard to break. Also the bonds are not polar. This means that alkanes are very unreactive toward reagents in water such as acids and alkalis, as well as oxidizing and reducing reagents. Three important reactions of alkanes are: *combustion, halogenation* and cracking (see *steam cracking* and *catalytic cracking*). Cracking and the halogenation of alkanes are examples of *free-radical chain reactions*.

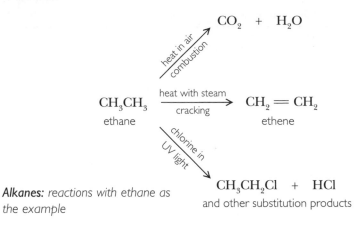

$$CO_2 \quad + \quad H_2O$$

heat in air
combustion

$$CH_3CH_3 \xrightarrow[\text{cracking}]{\text{heat with steam}} CH_2 = CH_2$$

ethane   ethene

chlorine in
UV light

$$CH_3CH_2Cl \quad + \quad HCl$$

and other substitution products

Alkanes: reactions with ethane as the example

alkenes, such as ethene and propene, are products of cracking oil fractions (see *catalytic cracking, steam cracking*). They are important starting points for making other chemicals because of the reactivity of their double bonds.

Alkenes are *unsaturated hydrocarbons* with the general formula C_nH_{2n}. The characteristic *functional group* of the alkenes is a carbon–carbon double bond. The presence of the double bond makes alkenes more reactive than *alkanes*.

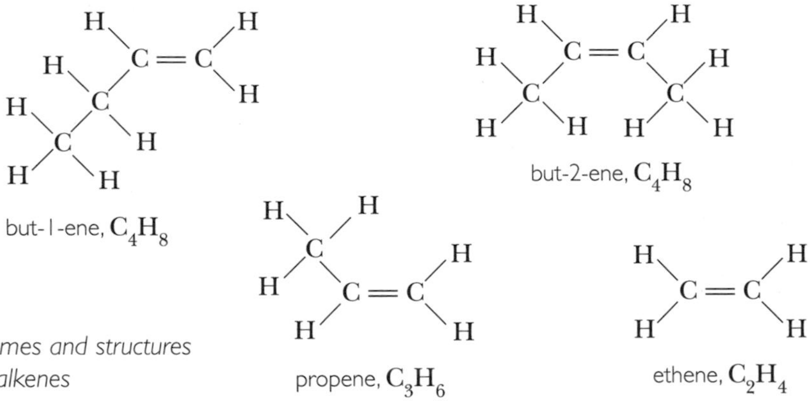

but-1-ene, C_4H_8

but-2-ene, C_4H_8

Names and structures of alkenes

propene, C_3H_6

ethene, C_2H_4

The name of an alkene is based on the name of the corresponding alkane with its ending changed to -ene. Where necessary, a number in the name shows the position of the double bond in the structure, as in the two structural *isomers* but-1-ene and but-2-ene. Counting starts from the end of the chain that will give the lowest possible number. The number in the name shows the first of the two atoms connected by the double bond. In but-1-ene, for example, the double bond is between the first and the second atoms in the carbon chain.

The boiling points of alkenes increase as the number of carbon atoms in the molecules increase. Ethene, propene and the butenes are gases at room temperature. Alkenes with more than four carbon atoms are liquids or even solids. Alkenes, like other hydrocarbons, do not mix with, or dissolve in, water.

The characteristic reactions of alkenes are *electrophilic addition* reactions.

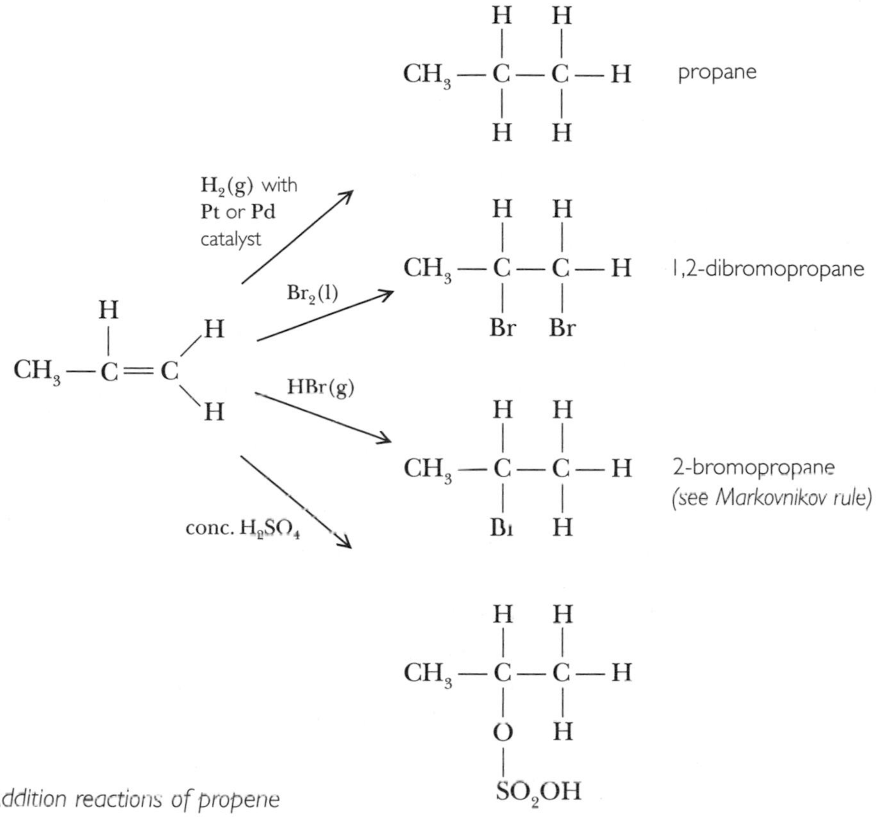

$$CH_3 - \underset{\underset{H}{|}}{\overset{\overset{H}{|}}{C}} - \underset{\underset{H}{|}}{\overset{\overset{H}{|}}{C}} - H \qquad \text{propane}$$

$$\underset{H}{\overset{H}{|}} \qquad H_2(g) \text{ with Pt or Pd catalyst}$$

$$CH_3 - C = C \qquad Br_2(l)$$

$$CH_3 - \underset{\underset{Br}{|}}{\overset{\overset{H}{|}}{C}} - \underset{\underset{Br}{|}}{\overset{\overset{H}{|}}{C}} - H \qquad 1,2\text{-dibromopropane}$$

HBr(g)

$$CH_3 - \underset{\underset{Br}{|}}{\overset{\overset{H}{|}}{C}} - \underset{\underset{H}{|}}{\overset{\overset{H}{|}}{C}} - H \qquad \begin{array}{l}2\text{-bromopropane}\\ \textit{(see Markovnikov rule)}\end{array}$$

conc. H_2SO_4

$$CH_3 - \underset{\underset{O}{|}}{\overset{\overset{H}{|}}{C}} - \underset{\underset{H}{|}}{\overset{\overset{H}{|}}{C}} - H$$
$$\underset{SO_2OH}{|}$$

Addition reactions of propene

alkoxides are metal *salts* of alcohols. Ethanol, for example, reacts with *sodium* to produce sodium ethoxide.

$$C_2H_5OH(l) + Na(s) \longrightarrow C_2H_5O^-Na^+(s) + H_2(g)$$

The ethoxide ion is a very *strong base*. It rapidly gains a proton if water is added to turn back to ethanol.

alkyl group: a group of carbon and hydrogen atoms that forms part of the structure of a molecule. The simplest example is the methyl group CH_3 —, which is methane with one hydrogen atom removed. In general, alkyl groups are *alkane* molecules minus one hydrogen atom.

alkyl group	formula
methyl	CH_3-
ethyl	CH_3CH_2-
propyl	$CH_3CH_2CH_2-$
butyl	$CH_3CH_2CH_2CH_2-$

A useful shorthand for any alkyl group is the capital letter R. Further alkyl groups are then represented by R′ or R″. So, for example, a tertiary *amine* with three different alkyl groups attached to the nitrogen atom can be written as:

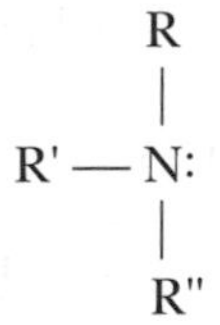

$$R' - N:$$
$$\underset{R''}{\overset{R}{|}}$$

General formula for a tertiary amine

alkylation is a reaction that introduces an *alkyl group* into a molecule by *addition reactions* or *substitution reactions*. Industrially the alkylation of alkenes produces branched alkanes needed to raise the octane number of *gasoline*.

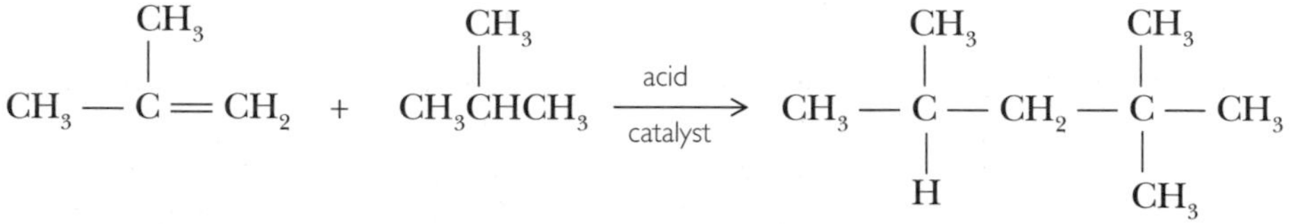

$$CH_3 - \underset{\underset{}{\overset{|}{C}}}{\overset{\overset{CH_3}{|}}{}} = CH_2 \; + \; CH_3CHCH_3 \; \xrightarrow[\text{catalyst}]{\text{acid}} \; CH_3 - \underset{\underset{H}{\overset{|}{C}}}{\overset{\overset{CH_3}{|}}{}} - CH_2 - \underset{\underset{CH_3}{\overset{|}{C}}}{\overset{\overset{CH_3}{|}}{}} - CH_3$$

methylpropene methylpropane   2,2,4-trimethylpentane

Production of a branched alkane by alkylation of an alkene

The *Friedel–Crafts reaction* adds alkyl groups to benzene rings in *arenes*.

alkynes are hydrocarbons with a triple bond between two carbon atoms. They are *unsaturated hydrocarbons* with the general formula C_nH_{2n-2}. The best-known example is ethyne (historically known as acetylene), the first member of the series.

The structure of ethyne $H - C \equiv C - H$

allotropes are different forms of the same element in the same physical state. *Oxygen* has gaseous allotropes with different molecular structures: normal diatomic oxygen (O_2) and *ozone* (O_3) (systematically called trioxygen). *Sulfur* has solid allotropes with the same molecular structure (S_8) but different crystal structures: rhombic and monoclinic sulfur.

Carbon has allotropes consisting of the different giant structures of atoms: diamond and graphite. Carbon also exists in molecular form as the *fullerenes*.

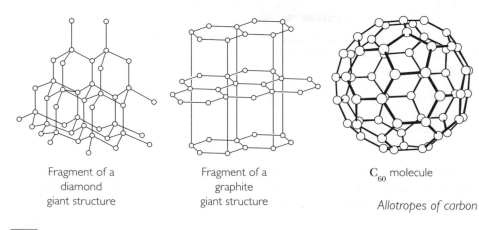

Fragment of a
diamond
giant structure

Fragment of a
graphite
giant structure

C_{60} molecule

Allotropes of carbon

Other elements with allotropes are *phosphorus* and *tin*. (See also *enantiotropy* and *monotropy*.)

alloys are usually mixtures of metals, but *steel* is an alloy of iron with the nonmetal carbon. Alloys are often more useful than pure metals. Controlling the composition of an alloy makes it possible to vary its properties. Examples of alloys are:

- mild steel – an alloy of iron with 0.12–0.25% carbon; it is relatively cheap, easily rolled into sheets and can be pressed into shape
- *brass* – an alloy of copper with less than 20% zinc; it is easily worked, has a gold color and does not corrode
- *bronze* – an alloy of copper with up to 12% tin; it is strong, hardwearing and resistant to corrosion
- solder – an alloy of lead and tin that melts at a low temperature and can be used to join metals
- duralumin – an alloy of 95% aluminum with 4% copper and smaller amounts of magnesium, iron and silicon; it is stronger, harder and more resistant to corrosion than pure aluminum.

alpha decay is the emission of an alpha particle from the nucleus of an atom of a *radioactive* element. Alpha decay produces an atom of an element two places to the left in the periodic table because the *proton (atomic) number* of the atom decreases by two. At the same time the *nucleon (mass) number* decreases by four. When an atom of uranium-238 decays by loss of an alpha particle it turns into an atom of thorium-234.

$$^{238}_{92}U \longrightarrow {}^{234}_{90}Th + {}^{4}_{2}He$$

alpha (α) particles consist of two protons and two neutrons and are identical with the nuclei of helium atoms. They are emitted from the nuclei of *radioactive* elements during alpha decay.

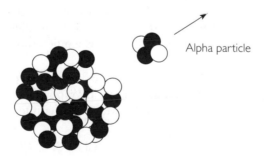

Alpha particle

An alpha particle emitted from a radioactive nucleus is usually represented as ${}^{4}_{2}He$ but chemically it is ${}^{4}_{2}He^{2+}$.

aluminum (Al) is a silvery metal. It is very useful because it has a relatively low density while being resistant to *corrosion* and is a good conductor of thermal energy and electricity.

Aluminum is the second element in group 3, coming below boron in the periodic table. The *electron configuration* of aluminum is [Ne]$3s^23p^1$. Aluminum has a cubic *close-packed giant structure* with the atoms held together by *metallic bonds*.

Aluminum is a reactive metal with a negative *standard electrode potential* such that $E^{\ominus} = -1.66$ V for the $Al^{3+}(aq)|Al(s)$ half-cell. This puts aluminum above zinc in the *electrochemical series*. A thin, tough and transparent layer of aluminum oxide on the surface of the metal stops most reactions. As a result aluminum does not corrode in air or dissolve in acids as might be expected. The oxide layer is so important that it is often thickened by *anodizing*.

The oxide layer protects the metal from dilute acids but aluminum is attacked by fairly concentrated hydrochloric acid.

$$2Al(s) + 6HCl(aq) \longrightarrow 2AlCl_3(aq) + 3H_2(g)$$

Concentrated nitric acid is an oxidizing agent that thickens the oxide layer making the metal less likely to react ("passive").

The oxide layer and the metal itself dissolve in concentrated, strong alkalis.

$$2Al(s) + 2OH^-(aq) + 6H_2O(l) \longrightarrow 2[Al(OH)_4]^- + 3H_2(g)$$

On heating, aluminum reacts directly with nonmetals, including oxygen, sulfur, nitrogen and the halogens. Aluminum combines very strongly with oxygen and is used to reduce the oxides of other metals in the *thermit reaction*.

Important aluminum compounds include *aluminum oxide* and hydroxide, *aluminum chloride* and salts containing the hydrated *aluminum(III) ion*. In all its compounds aluminum is in the *oxidation state* +3. The relatively high charge and small size of the Al^{3+} ion state help to account for the differences between aluminum compounds and the compounds of metals in group 1 and group 2. In some ways aluminum compounds have properties more characteristic of nonmetals than metals. Compared with the larger Na^+ ions, Al^{3+} ions have a strong tendency to polarize neighboring anions, giving rise to *polar covalent bonds* rather than *ionic bonding*. Only the fluoride and oxide are ionic. (See also *Fajan's rules*.)

aluminum chloride ($AlCl_3$) is an off-white solid that *sublimes* on heating and fumes in moist air because of *hydrolysis* to hydrogen chloride and the hydroxide. Aluminum chloride is manufactured on a large scale by injecting a stream of chlorine gas into molten aluminum at 800°C. At this temperature the product vaporizes and is collected as a solid in condensers.

Aluminum atoms in $AlCl_3$ have only six electrons and have a strong tendency to accept two more. As a result, aluminum chloride vapor contains Al_2Cl_6 dimers (see *dimerization*). Solid $AlCl_3$ has a layer lattice with bonding intermediate between ionic and covalent.

A dot and cross diagram for $AlCl_3$ and the bonding in an Al_2Cl_6 dimer. Lone pairs on chlorine atoms form dative bonds with aluminum atoms.

$AlCl_3$ is a strong acceptor of electron pairs, making it a powerful *Lewis acid*.

Aluminum chloride is the catalyst for *Friedel–Crafts* and related reactions. In industry this means that it is an important catalyst for the manufacture of a wide range of useful products including *polymers*, pigments, pharmaceuticals, *dyes* and *detergents*.

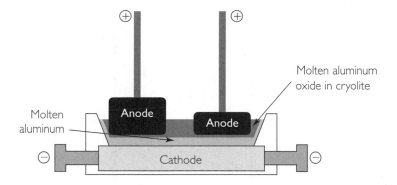

Cross sectional diagram of an electrolysis cell for extracting aluminum

aluminum extraction: *aluminum* is obtained by *electrolysis* of a solution of aluminum oxide in molten cryolite, Na_3AlF_6. Pure aluminum oxide for the process is obtained by purifying *bauxite*.

The discovery that aluminum oxide dissolves in molten cryolite was essential to the development of the process because the pure oxide melts at 2015°C – much too high for economic industrial processing.

Electrolysis takes place in carbon-lined steel tanks called "pots." The carbon lining is the *cathode* of the cell. The *anodes* are blocks of carbon. The currents used are high, of the order of 100 000 A, so the process is generally carried out where electricity is relatively cheap, often close to a source of hydroelectric power.

    Reduction at the cathode: $Al^{3+} + 3e^- \longrightarrow Al$

The aluminum is liquid at the temperature of the molten electrolyte (970°C) and it collects at the bottom of the pot. The molten metal is tapped off from time to time.

    Oxidation at the anode: $2O^{2-} \longrightarrow O_2 + 4e^-$

Much of the oxygen reacts with the carbon of the anodes, forming carbon dioxide. The anodes burn away and have to be replaced regularly.

Waste gas from the cell contains fluorides and has to be thoroughly cleaned to avoid pollution of the region surrounding the plant.

aluminum(III) ions are hydrated in aqueous solution and are present as a *complex ion* $[Al(H_2O)_6]^{3+}$. Six water molecules form *coordinate bonds* with each metal ion.

The electrons in the water molecules are pulled toward the highly polarizing aluminum ion, making it easier for the water molecules linked to the aluminum ion to give away protons. The hydrated aluminum ion is as strong an *acid* as ethanoic acid. The hydrated ion gives protons to water molecules, forming *oxonium ions*. The solution is acidic enough to release carbon dioxide when added to sodium carbonate.

$$[Al(H_2O)_6]^{3+} + H_2O \rightleftharpoons [Al(H_2O)_5OH]^{2+} + H_3O^+$$
$$[Al(H_2O)_5OH]^{2+} + H_2O \rightleftharpoons [Al(H_2O)_4(OH)_2]^+ + H_3O^+$$

Adding a base such as hydroxide ions to a solution of aluminum ions removes a third proton, producing an uncharged complex. The uncharged complex is much less

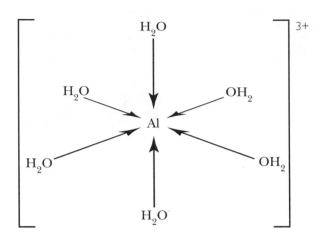

Structure of a hydrated aluminum ion showing the octahedral arrangement of water molecules. This is the hexaaquoaluminate(III) ion.

soluble in water and precipitates as a white jellylike precipitate – hydrated aluminum hydroxide.

$$[Al(H_2O)_4(OH)_2]^+ + OH^- \rightleftharpoons [Al(H_2O)_3(OH)_3](s)$$

Adding excess alkali removes yet another proton, now producing a negatively charged ion that is soluble in water so that the precipitate redissolves. This demonstrates the *amphoteric* properties of aluminum hydroxide.

$$[Al(H_2O)_3(OH)_3](s) + OH^- \rightleftharpoons [Al(H_2O)_2(OH)_4]^-(aq)$$

All these changes are reversed by adding a solution of a strong acid such as hydrochloric acid, which turns the hydroxide ions in the complex back to water molecules.

aluminum oxide (Al_2O_3) is a white solid with a very high melting point. Aluminum oxide exists naturally as a group of minerals called corundum. Corundum is an important abrasive; its hardness is 9 on the *Mohs scale of hardness*. Emery is a grayish-black variety of corundum made of aluminum oxide mixed with iron oxide minerals. Some gemstones are varieties of corundum including rubies, which are red because of the presence of some chromium(III) ions in place of aluminum(III) in the crystal structure. Sapphires are blue because some of the aluminum ions are replaced by a mixture of titanium(IV) and cobalt(II) or iron(II) ions.

Aluminum oxide is widely used as an engineering *ceramic*. It is used to make the insulator in spark plugs. A translucent, polycrystalline form of the compound encloses high-pressure, high-temperature sodium street lamps, which give a much whiter light than yellow low-pressure lamps.

Aluminum oxide is an *amphoteric compound* but the pure solid is insoluble and this property is more easily demonstrated by adding alkali to a solution of aluminum(III) ions. The amphoteric behavior is used in the production of the pure oxide from *bauxite*.

alums are *double salts* that crystallize easily from solutions in water, forming attractive octahedral crystals. Alums have the general formula $M(I)M(III)(SO_4)_2.12H_2O$. M(I) is an ion with a 1+ charge such as Na^+, K^+ or NH_4^+ and M(III) is a metal ion with a 3+ charge such as Al^{3+}, Cr^{3+} or Fe^{3+}.

amalgams are solutions of metals in mercury. Dentists make amalgams for filling teeth by dissolving silver, copper and tin in mercury.

amides are organic nitrogen compounds derived from *carboxylic acids* by replacing the hydroxide group with an — NH_2 group.

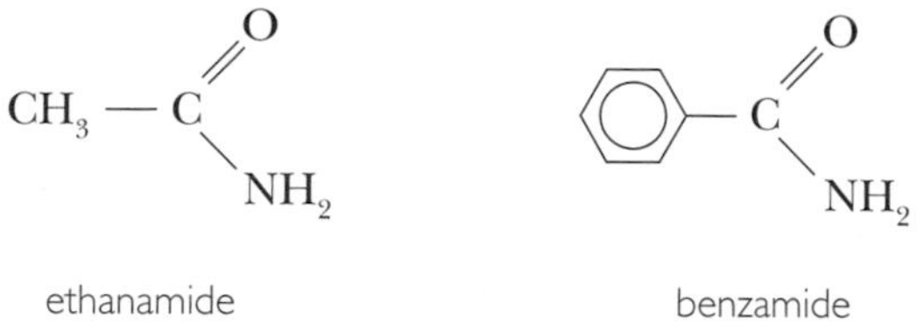

ethanamide   benzamide

Names and structures of amides

Amides are white crystalline solids at room temperature apart from methanamide, which is a liquid. Simple amides are soluble in water.

Amides form rapidly at room temperature when *acyl chlorides* or *acid anhydrides* react with ammonia. *Esters* react more slowly to form amides.

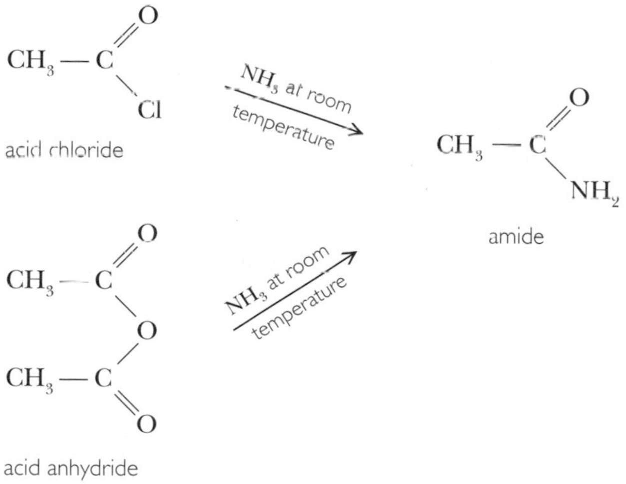

acid chloride

amide

acid anhydride

Reactions that produce amides

Another way of making amides is to convert a carboxylic acid to an ammonium salt and then to dehydrate the salt by heating it under reflux for several hours.

$$CH_3CO_2H + NH_3 \longrightarrow CH_3CO_2^-NH_4^+ \longrightarrow CH_3CONH_2 + H_2O$$

carboxylic   ammonia   ammonium salt   amide
acid

Unlike *amines*, amides are very weak bases. They give neutral solutions in water and do not form salts with acids such as hydrochloric acid. The lone pair of electrons on the nitrogen atom is delocalized with the carbonyl group.

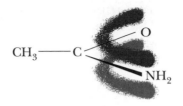

Delocalization of electrons in the amide group

Reduction converts an amide to an amine. A suitable procedure is to treat the amide with *lithium tetrahydridoaluminate(III)* in dry ethoxyethane and then add water.

$$CH_3CONH_2 \xrightarrow[\text{2. H}_2\text{O}]{\text{1. LiAlH}_4 \text{ in ether}} CH_3CH_2NH_2$$

Heating with dilute acid or dilute alkali hydrolyzes amides to the corresponding acid.

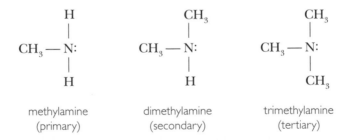

Hydrolysis of ethanamide

(See also *Hofmann degradation*.)

amines are nitrogen compounds in which one or more of the hydrogen atoms in ammonia (NH_3) is replaced by an *alkyl group* or *aryl group*. The number of alkyl groups determines whether the compound is a primary, secondary or tertiary amine.

The names of amines are based on the nature and number of alkyl groups attached to the nitrogen atom.

H | CH_3 — N: | H	CH_3 | CH_3 — N: | H	CH_3 | CH_3 — N: | CH_3
methylamine (primary)	dimethylamine (secondary)	trimethylamine (tertiary)

Names and structures of primary, secondary and tertiary amines. Note the meaning of primary, secondary and tertiary here – it is not the same as for alcohols and halogenoalkanes.

Amines can be very smelly. Ethylamine has a fishy smell. Animal flesh smells putrescent because it gives off diamines.

Primary amines like ammonia can act as *bases*, form *complex ions* with metal ions and react as *nucleophiles*.

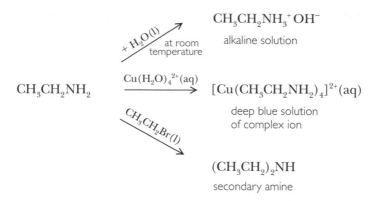

Reactions of the primary amine, propylamine

amino acids are compounds that join together in long chains to make *proteins*. They are carbon compounds with two *functional groups*: an amino group and a carboxylic acid group. Proteins consist of long chains of amino acids. There are about 20 different amino acids that link together to make proteins.

$$H_2N - \underset{\underset{H}{|}}{\overset{\overset{H}{|}}{C}} - CO_2H \qquad H_2N - \underset{\underset{H}{|}}{\overset{\overset{CH_3}{|}}{C}} - CO_2H \qquad H_2N - \underset{\underset{H}{|}}{\overset{\overset{CH_2OH}{|}}{C}} - CO_2H$$

glycine alanine serine

Examples of amino acids in proteins. Note that the amino group is attached to the carbon atom next to the carboxylic acid group.

Amino acids are crystalline solids. They are very soluble in water and crystallize as *zwitterions*.

Each of the amino acids in a protein has a central carbon atom attached to four other groups so, except for glycine, which has two hydrogen atoms, these are *chiral* molecules, which can exist in mirror-image forms. The natural amino acids all take the L-form.

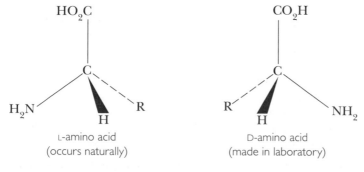

L-amino acid
(occurs naturally)

D-amino acid
(made in laboratory)

Mirror-image forms of an amino acid

amino group: the — NH_2 functional group found in primary *amines* and *amino acids*. As in *ammonia*, there is a *lone pair of electrons* on the nitrogen atom. The amino group, like ammonia, can act as a *base*, form *complex ions* with metal ions and react as a *nucleophile*.

ammines are *complex ions* formed between metal ions and ammonia molecules. Examples are the diamminesilver(I) ion and the tetraammine copper(II) ion. The *lone pair* on the nitrogen atom of each ammonia molecule forms a dative covalent bond with the central metal ion (see *coordinate bond*).

$$[Ag(NH_3)_2]^+$$

diamminesilver(I) ion

$$[Ca(NH_3)_6]^{2+}$$

hexaamminecobalt(II) ion

Ammine complexes

Ammine complexes are useful in *qualitative analysis*. Formation of a complex may produce a color change or redissolve a precipitate. Adding ammonia solution to a solution with copper(II) ions first produces a pale blue precipitate of the hydroxide, but with excess ammonia the precipitate dissolves to give a deep blue solution when the tetraammine complex forms.

Adding ammonia solution to a precipitate of a *silver halide* can distinguish the chloride from the bromide or iodide. Only silver chloride (the least insoluble) will freely dissolve in dilute ammonia solution to form the diammine complex.

ammonia (NH_3) is the simplest compound of nitrogen and hydrogen. It is a colorless gas with a pungent smell. It is the only common alkaline gas. The molecule has a pyramidal shape:

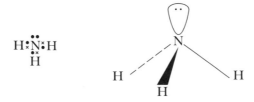

Dot and cross diagram for ammonia and the shape of an ammonia molecule. There are three bonding pairs and one lone pair in the outer shell the nitrogen atom. The four electron pairs point to the vertices of a distorted tetrahedron. The bond angle is less than the regular tetrahedral angle (109.5°) because repulsion between the lone pair and the bonding pairs is greater than the repulsion between bonding pairs (see shapes of molecules).

The properties of ammonia are affected by *hydrogen bonding*. Ammonia molecules can form hydrogen bonds with each other and with water molecules. As expected for a compound with small molecules, ammonia is a gas at room temperature but because of hydrogen bonding it is quite easily liquefied by cooling or increasing the pressure. Ammonia is also very soluble in water because of hydrogen bonding.

Many of the important properties of ammonia involve the lone pair of electrons on the nitrogen atom. The lone pair means that ammonia is:

- a *weak base*: $NH_3(g) + HCl(g) \longrightarrow NH_4^+Cl^-(s)$
- a *ligand* in *complex ions* (see *ammines*):

$$[Cu(H_2O)_6]^{2+}(aq) + 4NH_3(aq) \longrightarrow [Cu(NH_3)_4(H_2O)_2]^{2+}(aq)$$
$$+ 4H_2O(aq)$$

- a *nucleophile*: $CH_3CH_2CH_2Br + NH_3(aq) \longrightarrow CH_3CH_2CH_2NH_3^+Br^-(aq)$.

Other reactions of ammonia involve the N — H bonds. In particular, the reactions in which ammonia acts as a *reducing agent*. Ammonia burns in oxygen to form nitrogen and steam. It reacts with chlorine to form nitrogen and ammonium chloride. It reduces metal oxides, such as copper (II) oxide.

$$3CuO(s) + 2NH_3(g) \longrightarrow 3Cu(s) + N_2(g) + H_2O(l)$$

The catalytic oxidation of ammonia is important in *nitric acid manufacture*.

ammonia manufacture: the Haber process for the synthesis of ammonia combines nitrogen with hydrogen in the presence of an iron catalyst.

$$N_2(g) + 3H_2(g) \rightleftharpoons 2NH_3(g) \qquad \Delta H - -92.4 \text{ kJ mol}^{-1}$$

Hydrogen for the process comes from natural gas and steam (see *steam reforming*). The nitrogen comes from the air.

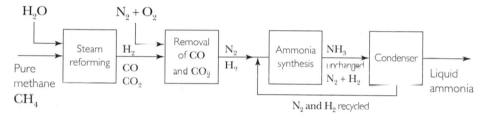

Flow diagram for the synthesis of ammonia

The reaction is very slow at room temperature. Raising the temperature increases the rate of reaction but the *reversible* reaction is *exothermic* so, according to *Le Chatelier's principle*, the higher the temperature, the lower the yield of ammonia at equilibrium. A catalyst makes it possible for the reaction to go fast enough without the temperature being so high that the yield is too low. Also, according to Le Chatelier's principle, increasing the pressure raises the percentage of ammonia at equilibrium.

The process typically operates at pressures between 70 atmospheres and 200 atmospheres with temperatures in the range 400°C to 600°C.

Fritz Haber applied theory to develop the process and made it work on a small scale. The key to success was to find the right conditions and to identify a suitable catalyst. Haber used platinum in his small-scale demonstration process. The engineering problems of manufacturing ammonia on a large scale were solved by Carl Bosch, who worked for the chemical company BASF. Bosch's team also carried out thousands of experiments to find a cheaper catalyst. They eventually developed a catalyst based on iron oxide mixed with small amounts of the oxides of other metals such as potassium, aluminum and magnesium. The first industrial plant went into production in 1913 near Mannheim in Germany.

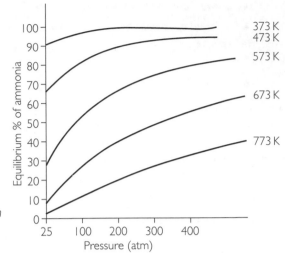

Graph showing how the equilibrium yield of ammonia varies with pressure and temperature

The main uses of ammonia are in making:

- *fertilizers* (80%)
- nylon (7%)
- *nitric acid* (5%).

ammonium hydroxide is the traditional name for ammonia solution or aqueous ammonia. The older name was used because a solution of *ammonia* in water contains some ammonium ions and hydroxide ions.

$$NH_3(aq) + H_2O(l) \rightleftharpoons NH_4^+(aq) + OH^-(aq)$$

However, ammonia is a *weak base,* so most of the ammonia in the solution is not ionized. Aqueous ammonia is a better name, because almost all the ammonia is present as dissolved molecules linked to water molecules by *hydrogen bonds.*

ammonium salts contain the ammonium ion (NH_4^+), formed when *ammonia* reacts with acids. Examples are ammonium chloride, ammonium sulfate and ammonium nitrate.

$$2NH_3(aq) + H_2SO_4(aq) \longrightarrow (NH_4)_2SO_4(aq)$$
$$NH_3(aq) + HNO_3(aq) \longrightarrow NH_4NO_3(aq)$$

An ammonium ion forms when the lone pair on the nitrogen atom in ammonia forms a dative bond with a hydrogen ion (proton) from an acid. The ammonium ion has four bonding electron pairs around the nitrogen atom so it has a tetrahedral shape.

Formation of an ammonium ion and the shape of the ammonium ion. Once formed, all four bonds are the same.

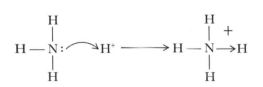

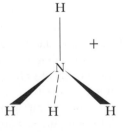

Ammonium salts such as ammonium sulfate and ammonium nitrate are soluble nitrogen compounds manufactured and used on a large scale as *fertilizers*. Ammonium nitrate is also used as an explosive.

amorphous solids have no regular crystal structure; their particles are in a random jumble. *Glasses* are amorphous solids.

amount of substance: the measurement that allows chemists to find formulas, write equations and make comparisons between equal numbers of atoms, molecules or ions.

Amount of substance is a physical quantity (symbol n) that is measured in the unit *mole* (symbol mol). In chemistry the word "amount" has this precise meaning. There is no measuring instrument for determining amounts directly, unlike balances for determining *masses* in kilograms or graduated glassware for measuring *volumes* in dm³ (liters). Instead, chemists first measure masses or volumes and then calculate the amount in moles given the *molar mass, concentration* or *molar volume* of the specified substance or *entity*.

For any pure substance:

$$\text{amount of substance (mol)} = \frac{\text{mass of substance (g)}}{\text{molar mass (g mol}^{-1})}$$

For a solution:

$$\text{amount of substance (mol)} = \text{volume of solution (dm}^3) \times \text{concentration of solution (mol dm}^{-3})$$

For a gas:

$$\text{amount of substance (mol)} = \frac{\text{volume of a gas at a specified temperature and pressure (m}^3)}{\text{molar volume of any gas under the same conditions (m}^3\text{ mol}^{-1})}$$

(See also the *Avogadro constant.*)

ampere: the SI unit of current. A current of one ampere is a flow of one *coulomb* of charge per second. $1 A = 1 C/s$.

amphetamines are *drugs* that stimulate the central nervous system and make people feel more alert. For a while amphetamines, such as Benzedrine, were used medicinally until it was found that they cause strong psychological dependence.

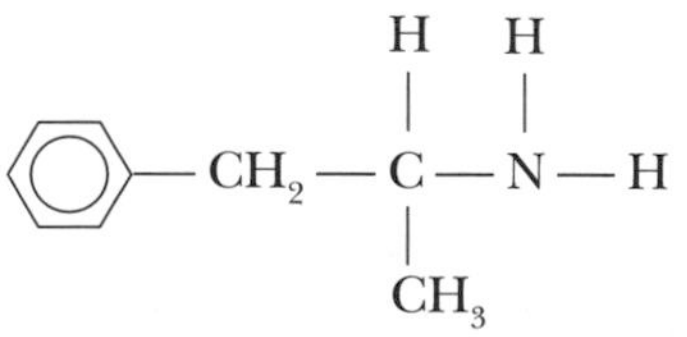

Molecular structure of Benzedrine

amphoteric compounds are substances that can behave both as *acids* and as *bases*. Water is an example. Water can both accept *protons* from acids forming *oxonium ions* and donate protons to stronger *bases* forming hydroxide ions.

Water acting as a base (taking protons from an acid):

$$H_2O(l) + H^+ \rightleftharpoons H_3O^+(aq)$$

from acid

Water acting as an acid (giving protons to a base):

$$H_2O(l) \rightleftharpoons OH^-(aq) + H^+$$
to base

Alternatively, these substances are described as being amphiprotic. Other examples are the hydrogencarbonate ion (HCO_3^-) and *amino acids*.

amphoteric oxides are oxides that react both like *acidic oxides* and *basic oxides*. Examples are: ZnO, Al_2O_3, Cr_2O_3, SnO, SnO_2, PbO, PbO_2. The anhydrous oxides are often relatively *inert* to aqueous reagents so that it is easier to demonstrate their amphoteric behavior on a test-tube scale with freshly formed samples of the metal hydroxides. Zinc hydroxide, for example, dissolves in acids to form *salts* (so acting as a *base*); it also dissolves in a solution of a strong alkali, forming zincate ions (thus acting as an *acid*).

$$Zn(OH)_2(s) + 2H^+(aq) \rightleftharpoons Zn^{2+}(aq) + 2H_2O(l)$$
$$Zn(OH)_2(s) + 2OH^-(aq) \rightleftharpoons ZnO_2^{2-}(aq) + 2H_2O(l)$$

amylases are *enzymes* that catalyze the *hydrolysis* of *starch* molecules to *sugars*. Amylases are found in saliva and in the juices secreted into the small intestine by the pancreas.

anaerobic respiration: see *respiration*.

analgesics: drugs that relieve pain. Analgesics may be mild like *aspirin* or powerful like morphine (from the opium poppy), which is a *narcotic*.

analytic chemistry is concerned with determining the *qualitative* and *quantitative* composition of substances.

anesthetics: total anesthetics are used in medicine to induce pain-free sleep during surgery. Early anesthetics were trichloromethane (chloroform), ethoxyethane (ether) and dinitrogen oxide (laughing gas). Since 1956 the most commonly used anesthetic has been halothane, $CF_3CHBrCl$. Local anesthetics, such as Novocaine, for minor surgery and dentistry prevent pain in the region of the body where they are applied or injected.

Ångström, Anders (1814–1874) was a Swedish spectroscopist who detected *hydrogen* in the Sun from a study of the lines in the spectrum of sunlight. He gave his name to the ångström unit, a non-*SI unit* of length that is sometimes used to measure the sizes of atoms and molecules and the wavelength of light. $1\,\text{Å} = 10^{-10}\,\text{m} = 0.1\,\text{nm}$.

anhydrides: see *acid anhydrides*.

anhydrous salts are the compounds left after removing the water from a *hydrated* salt. Hydrated copper(II) sulfate, for example, is blue. Heating drives off the *water of crystallization* as steam, leaving a white solid, anhydrous copper(II) sulfate.

$$CuSO_4.5H_2O(s) \longrightarrow CuSO_4(s) + 5H_2O(l)$$

aniline is the traditional name for *phenylamine*. Aniline and related compounds are used to make *azo dyes*, which are therefore also called aniline dyes.

anions are negative ions attracted to the *anode* during *electrolysis*.

charge	anion	symbol
1–	bromide	Br^-
	chloride	Cl^-
	ethanoate	$CH_3CO_2^-$
	hydrogencarbonate	HCO_3^-
	hydroxide	OH^-
	iodide	I^-
	nitrate [nitrate(V)]	NO_3^-
	nitrite [nitrate(III)]	NO_2^-
	manganate(VII)	MnO_4^-
2–	carbonate	CO_3^{2-}
	oxide	O^{2-}
	sulfate [sulfate(VI)]	SO_4^{2-}
	sulfide	S^{2-}
	sulfite [sulfate(IV)]	SO_3^{2-}
	thiosulfate	$S_2O_3^{2-}$
	dichromate(VI)	$Cr_2O_7^{2-}$
3–	nitride	N^{3-}
	phosphate	PO_4^{3-}

anion tests are used in *qualitative analysis* to identify the negative ions in salts. The tests use reagents that can produce color changes, gases and precipitates. Knowledge of the chemistry makes it possible to interpret the changes and identify the ions. See the table on page 36.

anisotropic solids have properties that depend on the direction in which they are measured. Examples of highly anisotropic substances are fibrous materials such as *asbestos*, and layer structures such as mica. The carbon atoms in graphite are arranged in layers. The properties of large single crystals of graphite show differences when measured parallel to the planes of atoms and at right angles to the planes of atoms.

annealing is a process of controlled heating and cooling used to modify the properties of a material, for which purpose it is kept for a time in a furnace at a temperature below its melting point. Annealing is used to remove internal stresses from *glass* objects after blowing or casting. Annealing is an important part of the heat treatment used to modify *crystal structures of metals* and hence control their properties.

anode: the *electrode* at which *oxidation* takes place. During *electrolysis* the external power supply removes electrons from the anode so that it becomes the positive electrode, attracting negative ions; the latter lose electrons (oxidation), thus turning into atoms or molecules.

The term anode is also sometimes used in *electrochemical cells*, where the oxidation process at this electrode in one of the *half-cells* forces electrons onto the electrode, which becomes the negative terminal of the cell.

Note that electrons flow out of the anode to the external circuit both during electrolysis and when a current is drawn from a chemical cell.

Test	Observations	Inference
Test for carbonate, sulfite and nitrite Add dilute hydrochloric acid to the solid salt. Warm gently if there is no reaction at first.	Gas that turns limewater milky white.	carbon dioxide from a carbonate
	Gas that is acidic, has a pungent smell and turns acid-dichromate paper from orange to green.	sulfur dioxide from a sulfite
	Colorless gas given off that turns brown where it meets the air.	nitrogen oxide (NO) from a nitrite turning to nitrogen dioxide (NO_2)
Test for halide ions Make a solution of the salt. Acidify with nitric acid, then add silver nitrate solution. Test the solubility of the precipitate in ammonia solution.	White precipitate soluble in dilute ammonia solution.	chloride
	Cream precipitate soluble in concentrated ammonia solution.	bromide
	Yellow precipitate insoluble in excess ammonia.	iodide
Test for sulfate and sulfite ions Make a solution of the salt. Add a solution of barium nitrate or chloride. If a precipitate forms add dilute nitric acid.	White precipitate that redissolves on adding acid.	sulfite
	White precipitate that does not redissolve in acid.	sulfate
Test for nitrates Make a solution of the salt, add sodium hydroxide solution and then a piece of aluminum foil or a little Devarda alloy. Heat.	Alkaline gas evolved that turns red litmus blue. Pungent smell.	ammonia from a nitrate (or nitrite)
Test for chromate ions Make a solution of the salt. Divide into three: • add dilute acid • add a solution of barium nitrate • add a solution of lead nitrate.	Yellow solution turns orange.	yellow chromate ions turning to orange dichromate
	Yellow precipitates forms with barium ions and lead ions.	precipitates of insoluble barium and lead chromates
		chromate

Anion tests

anodizing is an electrolytic process for thickening the oxide layer on the surface of *aluminum*. It is an example of anodic *oxidation*. In the process an aluminum sheet or component is the *anode* of an *electrolysis* cell containing sulfuric acid. The newly formed oxide layer can absorb dyes so that the surface of anodized aluminum is easily colored. The thicker oxide film helps to protect the metal, so anodized aluminum is more resistant to *corrosion*.

antacids are ingredients of indigestion tablets taken to neutralize acid in the stomach. After a meal the cells lining the stomach produce gastric juice that contains, among other things, a mixture of hydrochloric acid and enzymes to digest food. Antacids are *bases* that neutralize acids. Examples are sodium hydrogencarbonate, calcium carbonate, aluminum hydroxide and magnesium hydroxide.

antibiotics are chemicals that prevent *bacteria* growing or kill them. Thus antibiotics can cure bacterial diseases. Most antibiotics are the products of microorganisms. Some of the antibiotics used in medicine are natural but have been modified chemically, such as the semisynthetic penicillins. Other antibiotics are made entirely by chemical synthesis.

antifreeze is a chemical added to the cooling system of engines to prevent water freezing and damaging the engine during frosty weather. Antifreeze lowers the *freezing point* of water well below 0°C. Ethane-1,2-diol is used as antifreeze because it mixes freely with water but has a higher boiling point (198°C) so that it does not evaporate from the coolant when the engine is hot.

antiknock additives prevent knocking in engines by raising the octane number of *gasoline* and preventing the fuel from igniting too early. From the 1920s the main antiknock additive was the volatile lead compound tetraethyl lead, $Pb(C_2H_5)_4$. Lead compounds in exhaust gases are toxic and so poison the metal catalyst in *catalytic converters*. So petroleum companies now produce high-octane fuels by refining the fuel further and adding alcohols and *ethers* such as MTBE.

antiseptics are chemicals that kill microorganisms, but, unlike *disinfectants*, can safely be used on the skin. *Phenol* was the first antiseptic used in surgery, by Joseph Lister in 1857. Lister found that a spray of phenol controlled the growth of bacteria in open wounds but it also made the wounds difficult to heal so he moved on to other methods.

aqua regia was well known to alchemists for its ability to dissolve noble metals such as gold, hence its name, which is based on Latin for "royal water." It is a mixture of three parts concentrated *hydrochloric acid* with one part concentrated *nitric acid*.

aqueous solution: a solution of one or more *solutes* dissolved in water. The state symbol (aq) in *chemical equations* shows that a *species* is in aqueous solution.

arenes are *hydrocarbons* such as *benzene* with rings of carbon atoms stabilized by *delocalized electrons*. Traditionally, chemists have called the arenes "aromatic hydrocarbons," ever since Kekulé was struck by the fragrant smell of oils such as benzene. In the modern name, the "ar-" comes from aromatic and the ending "-ene" means that these hydrocarbons are unsaturated compounds like the *alkenes*.

As well as arenes related to benzene, there are others with fused ring systems such as naphthalene and anthracene.

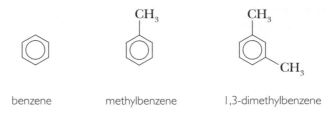

benzene   methylbenzene   1,3-dimethylbenzene

Structures of arenes. The circle in the benzene ring represents six delocalized electrons. This representation explains the shape and stability of benzene. The Kekulé structure is more helpful when describing the mechanism of the reactions of benzene.

Structure of naphthalene with fused rings, showing both the Kekulé structure and delocalization. The delocalized electrons are shared across both the rings.

Arenes are nonpolar. The forces between the molecules are weak *van der Waals forces*. The boiling points of arenes depend on the sizes of the molecules. The bigger the molecules, the higher the boiling points. Benzene and methylbenzene are liquids at room temperature. Naphthalene is a solid.

The important reactions of benzene and other arenes are very different from those of *alkenes* because of the delocalized electrons. Instead of *electrophilic addition* reactions, the useful changes are *electrophilic substitution* reactions.

Heating a mixture of an arene bearing a hydrocarbon side chain with alkaline potassium manganate(VII) oxidizes the side chain to a carboxylic acid group.

methylbenzene   benzoic acid

Oxidation of the hydrocarbon side chain of methylbenzene

argon (Ar) is the third member of the family of *noble gases* coming below neon in the periodic table with the *electron configuration* $[Ne]3s^23p^6$. It is a colorless, odorless gas consisting of single atoms.

Argon makes up about 0.9% of dry *air* but it was not identified until the late nineteenth century because of its inertness. It was discovered in the 1880s when the physicist Lord Rayleigh attempted to determine very accurately the densities of gases. He discovered a discrepancy of 0.1% between the density of the nitrogen he got from the air and the nitrogen made by decomposing ammonia gas. Prompted by this observation, William Ramsay set about removing all known gases from the air, including all the nitrogen. He found that he was left with an inert gas. When he looked at the emission spectrum of the gas he found lines in the spectrum that did not belong to any known element. Ramsay and Rayleigh amazed a group of scientists at Oxford in August 1894 by announcing the discovery of the new element. The chairman of the meeting christened the gas argon from the Greek word meaning idle, or lazy.

Argon is produced by the *fractional distillation* of liquid air. Ninety percent of the gas is used to provide an inert atmosphere for processes such as welding; the other 10% is used to fill filament lamps.

aromatic hydrocarbons: an older term for *arenes*.

aromatic substitution: another name for *electrophilic substitution* in arenes.

Arrhenius equation: an equation that describes how the rate constant for a reaction varies with temperature and makes it possible to determine the *activation energy* for the reaction (see *rate equation*). The *collision theory* of reaction rates helps to account for the form of the equation.

Arrhenius equation: $k = Ae^{-E_a/RT}$

k is the rate constant for the reaction, E_a is the activation energy, R is the gas constant and T the temperature in kelvin. A is another constant.

Putting the equation into logarithmic form (using *logarithms* to base e) makes it easier to use.

$$\ln k = \ln A - \frac{E_a}{RT} = \text{constant} - \frac{E_a}{RT}$$

This equation gives a straight line if $\ln k$ is plotted against $1/T$. The gradient of the line is $-E_a/R$.

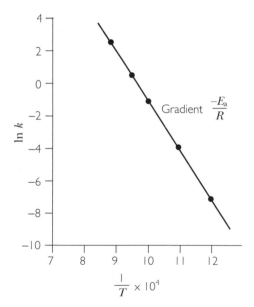

Plot of $\ln k$ *against* $1/T$ *for a reaction*

arsenic (As) is a grayish-white *metalloid* that forms very toxic compounds. The element comes below phosphorus in group 5 of the *periodic table* and has the *electron configuration* $[Ar]3d^{10}4s^24p^3$.

aryl group: a group of carbon and hydrogen atoms that forms part of the structure of a molecule. The simplest example is the *phenyl group*, C_6H_5 —, which is *benzene* with one hydrogen atom removed. In general aryl groups are arene molecules minus one hydrogen atom.

asbestos is the name given to various fibrous *silicate* minerals in which SiO_4 groups are linked into long chains. These minerals have very high melting points and they do not burn. The *fibers* are flexible enough to be woven into fabrics that are heat resistant, fireproof and do not conduct electricity. Breathing asbestos fibers can cause lung disease many years later, including asbestosis and mesothelioma (a form of cancer). For this reason the use of the asbestos has been phased out in many parts of the world, especially blue asbestos, which is particularly hazardous.

ascorbic acid (vitamin C) is a white crystalline compound found dissolved in the juices of fresh fruit and vegetables. Lack of ascorbic acid in the diet leads to scurvy. Ascorbic acid is relatively soluble in water and may be washed out of foods on cooking. It is thermally unstable and is progressively destroyed during cooking.

$$HO - \overset{\displaystyle \overset{H}{|}}{C} - CH_2OH$$

Structure of ascorbic acid

The ascorbic acid molecule does not contain a free *carboxylic acid* group because its carboxyl group reacts with its hydroxyl group, eliminating water to form a ring compound. Ascorbic acid is a good *reducing agent*. It is added to some processed foods as a preservative; as an antioxidant, it prevents oxidation of other food components.

aspirin is the common name for the most widely used medical drug. Chemically it is the ethanoyl (acetyl) *ester* of 2-hydroxybenzoic acid (salicylic acid). (See *acylation*.)

Aspirin is a mild painkiller (*analgesic*); it also helps to lower fevers and reduce inflammation of joints. Large-scale studies have shown that people who have had a heart attack are less likely to have a second attack if they take half an aspirin tablet a day.

assaying is a process of *quantitative analysis* that determines the amount of a substance in a given sample. So a piece of gold is assayed to see what proportion of the metal sample is gold. Gold and silver articles are assayed before being hallmarked. A range of assaying techniques has been developed to determine the purity or biological activity of drugs, enzymes and other substances that affect living things.

astatine (At) is the rarest element in the *halogen* family. It is the element below iodine in group 7 of the periodic table. It has the *electron configuration* $[Xe]4f^{14}5d^{10}6s^26p^5$. There are twenty known *isotopes* of astatine, all of which are highly *radioactive.* The longest lived is astatine-210 with a *half-life* of 8.3 hours. The element was discovered in 1940 when it was prepared artificially by bombarding bismuth with *alpha particles* in a cyclotron.

asymmetric molecules are molecules with no centers, axes or planes of symmetry. Asymmetric molecules are *chiral* and can exist in distinct mirror image forms, giving rise to *optical isomerism.* Any carbon atom with four different groups or atoms attached to it is asymmetric.

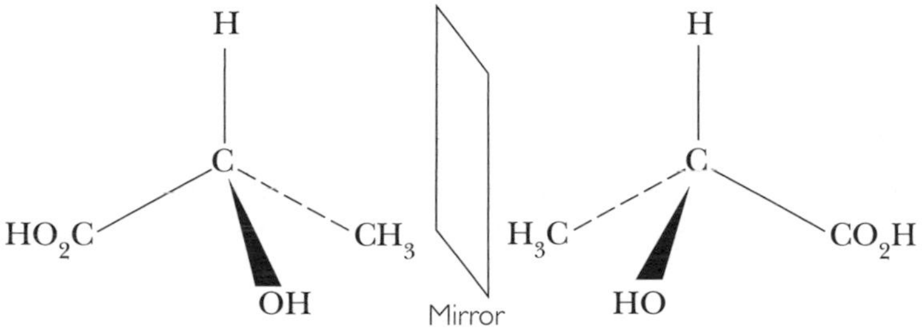

The mirror image forms of the asymmetric molecule, lactic acid

atactic polymer: a form of *addition polymer*, such as poly(propene), in which the side groups along the *polymer* chain are randomly orientated. Atactic poly(propene) is an *amorphous*, rubbery polymer of little value, unlike *isotactic* poly(propene).

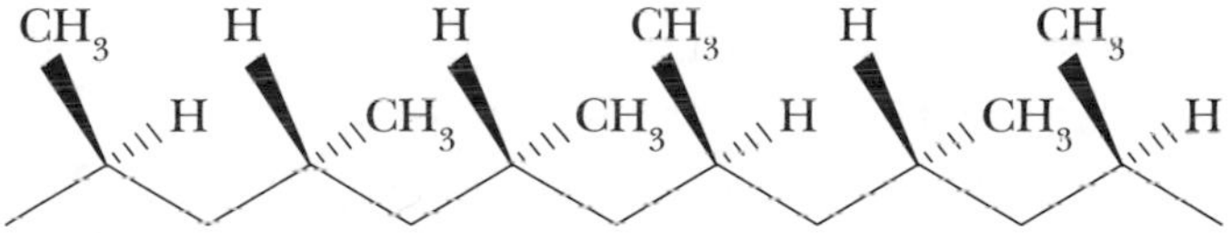

Part of a chain of atactic poly(propene)

atmosphere: the zone around the Earth that contains all the gases in the *air.* By convention the upper limit of the atmosphere is taken to be 1000 km above the Earth's surface. However, because of gravity, most of the air is concentrated in the lower regions. About 50% by mass lies within 5.6 km of the surface and 99% within 40 km. Most of the climate and weather processes take place in the troposphere, which extends up to about 17 km.

atmospheric pressure usually means the *pressure* of the atmosphere at ground level. Standard atmospheric pressure (1 atm) = 101 325 Nm^{-2} = 101.325 kPa. The choice of this value dates back to the days when atmospheric pressure was normally measured by a column of mercury in a barometer. A pressure of one atmosphere was defined as the pressure needed to support a column of mercury 760 mm high.

atom: the smallest particle of an element. An atom consists of a tiny nucleus surrounded by a cloud of electrons. The nucleus consists of protons and neutrons. All the atoms of the same element have the same *proton number.* The number of neutrons may vary and this accounts for the existence of *isotopes.*

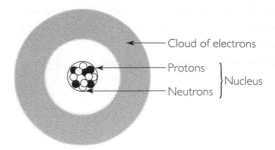

Atomic structure

Chemical reactions involve the electrons in the outer *shells* of atoms. As a result the *electron configuration* of an element helps to account for its chemical behavior.

Radioactivity and the changes in nuclear reactors involve the nuclei of atoms. When describing nuclear changes it helps to use symbols that show the *nucleon number* (mass number) and proton number.

Symbols for atoms. The proton number gives the number of protons in the nucleus. In a neutral atom the number of electrons is the same. The difference between the nucleon number and the proton number gives the number of neutrons in the nucleus.

atomic absorption spectroscopy is a technique of *quantitative analysis* for measuring the amount of an element in a sample. The procedure depends on the fact that the atoms absorb radiation at particular frequencies.

The sample is vaporized and split into gaseous atoms by a very hot flame at around 2000°C. Light from a special lamp produces radiation with a wavelength absorbed by the element to be measured.

By measuring the *absorbance* at a particular wavelength it is possible to determine the amount of certain elements in the sample. The procedure is calibrated using samples of known concentration.

Atomic absorption spectroscopy provides a sensitive and reliable method for determining more than 60 elements. Examples include the determination of traces of mercury in the environment, lead in blood, or heavy metals in the effluent from a factory. The technique is widely used in commercial laboratories, for example in the water industry.

atomic emission spectroscopy is a very sensitive method of analysis used to identify and measure the elements in a sample. Atomic emission spectra of pure elements also provide the evidence needed to determine the *energy levels* and *electron configurations* in atoms.

Carrying out a *flame test* and examining the colored light from the flame with a hand-held spectroscope is a simple demonstration of this type of spectroscopy.

The first step in a more sophisticated analysis is to vaporize the sample using a very hot flame or an electric spark to atomize the sample and produce a gas consisting of free atoms. Energy from the flame or spark also excites some of the electrons in the atoms so that they jump to higher energy levels. As the electrons drop back to lower levels they emit radiation. The radiation passes through a prism or diffraction grating to produce the *atomic spectrum* of the elements in the sample.

Important applications of atomic emission spectroscopy include the measurement of sodium, potassium, lithium and calcium ions in biological fluids such as blood and urine.

atomic number is the older term for *proton number.*

atomic orbitals are the subdivisions of the main electron shells in atoms. There is one orbital in the first shell, four in the second, nine in the third and sixteen in the fourth shell. Each orbital can contain up to two electrons.

Each orbital is defined by its:

- energy
- shape
- direction in space.

The study of *atomic spectra* makes it possible to determine the energies of atomic orbitals. The terms "energy level" and "orbital" are often used interchangeably.

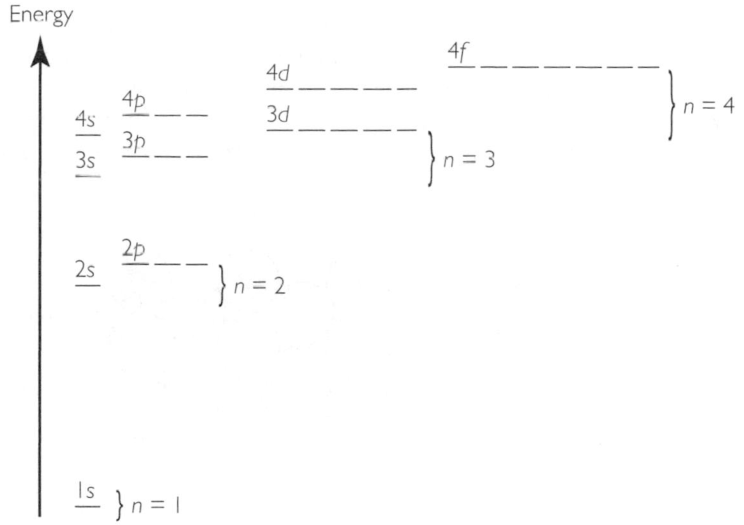

The energies of atomic orbitals in atoms. The labels s, p, d and f are left over from early studies of atomic spectra that used the words sharp, principal, diffuse and fundamental to describe different series of lines. The pattern of energy levels accounts for the electron configurations of atoms and the arrangement of elements in the periodic table.

The shapes of orbitals are derived from theory. The shapes are determined by solving a mathematical equation (the Schrödinger wave equation) that makes it possible to calculate the probability of finding an electron at any point in an atom.

The probable location of the electrons in the first shell is spherical. It is an example of an *s*-orbital (1*s*).

The four orbitals in the second shell are made up of one *s*-orbital (2*s*) and three dumbell shaped *p*-orbitals. The three *p*-orbitals ($2p_x$, $2p_y$, $2p_z$) are arranged at right angles to each other.

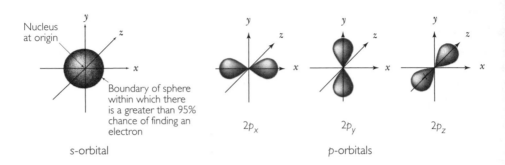

The shapes of s and p atomic orbitals

atomic radius: a measure of the size of an atom in a crystal or molecule. Chemists use *X-ray crystallography* and other techniques to measure the distance between the nuclei of atoms. The *atomic radius* of an atom depends on the type of bonding and on the number of bonds. Usually atomic radii for metals are calculated from the distances between atoms in metal crystals (metallic radii). Atomic radii for nonmetals are calculated from the lengths of covalent bonds in crystals or molecules (*covalent radii*).

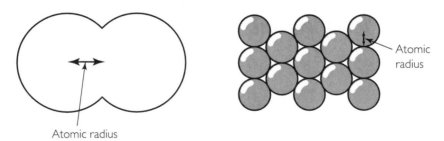

Atomic radii in a molecule and in a crystal

Atomic radii increase down any group in the periodic table as the number of electron shells increases. In *group 1* the metallic radii rise from 0.157 nm for lithium to 0.272 nm for cesium.

Atomic radii decrease from left to right across a period. Across the period Na to Ar, atomic radii fall from 0.191 nm for sodium to 0.099 nm for chlorine. From one element to the next across a period the charge on the nucleus increases by one as the number of electrons in the same outer shell increases by one. *Shielding* by electrons in the same shell is limited so the "effective nuclear charge" increases and the electrons are drawn more tightly to the nucleus.

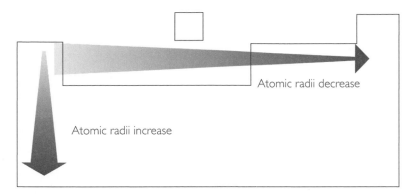

Trends in atomic radii in the periodic table

atomic spectrum: the pattern of lines seen with a spectroscope when the atoms of an element emit radiation. Atoms emit radiation when excited by heat or electricity.

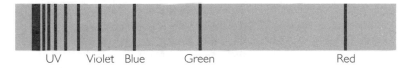

UV   Violet   Blue   Green   Red

The line emission spectrum for hydrogen in the visible and ultraviolet (UV) regions of the spectrum

Some elements emit radiation in the visible region of the spectrum and these are the elements that give colored flames in *flame tests.*

Quantum theory explains why atomic emission spectra consist of a series of sharp lines. Each line in an emission spectrum corresponds to an energy jump of a definite size as electrons drop back from a higher to a lower energy level.

Atoms also absorb radiation. If radiation passes through the vapor of an element and is viewed through a spectroscope, the absorption spectrum appears as dark lines where particular frequencies are absorbed from the continuous spectrum.

atomic theory: the theory that all matter is made up of very tiny particles called atoms. Modern atomic theory was foreshadowed in ancient Greek philosophy but chemists now trace the development of the theory back to the work of John Dalton. The significant ideas developed between 1800 and 1930. Studies of the structure of atomic nuclei continue with the help of huge particle accelerators such as those of CERN in Switzerland.

1804   John Dalton's theory of atoms as solid spheres explains the differences between elements and compounds. In this theory all the atoms of the same element weigh the same. It begins to be possible to determine chemical formulas by finding the combining masses of elements.

1896   Henri Becquerel discovers *radioactivity,* leading to the work of Marie and Pierre Curie who in the next few years separate and identify more radioactive elements.

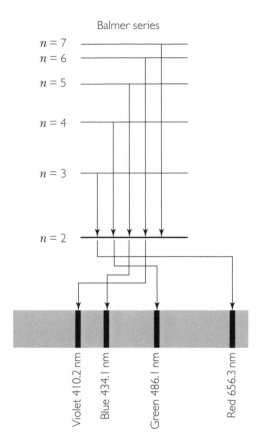

Balmer series

Atomic spectrum: electron jumps between energy levels in the hydrogen atom giving rise to the visible lines in the emission spectrum

1897   J J Thompson discovers the electron showing that atoms are themselves made up of even smaller particles.

1911   Hans Geiger and E Marsden's *alpha particle* scattering experiment leads to the Rutherford model of the atom with a tiny nucleus surrounded by orbiting electrons.

1913   Niels Bohr model explains the *atomic spectrum* of hydrogen by proposing that the electrons orbiting the nucleus could only have definite energies. According to *quantum theory* atoms absorb and emit radiation at particular frequencies depending on the size of the energy jumps between *energy levels*.

1919   Francis Aston uses his mass spectrograph to demonstrate the existence of *isotopes*, which had earlier been proposed by Soddy to describe atoms of the same element that have different masses.

1923   Louis-Victor de Broglie puts forward the theory that electrons have wave-like properties as well as particle properties. This theory is confirmed by experiment in 1927 when scientists in the USA and UK obtained diffraction effects with beams of electrons.

1926 Erwin Schrödinger publishes his mathematical theory of wave mechanics. The Schrödinger wave equation explains the pattern of energy levels in the hydrogen atoms and gives rise to the picture of electron in *atomic orbitals* with particular energies and shapes.

1932 James Chadwick discovers the neutron, making it possible to explain the existence of isotopes and radioactivity.

atomic weight is an outdated term now replaced by *relative atomic mass*.

atomization is a process in which an element or compound is converted into gaseous atoms. (See also *enthalpy change of atomization* and *bond enthalpies*.)

ATP (adenosine triphosphate) plays a crucial role in the *energy transfer* processes of living organisms. *Hydrolysis* of ATP, under the control of *enzymes*, splits off one of the three phosphate groups, releasing 31 kJ mol^{-1} to drive biochemical processes and for muscle movement.

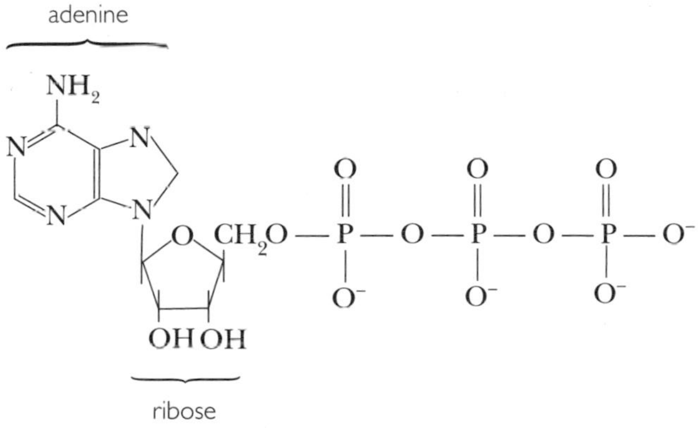

Structure of ATP

attacking group is a term used to describe the mechanism of chemical reactions. *Nucleophiles* and *electrophiles* are examples of attacking groups.

aufbau principle: the principle that the *electron configurations* of atoms build up according to a set of rules. The three rules are that:

- electrons go into the *orbital* at the lowest available *energy level*
- each orbital can only contain at most two electrons (with opposite *spins*)
- where there are two or more orbitals at the same energy, they fill singly before the electrons pair up.

autocatalysis is catalysis of a reaction by one of its products. An autocatalytic reaction starts slowly but then speeds up as the catalytic product starts to form. The oxidation of ethanedioate ions by manganate(VII) ions in acid solution is catalyzed by manganate(II) ions, thus:

$$2MnO_4^-(aq) + 5C_2O_4^{2-}(aq) + 16H^+(aq) \longrightarrow 10CO_2(g) + 2Mn^{2+}(aq) + 8H_2O(l)$$

At first bubbles of carbon dioxide appear very slowly but once the reaction produces some manganese(II) ions it speeds up and gas is evolved more rapidly.

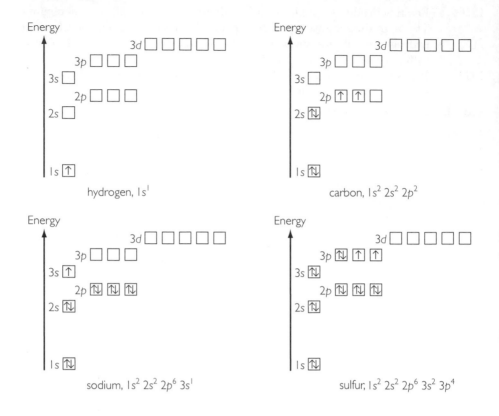

Aufbau principle: electrons in energy levels for four atoms to show the application of the aufbau principle

Avogadro constant: the number of atoms, molecules, ions or other chemical *entities* in one mole of a substance. The Avogadro constant (L) = 6.02×10^{23} mol^{-1}.

amount of substance (mol) × Avogadro constant (mol^{-1}) = number of specified entities

So 0.25 mol carbon atoms contains 1.50×10^{23} atoms while 0.5 mol oxygen molecules contains 3.10×10^{23} molecules.

Avogadro's law states that equal *volumes* of gases under the same conditions of temperature and *pressure* contain equal numbers of molecules. This means that one *mole* of any gas occupies the same volume under the same conditions. The volume occupied by a gas at 273 K (0°C) and one atmosphere pressure (101.3 kPa) is about 22.4 dm^3. These are the conditions of standard temperature and pressure (*stp*). In a warmish laboratory at 298 K (25°C) the volume of one mole of gas is about 24 dm^3.

Amadeo Avogadro (1776–1856) was the Italian scientist who proposed this law to account for *Gay-Lussac's law of combining volumes*.

azeotropic mixture: a mixture of liquids that on *boiling* produces a *vapor* with the same composition as the liquid. This means both that the liquids cannot be separated by fractional distillation and that azeotropes are constant boiling mixtures.

A mixture containing 95.6% ethanol with 4.4% water is an azeotrope that boils at 78.2°C. As a result it is not possible to produce pure ethanol (anhydrous or absolute ethanol) by distillation alone.

azo compound: a compound with the group $-N=N-$ in its structure.

azo dyes are made by coupling a *diazonium salt* with one of a variety of coupling agents. Benzene diazonium chloride, for example, couples with *phenylamine* to make a yellow azo compound.

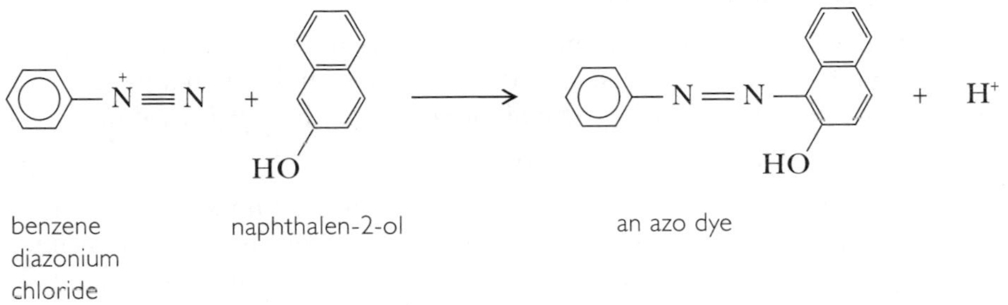

benzene
diazonium
chloride

naphthalen-2-ol

an azo dye

Equation for a coupling reaction to make an azo dye

Very many azo *dyes* are manufactured by linking combinations of 50 diazonium salts with 52 coupling agents. Most of the dyes are red, orange or yellow. The *acid–base indicator* methyl orange is an azo dye.

back titration is an analytical technique used when the reaction between the standard solution and the substance to be analyzed is slow. The procedure is to add a measured excess of the standard solution, allow time for the reaction to finish and then to use a titration with a second standard solution to measure how much of the first standard solution remains unused.

This technique is used to measure amounts of ammonium salts. An excess of a standard solution of sodium hydroxide is added to a sample and the mixture heated to drive off ammonia. In the process some of the sodium hydroxide is used up.

$$NH_4^+(aq) + OH^-(aq) \longrightarrow NH_3(g) + H_2O(l)$$

After all the ammonia has been driven off by boiling, a titration with standard hydrochloric acid measures the amount of unused sodium hydroxide remaining. This shows how much of the alkali was used to react with the ammonium salt in the sample and hence the amount of ammonium salt in the sample.

bacteria are a group of microorganisms. Some bacteria are harmful and responsible for diseases such as cholera, tuberculosis and food poisoning. Most bacteria play a vital part in ecological processes. Soil bacteria, for example, help to break down the remains of living things releasing the nutrient elements such as nitrogen, in a form that plants can use for growth.

Bacteria are the basis of much traditional and modern biotechnology. In a traditional process, for example, bacteria are used to make yogurt. In new methods they are altered by genetic engineering to produce substances such as human insulin for diabetics.

Bakelite is the phenol–methanal plastic discovered by the Flemish-born chemist Leo Baekland in 1905 who was then living in the USA. This was the start of the modern plastics industry. Bakelite is a cross-linked, *thermosetting polymer* formed when phenol and methanal (formaldehyde) are mixed and heated with an acid *catalyst*.

balanced equations show the amounts (in moles) of reactants and products involved in chemical reactions. There is no change in the total number of atoms of each element as reactants turn into products during a chemical reaction. Four steps lead to the balanced equation for a reaction. Take for example the reaction of sodium with water.

Step 1   Identify the reactants and products by name:

sodium reacts with water to form sodium hydroxide and hydrogen.

Step 2   Write down the correct formula for reactants and products:

$$Na + H_2O \longrightarrow NaOH + H_2$$

Step 3   Balance the numbers of atoms of each element by inspection and by writing numbers in front of the formula as necessary. In this example there has to be an even number of hydrogen atoms on the left (in H_2O molecules) so the number on the right must be even too.

$$2Na + H_2O \longrightarrow 2NaOH + H_2$$

Never change any of the formulas to balance an equation. Do not add an extra formula to balance an equation without carefully checking that it is right to do so.

Step 4   Add state symbols:

$$2Na(s) + H_2O(l) \longrightarrow 2NaOH(aq) + H_2(g)$$

The balanced equation shows the *amounts* (in moles) of reactants and products. In the example, 2 mol sodium atoms react with 1 mol water molecules to give 2 mol sodium hydroxide and 1 mol hydrogen. This is the *stoichiometry* of the reaction. (See also *redox reactions*.)

ball and stick models are used to show in three dimensions the structure and bonding of crystals, molecules and complex ions. They are better than *space-filling models* for showing bond angles, but they do not show the relative size of atoms and ions.

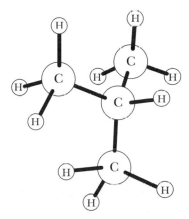

Ball and stick model of 2-methylpropane

Balmer series: a series of lines that appear in the visible region of the *hydrogen emission spectrum.*

barbiturates are drugs that depress the central nervous system. They are used as sedatives and sleeping pills. They are now prescribed much less than before since it was realized that they can produce dependence.

barium (Ba) is a silvery-white, soft metal that is one of the alkaline earth metals in *group 2* of the periodic table. Barium occurs naturally as barites ($BaSO_4$) and also as witherite ($BaCO_3$).

Barium sulfate absorbs X-rays strongly so it is the main ingredient in "barium meals" used to diagnose disorders of stomach or intestines. Soluble barium compounds are toxic but barium sulfate is very insoluble and so cannot be absorbed into the bloodstream from the gut. X-rays cannot pass through the "barium meal," which therefore creates a shadow on the X-ray film.

base: a molecule or ion that can accept a hydrogen ion (proton) from an acid. This is the usual definition based on the *Brønsted–Lowry theory*. A base has a *lone pair of electrons* that can form a *dative covalent bond* with a proton.

$$H\!:\!\overset{\cdot\cdot}{\underset{\cdot\cdot}{O}}\!:^{-} \quad \curvearrowright H^{+} \longrightarrow \quad H\!-\!\overset{\cdot\cdot}{\underset{\cdot\cdot}{O}}\!\rightarrow H$$

A hydroxide ion has a lone pair of electrons that can form a dative bond with a hydrogen ion.

Common bases are the oxide and hydroxide ions, *ammonia* and *amines,* as well as the carbonate and hydrogencarbonate ions. There is a lone pair on the nitrogen atom of ammonia that allows it to act as a base:

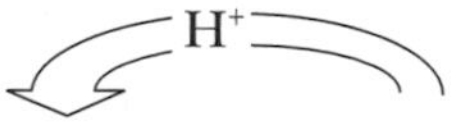

$$NH_3(g) \quad + \quad HNO_3(g) \longrightarrow NH_4^{+}NO_3^{-}(s)$$

base   acid

In *biochemistry* the term base often refers to one of the five nitrogenous bases that make up nucleotides and *nucleic acids* (DNA and RNA). These compounds (*adenine,* guanine, cytosine, uracil and thymine) are bases in the chemical sense because they have lone pairs on nitrogen atoms that can accept hydrogen ions.

base catalysis: any reaction speeded up by a base *catalyst*. One example is the base-catalyzed *hydrolysis* of a nitrile to the salt of a carboxylic acid.

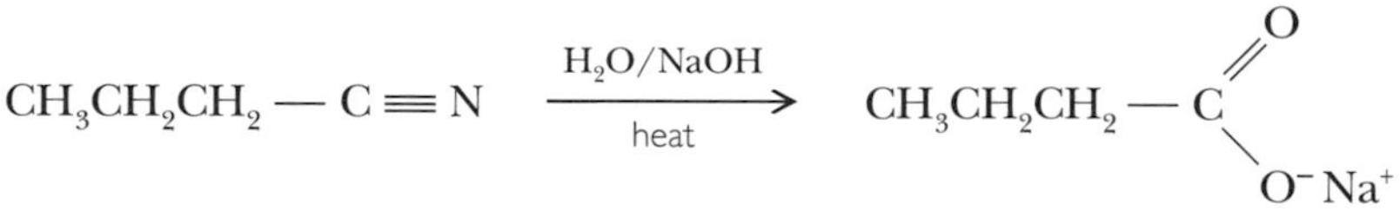

$$CH_3CH_2CH_2 - C \equiv N \quad \xrightarrow[\text{heat}]{H_2O/NaOH} \quad CH_3CH_2CH_2 - C \overset{\displaystyle O}{\underset{\displaystyle O^{-}Na^{+}}{\Big\backslash}}$$

Hydrolysis of propanenitrile to sodium butanoate with a base catalyst

base dissociation (ionization) constants measure the strength of bases by showing the extent to which they accept hydrogen ions in solution. Base dissociation constants are used to compare the strengths of relatively *weak bases.*

For the weak base ammonia: $NH_3(aq) + H_2O(l) \rightleftharpoons NH_4^{+}(aq) + OH^{-}(aq)$

The equilibrium constant, $K_c = \dfrac{[NH_4^{+}(aq)][OH^{-}(aq)]}{[NH_3(aq)][H_2O(l)]}$

In dilute solution the concentration of water is effectively constant, so the expression can be written in this form where K_b is the base dissociation constant:

$$K_b = \frac{[NH_4^{+}(aq)][OH^{-}(aq)]}{[HA](aq)}$$

Dissociation constants are shown below for some weak bases in order of base strength with the strongest of the bases at the top of the list.

Base	K_b/mol dm^{-3}
ethylamine, $C_2H_5NH_2$	5.4×10^{-4}
methylamine, CH_3NH_2	4.3×10^{-4}
ammonia, NH_3	1.8×10^{-5}
phenylamine, $C_6H_5NH_2$	3.8×10^{-10}

basic oxide: an oxide of a *metal* that reacts with acids to form salts and water. Copper(II) oxide, for example, reacts with acids to produce copper(II) salts.

$$CuO(s) + H_2SO_4(aq) \longrightarrow CuSO_4(aq) + H_2O(l)$$

Note that it is the oxide ion in the basic oxide that acts as a base by taking a hydrogen ion from the acid.

$$O^{2-} + 2H^+ \longrightarrow H_2O$$

Basic oxides that dissolve in water are *alkalis*. As the compound dissolves, the oxide ion, acting as a base, takes a hydrogen ion from water and forms a hydroxide ion.

$$CaO(s) + H_2O(l) \longrightarrow Ca(OH)_2(aq)$$

batch process: a process that produces a specified amount of a product in a single operation. In industry a batch process is used to manufacture chemicals needed in relatively small amounts so that a *continuous process* is not worthwhile. Batch processing is typically used to make fine chemicals on a scale of up to 100 tonnes per year. An industrial batch process is essentially a large-scale version of a synthesis carried out in laboratory glassware. After producing a batch of a chemical the apparatus is cleaned and used again.

Some metals are extracted by batch processes (see *chromium extraction* and *titanium extraction*).

battery: two or more *electrochemical cells* connected in series make up a battery of cells. This is the strictly correct meaning of the term battery. It is a term that scientists borrowed from the army, where a line of guns is still called a battery. An automobile battery consists of six rechargeable *lead–acid cells* connected in series to give a 12 volt supply. In everyday conversation, however, it is common to use the word "battery" when referring to a single cell.

bauxite: an ore of aluminum consisting of impure aluminum oxide. Impurities are removed by heating powdered bauxite with sodium hydroxide solution. Aluminum oxide, which is *amphoteric*, dissolves but other oxides such as iron(III) oxide and titanium(IV) oxide do not. After filtering, *seed crystals* are added and hydrated aluminum oxide crystallizes as the solution cools. Heating the hydrate crystals at 1000°C produces anhydrous aluminum oxide ready for *aluminum extraction*.

becquerel (Bq): the *SI unit* for measuring radioactivity. If one atomic nucleus decays per second the activity is one becquerel.

bench reagents are solutions traditionally kept on the laboratory bench for general chemical use such as *qualitative analysis*. The concentrations of bench reagents are only approximate. The concentration of bench acids and alkalis is often around 2 mol dm^{-3} for hydrochloric acid, nitric acid, sodium hydroxide and ammonia solutions but 1 mol dm^{-3} for sulfuric acid (which produces two moles of hydrogen ions per mole of acid).

Benedict's solution is a reagent for detecting *reducing sugars* and for distinguishing *aldehydes* from *ketones*. The deep blue reagent contains copper(II) ions complexed with citrate ions in alkaline solution. A reducing sugar or aldehyde reduces the reagent to copper(I) oxide. The blue color goes and a reddish-brown precipitate forms. The reagent is similar to Fehling's solution but safer to use because it is less corrosive. Also Benedict's solution is more stable and so does not have to be stored as two reagents.

benzene (C$_6$H$_6$) is the simplest *arene* hydrocarbon. It is a nonpolar liquid at room temperature and was once widely used as a solvent until it was known to be a *carcinogen*.

Three ways of representing the structure of benzene. Note that all the atoms in a benzene molecule are in the same plane. The molecule is planar.

At first sight benzene is an unsaturated compound with three double bonds and should be highly reactive like the *alkenes*. Benzene is far more stable and less reactive than the *Kekulé structure* suggests (see *stability of benzene*).

The "three double bonds" in the benzene ring are not isolated. The electron clouds in these double bonds overlap and merge to form a double doughnut-shaped electron cloud of *delocalized electrons* that sandwiches the six-sided carbon skeleton.

Like other arenes, benzene burns with a very smoky, yellow flame. The characteristic reactions of benzene are *electrophilic substitution* reactions.

Summary of the substitution reactions of benzene

beryllium (Be) is a strong metal with a high melting point that is very much less dense than iron. The element makes useful alloys with other metals. Beryllium is the first element in *group 2* of the periodic table. Its *electron configuration* is [He]2s^2. The element occurs naturally as beryl, an aluminosilicate mineral that is colorless if pure but a brilliant green (emerald) where chromium(II) ions replace some of the aluminum(III) ions.

Beryllium is not a typical group 2 element. Resemblances between the chemistry of beryllium and aluminum are examples of the *diagonal relationship*.

beta (β) particles are electrons given off from the nuclei of some *radioactive* atoms when they decay. During beta decay a neutron turns into a proton so the *proton number* of the atom increases by one while the *nucleon number* is unchanged. An atom of a new element forms. The new element is one place to the right in the *periodic table*.

$$^{228}_{88}\text{Ra} \longrightarrow \ ^{228}_{89}\text{Ac} + \ ^{0}_{-1}\text{e}$$

radium   actinium   beta
particle

The symbol $^{0}_{-1}$e for a beta particle means that the nucleon numbers and proton numbers balance on the two sides of the nuclear equation.

bicarbonate is the traditional name for hydrogencarbonate. Sodium bicarbonate can be used as an ingredient in baking powder and as an alkali in antacids.

bidentate ligands form two dative covalent bonds with metal ions in *complexes*. Examples of bidentate (or "two-toothed") *ligands* are: 1,2-diaminoethane, amino acids and the ethanedioate ion.

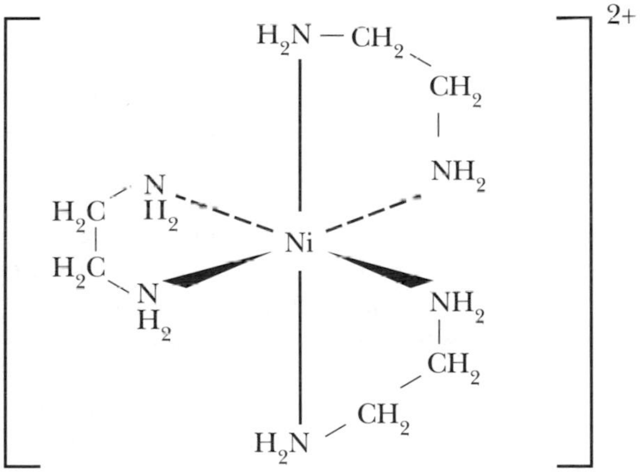

Structure of a complex formed by the bidentate ligand, 1,2-diaminoethane

bifunctional compounds are compounds with two *functional groups*. Important examples are the *amino acids*.

biochemistry is the study of chemical changes in living organisms. Metabolism describes the many chemical processes in all living things. Many of these *enzyme* catalyzed reactions are involved in the hydrolysis and oxidation of food. Others build up small molecules into the complex molecules that cells need as they grow. The techniques of molecular biology helped to transform biochemistry because they allowed scientists to work out the structures and shapes of large molecules such as proteins and nucleic acids and hence to begin to reveal the way in which genetic material in cells controls metabolism. The following timechart shows some highlights in the development of molecular biology. Bear in mind that it may have taken scientists up to ten or even twenty years to develop the new techniques and carry out the investigations leading to the discoveries at the dates shown.

1944	Oswald Avery shows that *DNA* is the genetic material in the chromosomes of bacteria.
1951	Linus Pauling interprets his *X-ray* studies to suggest that some protein molecules have a helical structure he calls the alpha helix.
1951	Erwin Chargaff shows that in a DNA molecule the number of cytosine units is the same as the number of guanine units while the number of adenine units equals the number of thymine units.
1953	Max Perutz devises the technique that makes it possible to use X-ray diffraction to work out the three-dimensional shapes of *proteins* such as hemoglobin and myoglobin.
1953	Francis Crick and James Watson propose the double-helix structure for DNA based on X-ray photographs by Rosalind Franklin and Maurice Wilkins.
1955	Frederick Sanger announces the full sequence of *amino acids* in the two chains of an *insulin* molecule.
1956	George Palade discovers ribosomes in cells and shows that they are the site of protein synthesis.
1956	Paul Berg finds the first example of transfer RNA, the molecules that identify amino acids during protein synthesis.
1961	Sydney Brenner, Francis Crick and others confirm that the genetic code is based on triplets of bases in *nucleic acids*.
1970	Har Khorana finishes the synthesis of the first artificial gene by producing bacterial DNA with a sequence of 126 *nucleotide* base pairs.
1970s	Hamilton Smith isolates restriction enzymes that break DNA molecules at specific points, allowing the development of genetic engineering and DNA sequencing.
1973	Herbert Boyer demonstrates a technique for splicing together genes from different bacteria. By the end of the 1970s this recombinant DNA technique makes it possible to modify bacteria to produce useful substances such as insulin and growth hormone.
1977	Frederick Sanger uses restriction enzymes, radioactive labeling and *electrophoresis* to work out the full sequence of bases in the DNA of a virus.
1984	Alec Jeffreys invents the technique of genetic fingerprinting.
1990	Human genome project starts.

biodegradable materials break down in the environment due to the action of microorganisms.

biogas is methane gas produced by the action of bacteria on animal and plant wastes in anaerobic conditions. Many sewage works produce biogas. Biogas also forms in landfill sites as the waste rots down. The gas can be a hazard unless collected and burnt. Small-scale biogas digesters are used in many parts of the world to supply nearby homes with gas for cooking.

biological oxygen demand (BOD) is a measure of water pollution by organic matter from sources such as sewage. BOD is the quantity of dissolved oxygen (measured in $mg\,dm^{-3}$) removed from a sample of water by microorganisms when incubated for five days at 20°C. A sample of water containing much organic matter will support large numbers of bacteria that use dissolved oxygen as they break down the pollutants.

biopolymers are naturally occurring *polymers* in living things. They include *polysaccharides, proteins* and *nucleic acids.*

biotechnology makes use of microorganisms or *enzymes* to produce useful products. Traditional biotechnology uses yeast to make beer, bread and wine as well as bacteria to make yogurt. Modern biotechnology, based on genetic engineering, makes it possible to use genetically modified bacteria to produce medically important substances such as insulin, growth hormone and the blood clotting agent, factor VIII.

Biuret test: a test to detect *proteins.* The procedure is to add sodium hydroxide to a test sample followed by a few drops of copper(II) sulfate solution. The solution turns mauve if protein is present. The test actually detects *peptide* bonds.

blank determinations are used in *quantitative analysis* to eliminate errors. The analyst works through the whole procedure with a blank solution containing the solvent and all the reagents but none of the sample. In a *titration* a blank determination makes it possible to allow for the volume of reagent needed to change the color of the indicator at the *end point.* Blank determinations in colorimetry and spectroscopy help to detect, and allow for, errors caused by contamination of reagents or the effects of the apparatus used.

blast furnace: a furnace for extracting metals, which depends on a blast of preheated air entering near the bottom of the furnace. *Iron extraction* is a large-scale, *continuous process* in blast furnaces.

bleaching is a process for destroying unwanted colors by *oxidation* or *reduction.* Domestic liquid bleach is a solution of sodium chlorate(I) formed by the reaction of *chlorine* with cold sodium hydroxide solution. Bleaching powder is calcium chlorate(I), $Ca(OCl)_2$, made by absorbing chlorine gas in calcium hydroxide. These are oxidizing bleaches. Another oxidizing bleach is *hydrogen peroxide.*

Oxidizing bleaches not only remove color but also kill microorganisms.

Sulfur dioxide and sodium sulfite are reducing bleaches. Paper bleached white by a reducing bleach may turn yellow with age as oxygen in the air reverses the process.

Color in organic compounds is caused by delocalized electrons in sequences of alternating double and single bonds (*conjugated systems*). Oxidizing bleaches break some of the double bonds. Reducing bleaches convert double bonds to single bonds.

body-centered cubic structure is a crystal structure with an atom at each corner of a cube surrounding one atom at the center of the cube. This structure is more open than the two *close-packed structures.*

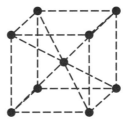

Body-centered cubic structure. Each metal atom is surrounded by eight nearest neighbors.

Metals with the body-centered cubic structure are the *group 1* metals lithium, sodium and potassium, also the *d-block* metals chromium, vanadium and tungsten.

boiling: a liquid boils when it is hot enough for bubbles of vapor to form within the body of the liquid. This happens when the *vapor pressure* of the liquid equals the external *pressure*.

The boiling point of a liquid varies with pressure. Raising the external pressure raises the boiling point. Boiling points are usually measured at atmospheric pressure. The normal boiling point is the temperature at which the vapor pressure of the liquid equals one atmosphere (101.3 kPa).

bomb calorimeter: an apparatus for measuring energy changes when compounds burn.

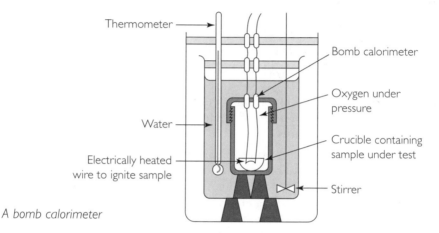

A bomb calorimeter

A measured amount of a sample burns in oxygen under pressure and the temperature rise of the whole apparatus is measured. The calorimeter is calibrated using benzoic acid for which the standard *enthalpy change of combustion* is known accurately.

A bomb calorimeter operates at constant volume so a correction is needed to convert the results to *enthalpy changes* at constant pressure.

bond angle is the angle between two *covalent bonds* in a molecule or *giant structure.* X-ray and electron diffraction studies make it possible to measure bond angles accurately. The results show that *covalent bonds* have a definite direction as well as length.

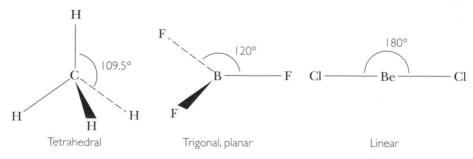

Molecules showing the bond angles

Electron pair repulsion theory makes it possible to predict the *shapes of molecules* and bond angles with great accuracy.

bond breaking: see *heterolytic bond breaking* and *homolytic bond breaking*. Note that it takes energy to break bonds. Bond breaking is an *endothermic change*.

bond dissociation enthalpy is the *enthalpy change* on breaking one mole of a covalent bond in a gaseous molecule. Energy is needed to break covalent bonds. Bond breaking is *endothermic* so the enthalpy change is positive.

Chemists use spectroscopy to measure bond dissociation enthalpies. The bond dissociation enthalpies for the hydrogen halides are as follows:

$$HX(g) \longrightarrow H(g) + X(g) \qquad \Delta H = +562 \text{ kJ mol}^{-1} \text{ for HF}$$
$$\Delta H = +432 \text{ kJ mol}^{-1} \text{ for HCl}$$
$$\Delta H = +366 \text{ kJ mol}^{-1} \text{ for HBr}$$
$$\Delta H = +299 \text{ kJ mol}^{-1} \text{ for HI}$$

For these compounds the bonds get easier to break as the halogen atoms get larger and the bonds get longer down group 7.

In molecules with two or more bonds between similar atoms, the successive bond dissociation enthalpies are not the same. In water, for example, the energy needed to break the first $O - H$ bond in $H - O - H(g)$ is 498 kJ mol^{-1} but the energy needed to break the second $O - H$ bond in $O - H(g)$ is only 428 kJ mol^{-1}.

bond enthalpies (or bond energies) are the mean values of *bond dissociation enthalpies* used in approximate calculations to estimate enthalpy changes for reactions. The mean values of bond enthalpies take into account the facts that:

- the successive bond dissociation enthalpies are not the same in compounds such as water or methane
- the bond dissociation enthalpy for a specific covalent bond varies slightly from one molecule to another.

Worked example:

Use mean bond enthalpies to estimate the enthalpy of formation of *hydrazine*.

Notes on the method

Write out the equation showing all the atoms and bonds in the molecules to make it easier to count the numbers of bonds broken and formed.

Look up the mean bond energies in a book of data. The symbol $E(N - H)$ stands for the bond energy of a covalent bond between a nitrogen atom and a hydrogen atom.

Answer

The equation for the reaction:

$$N \equiv N \; + \; 2\,H - H \; \longrightarrow \; \begin{array}{c} H \\ \diagdown \\ \diagup \\ H \end{array} N - N \begin{array}{c} H \\ \diagup \\ \diagdown \\ H \end{array}$$

The energy needed to break the bonds in the reactants

$$= E(N \equiv N) \text{ kJ mol}^{-1} + 2E(H - H) \text{ kJ mol}^{-1}$$

$$= 945 \text{ kJ mol}^{-1} + 2 \times 436 \text{ kJ mol}^{-1}$$
$$= 1817 \text{ kJ mol}^{-1}$$

The energy given out when the product forms

$$= E(\text{N}-\text{N}) \text{ kJ mol}^{-1} + 4E(\text{N}-\text{H}) \text{ kJ mol}^{-1}$$
$$= 158 \text{ kJ mol}^{-1} + 4 \times 391 \text{ kJ mol}^{-1}$$
$$= 1722 \text{ kJ mol}^{-1}$$

More energy is needed to break bonds than is given out when bonds are formed so the reaction is endothermic and the enthalpy change is positive.

$$\Delta H = +1817 \text{ kJ mol}^{-1} - 1722 \text{ kJ mol}^{-1} = +95 \text{ kJ mol}^{-1}$$

bond length: the distance between the nuclei of two atoms linked by one or more *covalent bonds*. For the same two atoms, *triple bonds* are shorter than *double bonds*, which in turn are shorter than single bonds.

Bond	Bond length/nm
C — C	0.154
C $=$ C	0.134
C $\equiv$ C	0.120
C $\cdots$ C in benzene	0.140

Bond lengths that are intermediate between single and double bonds, as in *benzene*, are a sign of electron *delocalization*.

bond polarity is the extent to which the shared pair of electrons in a *covalent bond* is attracted toward one of the atoms joined by the bond. Bonding electrons are pulled toward the more *electronegative* atom. The more electronegative atom carries a partial negative charge ($\delta-$) and the other atom carries a partial positive charge ($\delta+$).

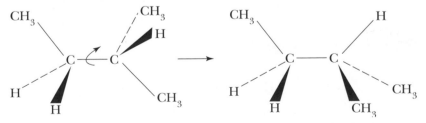

Examples of molecules with polar bonds

bond rotation is possible about single covalent bonds but is prevented under normal conditions by *double bonds* or *triple bonds*. The lack of rotation about double bonds gives rise to *geometric isomerism*.

The groups at the end of a single C — C bond can rotate freely relative to each other giving rise to different conformations of molecules.

bonding: see *metallic bonds, covalent bonds, ionic bonding, hydrogen bonding* and *intermolecular forces.*

bonding molecular orbital: a region in space in a molecule where there is a high probability of finding bonding electrons. Molecular orbitals, like *atomic orbitals,* are solutions to the Schrödinger wave equation. At a simplified, descriptive level, a molecular orbital forms by overlap of atomic orbitals of the atoms linked by a covalent bond.

When atomic, *s*-orbitals overlap the result is a sigma (σ) orbital. Two electrons can occupy a σ-orbital to form a *sigma bond.*

Formation of a sigma orbital   s-orbital   sigma bond

In ethene one of the bonds between the carbon atoms is a sigma bond. The second bond forms by sideways overlap of atomic *p*-orbitals. The bonding electrons are in a pi (π) orbital with two regions of increased electron density above and below the plane of the atoms.

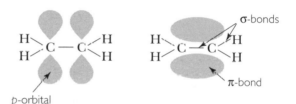

Sigma and pi bonds in ethene   p-orbital

A *pi bond* is not as strong as a sigma bond and so the double bond in ethene (or any other *alkene*) is not twice as strong as a single bond.

borax ($Na_2B_4O_7 \cdot 10H_2O$) is a naturally occurring mineral that has been used as a flux in metallurgy for hundreds of years. Molten borax cleans the surface of hot metals by dissolving metal oxides. This makes for good contact between metal surfaces when metals are welded or soldered together. Most borax is now used to make *borosilicate glass.*

Adding acid converts borax to boric acid (H_3BO_3), which is separated by cooling the solution in ice and filtering off the white crystals. Boric acid is a weak acid and mild antiseptic used in eye lotions and other medicines.

Born–Haber cycle: a thermochemical cycle that can be used to calculate the *lattice energy* for a compound of a metal with a nonmetal.

All the terms in the cycle can be measured experimentally. Applying *Hess's law* makes it possible to calculate the one unknown term, which is the lattice energy.

A Born–Haber cycle can help reveal the factors that determine the *stability* or instability of a compound. For a stable compound the lattice energy must be bigger than the total energy needed to produce gaseous ions from the elements.

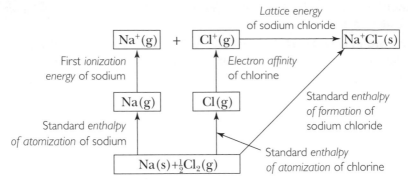

Born–Haber cycle for sodium chloride (see the separate entries for the definitions of the terms)

A Born–Haber cycle can also help to determine whether the bonding in a compound is truly ionic. The experimental lattice energy calculated from a Born–Haber cycle can be compared with the theoretical value calculated using the laws of electrostatics and assuming that the only bonding in the crystal is ionic.

Compound	Experimental lattice energy from a Born–Haber cycle/kJ mol^{-1}	Theoretical lattice energy calculated assuming that the only bonding is ionic/kJ mol^{-1}
NaCl	−780	−770
KCl	−711	−702
AgCl	−905	−833

The values in the table show that ionic bonding can account for the lattice energies of sodium and potassium chlorides. The lattice energy of silver chloride is greater than can be explained by ionic bonding. There must be a contribution from covalent bonding.

boron (B) is a hard, black solid with a high melting point and the only nonmetal in group 3 of the periodic table. Its *electron configuration* is [He]$2s^22p^1$. Boron is in oxidation state +3 in all its compounds. The bonding between boron and other elements is covalent.

Boron has become important as an element since the development of the nuclear industry. The *isotope* boron-10 absorbs neutrons strongly so the element was scattered over the Chernobyl nuclear reactor after the explosion to quench chain reactions.

Boron trichloride (BCl_3) is a colorless liquid and like *aluminum chloride*, it is a strong electron pair acceptor (*Lewis acid*).

Sodium tetrahydridoborate(III) ($NaBH_4$) is a useful reducing agent.

borosilicate glass is used to make oven glassware and laboratory equipment because it has a higher melting point than cheaper, soda lime glass and is much less likely to crack as it heats up or cools down. Borosilicate glass has a high refractive index, making it useful for the production of lenses.

Boyle's law states that the volume of a fixed amount of gas is inversely proportional to its pressure at constant temperature.

$$p \propto \frac{1}{V}$$ at constant temperature for a fixed amount of a gas

Hence $p_1V_1 = p_2V_2$ = constant

Brady's reagent is a solution of 2,4-dintrophenylhydrazine in acid used to detect and identify *carbonyl compounds*. Mixing an aldehyde or ketone with the reagent produces an yellow-orange precipitate. The *addition–elimination reaction* produces a 2,4-dinitro-phenylhydrazone. This solid derivative can be filtered off, recrystallized and identified by measuring its melting point, making it possible to identify the carbonyl compound.

brasses are *alloys* of copper (60–80%) and zinc (20–40%). Brass is easily worked, has an attractive gold color and does not corrode.

breathalyzer: an instrument for estimating the concentration of alcohol in blood. A breathalyzer measures the ethanol in a sample of air from the lungs. There is an equilibrium between ethanol dissolved in blood and ethanol vapor in the air in the lungs and the constant ratio at body temperature makes it possible to infer the blood alcohol concentration.

The first successful breathalyzer was based on the chemical reduction of orange dichromate(VI) ions to green chromate(III) ions as they oxidize ethanol to ethanal. The driver breathed through a tube containing the orange crystals and the extent to which they turned yellow was *calibrated* to measure the blood alcohol concentration.

Many of the roadside breathalyzers are now *fuel cells*. At one electrode ethanol is oxidized to ethanoic acid while at the other electrode oxygen is reduced to water. The higher the concentration of ethanol in the driver's breath, the greater the voltage of the cell.

brine is the term used industrially for a solution of sodium chloride in water. Brine is produced by "solution mining" of underground salt deposits. Water is pumped into the salt down one pipe. The mineral dissolves and flows to the surface through a second pipe.

Natural brines are solutions of a mixture of salts and can be a useful source of chemicals such as potassium, magnesium and bromine or their compounds.

bromination is a reaction that replaces a hydrogen atom in an organic molecule with a bromine atom. One example is the bromination of *alkanes* – a *free-radical chain reaction* initiated by ultraviolet radiation.

Another example is the bromination of *benzene* by bromine in the presence of iron bromide as the catalyst. This is an *electrophilic substitution* reaction.

bromine (Br) is a corrosive, dark red liquid that evaporates easily to give an orange vapor. It is the only liquid nonmetal at room temperature. Bromine is a halogen – the third element in *group 7* – with the *electron configuration* $[Ar]3d^{10}4s^24p^5$.

Bromine consists of diatomic molecules with pairs of atoms held together by single covalent bonds. The molecules are nonpolar so the *intermolecular forces* are relatively weak, *van der Waals forces*.

Bromine, like the other halogens, is an oxidizing element. It is a less powerful *oxidizing agent* than chlorine.

Bromine reacts with *s-block* metals to form ionic bromides in which the bromine atoms gain one electron to fill the $4p$ energy levels.

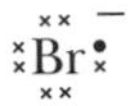

$$\overset{\times\times}{\underset{\times\times}{\times}Br\overset{-}{\underset{}{:}}}$$

Outer electron configuration of a bromide ion

Bromine oxidizes *nonmetals* such as sulfur and hydrogen on heating, forming covalent, molecular bromides.

$$H_2(g) + Br_2(g) \longrightarrow 2HBr(g)$$

$$H\overset{\times\times}{\underset{\times\times}{\,:\,}}Br\overset{\times}{\underset{}{\,}}$$

Covalent bonding in hydrogen bromide

Hydrogen bromide is a fuming, acidic gas. Like the other *hydrogen halides* it is very soluble in water and a strong acid.

Bromine only reacts with water to a limited extent but it reacts with sodium hydroxide, rapidly *disproportionating* at room temperature to form bromate(V) ions.

oxidized from 0 to +5

$$2Br_2(aq) \;+\; 6OH^- \;\longrightarrow\; 5Br^-(aq) \;+\; BrO_3^-(aq) \;+\; 3H_2O(l)$$

reduced from 0 to −1

Bromine oxidizes a range of ions or molecules in solution:

- iodide ions to iodine
- sulfite ions to sulfate ions
- thiosulfate ions to sulfate ions
- hydrogen sulfide to sulfur.

bromine extraction: a process for obtaining bromine from seawater or natural *brine*. The four-stage process concentrates and separates the bromine from seawater, which contains about 65 ppm of bromide ions. The process produces one tonne of bromine from 20 000 tonnes of seawater.

Stage 1 *Oxidation* of bromide ions to bromine.

Seawater is filtered and acidified to pH 3.5 to prevent chlorine and bromine reacting with water, then chlorine displaces bromine:

$$Cl_2 + 2Br^- \longrightarrow 2Cl^- + Br_2$$

Stage 2 Separation of bromine vapor.

A blast of air through the reaction mixture carries away the displaced bromine and helps to concentrate it.

Stage 3   Formation of hydrobromic acid.

The air with bromine vapor meets sulfur dioxide gas and a fine mist of water, producing hydrobromic acid, which is ionized in solution. After this stage the concentration of bromine in the solution is 1500 times greater than in seawater.

$$Br_2(g) + SO_2(g) + 2H_2O(l) \longrightarrow 4H^+(aq) + 2Br^-(aq) + SO_4^{2-}(aq)$$

Stage 4   Displacement and purification of bromine.

The solution from stage 3 now flows down a tower with a flow of chlorine gas and steam passing up it. The chlorine oxidizes bromide ions to bromine, which evaporates in the steam. The mixture of steam and bromine is cooled and condensed, producing a dense lower bromine layer under a layer of water.

Natural brines contain more bromine than seawater so that only stage 4 is needed to separate the bromine.

Bromine is used to make additives for leaded gasoline, flame retardants, agricultural chemicals, synthetic rubber for the inner lining of tubeless tires, dyes and a range of chemical intermediates. Silver bromide is the photosensitive chemical used in *photography*.

bromine water is the traditional name for a solution of bromine in water used as a laboratory reagent. The reagent is orange because it consists largely of a mixture of bromine molecules and water molecules, hence the preferred name "aqueous bromine." Bromine *disproportionates* in water to a very limited extent, unlike *chlorine*. Aqueous bromine is decolorized when shaken with excess *alkene* because the *addition reaction* produces colorless products. Aqueous bromine loses its orange color when mixed with *phenol* and gives a white precipitate of tribromophenol. This is an example of *electrophilic substitution* that happens more readily with phenol than with benzene.

Brønsted–Lowry theory: the theory that *acids* are hydrogen ion (proton) donors and that *bases* are hydrogen ion (proton) acceptors. Johannes Brønsted (1879–1947) was a Danish physical chemist. He published his theory in 1923 at the same time as Thomas Lowry (1874–1936) of the University of Cambridge but the two worked independently.

bronze is an *alloy* of copper with up to 12% tin. Bronze is a strong, hardwearing alloy with good resistance to corrosion. It is used to make gear wheels, bearings, propellers for ships, statues and coins.

Brownian motion is the rapid random motion of minute particles suspended in a liquid or gas. The phenomenon was first seen by the British botanist Robert Brown looking at pollen grains in water through a microscope. Brownian motion is evidence for the *kinetic theory*. The erratic random motion of pollen, smoke particles or other *colloid*-sized specks of matter is due to continuous bombardment by fast moving molecules that are too small to be seen through a light microscope.

Buchner flask and funnel: the apparatus used for filtering solutions especially when isolating and purifying solid products of reactions by *recrystallization*. A pump (usually a water pump) lowers the pressure inside the flask so that a pressure difference across the filter paper speeds up filtration.

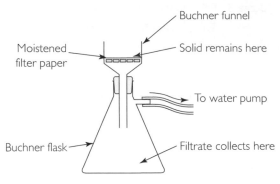

Moistened filter paper

Buchner funnel

Solid remains here

To water pump

Buchner flask

Filtrate collects here

Apparatus for Buchner filtration

buckminsterfullerene: a form of carbon consisting of C_{60} particles (see *allotropes*) and named after the architect Richard Buckminster Fuller, who designed the geodesic dome for Expo '67 in Montreal. The popular name for C_{60} molecules is "buckyballs."

Buckminsterfullerene was discovered in 1985 by Harry Kroto and his team at the University of Sussex. It was the first of a family of *fullerenes*.

buffer solutions are mixtures of molecules and ions in solution that help to keep *pH* more or less constant. A buffer solution cannot prevent pH changes but it evens out the large changes in pH that can happen without a buffer.

Buffers are important in living organisms. The pH of blood, for example, is closely controlled by buffers within the narrow range 7.38 to 7.42. Chemists use buffers when they want to investigate chemical reactions at a fixed pH.

Buffers are equilibrium systems that illustrate the practical importance of *Le Chatelier's principle*. A typical buffer mixture consists of a solution of a *weak acid* and one of its salts. For example, a mixture of ethanoic acid and sodium ethanoate. There must be plenty of the acid and its salt.

By choosing the right weak acid, it is possible to prepare buffers at any pH value throughout the pH scale. If the concentrations of the weak acid and its salt are the same, then the pH of the buffer is equal to pK_a for the acid.

$$CH_3CO_2H \ + \ H_2O \ \rightleftharpoons \ H_3O^+ \ + \ CH_3CO_2^-$$

| CH_3CO_2H acid molecules – a reservoir of H^+ ions | | H_3O^+ stays roughly constant – so the pH hardly changes | $CH_3CO_2^-$ base ions – with the capacity to accept H^+ ions |

Plenty of the weak acid to supply more H^+ ions if alkali is added

Plenty of the ions from the salt to combine with extra H^+ ions if acid is added

The action of a buffer solution

More generally the pH of a buffer mixture can be calculated with the logarithmic form of the equilibrium law (see *Henderson–Hasselbalch equation*).

$$pH = pK_a + \lg \frac{[salt]}{[acid]}$$

Diluting a buffer solution with water does not change the ratio of the concentrations of the salt and acid so the pH does not change (unless the dilution is so great that the assumptions made when deriving the equation no longer apply).

Worked example:

What is the pH of a buffer solution containing 0.40 mol dm^{-3} methanoic acid and 1.00 mol dm^{-3} sodium methanoate?

Notes on the method

Look up the value of pK_a in a book of data. The pK_a of methanoic acid is 3.8.

Answer

$$pH = 3.8 + \lg \frac{1.00}{0.40}$$

$$pH = 4.20$$

---

bumping is violent boiling that shakes the apparatus and can throw liquid from the container in which it is being heated. Adding a few fragments of porous pottery or some jagged antibumping granules cuts the risk of bumping by helping the bubbles of vapor to form smoothly.

Bunsen, Robert (1811–1899) was a German experimental and analytical chemist who was one of the pioneers of spectroscopy. When the gasworks opened in Heidelberg in 1854, gas burners could be used in the laboratories. Bunsen was unhappy with the available burners so he (or more likely one of his technicians) came up with the design still used all over the world today. The great advantage of the burner was that it could produce a hot and almost invisible flame. Bunsen liked to make his own glass apparatus and he noticed the way that flames turned yellow as he heated glass in them. He started heating a range of chemicals in burner flames and discovered the use of *flame tests* but realized that they could not be used to analyze mixtures. With his fellow scientist Kirchhoff he pioneered *atomic emission spectroscopy* for analysis and soon discovered two new elements in the waters of a local spa. He called them cesium and rubidium, the Latin names for sky blue and dark red, from the colors seen in their spectra.

burettes are graduated tubes, with taps or valves, used to measure the volumes of liquids or solutions during quantitative investigations such as *titrations*. The accuracy of a burette, when clean and properly used, depends on the precision with which it is manufactured and calibrated. Grade B burettes measuring up to 50 cm^3 have an allowed tolerance of ± 0.1 cm^3.

by-products are unwanted products of chemical synthesis or manufacturing. By-products are formed by side reactions that happen at the same time as the main reaction, reducing the yield of the product required.

In the laboratory preparation of 1-bromobutane from butan-1-ol, for example, the reagent is a mixture of sodium bromide and concentrated sulfuric acid. There are two side reactions that cut the yield. In the presence of acid, some of the butan-1-ol dehydrates to an alkene and some reacts to form an ether.

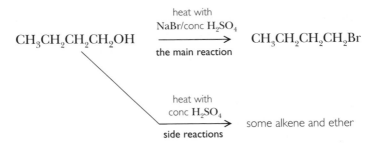

The main reaction and the side reactions

caffeine is a *drug* found in tea, coffee, chocolate and cola drinks. Caffeine gives people a "lift" and helps them to be mentally alert. The drug is used medically to stimulate the nervous, respiratory and cardiovascular systems. Caffeine is also added to medicines to counteract sleepiness caused by other ingredients.

Structure of caffeine (1,3,5-trimethylxanthine)

Caffeine can be isolated from tea or coffee as a white crystalline solid by *solvent extraction.*

calcium (Ca) is a reactive, metallic element in *group 2* of the periodic table. Its *electron configuration* is $[Ar]4s^2$. Samples of the silvery metal usually look gray because they are covered with a layer of calcium oxide.

Calcium burns brightly in air with a brilliant red flame, forming the white solid calcium oxide (CaO). The metal also reacts with cold water, producing hydrogen and a white precipitate of calcium hydroxide.

$$Ca(s) + 2H_2O(l) \longrightarrow Ca(OH)_2(s) + H_2(g)$$

Calcium forms ionic compounds with nonmetals in which the metal is in the +2 oxidation state as Ca^{2+}.

Calcium oxide is a white solid made by heating *calcium carbonate.* It is a *basic oxide.* Its reaction with cold water to make calcium hydroxide is highly *exothermic.* Calcium hydroxide is only sparingly soluble in water, forming an alkaline solution often called limewater.

Anhydrous calcium chloride ($CaCl_2$) is a cheap drying agent. The chloride crystallizes from solution as a hydrate, $CaCl_2.6H_2O$.

calcium carbonate occurs naturally as limestone, chalk and marble. Limestone is an important mineral. Some of the rock is quarried for road building and construction. Pure limestone is also used in the chemical industry. Heating limestone in a furnace at 1200 K converts it to calcium oxide (quicklime). The reaction of quicklime with water produces calcium oxide (slaked lime).

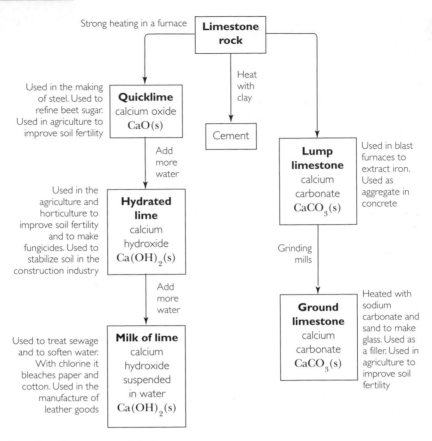

Strong heating in a furnace → **Limestone rock**

Heat with clay

Used in the making of steel. Used to refine beet sugar. Used in agriculture to improve soil fertility

Quicklime calcium oxide $CaO(s)$

Cement

Add more water

Used in the agriculture and horticulture to improve soil fertility and to make fungicides. Used to stabilize soil in the construction industry

Hydrated lime calcium hydroxide $Ca(OH)_2(s)$

Lump limestone calcium carbonate $CaCO_3(s)$

Used in blast furnaces to extract iron. Used as aggregate in concrete

Grinding mills

Add more water

Used to treat sewage and to soften water. With chlorine it bleaches paper and cotton. Used in the manufacture of leather goods

Milk of lime calcium hydroxide suspended in water $Ca(OH)_2(s)$

Ground limestone calcium carbonate $CaCO_3(s)$

Heated with sodium carbonate and sand to make glass. Used as a filler. Used in agriculture to improve soil fertility

Products from limestone and their uses

calibration: a procedure used in quantitative analysis. Calibration makes it possible to convert the measurement of temperature, volume or light absorption into an

Calibration curve used to determine the concentration of copper(II) ions in aqueous solution obtained by taking instrument readings with a series of standard solutions. The instrument reading for an unknown sample is 60.0. The concentration of the sample can be read from the graph. The concentration of copper(II) ions in the sample is 5.5 × 10⁻³ mol dm⁻³.

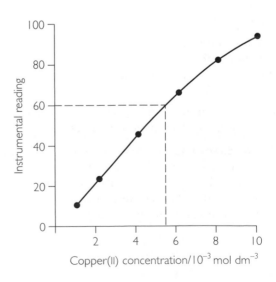

accurate *concentration* in moles per liter. When using colorimeters or spectrometers, for example, it is common to plot a calibration curve. Instrument readings are taken for a series of *standard solutions* of known concentration.

calorimeter: an apparatus for measuring the energy change during a chemical reaction. Typically a calorimeter is insulated from its surroundings and contains water. The energy from the reaction heats up the water and rest of the apparatus. An accurate thermometer measures the temperature rise. The apparatus is *calibrated* to determine its overall *specific heat capacity* by measuring the temperature rise for a reaction with a known *enthalpy change*.

Enthalpy changes of combustion are measured using a *bomb calorimeter*.

Enthalpy changes for reactions in solution can be compared quickly using an expanded polystyrene cup with a lid, as the calorimeter. Expanded polystyrene is an excellent insulator and has a negligible specific heat capacity. If solutions are dilute it is sufficiently accurate to assume that their density and specific heat capacity are the same as those of water.

Worked example:

When 50 cm^3 of 2.0 mol dm^{-3} hydrochloric acid mixes with 50 cm^3 2.0 mol dm^{-3} sodium hydroxide in a polystyrene cup the temperature rise is 13.5°C. What is the enthalpy change for the neutralization reaction?

Notes on the method

Assume that the density of the solutions is the same as water = 1 g cm^{-3} and that for both the specific heating capacity, like water, is 4.18 J g^{-1} K^{-1}.

Note that the total volume of solution is 100 cm^3 so the mass of solution heating up can be taken as 100 g.

The enthalpy change is the energy exchanged with the surroundings when a reaction proceeds as constant temperature and pressure. Here the energy from the exothermic reaction is kept in the system to heat up the water. The calculation shows the energy that would otherwise be lost to the surroundings during a constant temperature change.

The enthalpy change for a reaction, ΔH, is the energy change for the amounts (in moles) shown in the chemical equation.

Answer

The amount of hydrochloric acid $=$ the amount of sodium hydroxide

$$= \frac{50}{1\ 000}\ dm^3 \times 2.0\ mol\ dm^{-3}$$

$$= 0.1\ mol$$

Energy given out by the reaction and used to heat the water in the cup

$$= 4.18\ J\,g^{-1}\,K^{-1} \times 100\ g \times 13.5\ K$$

$$= 5643\ J$$

Energy given out per mole of acid $= \dfrac{5643\ J}{0.1\ mol} = 56\ 430\ J\ mol^{-1}$

$$= 56.4\ kJ\ mol^{-1}$$

The reaction is exothermic so the enthalpy change for the system is negative.

$$NaOH(aq) + HCl(aq) \longrightarrow NaCl(aq) + H_2O(l) \quad \Delta H = -56.4 \text{ kJ mol}^{-1}$$

capillary rise is an effect seen when a fine capillary tube is dipped into a liquid. The liquid normally rises up the tube. The larger the surface tension of the liquid and the thinner the tube, the greater the effect.

More generally capillary action draws liquids, especially water, through any material that is riddled with fine crevices. Capillary action draws solvent up the paper during *paper chromatography*.

carbocations are *intermediates* formed during organic reactions in which a carbon atom carries a positive charge. Carbocations form, for example, during *nucleophilic substitution* by the S_N1 mechanism and during *electrophilic addition* to alkenes.

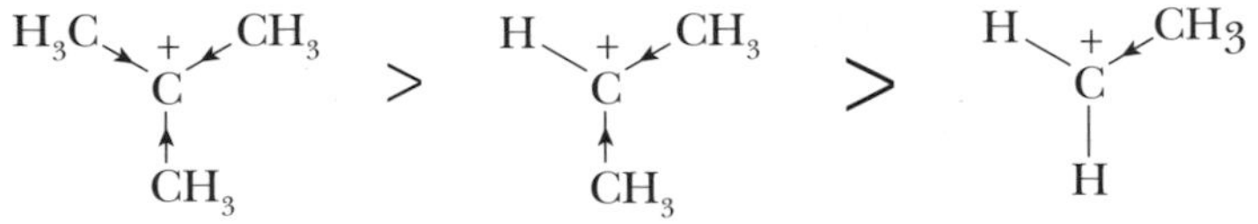

Three carbocations showing the order of stability: tertiary>secondary>primary. The inductive effect of electron-releasing alkyl groups (shown by arrows on the bonds) helps to spread the positive charge and stabilize the ion. The more alkyl groups, the more stable the carbocation.

carbohydrates are compounds of carbon, hydrogen and oxygen. They include sugars, starch and cellulose. The name carbohydrate arises from the formulas in which

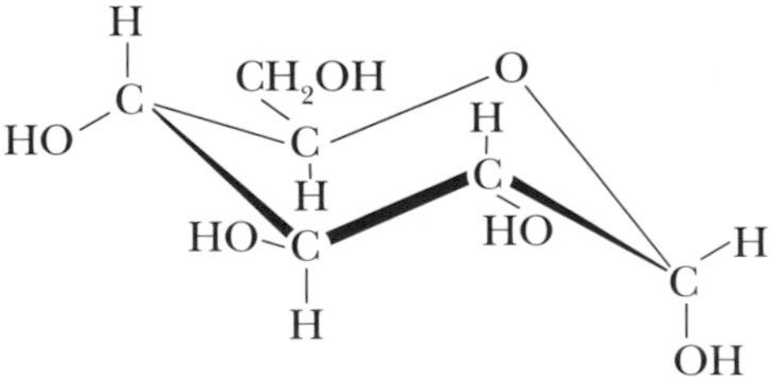

glucose

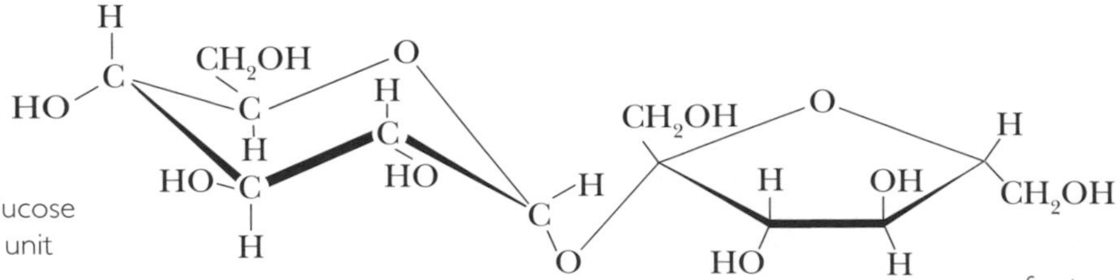

sucrose

Structures of glucose and sucrose (table sugar)

hydrogen is usually present in the same ratio as in water. The formula for glucose, for example, is $C_6H_{12}O_6$, which could be written $C_6(H_2O)_6$. Neither way of writing the formula gives any idea of how the atoms are arranged in a glucose molecule.

Glucose is a monosaccharide. Sucrose, with two sugar units joined together, is a disaccharide.

Starch and cellulose are polysaccharides. They both consist of long chains of glucose units. The difference lies in the links between the units.

Plants make glucose by *photosynthesis*. Some of the glucose they store as starch, a reserve of energy food. Some of the glucose builds up the cellulose cell walls as the plants grow. When people eat parts of plants, such as potatoes or rice, they can digest starch but not cellulose. Cows feed on grass but rely on bacteria in their guts to break down the cellulose to glucose. Cows chew the cud to give bacteria time to digest the long chain molecules.

carbon (C) is a nonmetal element with three solid *allotropes*: diamond, graphite and *buckminsterfullerene*. *Charcoal* is an impure form of carbon. Carbon is the first element in *group 4* of the periodic table. Its *electron configuration* is $[He]2s^22p^2$.

Carbon's remarkable ability to form stable chains and rings of atoms with single, double and triple bonds gives rise to *organic chemistry*.

Carbon forms two oxides, both of which are colorless, molecular gases with no smell. Carbon monoxide (CO) is a *neutral oxide*. It is highly poisonous because it is held more strongly by hemoglobin than oxygen. Carbon monoxide is used as a reducing agent in metallurgy, for example during *iron extraction* in a blast furnace.

Carbon monoxide is also used on a large scale to manufacture methanol. Steam reacts with methane in natural gas in the presence of a nickel oxide catalyst to produce a mixture of carbon monoxide and hydrogen (see *steam reforming*). The mixture of carbon monoxide and hydrogen combines to make methanol at about 250°C over a copper-based catalyst.

$$CO(g) + 3H_2(g) \rightleftharpoons CH_3OH(l)$$

Carbon dioxide (CO_2) is an *acidic oxide*. It dissolves in water, forming carbonic acid, which is a weak acid.

$$CO_2(g) + H_2O(l) \rightleftharpoons H_2CO_3(aq)$$

The gas is strongly absorbed by alkalis such as potassium hydroxide.

The simplest chloride of carbon, tetrachloromethane (CCl_4), is a colorless liquid with tetrahedral molecules. Unlike many other nonmetal chlorides it is not hydrolyzed by water or by alkalis. Carbon does not react directly with chlorine so tetrachloromethane is made by the reaction of carbon disulfide with chlorine.

carbon cycle: the cycling of the element carbon in the natural environment as carbon compounds move between the main reservoirs of carbon in the atmosphere, the oceans and on land (see *environmental chemistry*).

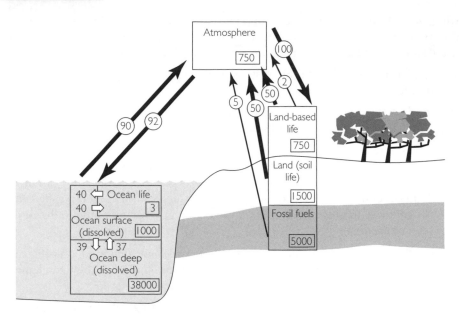

A highly simplified carbon cycle with estimates of the quantities in the main reservoirs where the figures are in gigatonnes of carbon (1 Gt = 1000 million tonnes). Also shown are estimates of the flows of carbon in gigatonnes per year (Gt yr⁻¹).

carbonium ions: see *carbocations*.

carbonyl compounds contain the carbonyl group ($C = O$). The two main classes of carbonyl compounds are the *aldehydes* and the *ketones*. The $C = O$ double bond is polar with the electrons drawn toward the more electronegative oxygen atom. The characteristic reactions of carbonyl compounds are *nucleophilic addition reactions* and *addition–elimination reactions*.

The carbonyl group in aldehydes and ketones

$$\ce{\overset{\delta+}{C} = \overset{\delta-}{O}}$$

carborundum is the common name for silicon carbide (SiC), a shiny, black solid made by heating silicon dioxide with carbon at 2000°C. It has the same crystal structure as diamond but with every other carbon atom replaced by a silicon atom. Carborundum is a useful abrasive, being harder than corundum (*aluminum oxide*) but not as hard as diamond. Like diamond, carborundum has a very high melting point, making it a useful *refractory*.

carboxylic acids are compounds with the formula $R — CO_2H$ where R represents an *alkyl group*, *aryl group* or a hydrogen atom. The carboxylic acid group ($— CO_2H$) is the *functional group* that gives the acids their characteristic properties.

Carboxylic acids are named by changing the ending of the corresponding *alkane* to -oic acid. So ethanol becomes ethanoic acid.

Even the simplest acids such as methanoic and ethanoic acid are liquids at room temperature because of *hydrogen bonding* between the carboxylic acid groups. Also because

methanoic acid   ethanoic acid   propanoic acid

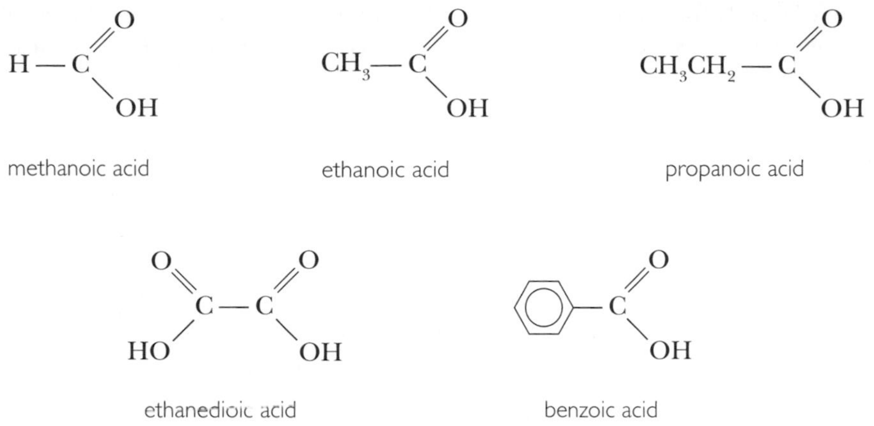

ethanedioic acid   benzoic acid

Names and structures of carboxylic acids

of hydrogen bonding, these acids mix freely with water. Benzoic acid is a solid at room temperature. It is only very slightly soluble in cold water but more soluble in hot water.

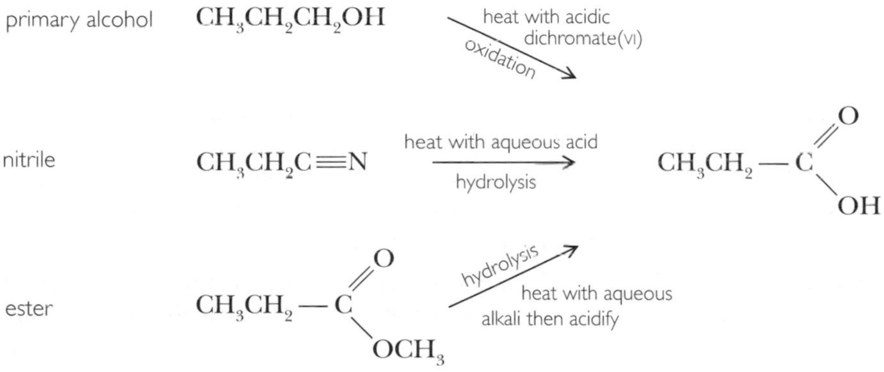

primary alcohol $CH_3CH_2CH_2OH$ heat with acidic dichromate(VI)
oxidation

nitrile $CH_3CH_2C{\equiv}N$ heat with aqueous acid hydrolysis $CH_3CH_2 - C{\Large\langle}{\substack{O \\ OH}}$

ester $CH_3CH_2 - C{\Large\langle}{\substack{O \\ OCH_3}}$ hydrolysis heat with aqueous alkali then acidify

Reactions that produce carboxylic acids

Carboxylic acids are *weak acids*. The hydroxyl part of the carboxylic acid group is more acidic than the hydroxyl group in *alcohols* because the carboxylate ion formed is stabilized by *delocalization of electrons*. Carboxylic acids are sufficiently acidic to produce carbon dioxide when added to a solution of sodium carbonate. This reaction distinguishes carboxylic acids from weaker acids such as *phenols*.

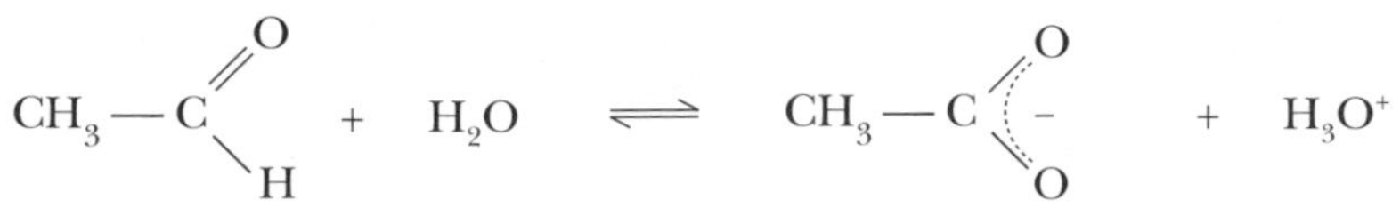

$$CH_3 - C{\Large\langle}{\substack{O \\ H}} \; + \; H_2O \; \rightleftharpoons \; CH_3 - C{\Large\langle}{\substack{O \\ O}}^- \; + \; H_3O^+$$

Ionization of ethanoic acid. Delocalization of electrons stabilizes the carboxylate ion and favors ionization of the acid.

Carboxylic acids form a number of related compounds (derivatives): *acyl chlorides, acid anhydrides, esters* and *amides*. The reactions of ethanoic acid are typical of carboxylic acids.

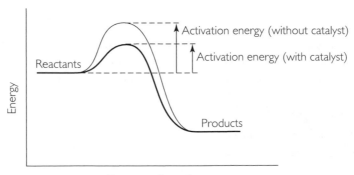

Reactions of ethanoic acid

carcinogens are compounds that can cause cancer. In a healthy body, the rate at which cells divide to produce new cells is strictly controlled. Cancer is a disorder that happens when some cells somehow escape from the normal control and multiply to produce a growth, or tumor. Chemicals that cause cancer probably produce changes (mutations) in the genes that control cell division.

catalysts speed up the rates of chemical reactions without themselves changing permanently. Catalysts can be recovered at the end of the reaction. Often a small amount of catalyst is effective.

Catalysts work by lowering the *activation energy* for reactions. Lowering the activation energy increases the proportion of molecules with enough energy to react.

Diagram showing the effect of a catalyst on the activation energy of a reaction

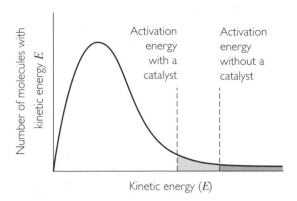

Distribution of molecular energies showing how the proportion of molecules able to react increases when a catalyst lowers the activation energy

Often a catalyst changes the *mechanism of a reaction* and makes reactions more productive by increasing the yield of the desired product and reducing waste.

Many catalysts are specific to a particular reaction. This is especially true of *enzymes*. If the catalyst is in the same phase as the reactants it is a *homogeneous catalyst*. If the catalyst is in a different phase it is a *heterogeneous catalyst*.

Catalysts speed up reactions but they do not change the position of equilibrium for a reversible reaction.

Highlights in the development of industrial catalysts include:

- 1908 Fritz Haber discovered how to make *ammonia* from nitrogen and hydrogen with a modified iron catalyst.
- 1912 Paul Sabatier first used a nickel catalyst to *hydrogenate* unsaturated *vegetable oils* and turn them to solid *fats* for margarine.
- 1930 Eugene Houdry developed *catalytic cracking* of oil fractions to make *gasoline*.
- 1942 Vladimir Ipatieff and Herman Pines found a catalytic method of alkylating *hydrocarbons* to produce branched hydrocarbons with high octane numbers to prevent *knocking* in gasoline engines.
- 1976 General Motors and the Ford Motor Corporation developed *catalytic converters* to cut pollution from motor vehicles.

catalytic converter: a device in the exhaust system of an automobile that contains a *catalyst* to covert pollutants in the exhaust gases to less harmful substances. Vehicle exhausts pollute the air because the engine does not burn all the fuel and because the temperature and pressure in the cylinders are high enough for nitrogen from the air to react with oxygen.

Pollutant	Origin of the pollutant
carbon dioxide, CO_2	Complete combustion of hydrocarbons in *gasoline*
carbon monoxide, CO	Incomplete combustion of fuel
hydrocarbons, C_xH_y	Unburnt fuel
nitrogen oxides, NO_x	Reaction of nitrogen and oxygen from the air in the hot engine
lead compounds	From antiknock additives in leaded gasoline

Unleaded fuel must be used in vehicles fitted with a catalytic converter because lead would poison the catalyst and stop it working.

The catalyst is a finely divided alloy of platinum and rhodium supported on an inert ceramic, pierced with many fine tubes to give a very large surface area. Once the catalyst is hot enough it converts the pollutants to steam, carbon dioxide and nitrogen.

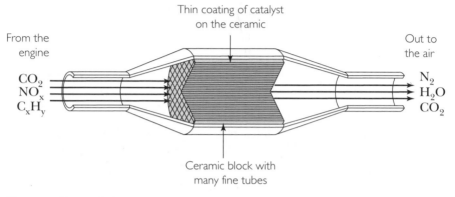

Thin coating of catalyst on the ceramic

From the engine

CO_2
NO_x
C_xH_y

Out to the air

N_2
H_2O
CO_2

Ceramic block with many fine tubes

Diagram of a catalytic converter

catalytic cracking: a process in an oil refinery for converting fractions from the *fractional distillation of oil* into more useful products by breaking up larger molecules into smaller ones. The problem in refining is to produce the oil products in the

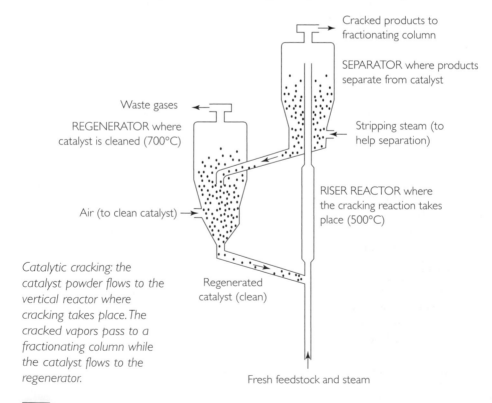

Cracked products to fractionating column

SEPARATOR where products separate from catalyst

Waste gases

REGENERATOR where catalyst is cleaned (700°C)

Stripping steam (to help separation)

RISER REACTOR where the cracking reaction takes place (500°C)

Air (to clean catalyst) →

Catalytic cracking: the catalyst powder flows to the vertical reactor where cracking takes place. The cracked vapors pass to a fractionating column while the catalyst flows to the regenerator.

Regenerated catalyst (clean)

Fresh feedstock and steam

amounts needed by customers. Generally crude oil contains too much of the high-boiling fractions (bigger molecules) and not enough of the low-boiling fractions (smaller molecules) needed for fuels such as *gasoline*.

Catalytic cracking is a *continuous process*. The finely powdered catalyst made of silicon and aluminum oxides gradually gets coated with carbon so it circulates through a regenerator where the carbon burns away in a stream of air (see figure).

catenation: the ability of the atoms of an element to join together in long chains or rings. *Carbon* atoms have an exceptional ability to catenate – hence the wide range of organic compounds. *Silicon*, the second element in group 4, does not have the same ability to catenate. Silicon forms *hydrides*, Si_nH_{2n+2}, analogous to the *alkanes* but the largest known molecule has n equal to eight, and only silane (SiH_4) is stable for any length of time.

Sulfur atoms can catenate. Both the rhombic and monoclinic *allotropes* consist of S_8 rings. Plastic sulfur is a tangled mass of long chains of sulfur atoms but it rapidly reverts to the rhombic form at room temperature.

cathode: the *electrode* at which *reduction* takes place. During *electrolysis* the external power supply adds *electrons* to the cathode so that it becomes the negative electrode attracting positive ions, which gain electrons (reduction) turning into atoms or molecules.

The term cathode is also sometimes used in *electrochemical cells* where the reduction process at this electrode in one of the *half-cells* takes electrons from the electrode, which becomes the positive terminal of the cell.

Note that electrons flow into the cathode from the external circuit both during electrolysis and when a current is drawn from a chemical cell.

cathodic protection: an electrochemical method of preventing *corrosion* used with pipelines, oil rigs and the hulls of ships. Steel corrodes where it is oxidized. This happens wherever the metal is an *anode*. In anodic regions the iron atoms give up electrons, turning into ions. Attaching a more reactive metal, such as zinc or magnesium, to iron creates an electrochemical cell in which the iron is the *cathode* so the more reactive metal corrodes.

cations: are *positive ions* attracted to the *cathode* during *electrolysis*. (See *cation tests* for examples of common cations.)

cation tests are used in qualitative analysis to identify the positive ions in salts. Adding sodium hydroxide produces a precipitate if the metal hydroxide is insoluble. The precipitate dissolves in excess of the alkali if the hydroxide is *amphoteric*.

Adding *ammonia* solution also precipitates insoluble hydroxides. These redissolve in excess if the metal ion forms stable *complex ions* with ammonia molecules.

These tests can be supplemented with *flame tests* to identify metal ions such as sodium and potassium, which do not give precipitates (see table on page 81).

cell: see *electrochemical cells*.

Celsius temperature scale: a scale in which the melting point of ice is set at $0°C$ and the boiling point of water at $100°C$. The scale is based on the absolute or *kelvin* temperature scale.

Temperature in $°C$ = absolute temperature (K) – 273 K

cement is manufactured by heating clay with powdered limestone in a rotating kiln and then grinding the lumps of product to a fine powder. Cement is a complex mixture of calcium silicates and calcium aluminosilicates that becomes hydrated and sets when mixed with water. Stirring cement with sand, gravel and water makes concrete.

ceramics are materials such as pottery, glasses, cement, concrete and graphite. Ceramics also include a wide range of crystalline materials such as *carborundum*, silicon nitride, *aluminum oxide* and magnetic *ferrites*. What all these materials have in common is that they are nonmetallic, inorganic materials that are heated to a high temperature in a furnace at some stage during their manufacture.

Typical advantages of ceramics are that they are:

- very hard
- strong in compression
- chemically *inert*
- *refractories*
- electrical insulators.

Typical disadvantages of many ceramics are that they are:

- weak in tension
- brittle
- liable to crack if there is a sudden temperature change.

cesium chloride structure is the cubic crystal structure of the ionic compound cesium chloride (CsCl). In general it is a structure for a compound M^+X^- in which each positive ion is surrounded by eight nearest neighbors at the corners of a cube and each negative ion is similarly surrounded by eight positive ions. So the *coordination numbers* for both elements is 8.

○ Cl

● Cs

Structure of cesium chloride showing 8:8 coordination. The structure consists of a simple cubic array of positive ions interpenetrating a cubic array of negative ions.

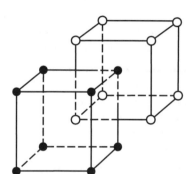

Other compounds with this structure include CsBr, CsI and NH_4Cl.

This structure is only possible in compounds with a positive ion that is relatively large so it can be in contact with eight neighboring negative ions. Cesium, in period 6 of the periodic table, forms larger ions than, for example, sodium. (See also *unit cell*.)

CFCs (chlorofluorocarbons) such as CCl_3F, CCl_2F_2 and CCl_2FCClF_2 are compounds containing carbon, chlorine and fluorine. They have advantages: they are unreactive, do not burn and are not *toxic*. Also it is possible to make CFCs with different boiling points to suit different applications. These properties make CFCs ideal as the working fluid in refrigerators and air conditioning units. They are also used to make the bubbles in expanded plastics and insulating foams. CFCs make good solvents for dry cleaning and removing grease from electronic equipment.

The problem with CFCs is that they escape into the *atmosphere* where they are so stable that they last for many years, long enough for them to diffuse up to the stratosphere. In the stratosphere the intense ultraviolet light from the Sun splits CFCs into *free radicals* including chlorine atoms. Chlorine atoms react with *ozone*:

$$Cl\bullet + O_3 \longrightarrow ClO\bullet + O_2$$
$$ClO\bullet + O\bullet \longrightarrow Cl\bullet + O_2$$

The first reaction is much faster than other reactions in the stratosphere. The second reaction involves oxygen atoms that are common in the stratosphere and this recreates the chlorine atom. This means in effect that one chlorine atom can rapidly destroy many ozone molecules.

Now that the damaging effects of CFCs are known they are being phased out where possible. The hunt is on for alternative compounds with the desirable properties of CFCs but without the environmental problems.

Positive ion in solution	Observations on adding sodium hydroxide solution drop by drop and then in excess	Observations on adding ammonia solution drop by drop and then in excess
calcium, Ca^{2+}	white precipitate but only if the calcium ion concentration is high	no precipitate
magnesium, Mg^{2+}	white precipitate insoluble in excess reagent	white precipitate insoluble in excess reagent
barium, Ba^{2+}	no precipitate	no precipitate
aluminum, Al^{3+}	white precipitate that dissolves in excess reagent	white precipitate insoluble in excess reagent
chromium(III), Cr^{3+}	green precipitate that dissolves in excess to form a dark green solution	green precipitate insoluble in excess reagent
manganese(II), Mn^{2+}	off-white precipitate insoluble in excess reagent	off-white precipitate insoluble in excess reagent
iron(II), Fe^{2+}	green precipitate insoluble in excess reagent	green precipitate insoluble in excess reagent
iron(III), Fe^{3+}	browny-red precipitate insoluble in excess reagent	browny-red precipitate insoluble in excess reagent
copper(II), Cu^{2+}	pale blue precipitate insoluble in excess	pale blue precipitate dissolving in excess to form a dark blue solution
zinc, Zn^{2+}	white precipitate that dissolves in excess reagent	white precipitate that dissolves in excess reagent
lead, Pb^{2+}	white precipitate that dissolves in excess reagent	white precipitate insoluble in excess reagent
ammonium, NH_4^+	alkaline gas (ammonia) given off on heating	no visible change

Cation tests

changes of state are changes from one state of matter to another. The following are all examples of changes of state:

- a solid melting to a liquid
- a liquid freezing to a solid
- a liquid evaporating and becoming a gas
- a gas condensing to a liquid.

Energy is taken in from the surroundings during melting and evaporating (they are *endothermic* processes). The energy is needed to break the bonds between atoms, molecules or ions.

Energy is given out to the surroundings during freezing or condensing (they are *exothermic* processes). Energy is given out as the bonds between particles reform.

A few solids turn directly to gas when heated at atmospheric pressure. On cooling the vapor turns directly back to a solid. This is *sublimation.*

charcoal is a form of *carbon* made by heating wood or bones in the absence of air. Charcoal consists of minute graphite crystals. Heating charcoal in steam at about 1000°C produces activated charcoal by driving out volatile compounds from the pores of the solid. Activated charcoal is an excellent absorbent used to filter out impurities from gases and solutions.

Charles's law states that the volume of a fixed amount of gas at constant pressure is proportional to its absolute temperature.

$$V \propto T \text{ or } \frac{V}{T} = \text{constant}$$

The law follows from the *ideal gas* equation $pV = nRT$ if p and n are constant. Real gases deviate from ideal gas behavior. Note that the law only applies if there is no chemical change altering the number of gas molecules as the gas gets hotter or colder.

chelates are *complex ions* in which each *ligand* molecule or ion forms more than one *dative covalent bond* with the central metal ion. Chelates are formed by *bidentate* and *polydentate* ligands such as *edta*. The term chelate comes from the Greek word for a crab's claw, reflecting the claw-like way in which chelating ligands grab hold of metal ions. Chelate complexes are generally more stable than complexes formed by mono-dentate ligands (see *stability constants*). Powerful chelating agents trap metal ions and effectively isolate them in solution.

chemical equations describe what happens during reactions by identifying the reactants and products. State symbols show the *states of matter* of the chemicals involved. Equations may also show the reaction conditions by including information about temperature, pressure and catalysts above or below the arrow leading from reactants to products. There are various types of chemical equation.

- Word equations simply name the reactants and products:
  hydrogen + oxygen $\longrightarrow$ water

- *Balanced equations* with formulas are used to calculate the amounts of reactants and products:
  $$2H_2(g) + O_2(g) \longrightarrow 2H_2O(l)$$

- *Ionic equations* are balanced equations leaving out any *spectator ions* that do not change:

$$H^+(aq) + OH^-(aq) \longrightarrow H_2O(l)$$

- *Half-equations* are balanced equations that show part of a *redox* reaction:

$$2H^+(aq) + 2e^- \longrightarrow H_2(g)$$

- Unbalanced symbol equations show just the main starting chemical and the main product with the conditions for reaction written by the arrow:

$$C_2H_5OH \xrightarrow[\text{heat}]{Cr_2O_7{}^{2-}/H^+} CH_3CO_2H$$

- Mechanistic equations show intermediate steps in the *mechanism* for a reaction:

$$H_2 + Br\bullet \longrightarrow HBr + H\bullet$$

chemical industry: the industry that converts raw materials such as crude oil, natural gas and minerals into useful products such as pharmaceuticals, *fertilizers*, *detergents*, paints and *dyes*.

A chemical plant consists not only of the reaction vessels and equipment for separating and purifying products, but also the storage vessels, pumps and pipes, sources of energy and heat exchangers together with the control room.

Bulk chemicals are manufactured on a scale of thousands or even millions of tonnes per year. Examples are ethene, sulfuric acid, ammonia and chlorine. They are mainly used as the starting point for making other substances. Fine chemicals such as pesticides and pharmaceuticals are made on a much smaller scale – a few tonnes or hundreds of tonnes per year.

Specialty chemicals are manufactured for their particular properties as thickeners, stabilizers, flame retardants and so on (see table on page 84).

chemotherapy is the use of chemicals to treat disease. Chemotherapy began with the work of Paul Ehrlich (1854–1915) who had the idea that it might be possible to find chemicals that kill the microorganisms that cause disease without harming healthy living cells. Paul Ehrlich worked as an assistant to Robert Koch (1843–1910) who pioneered the use of *dyes* to stain and identify *bacteria*. Ehrlich was particularly interested in selective dyes. Some dyes, for example, take well on cotton but not on wool. Ehrlich found that methylene blue would dye nerve cells well but not other parts of the body. This inspired him to search for chemical "magic bullets" to target microorganisms and diseased cells. After a long series of experiments Ehrlich and his Japanese colleague Sahachiro Hata finally discovered an arsenic compound that cured syphilis. For the first time a synthetic chemical was used to cure a bacterial disease.

The high hopes raised by Ehrlich's work led to many disappointments until 1932 when Gerhard Domagk was involved in testing the medical effects of new dyes produced by a German chemical company. He found that the dye Prontosil red was remarkably effective against streptococcal infections in mice. Domagk saved his daughter's life with the new drug when she accidentally picked up a serious infection by pricking her finger in his laboratory. This led to the development of sulfonamide drugs that were used to treat bacterial diseases until the discovery of *antibiotics*.

Today chemotherapy is widely used to treat cancer but few drugs are "magic bullets." If they are effective in destroying cancerous cells they are generally toxic and damage other parts of the body too (see *cisplatin*).

Main raw materials	Large-scale processes and products	Uses of the products
Crude oil and *natural* gas for the petrochemical industry	*Fractional distillation, steam cracking, steam reforming* and *isomerization* and many other processes to produce the building blocks for the industry such as *ethene*, propene and *benzene*	Manufacture of *polymers*, solvents, pharmaceuticals, *agrochemicals, dyes*, pigments and *detergents*
Salt (sodium chloride) and limestone for the chlor-alkali industry	*Electrolysis of brine* for making chlorine, sodium hydroxide and hydrogen. Solvay process to make sodium carbonate	Manufacture of *bleaches, disinfectants*, solvents, some polymers and in the *glass* and paper industries
Sulfur from underground deposits of the element or from the purification of oil and gas plus oxygen from the air	Contact process for *sulfuric acid manufacture*	Manufacture of *paints*, pigments, *fertilizers*, detergents, *plastics* and many uses in the chemical, metallurgical and petrochemical industries
Nitrogen from the air, natural gas and oil fractions	Haber process for *ammonia* manufacture and catalytic oxidation of ammonia for *nitric acid manufacture*	Manufacture of fertilizers, dyes, pigments, detergents, *explosives*, plastics and *fibers*
Calcium phosphate rock	Treatment of phosphate rock with concentrated sulfuric acid to make *phosphoric(V) acid* and phosphates	Fertilizer industry, manufacture of washing powders, toothpaste, food industry, enamels and glazes
Fluorite (calcium fluoride)	Action of concentrated sulfuric acid on fluorite to make hydrogen fluoride; electrolysis of fluorides in hydrogen fluoride to make fluorine	Etching and polishing glass and integrated circuits; manufacture of fluorocarbons and hydrofluorocarbons (to replace *CFCs*); pharmaceuticals and the polymer ptfe

Chemical industry

chiral compounds are *asymmetric* so that they have mirror-image forms that are not identical. The most common chiral compounds have a carbon atom attached to four different atoms or groups. The two mirror-image forms are known as enantiomers.

$$CO_2H$$

C

H   · OH

$$CH_3$$ Mirror

$$HO_2C$$

C

HO ·   H

$$H_3C$$

Mirror-image forms of 2-hydroxypropanoic acid (lactic acid)

Enantiomers behave identically in ordinary chemical reactions and their main physical properties are the same. They differ in their effect on polarized light – they are optically active. One mirror-image form rotates the plane of polarized light in one direction. The other form has the opposite effect. They are *optical isomers*.

Chirality is very important in living organisms. Living cells are full of messenger and carrier molecules that interact selectively with the active sites and receptors in other molecules such as *enzymes*. The messenger and carrier molecules are all chiral and the body works with only one of the mirror-image forms. In most living things all the *amino acids*, for example, are L amino acids.

The importance of chirality in living things was brought home to people forcibly by the impact of the thalidomide tragedy. Thalidomide was a sedative used in the early 1960s. Doctors believed that it was very safe and prescribed it widely. Sadly it was soon discovered that thalidomide could harm babies if taken by mothers during the early months of pregnancy.

Thalidomide is chiral. One isomer is the effective sedative. The other isomer causes malformations in babies (it is a *teratogen*). Ever since the thalidomide affair, the pharmaceutical and agrochemical industries have to test the mirror-image forms of chiral chemicals separately before they can be used as drugs or agrochemicals.

Some complex ions are chiral.

Mirror-image forms of a complex between chromium(III) ions and 1,2-diaminoethane, en (see bidentate ligands). Three-dimensional models make it easier to see that they are non-superimposable.

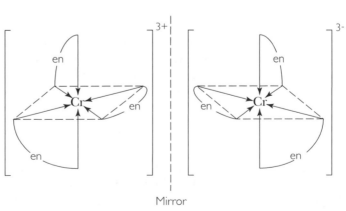

Mirror

85

chlorination is a reaction that replaces a hydrogen atom in an organic molecule with a chlorine atom. One example is the chlorination of *alkanes* – a *free-radical chain reaction* initiated by *ultraviolet radiation*.

Another example is the chlorination of *benzene* by chlorine in the presence of an iron chloride catalyst. This is an *electrophilic substitution* reaction.

chlorine (Cl) occurs as a greenish, toxic gas consisting of Cl_2 molecules. It is the second element in the family of nonmetals called the halogens (*group 7*). Its *electron configuration* is $[Ne]3s^23p^5$.

Chlorine is manufactured on a large scale by the *electrolysis of brine*.

Chlorine is a powerful *oxidizing agent* that reacts directly with most elements. In its compounds chlorine is usually present in the −1 oxidation states but chlorine can be oxidized to positive oxidation states by oxygen and fluorine.

+7	ClO_4^-	$KClO_4$
+5	ClO_3^-	$KClO_3$
+3	ClO_2^-	$KClO_2$
+1	ClO^-	HOCl
0	Cl_2	
−1	Cl^-	HCl

Oxidation states of chlorine

Chlorine forms ionic chlorides with metals.

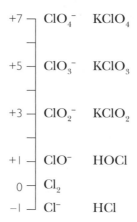

Formation of ions in magnesium chloride when chlorine reacts with magnesium

Chlorine forms covalent, molecular chlorides with most nonmetals but it does not react directly with carbon, oxygen or nitrogen. Hydrogen burns in chlorine to produce the colorless, acidic gas hydrogen chloride, HCl. Hydrogen chloride is very soluble in water, forming *hydrochloric acid*.

Reaction of hydrogen with chlorine to produce hydrogen chloride molecules

$$H:H \quad + \quad \overset{\times\times}{\underset{\times\times}{\times Cl}}\overset{\times\times}{\underset{\times\times}{\times Cl\times}} \quad \longrightarrow \quad 2\ H\overset{\times\times}{\underset{\times\times}{:Cl\times}}$$

Chlorine dissolves in water. It reacts reversibly with water, forming a mixture of weak chloric(I) acid and strong hydrochloric acid. This is an example of a *disproportionation reaction*.

$$Cl_2(aq) + H_2O(l) \rightleftharpoons HOCl(aq) + Cl^-(aq) + H^+(aq)$$

Chlorine oxidizes a range of ions or molecules in solution:

- iron(II) ions to iron(III) ions
- bromide ions to bromine
- iodide ions to iodine
- sulfite ions to sulfate ions
- thiosulfate ions to sulfate ions
- hydrogen sulfide to sulfur.

chlorine oxoanions form when chlorine reacts with water and alkalis. In these compounds chlorine is oxidized to positive oxidation states through a series of *disproportionation reactions.*

When chlorine dissolves in potassium (or sodium) hydroxide solution at room temperature it produces chlorate(I) and chloride ions.

$$Cl_2(aq) + 2OH^-(aq) \longrightarrow ClO^-(aq) + Cl^-(aq) + H_2O(l)$$

On heating the chlorate(I) ions disproportionates to chlorate(V) and chloride ions:

$$3ClO^-(aq) \longrightarrow ClO_3^-(aq) + 2Cl^-(aq)$$

Potassium chlorate(III) can be crystallized from the solution. Careful heating just above the melting point converts potassium chlorate(V) to potassium chlorate(VII) and potassium chloride.

$$KClO_3(s) \longrightarrow 3\ KClO_4(s) + KCl(s)$$

cholesterol is a *steroid* that plays an important part in metabolism. It is a part of cell membranes and the precursor of steroid hormones such as testosterone and progesterone.

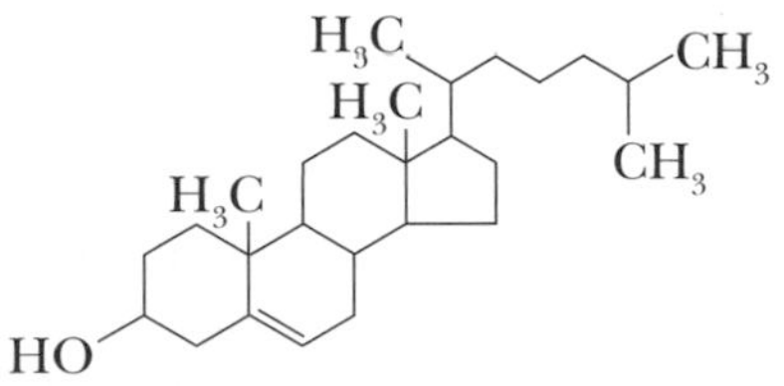

Structure of cholesterol

High levels of cholesterol in the blood may lead to deposits building up in arteries, resulting in heart disease. Cholesterol levels are monitored in some older people and in those thought likely to suffer from heart disease.

chromatography is a method for separating and identifying the chemicals in a mixture. Chromatography can be used to:

- separate and identify the chemicals in a mixture
- check the purity of a chemical product
- identify impurities in a product
- purify a chemical product (on a laboratory or industrial scale).

All types of chromatography have a stationary phase (a solid or a liquid held by a solid) and a mobile phase (a liquid or gas). The components of a mixture separate as the mobile phase moves through the stationary phase. Components that tend to mix with the mobile phase move faster. Components that tend to be held by the stationary phase move slower.

The basic principle underlying the separation is:

- *adsorption* when the stationary phase is a solid
- *partition* when the stationary phase is a liquid held as a thin layer on the surface of a solid.

There are several types of chromatography including: *liquid chromatography, high-performance liquid chromatography* (hplc), *paper chromatography, thin-layer chromatography* (tlc) and *gas–liquid chromatography* (glc).

chromium (Cr) is a hard, silvery *d-block* metal with the *electron configuration* $[Ar]3d^54s^1$. This electron configuration is an exception to the normal $[Ar]3d^x4s^2$ pattern for the first series of *d*-block elements. Energetically it is more favorable to have one electron in each *d*-orbital and thus to half-fill the *d*-subshell.

In solution chromium forms ion in the +2, +3 and +6 *oxidation states.*

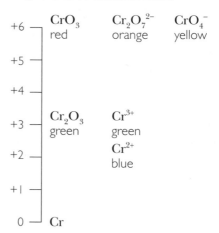

Oxidation states of chromium

There is an equilibrium between yellow chromate(VI) ions and orange dichromate(VI) ions in aqueous solution. The position of equilibrium depends on the pH. In acid the hydrogen ion concentration is high so the solution is orange because dichromate ions predominate. Adding alkali removes hydrogen ions and turns the solution yellow as chromate ions form. These shifts in the position of equilibrium are as predicted by *Le Chatelier's principle.* Note that this is not a redox reaction. Chromium is in the +6 state on both sides of the equation.

$$2CrO_4^-(aq) + 2H^+(aq) \rightleftharpoons Cr_2O_7^{2-}(aq) + H_2O(l)$$

Dichromate ions in acid solution are used to oxidize *alcohols* and *aldehydes*. Paper moistened with dichromate(VI) solution is used in the *gas test* for sulfur dioxide. The paper turns from orange to green as dichromate(VI) ions are reduced to chromium(III) ions. Potassium dichromate(VI) is used as a *primary standard* in *redox titrations.*

$$Cr_2O_7^{2-}(aq) + 14H^+(aq) + 6e^- \longrightarrow 2Cr^{3+}(aq) + 7H_2O(l)$$

Zinc reduces a green solution of chromium(III) to a blue solution of chromium(II) ions. Chromium(II) is a powerful *reducing agent* and is quickly converted to chromium(III) by oxygen in the air.

chromium extraction: chromium is extracted from chromium(III) oxide in a *batch process* using aluminum as the reducing agent. The commercial ore is chromite, which contains other metals as well as chromium, especially iron. The first step is to convert the ore to pure chromium(III) oxide. A mixture of the oxide with powdered aluminum is then ignited in a reaction vessel. The *exothermic reaction* produces 97–99% pure metal.

$$Cr_2O_3(s) + 2Al(s) \longrightarrow 2Cr(s) + Al_2O_3(s)$$

Carbon can reduce chromium oxide but the metal contains carbon as an impurity, which makes the metal brittle and less resistant to corrosion.

Chromium, like aluminum, is protected from corrosion by a thin layer of oxide on the metal surface. The main use of chromium is to make *alloys* with iron (stainless steels). Electroplating with chromium gives a shiny, corrosion-resistant finish to metals.

chromophore: the part of a molecule that gives rise to its color. Chromophores in carbon compounds have an extended system of *delocalized electrons*. Families of dyes with the same chromophore are made by attaching different *functional groups* to modify the color. Functional groups linked to a chromophore may also make the dye more soluble in water and help it stick to the fibers of a textile

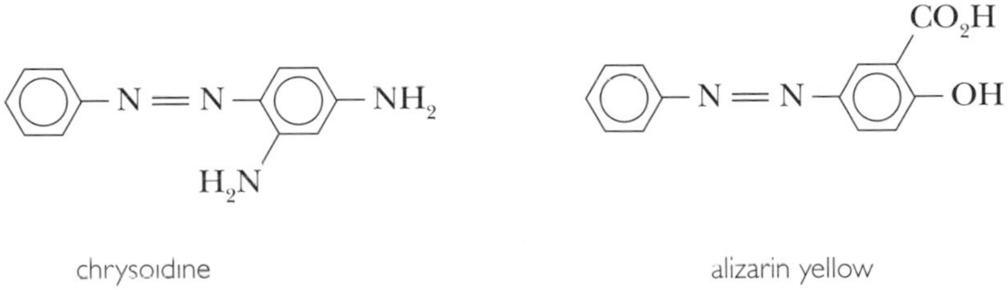

chrysoidine   alizarin yellow

Two dyes based on the same chromophore

cisplatin is an anticancer drug consisting of a complex ion of platinum, $Pt(NH_3)_2Cl_2$. The ion is planar and can exist as *cis* and *trans* isomers (see *geometrical isomerism*). The *cis* isomer inhibits cell division but does not prevent cell growth. This makes it a useful treatment for cancer. Unfortunately cisplatin is toxic and has unpleasant side effects.

Structure of the cis and trans isomers of Pt(NH₃)₂Cl₂

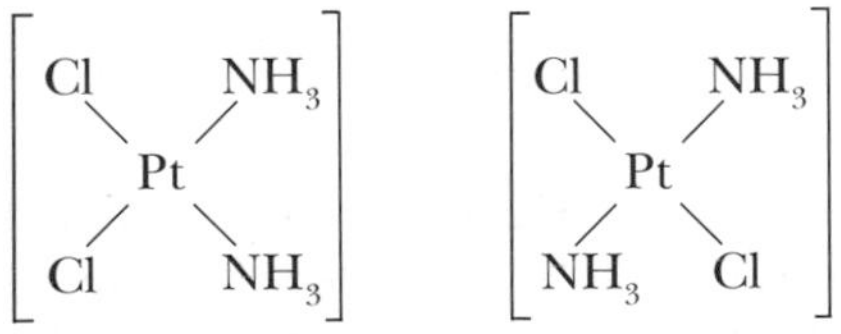

cis isomer   trans isomer

cis–trans isomerism: see *geometrical isomerism*.

clay minerals are hydrated aluminosilicates formed by the *weathering* of feldspars in igneous rocks. Kaolinite is the main component of kaolin, which is used as a coating agent and filler. Kaolinite is also the main constituent of ball clay used to make *ceramic* tableware, porcelain and wall tiles.

Kaolinite has a layer structure. Each layer consists of a sheet of *silicate* (SiO_4) tetrahedra interlocked with an aluminate sheet.

close-packed structures are found in metal crystals. In a layer of close-packed spheres each atom has six other spheres touching it. In three dimensions, layers of close-packed atoms stack up in two possible ways. In hexagonal close packing the third layer is directly over the first layer (aba). In cubic close packing it is the fourth layer that corresponds with the first layer (abca). In the two structures each atom touches 12 nearest neighbors, so for both the *coordination number* is 12.

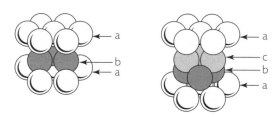

Hexagonal and cubic close packing of metal atoms

The *unit cell* of the cubic close-packed structure is a face-centered cube.

coal is a fossil fuel formed by the action of heat and pressure on the remains of plant buried under sediments. Heating coal in the absence of air at 1000°C drives off coal tar, ammonia and coal gas, leaving a residue of coke. Coke is required for a range of industrial processes including *iron extraction* in blast furnaces. Coal tar was a major source of organic chemicals until crude oil took over in the 1940s. Coal tar is a rich source of *arenes* and was the main source of *benzene* when William Perkin was pioneering the production of synthetic dyes.

cobalt (Co) is a hard, silvery *d-block* metal that is less reactive than iron. It has the *electron configuration* $[Ar]3d^74s^2$.

Cobalt is an ingredient of alloy *steels* such as the ferromagnetic alloy, Alnico, which makes excellent permanent magnets.

In solution cobalt forms ions in the +2 and +3 oxidation states. Cobalt(II) is the more stable state. Anhydrous cobalt(II) chloride is blue but it turns pink on adding water as the cobalt ions are hydrated to the $[Co(H_2O)_6]^{2+}$ ion. This is used as a test to detect water. The granules of the drying agent "self-indicating *silica gel*" are blue because they contain anhydrous cobalt ions. When the gel's drying action is exhausted the granules turn pink.

A dilute solution of cobalt chloride is pink because the cobalt(II) ions are hydrated. A concentrated solution is blue. A dilute solution also turns blue on adding concentrated hydrochloric acid. The color change is due to a *ligand* exchange reaction as chloride ions replace the water molecules. The reaction is reversible:

$$[Co(H_2O)_6]^{2+} + 4Cl^-(aq) \rightleftharpoons [CoCl_4]^{2-} + 6H_2O(aq)$$

It is normally very difficult to oxidize aqueous cobalt(II) to cobalt(III) but the reaction goes readily if the cobalt(II) ions are complexed with ammonia molecules. The Co(III) complex with ammonia is more stable than the Co(II) complex. The value for the *standard electrode potential* shows that aqueous Co(III) is a stronger oxidizing agent than potassium manganate(VII) in acid solution:

$$[Co(H_2O)_6]^{3+} + e^- \rightleftharpoons [Co(H_2O)_6]^{2+} \qquad E^\ominus = +1.82\ V$$

When the two states are complexed with ammonia the standard electrode potential shifts to a value that shows that the Co(III) state is much more stable. Cobalt(II) is now a reducing state and can be oxidized to Co(III) by oxygen or hydrogen peroxide.

$$[Co(NH_3)_6]^{3+} + e^- \rightleftharpoons [Co(NH_3)_6]^{2+} \qquad E^\ominus = +0.10\ V$$

colligative properties are the properties of solutions that depend on the concentration of solute particles but not on the nature of the particles. Dissolving salt, sugar or any other solute in water lowers its *vapor pressure*, raises its boiling point, lowers its *freezing point* and increases its *osmotic pressure*. The extent of these changes depends only on the *mole fraction* of solute particles and not on the nature of the dissolved molecules or ions.

collision theory accounts for the effects of concentration, temperature and *catalysts* on *reaction rates*. The idea is that a chemical reaction happens when the molecules or ions of reactant collide, making some bonds break and allowing new bonds to form.

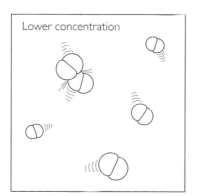
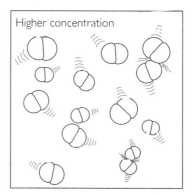

Raising the concentration means that the reacting particles are closer together. There are more collisions and reactions are faster.

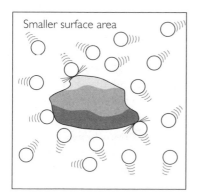
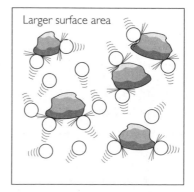

In a heterogeneous reaction of a solid with either a liquid or gas the reaction is faster if the solid is broken up into smaller pieces. Crushing the solid increases its surface area, collisions can be more frequent and the rate of reaction is bigger.

It is not enough for the molecules to collide. In soft collisions the molecules simply bounce off each other. Molecules are in rapid random motion and if every collision led to reaction all reactions would be explosively fast. Only pairs of molecules that collide with enough energy to stretch and break chemical bonds can lead to new products. Reactant molecules have to overcome the *activation energy*.

Collision theory refers to the *Maxwell–Boltzman distribution* of energies of molecules to explain the effects of temperature and catalysis on reaction rates.

colloids consist of fine particles (the disperse *phase*) of one substance finely dispersed in another (the continuous phase). The dispersed particles in liquids and gases are large enough to scatter light but they do not settle out and they show *Brownian motion*. The diameter of colloid particles is typically around 10 to 1000 nm (much larger than atomic diameters, which are around 0.2 nm).

Continuous phase	Disperse phase	Type	Example
gas	liquid	liquid aerosol	mist
gas	solid	solid aerosol	smoke
liquid	gas	foam	whipped cream
liquid	liquid	emulsion	hand cream, mayonnaise
liquid	solid	sol	paint, muddy river water, sewage
solid	gas	solid foam	pumice
solid	liquid	gel or solid emulsion	jelly, butter
solid	solid	solid sol	pearl, pigmented plastics

colored compounds in many instances get their color by absorbing some of the radiation in the visible region of the electromagnetic spectrum with wavelengths between 400 nm and 700 nm.

It is the electrons in colored compounds that absorb radiation as they jump from their normal state to a higher excited state. According to *quantum theory* there is a fixed relationship between the size of the energy jump and the wavelength of the radiation absorbed. In many compounds the jumps are so big that they absorb in the ultraviolet part of the spectrum. These compounds are colorless.

Color in transition metal ions arises from electronic transitions between *d-orbitals*. In a free atom all of the five *d*-orbitals have the same energy. When a transition metal ion forms complex ions the *d*-orbitals split into two groups with different energies. The size of the split depends on the number and nature of the ligands in the complex. This helps to account for color changes.

If all the *d*-orbitals are full there is no possibility of electronic transitions between them. This explains why Zn^{2+} and Cu^+ ions are colorless.

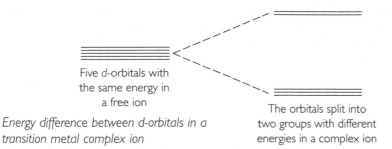

Five d-orbitals with
the same energy in
a free ion

Energy difference between d-orbitals in a transition metal complex ion

The orbitals split into
two groups with different
energies in a complex ion

Color in organic compounds is often associated with *delocalized electrons*. The energy jumps between molecular orbitals absorb visible radiation in molecules with extended systems of alternating double and single bonds (see *conjugated system*).

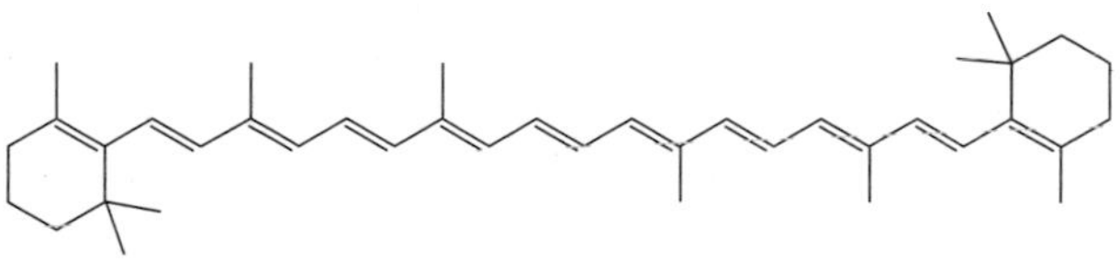

Skeletal formula of β–carotene, the main orange color in carrots, used as a colorant in foods, drugs and cosmetics

Some colors are caused by physical effects rather than electronic transitions. Examples of such effects are:

- light scattering – moonstones, blue skies
- interference – soap bubbles and oil films on water
- diffraction – opal, liquid crystals
- refraction of some wavelengths more than others – "fire" in gemstones.

colorimetry is a method for measuring the *concentration* of compounds in solution that can be used with chemicals that are themselves colored or which give a color when mixed with a suitable reagent.

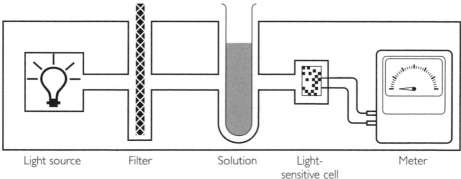

| Light source | Filter | Solution | Light-sensitive cell | Meter |

Diagram of a colorimeter

The filter lets through light, which is strongly absorbed by the solution. The extent of absorption depends on the path length of the light through the solution (which is a constant for the sample chamber used) and on the concentration of the solution. The instrument is *calibrated* by measuring the *absorbance* of a series of *standard solutions*. It can then be used to measure the concentration of unknown samples.

combustion is the reaction of a fuel with oxygen to release energy. Carbon in the fuel turns to carbon dioxide and hydrogen turns to steam (water). Any sulfur in the fuel is oxidized to sulfur dioxide. Nitrogen in a fuel may end up as the element after combustion or if the temperature is high enough, combined with oxygen to form a mixture of *nitrogen oxides.*

combustion analysis is a method for determining the *empirical formulas* of organic compounds. A weighed sample of the compound is burnt in excess oxygen mixed with helium. This converts the carbon to carbon dioxide and the hydrogen to water. A catalyst ensures that combustion is complete. The inert helium carries the products of combustion and the excess oxygen through a tube that contains chemicals to remove any volatile halogen, sulfur or phosphorus compounds. Oxides of nitrogen are converted to nitrogen gas and the excess oxygen combines with copper.

The water vapor is absorbed in magnesium chlorate(VII). Carbon dioxide is absorbed in soda lime. In a modern instrument, measurements of the thermal conductivity of the helium before and after absorption make it possible to determine the masses of water, carbon dioxide and nitrogen formed by burning the sample.

From the results it is possible to calculate the *percentage composition* of the compound. Any mass of the sample not accounted for is assumed to be due to oxygen.

Worked example:

Complete combustion of 0.15 g of a liquid compound produced 0.22 g of carbon dioxide and 0.09 g water. What is the empirical formula of the compound?

Notes on the method

The *molar mass* of carbon dioxide, CO_2 = 44 g mol^{-1} of which carbon is 12 g mol^{-1}

The molar mass of water, H_2O = 18 g mol^{-1} of which hydrogen is 2 g mol^{-1}

Answer

The mass of carbon in the sample = $\frac{12}{44}$ × 0.22 g = 0.06 g

The mass of hydrogen in the sample = $\frac{2}{18}$ × 0.09 g = 0.01 g

The total mass of carbon and hydrogen = 0.07 g in a sample with mass 0.15 g

So the difference gives the mass of oxygen in the sample, which is 0.08 g

These are the *amounts* of the elements in the sample:

carbon: 0.06 g ÷ 12 g mol^{-1} = 0.005 mol

hydrogen: 0.01 g ÷ 1 g mol^{-1} = 0.01 mol

oxygen: 0.08 g ÷ 16 g mol^{-1} = 0.005 mol

The ratio C:H:O is 1:2:1

The empirical formula of the compound is CH_2O.

---

common ion effect: the change in equilibrium position observed on adding an ionic compound that contains one of the ions involved in the equilibrium.

The common ion effect can change the extent of the ionization of *weak acids* and *weak bases*. The effect influences the behavior of *buffer solutions*. In a typical buffer solution a weak acid, such as ethanoic acid, is mixed with one of its salts, such as sodium ethanoate. In this example the common ion is the ethanoate ion. Ethanoate ions from the salt suppress the ionization of the acid as predicted by the *equilibrium law*. The added common ion from the sodium ethanoate shifts the equilibrium to the left and lowers the concentration of aqueous hydrogen ions.

$$CH_3CO_2H(aq) + H_2O(l) \rightleftharpoons CH_3CO_2^-(aq) + H_3O^+(aq)$$

$$\uparrow$$

$$CH_3CO_2^-(aq) \text{ common ion}$$
$$\text{from sodium ethanoate}$$

For a 0.25 mol dm^{-3} solution of ethanoic acid the pH = 2.7. In the presence of 0.1 mol dm^{-3} sodium ethanoate the concentration of H$_3$O$^+$(aq) falls markedly and the pH = 4.4.

This effect can also alter the solubility of sparingly soluble salts, making it possible to control their precipitation.

complex-forming titration is a practical technique used to determine the concentration of metal ions. A *titration* measures the volume of a *standard solution* of a complex-forming reagent needed to react exactly with a measured volume of the unknown solution of metal ions, such as zinc ions.

Complex-forming titrations often use a standard solution of *edta*, which forms very stable *complex ions* with metal ions. The procedure is the same as for any other titration.

To find the end point the analyst adds an indicator and a *buffer solution*, which forms a colored but unstable complex with the metal ion in the flask. A suitable indicator is Eriochrome black T, which is blue in solution at pH 10. At the start of the titration it produces a wine-red complex. Edta from a burette forms a more stable complex with zinc ions and so takes the metal ions from the indicator. At the end point all the zinc ions have been complexed by titration with edta. The last drop of edta leaves no Zn^{2+} ions to form the red complex with the indicator so the indicator turns blue again.

Worked example:
>
> An alkaline buffer and a few drops of Eriochrome black T indicator were added to 25.0 cm^3 of a solution of zinc sulfate. In the titration 23.2 cm^3 of 0.010 mol dm^{-3} edta were run in from a burette until the indicator changed from red to blue. What was the concentration of the zinc ions?
>
> Notes on the method
>
> Always start by writing the equation for the reaction. See *titration* for a general method for the calculations.
>
> Remember to convert volumes in cm^3 to volumes in dm^3 by dividing by 1000.
>
> In any titration there is one unknown – in this case the concentration of the zinc ions, c_A.

Answer

The equation for the reaction is:

$$Zn^{2+}(aq) + edta^{4-}(aq) \longrightarrow [Zn(edta)]^{2-}(aq)$$

The volume of zinc sulfate solution in the flask, $V_A = \dfrac{25.0}{1000}$ dm^3

Let the concentration of zinc ions be c_A.

The volume of hydrochloric acid added from the burette, $V_B = \dfrac{23.2}{1000}$ dm^3

The concentration of hydrochloric acid, $c_B = 0.010$ mol dm^{-3}

$$\frac{V_A \times c_A}{V_B \times c_B} = \frac{n_A}{n_B}$$

$$\frac{^{25}\!/_{1000} \times c_A}{^{23.2}\!/_{1000} \times 0.010} = \frac{1}{1}$$

Therefore $c_A = \dfrac{23.2 \times 0.010}{25.0} = 0.0928$ mol dm^{-3}

The concentration of the zinc ions was 0.0928 mol dm^{-3}.

---

complex ions consist of a central metal ion linked to a number of molecules or ions with *lone pairs of electrons*. The surrounding molecules or ions are *ligands*, which use their lone pair of electrons to form a *coordinate bond* with the metal ion. The number of ligands in a complex ion is typically two, four or six.

The overall charge of a complex ion is the sum of the charges on the metal ion and its ligands. (See also *shapes of complex ions*.)

composites are made by combining two or more materials to create a new material. A composite combines the desirable properties of its constituents and compensates for their disadvantages. Steel-reinforced concrete is a composite material as is galvanized steel. Kitchen worktops are composites consisting of chipboard covered with paper impregnated with a polymer such as a *thermosetting* melamine–methanal resin.

Many important composites consist of fibers of one material, such as *glass*, aramids, or graphite, embedded in a *polymer*, *metal* or *ceramic* matrix. The combinations are designed to give new materials with better properties, especially high stiffness per unit weight, which is important in road and rail transport, aircraft, sporting goods and many other applications.

Glass fibers in a *polyester* matrix (so-called fiberglass) are used to make boat hulls and automobile bodies. Parts of aircraft and some sports gear are made from carbon fibers in an epoxy matrix.

concentrations of solutions are usually measured in moles per liter of solution (mol dm^{-3}). There are small volume changes when chemicals dissolve in water so it is important to note that concentrations normally refer to liters of solution, not to liters of the solvent.

$$\text{concentration/mol dm}^{-3} = \frac{\text{amount of solute/mol}}{\text{volume of solution/dm}^3}$$

Writing the formula of a chemical in square brackets is the usual shorthand for "concentration in mol dm^{-3}." (For example: $[CaCl_2]$ = 0.1 mol dm^{-3}.)

When ionic crystals dissolve the ions separate and become independent.

$$CaCl_2(s) + aq \longrightarrow Ca^{2+}(aq) + 2Cl^-(aq)$$

So if $[CaCl_2]$ = 0.1 mol dm^{-3}, then $[Ca^{2+}]$ = 0.1 mol dm^{-3} but $[Cl^-]$ = 0.2 mol dm^{-3}.

Other ways of measuring the concentrations are to use *mole fractions* or *parts per million, ppm.*

Worked example:

What is the concentration of a solution of potassium manganate(VII) made by dissolving 3.95 g of the solid in water and making the solution up to 500 cm^3?

Answer

The molar mass of potassium manganate(VII), $(KMnO_4)$ = 158.0 g mol^{-1}

$$\text{Amount of } KMnO_4 \text{ in solution } = \frac{3.95 \text{ g}}{158.0 \text{ g mol}^{-1}} = 0.025 \text{ mol}$$

$$\text{Volume of the solution } = \frac{500}{1000} \text{ dm}^3 = 0.5 \text{ dm}^3$$

$$\text{Concentration of the solution } = \frac{0.025 \text{ mol}}{0.5 \text{ dm}^3} = 0.05 \text{ mol dm}^{-3}$$

---

condensation polymers are produced by a series of condensation reactions splitting off water between the functional groups of the *monomers*. Examples of condensation polymers are *polyamides* and *polyesters*. Where each monomer has two function groups this type of polymerization produces chains.

Cross-linking is possible if one of the monomers has three functional groups.

condensation reaction: a reaction in which molecules join together by splitting off a small molecule such as water. The *addition–elimination reactions* of carbonyl compounds are examples of condensation reactions. The formation of an ester from an acid and an alcohol is also a condensation reaction.

$$CH_3-C\overset{O}{\underset{OH}{\big<}} + HO-C_2H_5 \longrightarrow CH_3-C\overset{O}{\underset{O-C_2H_5}{\big<}} + H_2O$$

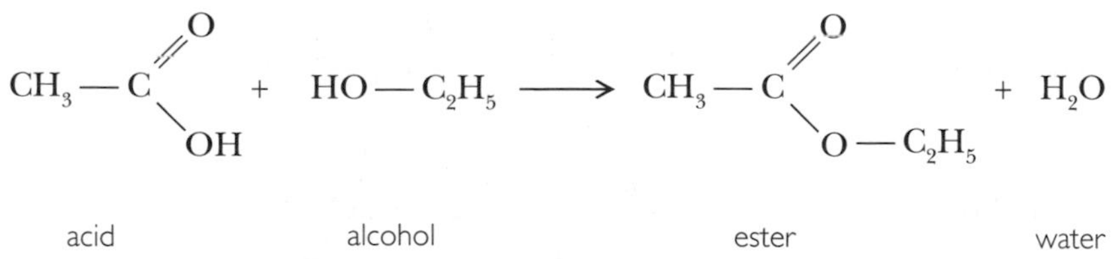

| acid | alcohol | ester | water |

Condensation reaction to form the ester ethyl ethanoate

conductiometric titrations use a conductivity cell and meter to measure the conductivity of the reaction mixture during a titration and hence to determine the end point. The conductivity can change during a titration because there is a change in:

- the ability of the ions present to move through the solution and conduct electricity

- the proportion of electrolytes that are only slightly ionized relative to electrolytes that are fully ionized.

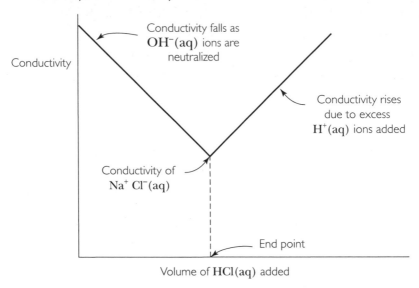

Changes in conductivity during a titration of *NaOH(aq)* with *HCl(aq)*. In water *H⁺(aq)* and *OH⁻(aq)* ions are very mobile so they conduct electricity very well.

confidence limits are the limits around an experimental mean value within which there is a high probability that the true mean lies.

Statistical analysis shows that there is a 95% probability that the true mean lies within $\pm 1.96\sigma$ of the experimental mean, where σ is the standard deviation.

Normal distribution of a large number of experimental results spread randomly about a mean value $\bar{x}$ where σ is the standard deviation

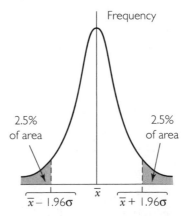

conformation of molecules: the possible shapes of molecules that can arise because of *rotation about covalent bonds.* Cyclohexane molecules, for example, shift to and fro between "chair" and "boat" forms. In both conformations the four single bonds around each carbon atom are arranged tetrahedrally as normal. The chair form is preferred because it is a little more stable. The energy difference between conformations is not large enough for them to be separated as distinct compounds.

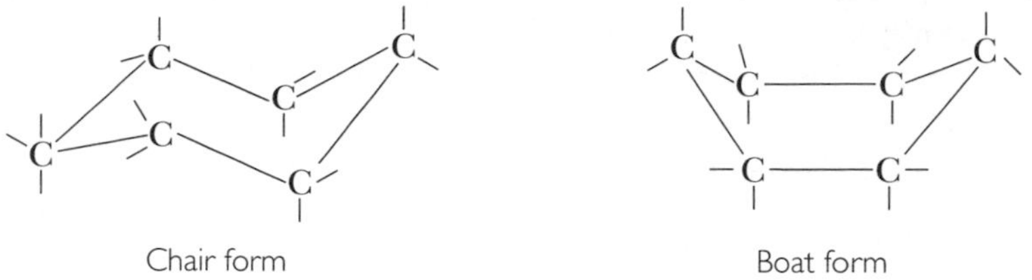

Chair form   Boat form

Chair and boat forms of cyclohexane

conjugate acid–base pairs: see *acid–base equilibria*.

conjugated system: a system of alternate double and single bonds in a molecule. Organic molecules with extended conjugated systems absorb radiation in the visible part of the spectrum and are therefore colored. Examples are the orange β-carotene molecule in carrots and the indicator phenolphthalein in alkali (see *colored compounds*).

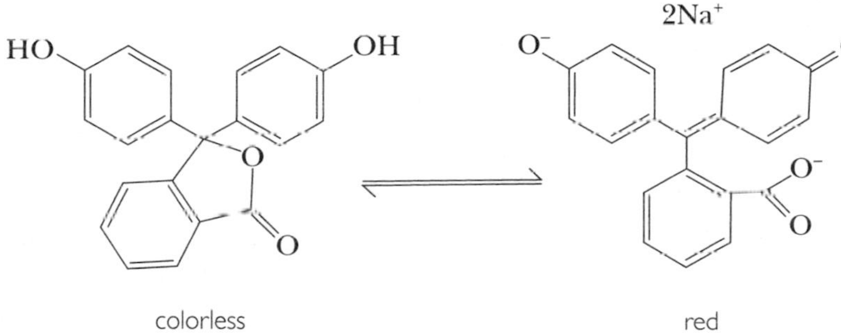

colorless   red

Structures of phenolphthalein in acid and alkali

conservation of mass (law of): the law that chemists now take for granted every time they write a balanced chemical equation. The law states that matter is neither created or destroyed during a chemical reaction.

constant-boiling mixture: see *azeotropic mixture*.

contact process: see *sulfuric acid manufacture*.

continuous processes manufacture chemicals on a large scale in industrial plants that operate for 24 hours in the day. Raw materials are constantly fed into the plant and products continuously removed. Examples of continuous processes are the *fractional distillation of oil*, the Haber process for *ammonia manufacture*, *iron extraction* in a blast furnace and the contact process for *sulfuric acid manufacture*.

conversion of units is often needed to make sure that the units are consistent before carrying out calculations. Typically the units of measurement (such as cm³) have to be converted to different units for calculation (in this case dm³).

Worked example:

In a titration, the volume of acid added from the burette was 23.5 cm³. What is the volume in liters (dm³)?

Notes on the method

Multiply by an appropriate factor to convert from the unit used for measurement to the unit needed for the calculation. Find the factor by:

• writing down the relationship between the two units, then by
• writing the relationship as a ratio, so that the units cancel when it multiplies the measurement, such that the original unit is replaced by the unit required.

Answer

$1 \text{ dm}^3 = 1000 \text{ cm}^3$

Hence $23.5 \text{ cm}^3 \times \dfrac{1 \text{ dm}^3}{1000 \text{ cm}^3} = 0.0235 \text{ dm}^3$

---

coordinate bond: a covalent bond formed when one atom contributes both of the shared pair of electrons. The alternative name is "dative covalent bond" since one atoms gives both the electrons to the bond. Once formed there is no difference between a coordinate bond and any other *covalent bond.*

Ammonia forms a coordinate bond with a hydrogen ion when it is acting as a *base.*

Formation of an ammonium ion

Coordinate (dative) bonding also accounts for the structures of carbon monoxide and the Al_2Cl_6 molecules in *aluminum chloride* vapor.

oxonium ion   nitric acid   carbon monoxide

Examples of coordinate (dative) bonds

Ligands form coordinate bonds with the central metal ions in *complex ions.*

coordination compounds contain complexes that may be cations, anions or neutral molecules. In a coordination compound, ligand molecules or negative ions form *coordinate bonds* with a metal ion.

Examples of coordination compounds:

• $K_3[Fe(CN)_6]$ containing the negatively charged complex ion $[Fe(CN)_6]^{3-}$

- $[Ni(NH_3)_6]Cl_2$ containing the positively charged complex ion $[Ni(NH_3)_6]^{2+}$
- $Ni(CO)_4$ a neutral complex between nickel atoms and carbon monoxide molecules.

coordination number: the number of nearest neighbors of an atom or ion in a crystal structure or the number of ligands bonded to a metal ion in a *complex ion*.

copolymerization is used to modify the properties of *polymers* by producing polymer chains from a mixture of monomers. ABS, for example, is a rigid, tough plastic widely used for the casing of domestic equipment and for parts of auto-mobiles. It is a copolymer of **A**crylonitrile $(CH_2=CH-CN)$, **B**utadiene $(CH_2=CH-CH=CH_2)$ and **S**tyrene $(C_6H_5-CH=CH_2)$.

copper (Cu) is a ductile metal with a familiar reddish color. It has the *electron configuration* $[Ar]3d^{10}4s^1$. This electron configuration is an exception to the normal $[Ar]3d^84s^2$ pattern for the first series of *d-block elements*. Energetically it is more favorable to have fill the *d*-subshell and leave only one electron in the 4s.

Copper is relatively unreactive. It corrodes very slowly in moist air and is not attacked by dilute nonoxidizing acids. Copper is a good conductor of electricity; it is widely used in electricity cables and for domestic water pipes.

Copper's mechanical properties are enhanced by making alloys such as *brass* and *bronze*.

Copper forms compounds in the +1 and +2 states. Under normal conditions copper(II) is the stable state in aqueous solution. Copper(I) disproportionates in aqueous solution.

$$2Cu^+(aq) \rightleftharpoons Cu^{2+}(aq) + Cu(s)$$

The equilibrium lies well to the right. Copper(I) in the presence of water can exist as very insoluble compounds such as Cu_2O, CuI or CuCl. Iodide ions, for example, reduce copper(II) to copper(I) ions, which immediately precipitate with more iodide ions as white copper(I) iodide.

$$2Cu^{2+}(aq) + 4I^-(aq) \longrightarrow 2CuI(s) + I_2(s)$$

Copper(I) can exist in aqueous solution as stable complexes such as $[Cu(NH_3)_2]^+$ or $[Cu(CN)_4]^{3-}$.

Fehling's solution and *Benedict's solution* contain deep blue copper(II) complexes in alkali. The reagents are used to detect *reducing sugars* and to distinguish *aldehydes* from *ketones*. A reducing sugar or aldehyde reduces the reagent on heating to copper(I) oxide. The blue color goes and a reddish-brown precipitate forms.

copper refining uses electrolysis to turn copper that is 99.5% pure into 99.99% pure metal. High purity is important especially when copper is to be used as an electrical conductor.

Impure copper is cast into anodes while the cathodes are thin sheets of pure copper. The electrolyte is a mixture of copper(II) sulfate and sulfuric acid.

At the anodes: $Cu(s) \longrightarrow Cu^{2+}(aq) + 2e^-$

At the cathodes: $Cu^{2+}(aq) + 2e^- \longrightarrow Cu(s)$

Valuable impurities such as gold and silver are recovered from the bottom of the electrolysis cell because they do not dissolve in the electrolyte.

corrosion of a metal is a redox process in which oxygen, water and acids attack metals. Most metals are extracted from oxides. Corrosion turns them back into oxides.

The most familiar and economically serious example of corrosion is the rusting of iron. Rusting is an electrochemical reaction.

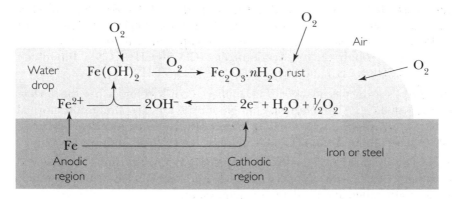

An electrochemical cell on the surface of iron in contact with water and the air. Regions rich in oxygen are cathodic. In these regions oxygen is reduced to hydroxide ions. Other parts of the metal surface are anodic. In these regions iron is oxidized to iron(II) ions. Iron(II) ions and hydroxide ions diffuse together and form a precipitate of iron(II) hydroxide, which is then oxidized to rust, hydrated iron(III) oxide.

coulomb (symbol C) is the *SI unit* of electric charge.

$$\text{electric charge (C)} = \text{current (C s}^{-1}) \times \text{time (s)}$$

A coulomb is the amount of electric charge flowing each second past a point in a circuit when the current is one ampere ($1\,A = 1\,C\,s^{-1}$).

covalent bonds form when atoms share electrons. The atoms are held together by the attraction between the positive charges on their nuclei and the negative charge on the shared electrons.

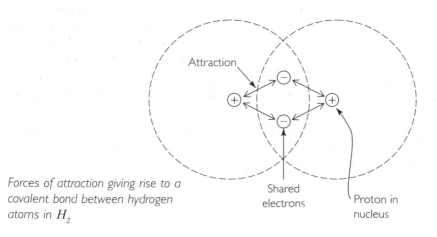

Forces of attraction giving rise to a covalent bond between hydrogen atoms in H_2

Covalent bonding holds together the atoms of nonmetals in molecules and *giant structures*. Molecules have a definite shape because covalent bonds have a definite length and direction.

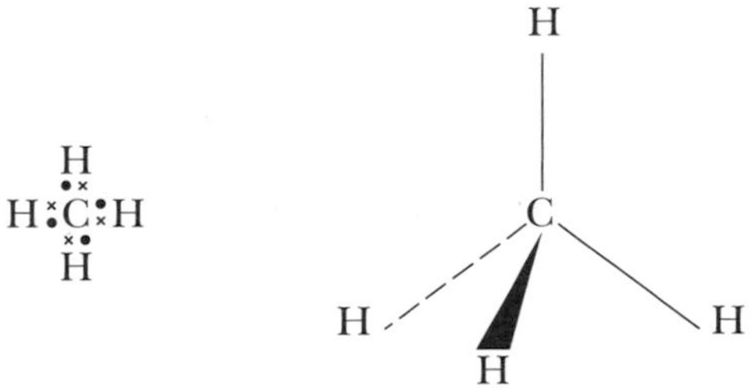

H
••×
H:C:H
×•
H

H
|
C
H —   H
H

Electron sharing in methane and the shape of a methane molecule

One shared pair of electrons gives rise to a single bond. *Double bonds* and *triple bonds* are also possible with two or three shared pairs.

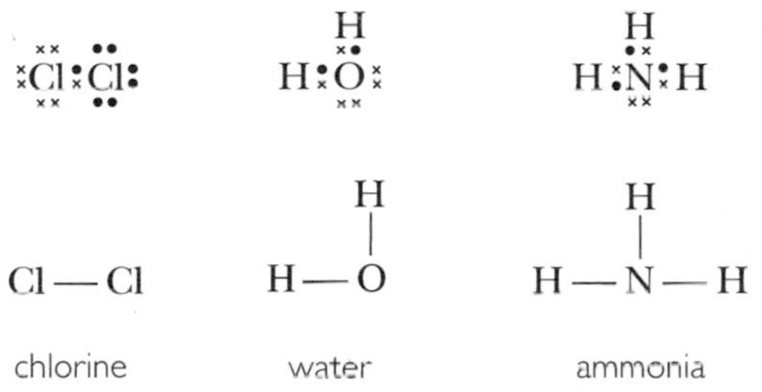

×× ••
×Cl:Cl×
×× ••

H
×•
H:O×
××

H
••×
H:N:H
××

H
|
Cl — Cl   H — O   H — N — H

chlorine   water   ammonia

Dot and cross diagrams to show single covalent bonding in molecules. Also shown is a simpler way of showing the bonding in molecules. A line between two symbols represents a covalent bond.

The nonmetals common in organic chemistry generally form a fixed number of covalent bonds. This helps us to determine the structures of molecules.

Element	Number of covalent bonds	Examples		
carbon, C	4	H — C — H (with H above and H below)	$\begin{array}{c}H\\\\H\end{array}$C=O	O=C=O
hydrogen, H	1	$\begin{array}{c}H\\\\H\end{array}$O	H — N — H (with H above)	H — Cl
oxygen, O	2	O=O	$\begin{array}{c}H\\\\H\end{array}$O	H — C (with O double bond and O—H)

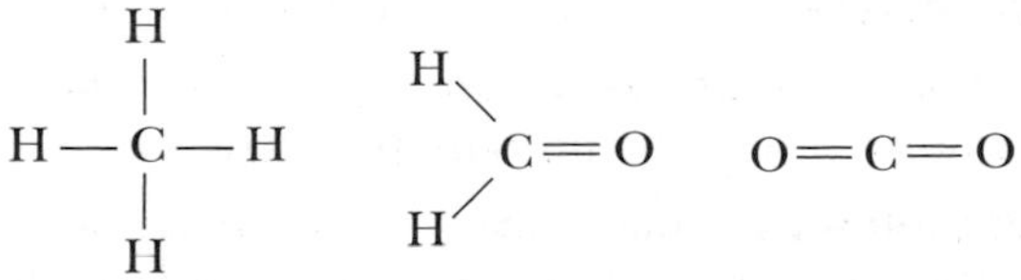

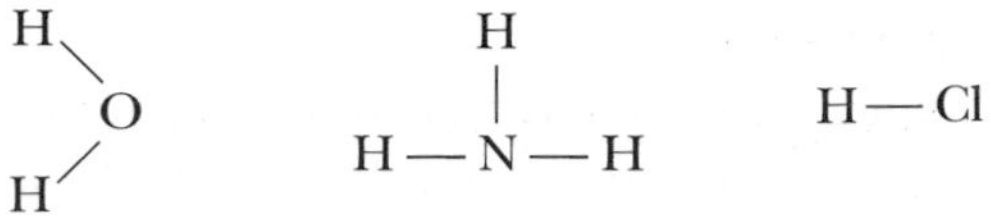

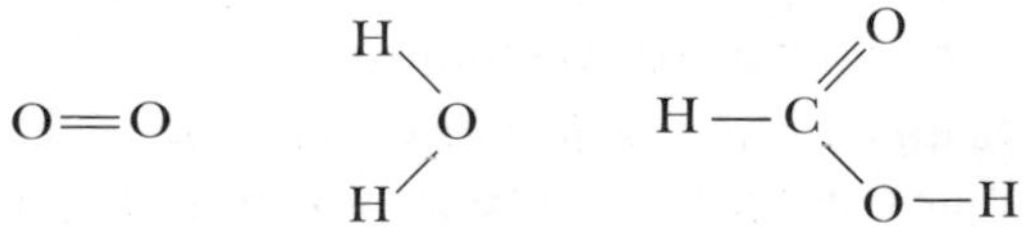

nitrogen, N	3	$N\equiv N$	$Cl-\overset{\displaystyle Cl}{\underset{\displaystyle |}{N}}-Cl$	$CH_3-N\overset{\displaystyle H}{\underset{\displaystyle H}{}}$
halogens, F, Cl, Br, I	1	$H-Br$	$Cl-\overset{\displaystyle Cl}{\underset{\displaystyle Cl}{C}}-Cl$	$H-\overset{\displaystyle H}{\underset{\displaystyle H}{C}}-I$

covalent radius: the covalent radius of an element is half the *bond length* when two atoms of the element are linked by a single covalent bond.

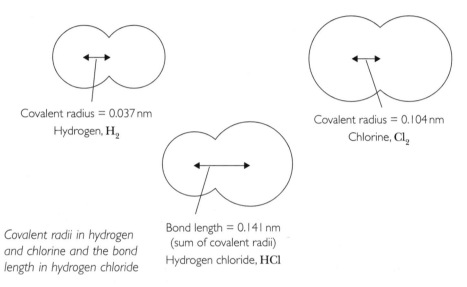

Covalent radius = 0.037 nm
Hydrogen, H_2

Covalent radius = 0.104 nm
Chlorine, Cl_2

Bond length = 0.141 nm
(sum of covalent radii)
Hydrogen chloride, HCl

Covalent radii in hydrogen and chlorine and the bond length in hydrogen chloride

The length of a single covalent bond between atoms of different elements can be estimated fairly accurately by adding the covalent radii for the two atoms.

cracking: see *catalytic cracking* and *steam cracking*.

critical temperature is the temperature above which it is impossible to liquefy a gas however high the pressure (see *vapors*).

cross-linking is the formation of chemical bonds between polymer chains to modify the properties of polymers such as *thermosetting* plastics as well as natural *rubber* during vulcanizing.

Cross-linking determines the three-dimensional shape of *proteins*. Cross-links in protein molecules take various forms including:

- *hydrogen bonding* between amino acid side-chains
- disulfide bridges formed by *covalent bonding* between cystine side-chains.

crude oil is a complex mixture of *hydrocarbon* molecules formed over millions of years when the remains of microscopic sea creatures trapped in sediments were converted by heat and pressure to petroleum. Crude oil is now the main source of *fuels* and organic compounds. The composition of crude oil varies from one oilfield to another. Some crudes contain significant quantities of sulfur and nitrogen compounds as well as traces of various metals. *Fractional distillation of oil* is the first step in refining to produce fuels and *lubricants* as well as feedstocks for the *petrochemical industry*.

crystallinity of polymers arises when the long-chain molecules are regular enough to lie more or less parallel to each other in some regions of the solid. The rest of the solid where the chains are tangled together is *amorphous*.

The crystallinity of *polymers* with regular, unbranched chains is generally higher than in polymers with branched or irregular molecules. Relatively strong *intermolecular forces* between chains also favor crystallinity. Highly crystalline polymers are stronger and less flexible than more amorphous polymers.

Crystalline region

Amorphous region

Crystalline and amorphous regions in a polymer

crystal structures of ionic compounds include the *sodium chloride, cesium chloride, fluorite, zinc blende, wurtzite* and *rutile* structures. In an ionic crystal the ions behave like charged spheres in contact. The structures are only stable if each ion is in contact with its nearest neighbors. The cesium ion is large enough to have eight chloride ions around it as in the cesium chloride structure. Sodium ions are smaller and only big enough to touch six neighboring chloride ions as in the sodium chloride structure.

Use of the *Born–Haber cycle* to determine experimental lattice energies makes it possible to decide whether the bonding in a crystal is purely ionic, due to *electrostatic forces* between ions.

crystal structures of metals: the important metal structures are the two *close-packed structures* and the *body-centered cubic structure*.

crystal structures of nonmetals: most solid *nonmetals*, such as *iodine, sulfur* and white *phosphorus* are molecular so the forces between the particles in the crystals are weak *van der Waals forces*. The crystals easily melt or turn to vapor on gentle heating.

Some nonmetals consist of giant structures of atoms held together by *covalent bonds*. Examples are *carbon* (as graphite or diamond) and *silicon*. Covalent bonds are strong and point in a definite direction so these structures have very high melting points.

Diamond is very hard. Graphite, the other *allotrope* of carbon with a giant structure, has a layer lattice. It too has a high melting point but it can be used as a *lubricant* because the forces between the layers are weak and they can slide over each other.

curly arrows are used to describe the movement of electrons as bonds break and form in the steps that describe the mechanism of a reaction. A curly arrow with both halves of the arrow head shows the movement of a pair of electrons. Note that the tail of the arrow starts where the electron pair begins. The head of the arrow points to where the electron pair will be after the change.

Movement of an electron pair during heterolytic *bond breaking*

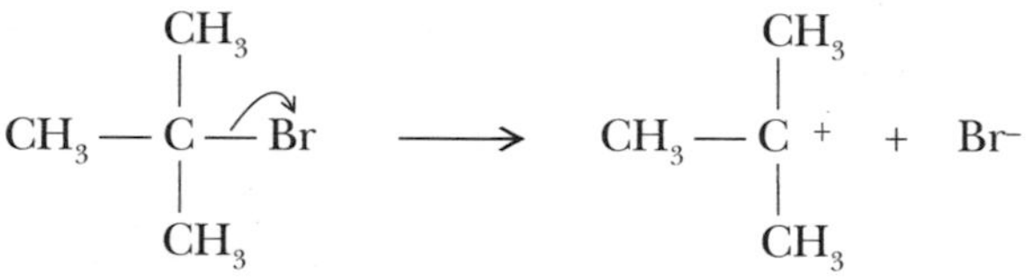

$$CH_3 - \underset{\underset{CH_3}{|}}{\overset{\overset{CH_3}{|}}{C}} \curvearrowright Br \longrightarrow CH_3 - \underset{\underset{CH_3}{|}}{\overset{\overset{CH_3}{|}}{C}} ^+ \ + \ Br^-$$

A curly arrow with only half an arrow head indicates the movement of a single electron.

Movement of single electrons during homolytic bond breaking

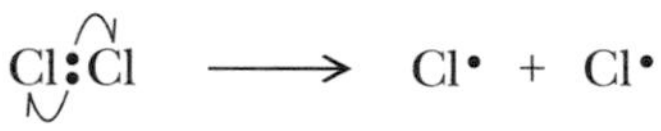

$$Cl \!:\! Cl \longrightarrow Cl^\bullet \ + \ Cl^\bullet$$

current is a flow of electric charge and is measured in *amperes*. In a metal the flow of charge is carried by electrons. In an electrolyte the charge carriers are negative ions moving toward the anode and positive ions moving toward the cathode.

cyanohydrins are the products formed when hydrogen cyanide adds to carbonyl groups in *aldehydes* and *ketones*. The modern name is hydroxynitriles.

dative covalent bond: see *coordinate bond*.

***d*-block elements** are the elements in the three horizontal rows of elements in periods 4, 5 and 6 of the *periodic table* for which the last electron added to the atomic structure goes into a *d-orbital*. In period 4, the *d*-block elements run from scandium $(1s^2 2s^2 2p^6 3s^2 3p^6 3d^1 4s^2)$ to zinc $(1s^2 2s^2 2p^6 3s^2 3p^6 3d^{10} 4s^2)$.

The changes in the properties across a series of *d*-block elements are much less marked than the big changes across a *p-block* series. This is because from one element to the next, as the *proton number* of the nucleus increases by one, the extra electron goes into the inner *d*-subshell. In period 4, the outer shell is always the 4s orbital, which is filled before the 3d starts to fill.

		3d	4s
Sc	[Ar]	↑ _ _ _ _	↑↓
Ti	[Ar]	↑ ↑ _ _ _	↑↓
V	[Ar]	↑ ↑ ↑ _ _	↑↓
Cr	[Ar]	↑ ↑ ↑ ↑ ↑	↑
Mn	[Ar]	↑ ↑ ↑ ↑ ↑	↑↓
Fe	[Ar]	↑↓ ↑ ↑ ↑ ↑	↑↓
Co	[Ar]	↑↓ ↑↓ ↑ ↑ ↑	↑↓
Ni	[Ar]	↑↓ ↑↓ ↑↓ ↑ ↑	↑↓
Cu	[Ar]	↑↓ ↑↓ ↑↓ ↑↓ ↑↓	↑
Zn	[Ar]	↑↓ ↑↓ ↑↓ ↑↓ ↑↓	↑↓

Electron configurations of d-block elements as free atoms. Note that orbitals fill singly before the electrons start to pair up. Note that the configurations chromium and copper do not fit the general pattern.

The chemistry of an atom is to a large extent determined by its outer electrons because they are the first to get involved in reactions. So the elements Sc to Zn in period 4 are similar in many ways.

All the *d*-block elements are *metals* with useful properties for engineering and construction. Most have high melting points. A plot of *physical properties* against proton number often has two peaks corresponding to the half-filling and then filling of the *d*-shell. (See figure.)

Some, but not all, of the *d*-block elements are classified as *transition elements*.

decantation involves gently pouring off most of a liquid or solution from a solid after centrifuging or simply allowing it to settle to the bottom of a container.

Filtering is often quicker if the solid is first allowed to settle and then most of the liquid decanted through the filter paper before pouring in the bulk of the solid. As a result most of the liquid passes through the filter paper before its pores are clogged by solid particles.

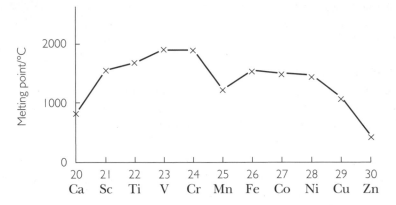

d-block elements: plot of melting point against proton number for the elements Ca to Zn

decay series: a series formed as a radioactive element decays to a daughter element that is also radioactive and itself decays, and so on until decay produces a stable atom. For example, the decays series for thorium-232 involves alpha and beta decay steps ending up with lead-208.

$$^{232}_{90}\text{Th} \xrightarrow{\alpha} {}^{228}_{88}\text{Ra} \xrightarrow{\beta} {}^{228}_{89}\text{Ac} \xrightarrow{\beta} {}^{228}_{90}\text{Th} \longrightarrow$$

Alpha decay and beta decay in the decay series for thorium-232. Note the changes of nucleon number and proton number.

decomposition is a reaction in which compounds break down into simpler substances, which may be compounds or elements. Heating is often necessary for decomposition (see *thermal decomposition*).

dehydration removes the elements of water from a compound to form a new compound. Concentrated sulfuric acid is a powerful dehydrating agent. It dehydrates blue copper sulfate crystals, sucrose and ethanol.

$$\text{CuSO}_4 \cdot 5\text{H}_2\text{O}(s) \xrightarrow{-5\text{H}_2\text{O}} \text{CuSO}_4(s)$$
$$\text{blue} \qquad\qquad\qquad\qquad\qquad \text{white}$$

$$\text{C}_{12}\text{H}_{22}\text{O}_{11}(s) \xrightarrow{-11\text{H}_2\text{O}} 12\text{C}(s)$$
$$\text{sucrose, white} \qquad\qquad\qquad \text{black}$$

$$\text{C}_2\text{H}_5\text{OH}(l) \xrightarrow{-\text{H}_2\text{O}} \text{CH}_2 = \text{CH}_2(g)$$
$$\text{ethanol} \qquad\qquad\qquad\qquad \text{ethene}$$

deliquescent substances take up water vapor from the air and dissolve in it. Examples are calcium chloride, potassium hydroxide and sodium hydroxide. Deliquescent substances make good drying agents in *desiccators*.

Deliquescent substances cannot be used as *primary standards* in volumetric analysis because they cannot be weighed accurately.

delocalized electrons are bonding electrons that are not fixed between two atoms in a bond but are shared between three or more atoms. Electron delocalization accounts for the shape, stability and properties of *benzene* rings, *nitrate* ions and other oxoanions, the acidity of *carboxylic acids* and *phenols*, and the color of some organic compounds.

Electron delocalization takes places in molecules where the conventional structure shows alternating double and single bonds. Delocalization also affects ions where an atom with a lone pair of electrons and a negative charge is separated by a single bond from a double bond.

An extreme example of delocalization is *metallic bonding* where electrons are shared between all the atoms in a crystal. Extended delocalization over the planes of carbon atoms explains the electrical conductivity of graphite.

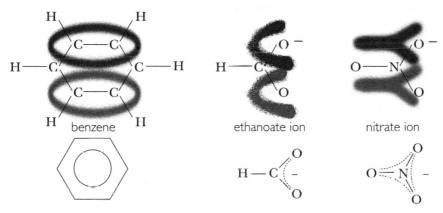

benzene   ethanoate ion   nitrate ion

Examples of delocalization in molecules and ions

denaturation of proteins happens when the three-dimensional shape of a *protein* is disrupted by heating or by extremes of *pH*. The chemical activity of protein molecules is linked to their shape. Changing the structure of proteins means that they lose their normal activity. *Enzymes*, for example, cease to act as *catalysts* when denatured.

density is the mass per unit volume of a material.

$$\text{density} = \frac{\text{mass}}{\text{volume}}$$

The symbol for density is ρ and the SI unit is $kg\ m^{-3}$. In chemistry densities are generally given in $g\ cm^{-3}$. The densities for most solids and liquids are in the range 0.5 to 10 $g\ cm^{-3}$.

The density of water at $0°C$ is 1.00 $g\ cm^{-3}$ and in approximate laboratory work it is common to assume that dilute aqueous solutions have the same density as water. Solids and immiscible liquids float if they are less dense than water. The density of *ice* at the same temperature is 0.917 $g\ cm^{-3}$ so ice floats on water.

At room temperature and pressure the densities of gases are about a thousand times smaller than those of solids and liquids. Measurement of gas densities can be used to calculate the *molar masses* of gases.

depression of freezing point: see *colligative properties.*

desalination is a process for obtaining pure water from seawater or other sources of water containing dissolved salts. Methods of desalination include *distillation* at low pressure, freezing, reverse *osmosis*, electrodialysis and *ion exchange.*

desiccator: a container with a *drying agent* used to remove the moisture (or other liquids) from chemical products that decompose if warmed in an oven. Chemicals that can be oven dried may also be stored in a desiccator as they cool to stop them picking up moisture from the air. A desiccator is a useful place to store chemicals that must be kept dry.

Vacuum desiccators are fitted with a tap so that air can be pumped out. The partial vacuum speeds up evaporation and diffusion of the vapor to the drying agent.

detergents clean things by removing dirt from surfaces. The chemicals that act as detergents are surface-active agents or *surfactants.* Water is a polar solvent with a high *surface tension.* This means that water alone it is not good at removing dirt and grease. Detergents help to clean by:

- lowering the surface tension of water so that it spreads out and wets the surface
- separating grease and particles from the surface
- suspending the dirt in water so that it can be rinsed away.

There are two main types of detergent:

- soap detergents (usually just called *soaps*) made from animal *fats* or *vegetable oils*
- soapless detergents (usually just called detergents), which are made using chemicals from oil.

Washing powders or liquids for clothes are complex formulations that may include:

- detergents to increase wetting power, separate grease from fabrics and keep dirt in suspension
- *sequestering agents* such as sodium polyphosphate to soften *hard water*
- *enzymes* to break down protein stains such as blood stains
- optical brighteners to keep white fabrics looking bright and white
- oxygen *bleach* such as sodium peroxoborate(III), which only acts above 60°C
- *perfume* and color to make the product distinctive and attractive to customers.

Zeolites are replacing phosphates to aid the action of detergents in hard water. The problem with phosphates is that they contribute to *eutrophication* of rivers and lakes.

deuterium is the *isotope* of hydrogen with proton number 1 but nucleon (mass) number 2. The symbols used for deuterium are ^2_1H or D. About 0.015% of natural hydrogen is the deuterium isotope. Deuterium oxide (heavy water) is D_2O.

The relative mass of D is twice that of H and this difference means that deuterium compounds react more slowly than their normal hydrogen equivalents. During *electrolysis* of acidified water H_2 is formed at the cathode more readily than D_2 so the concentration of deuterium increases as electrolysis continues. Eventually it is possible to make almost pure heavy water; this is used as a moderator in some nuclear power stations.

diagonal relationship: the similarities between the first member of one group in the *periodic table* with the second element in the next group, to the right, found particularly with these three pairs of elements: Li–Mg, Be–Al, and B–Si.

The diagonal relationship is a consequence of the relatively small size of the ions of the elements in the second short period. The polarizing power of the positive ion of an element determines to a large extent the type of bonding between the element with nonmetals such as oxygen and chlorine and hence the chemical characteristics of the compounds (see *Fajan's rules*).

These are some of the similarities between beryllium and aluminum that are not shared by the other group 2 elements:

- their bonding in compounds is mainly covalent
- their oxides and hydroxides are amphoteric
- their anhydrous chlorides vaporize easily and form dimers in the vapor phase (Be_2Cl_4 and Al_2Cl_6).

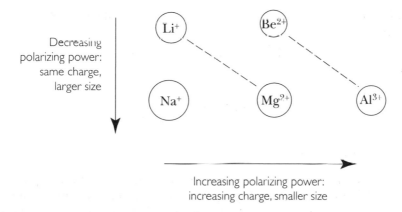

Decreasing polarizing power: same charge, larger size

Increasing polarizing power: increasing charge, smaller size

Diagonal relationships related to polarizing power

dialysis is used to separate dissolved ions and small molecules from *colloid* particles. Dialysis uses a *selectively permeable membrane*, which lets through the small ions and molecules but traps larger colloid particles. Dialysis is used in medicine to treat the blood of patients with kidney failure. Dialysis removes the waste products of metabolism from blood and helps to adjust the concentration of ions. Blood cells and colloidal sized protein molecules cannot pass through the membrane. (See figure.)

diatomic molecule: strictly a molecule with two atoms such as N_2 or HCl but the term is generally used for the molecules of elements with two identical atoms. Examples of diatomic elements are oxygen, O_2, nitrogen, N_2, and the halogens, F_2, Cl_2, Br_2 and I_2.

diazonium salts: salts formed when aryl amines, such as *phenylamine*, react with *nitrous acid* (HNO_2) below about 10°C.

Diazonium salts are unstable so they are made as needed and kept cold. Above 10°C, benzene diazonium chloride decomposes to phenol and nitrogen.

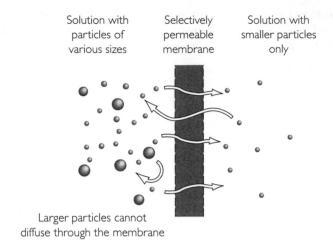

Solution with particles of various sizes

Selectively permeable membrane

Solution with smaller particles only

Larger particles cannot diffuse through the membrane

Dialysis

The commercial importance of diazonium salts is based on their coupling reactions to form *azo dyes*.

Diazonium salts are also useful intermediates that make it possible to form derivatives of arenes.

Formation of benzene diazonium chloride

dienes are hydrocarbons with two double bonds. Buta-1,3-diene is a product of *steam cracking* and is a useful intermediate for making other organic compounds. Synthetic *rubbers* are copolymers of butadiene, or one of its derivatives, with other unsaturated compounds such as styrene.

diffusion is a spreading out and mixing process in gases or solutions as molecules or ions mingle with each other. Molecules diffuse from a region where they are more concentrated to a region where their concentration is lower. Eventually diffusion evens out differences in concentration. The smaller the molecules or ions, the faster they diffuse. Diffusion is a consequence of the rapid random motion of molecules in gases and liquids. Diffusion through membranes is important in *dialysis* and *osmosis*.

dilution is the process of adding more solvent to a solution to lower the concentration.

Quantitative dilution is an important procedure in analysis. The purpose is to make a solution with known concentration by accurately diluting a *standard solution*. Successive dilutions provide a series of solutions that can be used to calibrate instruments such as *colorimeters*.

The procedure is to take a measured volume of the more concentrated solution with a pipette and run it into a graduated flask. The flask is then carefully filled to the mark with purified water.

The key to calculating the volumes to use when diluting a solution is to remember that the amount in moles of the reagent in the final solution must equal the amount in moles of the sample taken from the concentrated solution. If c is the concentration in mol dm^{-3} and V is the volume in dm^3:

- the amount in moles of the reagent in the concentrated solution = $c_A V_A$
- the amount in moles of the reagent in the diluted solution = $c_B V_B$.

So: $c_A V_A = c_B V_B$

Worked example:

What volume of a 1.00 mol dm^{-3} solution of copper(II) sulfate is needed to prepare 100 cm^3 of a 0.1 mol dm^{-3} solution?

Notes on the method

Start by a conversion to give the volume of the diluted solution in dm^3.

V_A can be calculated because all the other terms in the relationship $c_A V_A = c_B V_B$ are known.

Answer

Final volume of the diluted solution is to be: $100 \text{ cm}^3 \times \dfrac{1 \text{ dm}^3}{1000 \text{ cm}^3} = 0.1 \text{ dm}^3$

$1.0 \text{ mol dm}^{-3} \times V_A = 0.1 \text{ mol dm}^{-3} \times 0.1 \text{ dm}^3$

$V_A = \dfrac{0.1 \text{ mol dm}^{-3} \times 0.1 \text{ dm}^3}{1.0 \text{ mol dm}^{-3}} = 0.01 \text{ dm}^3 = 10 \text{ cm}^3$

Pipetting 10 cm^3 of the concentrated solution into a 100 cm^3 graduated flask and making it up to the mark gives the required dilution.

---

dimerization: two molecules linking together. Dimers may be held together by *covalent bonds* (see *aluminum chloride*) or by *hydrogen bonding*.

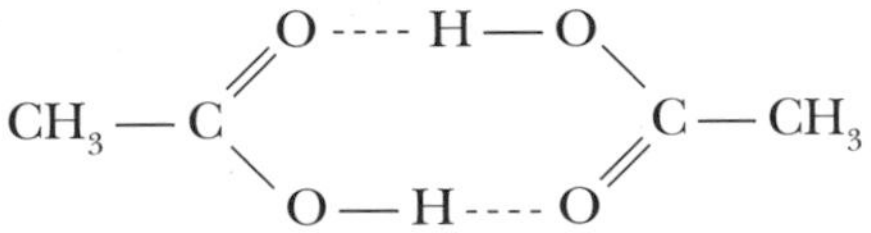

An ethanoic acid dimer in a nonpolar solvent. In aqueous solution, ethanoic acid does not dimerize because there are so many water molecules with which they can form hydrogen bonds.

diols are alcohols with two —OH groups. An example is ethan-1,2-diol, used as antifreeze.

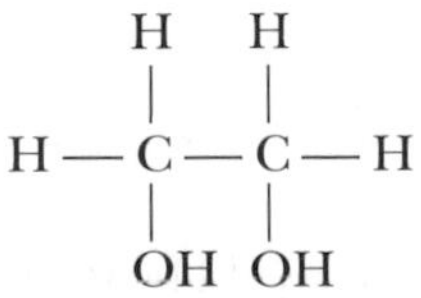

Structure of ethan-1,2-diol

dipole–dipole interactions are *intermolecular forces* involving *polar molecules* with permanent dipoles. The cohesive forces are stronger than *dispersion forces* and account for the fact that compounds such as propanone are liquids at room temperature while comparable nonpolar hydrocarbons are gases.

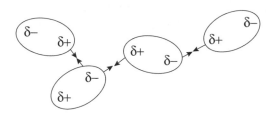

Attractions between molecules with permanent dipoles

diprotic acid: an *acid* such as sulfuric acid (H_2SO_4) that can give away two *protons* (H^+).

disaccharides: see *carbohydrates*.

disinfectants are chemicals that destroy microoganisms. Chlorine and oxygen *bleaches* are used as disinfectants. Unlike *antiseptics*, disinfectants cannot be used on skin and other living tissues.

disperse phase: see *colloids*.

dispersion forces are the weakest *intermolecular forces* that affect all molecules but particularly account for the attractions between nonpolar molecules such as the molecules of iodine, alkane molecules and between the atoms of noble gases. Intermolecular attractions explain why nonpolar substances can be liquids or solids.

When nonpolar atoms or molecules meet there are fleeting repulsions and attractions between the nuclei of the atoms and the surrounding clouds of electrons. Temporary displacements of the electrons lead to temporary dipoles. Dispersion forces are the attractions between induced dipoles that give rise to the tendency for the molecules to cohere.

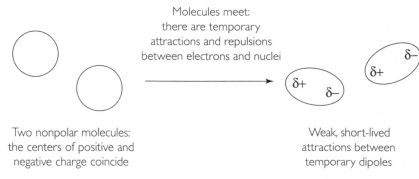

Diagram to illustrate the origins and effect of temporary induced dipoles

The greater the number of electrons, the greater the *polarizability* of the molecule and the greater the possibility for temporary, induced dipoles. This explains why the boiling points rise down *group 7* (the halogens) and *group 8* (the noble gases). For the same reason the boiling points in *alkanes* increase with the increasing number of carbon atoms in these hydrocarbon molecules.

displacement reactions are redox reactions that can be used to compare the relative strengths of metals as *reducing agents* and nonmetals as *oxidizing agents*.

A more reactive metal displaces a less reactive metal from one of its salts. Zinc, for example, displaces copper from a copper(II) sulfate. The zinc atoms reduce the copper ions.

$$Zn(s) + Cu^{2+}(aq) \longrightarrow Zn^{2+}(aq) + Cu(s)$$

In *group 7*, a more reactive halogen displaces a less reaction halogen. The order of reactivity for the halogens is Cl>Br>I. The more reactive halogen oxidizes the ions of a less reactive halogen.

$$Br_2(aq) + 2I^-(aq) \longrightarrow 2Br^-(aq) + I_2(s)$$

Standard electrode potentials make it possible to predict the direction of change in a displacement reaction (see *electrochemical series*).

displayed formulas show all the atoms and bonds in a molecule (see also *structural formulas*).

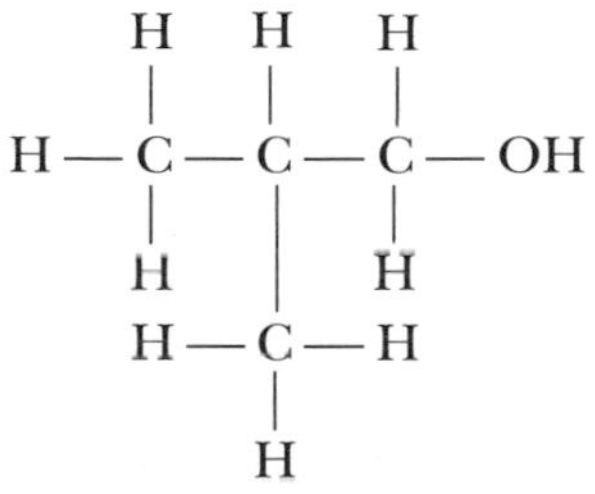

2-methylpropan-1-ol 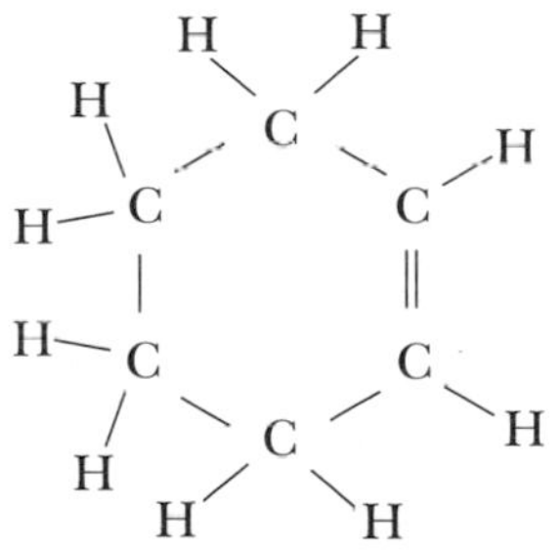   cyclohexene

Examples of displayed formulas

disproportionation reaction: a reaction in which the same element both increases and decreases its *oxidation number*. Copper(I) ions disproportionate in aqueous solution to a mixture of $Cu^{2+}(aq)$ ions and *copper* atoms. A series of disproportionation reactions is used to make *chlorine oxoanions*. *Hydrogen peroxide* disproportionates when it decomposes.

dissociation: a reaction in which a compound splits into two or more smaller products that can recombine to form the original compound if the conditions change.

Some compounds dissociate on heating. Examples are ammonium chloride and dinitrogen tetroxide. These *thermal dissociation* reactions are *reversible*. On cooling, the original compounds reform.

$$NH_4Cl(s) \underset{cool}{\overset{heat}{\rightleftharpoons}} NH_3(g) + HCl(g)$$

$$N_2O_4(g) \underset{\text{cool}}{\overset{\text{heat}}{\rightleftharpoons}} 2NO_2(g)$$

Acids dissociate into ions on solution in water. The extent to which they ionize distinguishes strong and weak acids and this is measured by the *acid dissociation constant.*

distillation: a technique for separating and purifying a liquid by heating to vaporize the liquid and then cooling to condense it. Simple distillation is used to purify water, to recover pure solvents and to separate liquid product from reaction mixtures. Substances that do not evaporate are left behind in the distillation flask.

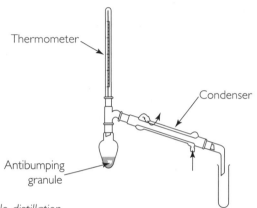

Apparatus for simple distillation

One of the easiest ways to determine the boiling point of a liquid is to distill a pure sample of the liquid in an apparatus with a thermometer.

(See also *fractional distillation*, *steam distillation* and *vacuum distillation*.)

DNA (deoxyribonucleic acid) is a double helix made up of two poly*nucleotide* chains. Both chains have a sugar phosphate backbone. Every sugar unit has one of four bases linked to it. The four bases are *adenine* (A), cytosine (C), guanine (G) and thymine (T). The links between the chains are formed by *hydrogen bonding* between pairs of bases: A pairs with T and C pairs with G. (See figure.)

A gene is a region of DNA with a discrete function, found in the chromosomes of cells.

dolomite is a carbonate mineral with the composition $MgCO_3.CaCO_3$. It is a raw material for the production of magnesium and its salts.

d-orbitals are the five atomic orbitals in a *d*-subshell. In a free atom or ion the five *d*-orbitals are at the same energy level. The five orbitals are not the same shape and they split into two groups with different energies when a *d-block element* ion is surrounded by molecules or ions in a complex ion. This helps to account for the color of complex ions.

dot and cross diagrams show the way in which the outer electrons of atoms are shared or transferred when *covalent bonds* and *ionic bonds* form. Dots, crosses and small circles help to keep count of the number of electrons contributed by each atom to bonding.

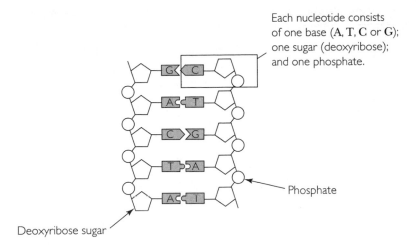

Each nucleotide consists of one base (**A**, **T**, **C** or **G**); one sugar (deoxyribose); and one phosphate.

Phosphate

Deoxyribose sugar

DNA: representation of part of a DNA double helix

Dot and cross diagrams for molecules show both bonding and lone pairs of electrons; they help to predict the *shapes of molecules.*

Despite the use of dots and crosses for the electrons coming from different atoms, all the electrons are the same. Once bonds form it is impossible to say which electron came from which atom.

double bond: two covalent bonds between two atoms as in *oxygen, alkenes* and *ketones.* With two electron pairs involved in bonding, there is a region of high electron density between two atoms joined by a double bond.

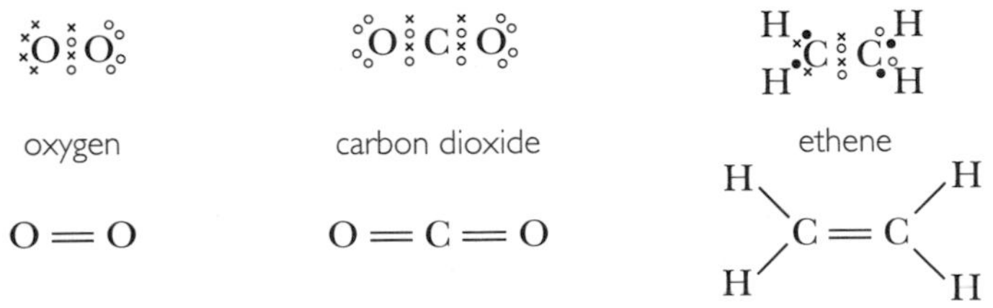

oxygen

$$O = O$$

carbon dioxide

$$O = C = O$$

ethene

$$H_2C = CH_2$$

Examples of molecules with double bonds

The molecular orbital model for a double bond shows that one of the bonds is a normal *sigma bond* while the second bond is a *pi bond* (see *bonding molecular orbital*).

double salts are solid ionic *salts* with two different metal cations in a lattice of negative ions. Crystalline double salts are not mixtures but distinct compounds with a definite structure.

When dissolved in water, double salts behave just like a mixture of two simple salts. The usual way of making a double salt is to mix equal amounts (in moles) of the two single salts in solution and then to crystallize the double salt. Examples of double salts are the *alums.*

drug: in medicine, a substance used for the treatment, relief, diagnosis or prevention of disease. There are many classes of medical drugs, which include:

- drugs that act on the central nervous system such as hypnotics, sedatives, tranquilizers, antidepressants, *narcotics, anesthetics* and *analgesics*
- drugs that kill bacteria such as *antibiotics* and sulfonamides (see *chemotherapy*)
- antiviral drugs such as those used to suppress HIV
- cardiovascular drugs that help to lower blood pressure, stimulate the heart or control the heart beat
- drugs such as *cisplatin* used in cancer treatment
- drugs used for the digestive system such as *antacids*, laxatives and drugs to treat ulcers
- *hormones* such as *insulin*, growth hormone and *steroids*.

People also take drugs for pleasure, stimulation and relaxation. Some recreational drugs such as alcohol and nicotine are legal. Others such as marijuana, cocaine and opiates are illegal. Drugs used to treat disease may also be exploited to enhance performance in sport. Sensitive methods of chemical analysis are widely used to detect traces of drugs in blood, breath and urine (see *breathalyzer*).

drug development is the research and development program that leads to the launch of a new drug. Ibuprofen, for example, is a drug that was developed to reduce inflammation in the joints of people suffering from rheumatoid arthritis. Testing showed that the drug was also an effective pain reliever and a rival to aspirin. The research and development (R & D) program took 30 years.

Before a new compound can become a marketable drug it has to show that:

- it meets a definite need of patients and their doctors
- it is technically possible to make it on a large scale
- there is a big enough market to make it commercial
- it is safe.

dry cells are *electrochemical cells* in which the electrolyte is made into a paste to stop it leaking out. The commonest cell for everyday use is the zinc–carbon dry cell, which produces an *emf* of 1.5 V. (See figure.)

At the negative terminal zinc atoms are oxidized into zinc ions:

$$Zn(s) \longrightarrow Zn^{2+}(aq) + 2e^-$$

At the positive terminal hydrogen is reduced from the +1 state but is then oxidized by manganese(VI) oxide:

$$2NH_4^+(aq) + 2e^- \longrightarrow 2NH_3(aq) + H_2(g)$$
$$2MnO_2(s) + H_2(g) \longrightarrow Mn_2O_3(s) + H_2O(l)$$

The voltage of the cell falls at high currents because hydrogen forms faster than it can be oxidized by the manganese(IV) oxide. This makes the cell unsuitable for high-power uses, for which *alkaline cells* are preferred.

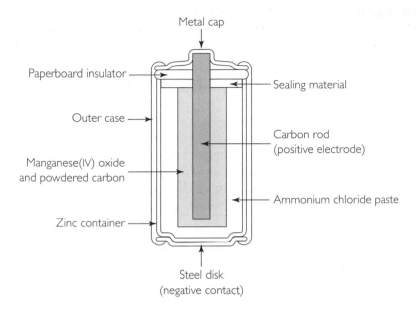

Metal cap

Paperboard insulator

Sealing material

Outer case

Carbon rod
(positive electrode)

Manganese(IV) oxide
and powdered carbon

Ammonium chloride paste

Zinc container

Steel disk
(negative contact)

Cross section of a dry cell

dry ice is solid carbon dioxide. Above −79°C it sublimes to carbon dioxide gas (see *sublimation*). This makes it a useful coolant.

drying agents remove water from moist liquids and gases. Liquid products of organic preparations are often dried with small amounts of anhydrous sodium sulfate or anhydrous magnesium sulfate before the final distillation step. Gases made with laboratory reagents are often moist and can be dried by bubbling them through concentrated sulfuric acid, or more safely by passing them though a U-tube containing *silica gel*. Anhydrous calcium chloride is frequently used in *desiccators* to absorb water, alcohols or amines.

drying oils are oils such as linseed oil that polymerize and set when exposed to air. As a drying oil linseed oil is used in the manufacture of *paints* and varnishes.

ductility is a property of materials, especially metals, that can be drawn out under tension without breaking. *Copper* is a ductile metal that can be pulled through a die (narrow hole) to make thin wire.

dyes are colored materials used to dye fabrics and other materials such as paper, hair, leather and food. A good dye is a fast dye, which means that it is not only colored but can also attach itself strongly to a material so that it does not wash out nor should it fade in the light.

Plants were the main source of natural dyes until William Perkin chanced on the first synthetic dye, mauveine, in 1856. Alizarin and indigo are plant dyes that were the basis of large-scale industries. The discovery of synthetic routes to these dyes in the late nineteenth century was an early triumph for *organic chemistry*.

Examples of synthetic dyes are *azo dyes, vat dyes* and *fiber reactive dyes*.

dynamic equilibrium: the state of balance in a *reversible* process when neither the forward change nor the backward change is complete; both changes are still going on at equal rates so that they cancel each other out and there is no overall change.

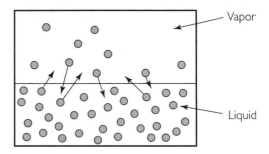

Dynamic equilibrium between a liquid and its vapor

Examples of systems that can be in dynamic equilibrium include:

- water and ice at 0°C, or more generally the liquid and solid states of a substance at its melting point
- a liquid with its saturated *vapor* in a closed container
- a solid with a *saturated solution* of the solid
- a solute distributed between two immiscible solvents
- a *weak acid* in aqueous solution, or any other reversible reaction at constant temperature and pressure.

edta is the common abbreviation for a particular ion that binds so firmly with metal ions that it holds them in solution and effectively makes them chemically inactive. A very little edta is added to salad dressing to trap traces of metal ions that otherwise would catalyze the oxidation of oils. Another practical application is where edta is included in bathroom cleaners to help remove scale by dissolving deposits of calcium carbonate left by hard water. Thanks to this ability to act as a *chelating agent*, edta can be used to treat lead poisoning.

In laboratories edta is the disodium salt of **e**thylene **d**iaminetetraacetic **a**cid (or as it is now called 1,2-bis[bis(carboxymethyl)amino]ethane). The ion can fold itself round metal ions so that four oxygen atoms and two nitrogen atoms can present lone pairs to form coordinate bonds with the metal ion. It is a hexadentate *ligand*.

(See also *complex-forming titration*.)

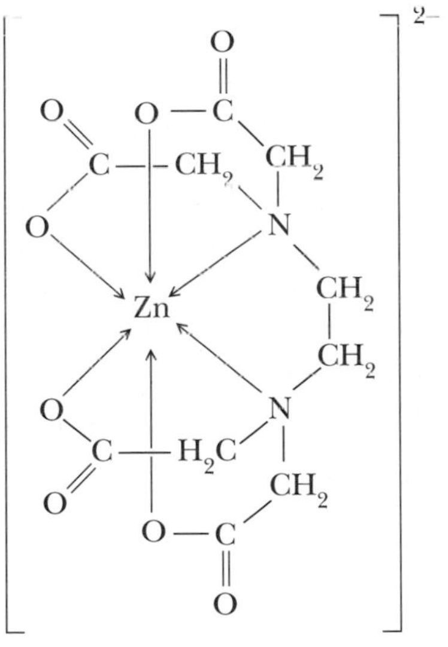

Complex ion formed by edta with a metal ion. For simplicity the disodium salt is often represented as Na_2Y.

efflorescence is the loss of *water of crystallization* from a hydrated salt kept in an open container. Hydrated crystals of sodium carbonate (sal soda, $Na_2CO_3.10H_2O$) turn powdery in an unsealed container as they gradually lose most of their water.

elastomers are *polymers* that can be stretched to several times their normal length and recover their original size and shape when released. They are elastic materials. Natural *rubber* is an elastomer, as are synthetic rubbers such as the *copolymer* of butadiene and styrene.

electric arc furnace: a furnace for making *steel* by recycling scrap iron and steel. The heat of an arc from carbon electrodes melts the metal. Added lime combines with impurities to form a *slag*. Other ingredients are added as necessary. The process can be precisely controlled to give small batches of steel matched to a specified composition.

electrical conductors are solids, liquids or gases that conduct electricity because they contain charged particles that are free to move. They include:

- metals and graphite in which the charge carriers are *delocalized electrons*
- electrolytes in which the charge carriers are positive and negative ions.

electrical insulators are solids, liquids or gases that do not conduct electricity because they contain no free-moving charged particles. Increasing the applied voltage may turn an insulator into a conductor if the voltage becomes high enough to ionize the atoms or molecules.

electrochemical cells produce an electric potential difference from a *redox reaction*. Some electrochemical cells are designed for practical use. Examples include *dry cells*, *alkaline manganese cells* and rechargeable *nickel–cadmium* (NiCad) and *lead–acid cells*.

The reaction of zinc metal with aqueous copper(II) ions is a redox reaction that can be described by two half-equations. Zinc is oxidized to zinc ions as copper(II) ions are reduced to copper metal.

$$Zn(s) \longrightarrow Zn^{2+}(aq) + 2e^-$$
$$Cu^{2+}(aq) + 2e^- \longrightarrow Cu(s)$$

In an electrochemical cell the two half-reactions happen in separate *half-cells*. The electrons flow from one cell to the other through a wire connecting the electrodes. The electric circuit is completed by a *salt bridge* connecting the two solutions.

The tendency for the current to flow is measured with a high-resistance voltmeter that measures the cell's *emf* when no current is flowing. In the example shown electrons tend to flow out of the zinc electrode (negative) round the circuit and into the copper electrode (positive). The emf of the cell is 1.14 V under standard conditions (298 K and concentrations of 1.0 mol dm^{-3}).

There is a convenient shorthand for describing cells. The standard emf of the cell, $E^{\ominus}_{cell}$, is written alongside the cell diagram. The agreed convention is that the sign of $E^{\ominus}_{cell}$ is the charge on the right-hand electrode.

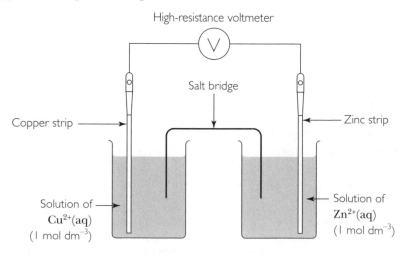

High-resistance voltmeter

Salt bridge

Copper strip

Zinc strip

Solution of Cu^{2+}(aq) (1 mol dm^{-3})

Solution of Zn^{2+}(aq) (1 mol dm^{-3})

Diagram of an electrochemical cell

$$Zn(s)| Zn^{2+}(aq) \parallel Cu^{2+}(aq)|Cu(s) \qquad E^{\ominus}_{cell} = +1.14\,V$$

If the cell emf is positive the reaction tends to go according to the cell diagram read from left to right. As a current flows in a circuit connecting the two electrodes, zinc atoms turn into zinc ions and dissolve, as copper ions turn into copper atoms and deposit on the copper electrode.

$$Zn(s) + Cu^{2+}(aq) \longrightarrow Zn^{2+}(aq) + Cu(s)$$

$E^{\ominus}_{cell}$ values can be calculated for any redox reaction with the help of a table of *standard electrode potentials.*

$$E^{\ominus}_{cell} = E^{\ominus}_{(right\text{-}hand\ electrode)} - E^{\ominus}_{(left\text{-}hand\ electrode)}$$

electrochemical series: a series showing half-reactions for oxidation and reduction with the most powerful *reducing agent* at the top of the list and the most powerful *oxidizing agent* at the bottom of the list.

The order of the half-reactions is determined by their *standard electrode potentials.* The *half-cell* with the most negative electrode potential is at the top of the list. The most negative electrode has the greatest tendency to give up electrons so it is powerfully reducing.

The half-cell with the most positive electrode potential is at the bottom of the list. The most positive electrode has the greatest tendency to gain electrons so it is the most powerfully oxidizing.

Half cell	Half-reaction	$E\,/V$
$Na^+(aq)| Na(s)$	$Na^+(aq) + e^- \rightleftharpoons Na(s)$	-2.71
$Mg^{2+}(aq)| Mg(s)$	$Mg^{2+}(aq) + 2e^- \rightleftharpoons Mg(s)$	-2.37
$Zn^{2+}(aq)| Zn(s)$	$Zn^{2+}(aq) + 2e^- \rightleftharpoons Zn(s)$	-0.76
$2H^+(aq)|H_2(g)$	$2H^+(aq) + 2e^- \rightleftharpoons H_2(g)$	0.00 (by definition)
$Cu^{2+}(aq)|Cu(s)$	$Cu^{2+}(aq) + 2e^- \rightleftharpoons Cu(s)$	$+0.34$
$[I_2(aq),2I^-(aq)]|Pt$	$I_2(aq) + 2e^- \rightleftharpoons 2I^-(aq)$	$+0.54$
$[Br_2(aq),2Br^-(aq)]|Pt$	$Br_2(aq) + 2e^- \rightleftharpoons 2Br^-(aq)$	$+1.09$
$[Cl_2(aq),2Cl^-(aq)]|Pt$	$Cl_2(aq) + 2e^- \rightleftharpoons 2Cl^-(aq)$	$+1.51$

The top part of the given electrochemical series shows half-reactions for metal ions and metals. Sodium is the most reactive of the metals when it reacts as a reducing agent forming metal ions, and copper is the least reactive. This broadly corresponds to the *activity series* for metals and the order of reaction shown by metal/metal ion *displacement reactions.*

The bottom part of the series shows half-reactions for halogens and halide ions. Chlorine is the most reactive of these halogens when it acts as an oxidizing agent forming chloride ions. Iodine is the least reactive. This corresponds to the order of reactivity of the halogens as shown by their displacement reactions.

The "counterclockwise rule" is a quick and easy reminder of the direction of change from the electrochemical series based on electrode potentials. First identify the two half-equations. Write them down with the more negative standard electrode potential on the top. The more positive half-reaction tends to go from right to left oxidizing the more negative half-reaction from right to left.

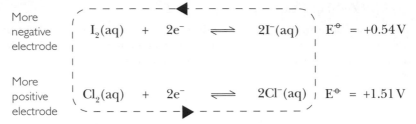

The counterclockwise rule predicts that chlorine will oxidize iodide ions.

Electrode potentials predict the direction of change but say nothing about the rate of change. A reaction that is feasible may not in fact happen because it is so slow.

electrode: see *anode* and *cathode*.

electrode potential: see *standard electrode potential*.

electrolysis is a process that uses an electric current to decompose a molten ionic compound or a solution of ions into elements. Ions can only conduct electricity when they are free to move, which is why electrolytes are molten compounds or solutions.

Large-scale manufacturing processes that use electrolysis include *aluminum manufacture* and the *electrolysis of brine*. *Electroplating, copper refining* and *anodizing* are also electrolytic processes.

During the electrolysis of molten salts, such as molten lead bromide:

- metal deposits appear at the cathode, e.g. $Pb^{2+} + 2e^- \rightarrow Pb$
- nonmetals appear at the anode, e.g. $2Br^- \rightarrow Br_2 + 2e^-$.

During the electrolysis of a solution of a salt in water the change at the *cathode* depends on the type of metal ion in the salt. If the metal is:

- low in the electrochemical series, it forms at the cathode, e.g.:
  $Cu^{2+}(aq) + 2e^- \rightarrow Cu(s)$
- high in the electrochemical series, the product at the cathode is hydrogen, from hydrogen ions produced by the ionization of water:
  $2H^+(aq) + 2e^- \rightarrow H_2(g)$.

During the electrolysis of a salt solution in water the change at the *anode* may depend on the type of electrode. If the anode is made of carbon or platinum the products are:

- halogen molecules if the ions in the solution are chloride, bromide or iodide ions, e.g.:
  $2Cl^-(aq) \rightarrow Cl_2(g) + 2e^-$
- otherwise oxygen from the water:
  $4OH^-(aq) \rightarrow O_2(g) + 2H_2O(l) + 4e^-$.

The concentration of the solution can affect the product at the anode. Chlorine forms at the anode during electrolysis of a concentrated solution of sodium chloride but as the solution gets more dilute increasing amounts of oxygen form.

If the anode is a metal such as copper or silver, the atoms in the electrode turn into ions, e.g. $Cu(s) \rightarrow Cu^{2+}(aq) + 2e^-$.

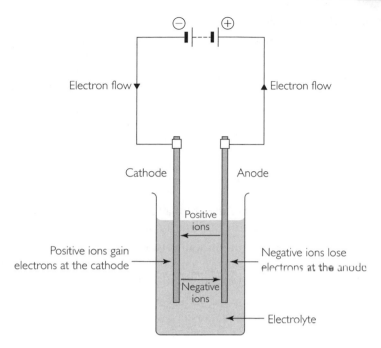

Changes during electrolysis in an electrolytic cell. Positive ions gain electrons at the negative electrode (cathode) and turn into atoms. This is reduction. Negative ions lose electrons at the positive electrode (anode). This is oxidation.

The amount of change at an electrode depends on:

- the charge on the ions
- the amount of electric charge that flows.

The extent of change at an electrode can be calculated from the ionic equation for the electrode process.

Worked example:

Sodium is manufactured by the electrolysis of molten sodium chloride (mixed with other salts to lower the melting point). In a commercial cell the current is 30 000 A. What mass of sodium is formed in an hour at the steel cathode?

Notes on the method

Two relationships are needed involving electric charge and the *Faraday constant*.

- quantity of electric charge/C $=$ current/A $\times$ time/s, since 1 A $=$ 1 C s^{-1}

- amount of electrons/mol $= \dfrac{\text{amount of electric charge/C}}{\text{Faraday constant/C mol}^{-1}}$

The value of the Faraday constant $= 96\,480$ C mol^{-1}.
The molar mass of sodium $= 23$ g mol^{-1}.

Answer

The equation for the electrode process: $\text{Na}^+ \; + \; \text{e}^- \; \rightarrow \; \text{Na}$

 1 mol $\quad$ 1 mol

Time of electrolysis $= 60 \times 60 \text{ s} = 3600 \text{ s}$

Quantity of electric charge passed per hour $= 30\,000 \text{ C/s} \times 3600 \text{ s}$
$= 108\,000\,000 \text{ C}$

Amount of electrons $= \dfrac{108\,000\,000 \text{ C}}{96\,480 \text{ C mol}^{-1}} = $ amount of sodium formed per hour

Mass of sodium formed per hour $= \dfrac{108\,000\,000 \text{ C}}{96\,480 \text{ C mol}^{-1}} \times 23 \text{ g mol}^{-1} = 25\,750 \text{ g}$

$= 25.75 \text{ kg}$

electrolysis of brine is the basis of the chlor-alkali industry. *Electrolysis* of brine is used to manufacture *chlorine, hydrogen* and *sodium hydroxide.*

Brine is a solution of sodium chloride in water. During electrolysis chlorine forms at the positive electrode (anode). Hydrogen bubbles off the negative electrode (cathode) while the solution turns into sodium hydroxide.

The cell used for electrolysis of brine has to be carefully designed because chlorine reacts with sodium hydroxide. The cell has to keep the chlorine and sodium hydroxide apart.

The types of cell used for the process include the flowing mercury cell and the membrane cell.

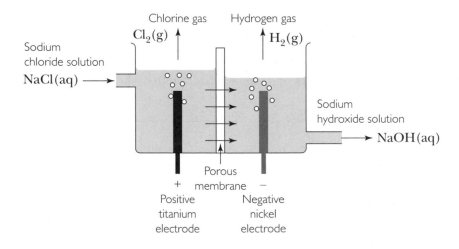

Main inputs and outputs of a membrane cell. The membrane allows the solution to pass through but stops the chlorine mixing with the alkali. The membrane has ion exchange properties; it lets positive ions through but not negative ions.

electromagnetic radiation is radiation such as X-rays, ultraviolet radiation, visible light and infrared rays that can travel through space as oscillating electric and magnetic waves.

There is a spectrum of types of electromagnetic radiation that differ only by their *wavelength*, λ, and *frequency*, ν. In space all radiation travels at the same speed, that of light, $c = 2.99 \times 10^8$ m s^{-1}.

$$\lambda = \frac{c}{\nu} = \frac{2.99 \times 10^8 \text{ m s}^{-1}}{\nu}$$

	radio frequency		microwave		infrared	visible	ultraviolet	X-rays	γ-rays

Frequency ν/Hz	10^5	10^6	10^7	10^8	10^9	10^{10}	10^{11}	10^{12}	10^{13}	10^{14}	10^{15}	10^{16}	10^{17}	10^{18}	10^{19}	10^{20}
Wavelength λ/m	10^3		1			10^{-3}			10^{-6}			10^{-9}				

The electromagnetic spectrum

When electromagnetic radiation interacts with matter it behaves as if made up of packets of energy. These energy quanta are also called photons. The higher the frequency of the radiation, the higher the energy of the quanta, given by $E = h\nu$. The higher-energy photons of ultraviolet radiation and X-rays can have a much greater chemical effect than lower-energy photons of infrared and radio waves.

electron affinity: the *enthalpy change* when gaseous atoms of an element gain electrons to become negative ions. Electron affinities are precisely defined and only used in thermochemical cycles such as the *Born–Haber cycle*. Chemical reactions in laboratories do not normally involve free gaseous atoms and ions.

The first electron affinity of an element is the enthalpy change when one mole of gaseous atoms gains electrons to form one mole of gaseous ions. These two equations define the first and second electron affinities for oxygen:

$$O(g) + e^-(g) \longrightarrow O^-(g) \qquad \Delta H^{\ominus} = -141 \text{ kJ mol}^{-1}$$
$$O^-(g) + e^-(g) \longrightarrow O^{2-}(g) \qquad \Delta H^{\ominus} = +798 \text{ kJ mol}^{-1}$$

The gain of the first electron is exothermic but adding the second electron to a negatively charged particle is an endothermic process. Overall adding two electrons to a gaseous oxygen atom is endothermic.

electron configuration: the number and arrangement of electrons in an atom of an element. Electrons fill energy levels according to the *aufbau principle*.

The electron configuration helps to make sense of the chemistry of an element. The electrons in the outer shell largely determine the chemical properties of an element. Elements in the same *group* of the periodic table have similar properties because they have the same outer electron configuration. There are trends in properties down a group because of the *shielding* effect of the increasing number of inner full shells.

There are several common conventions for writing electron configurations.

A shortened form of electron configuration uses the symbol of the previous *noble gas* to stand for the inner full shells. According to this convention the electron configuration of sodium is [Ne]$3s^1$.

Representations of the electron configuration of sodium, $1s^2 2s^2 2p^6 3s^1$

electron density maps show the whereabouts of electrons in crystals. The lines in the maps connect points with equal electron densities. Each map shows the pattern of electron density for a two-dimensional slice through the crystal. The maps are an interpretation of the information from X-ray diffraction studies. This is possible because it is the electrons in a crystal that scatter X-rays (see *X-ray crystallography*).

Electron density maps for an ionic crystal provide evidence for electron transfer from the metal to the nonmetal. The ions show up as distinct particles. Electron density maps for molecules show electrons shared between atoms in *covalent bonds*.

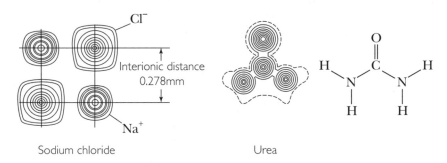

Sodium chloride   Urea

Electron density maps for an ionic crystal and for a molecule

electron-pair repulsion theory: see *shapes of molecules*.

electron transfer takes place during *redox reactions*. An atom, molecule or ion loses electrons when oxidized (**o**xidation **i**s **l**oss). The electrons are transferred to the atom, molecule or ion being reduced (**r**eduction **i**s **g**ain). Hence the memory aide: OIL RIG. *Oxidation numbers* and *half-equations* for redox reactions help to keep track of electron transfer reactions.

electronegativity measures the pull of an atom of an element on the electrons in a chemical bond. The stronger the pulling power of an atom, the higher its electronegativity. There are two quantitative scales of electronegativity; one devised by Linus Pauling and the other by Robert Mulliken. However, the term electronegativity is generally used to compare one element with another qualitatively so it is enough to know the trends in values across and down the periodic table.

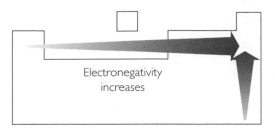

Trends in electronegativity for s- and p-block elements

The highly electronegative elements, such as fluorine and oxygen, are at the top right of the periodic table. The least electronegative elements, such as cesium, are at the bottom left.

The bigger the difference in the electronegativity of the elements forming a bond, the more polar the bond. Oxygen is more electronegative than hydrogen so an O — H bond is *polar* with a slight negative charge on the oxygen atoms and a slight positive charge on the hydrogen atom.

$$\overset{\delta+}{H} - \overset{\delta-}{Cl} \qquad\qquad \overset{H}{\underset{H}{>}}\overset{\delta+}{C} = \overset{\delta-}{O} \qquad\qquad \overset{\delta+}{H} - \overset{2\delta-}{O}$$

Examples of polar bonds between atoms with different electronegativities

The bonding in a compound becomes ionic if the difference in electronegativity is large enough for the more electronegative element to remove completely electrons from the other element. This happens in compounds such as sodium chloride, magnesium oxide or calcium fluoride.

electrophiles are reactive ions and molecules that attack parts of molecules that are rich in electrons. They are "electron-loving" reagents. Electrophiles form a new bond by accepting a pair of electrons from the molecule attacked during a reaction.

Examples of electrophiles are the H^+ and the NO_2^+ ions. Other electrophiles are the atoms at the $\delta+$ end of a *polar covalent bond*. See *electrophilic addition* and *electrophilic substitution*.

electrophilic addition takes place when *alkenes* undergo *addition reactions*. The electrophile attacks the electron-rich region of the double bond between two carbon atoms. Electrophiles that add to alkenes include hydrogen bromide, bromine and water (in the presence of an acid catalyst).

Hydrogen bromide molecules are *polar*. The hydrogen atom, with its $\delta+$ charge, is the electrophilic end of the molecule.

Bromine molecules are not polar but they become polarized as they approach the electron-rich double bond. Electrons in the double bond repel electrons in the bromine molecule. The $\delta+$ end of the molecule is electrophilic.

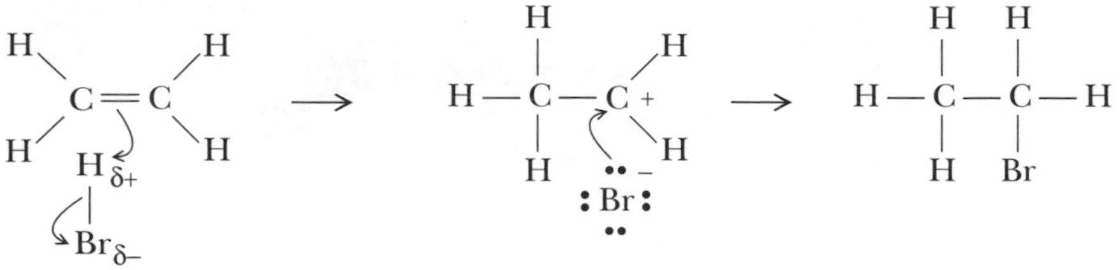

Electrophilic addition of hydrogen bromide to ethene. The reaction takes place in two steps. The intermediate has a positive charge on a carbon atom. It is a carbocation. *Curly arrows show the movement of a pair of electrons. Bond breaking is* heterolytic *and the intermediates ions.*

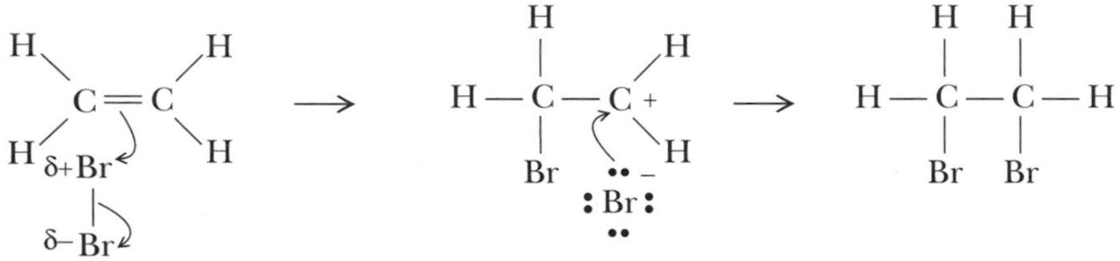

Electrophilic addition of bromine to ethene

electrophilic substitution is the characteristic reaction of arenes such as benzene. The electrophile attacks the electron-rich benzene ring with its six *delocalized electrons*. When describing the mechanism of this type of reaction it is easier to keep track of what is happening to the electrons using the *Kekulé structure* for *benzene*.

Electrophilic substitution of bromine in benzene is rapid in the presence of iron. Iron reacts with some bromine to form iron(III) bromide, which is the catalyst. Iron(III) bromide is an electron pair acceptor (*Lewis acid*) that produces the electrophile, Br^+.

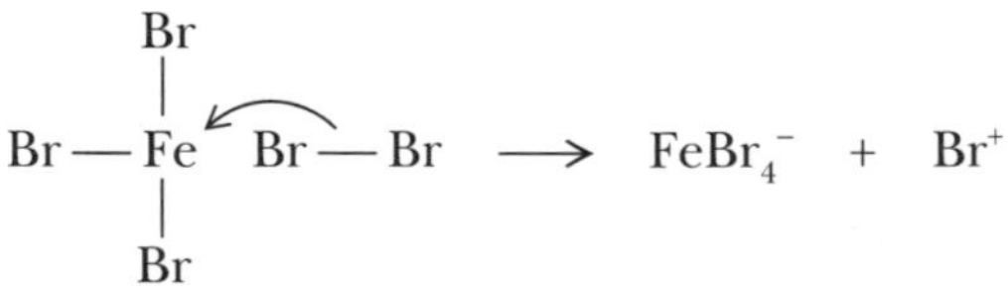

Formation of the electrophile

The first step of electrophilic substitution in benzene is very similar to the first step of *electrophilic addition* to alkenes. The intermediate could then complete the reaction by adding a bromide ion but in fact what happens is the loss of H^+ leading to substitution. Loss of H^+ is preferred because it keeps the stable benzene ring stabilized by six delocalized electrons.

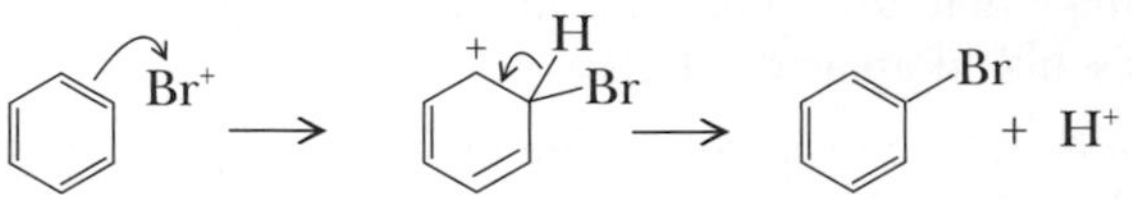

The mechanism of electrophilic substitution. Note that an alternative second step (addition of a bromide ion) is not favored because it gives a product that does not have a stable benzene ring.

Other examples of electrophilic substitution are the *nitration of benzene*, the *sulfonation of benzene* and the *Friedel–Crafts reaction*.

electrophoresis is a technique for separating and identifying organic compounds. It can be used to separate compounds such as amino acids that become electrically charged when dissolved in water at a particular pH. Electrophoresis is used in hospitals to diagnose disease. It is important in genetic profiling to separate out the bands that form the "fingerprint." It is also used in research to study the structures of *proteins* and *nucleic acids*.

Electrophoresis takes place on strips of a gel soaked in a buffer solution to keep the pH constant. Small spots of several samples can be put on each gel. The charged molecules move when an electric voltage is connected between the ends of the gel and they separate into bands according to their size and charge. Most samples are colorless so, once the separation is complete, the gel is dipped into a stain to show up the bands.

electroplating uses *electrolysis* to coat one metal with another. The process is often used to coat metals with thin layers of copper, nickel, chromium, silver and zinc. The object to be plated forms the cathode in an electrolysis cell containing a solution of ions of the metal to be plated. Good results depend on careful control of the conditions including the composition and concentration of the electrolyte, the temperature and the size of the current.

electrostatic forces are the forces between charged particles. Unlike charges attract each other. Positive ions, for example, attract negative ions in ionic compounds. Like charges repel each other. Positive ions in an electrolyte are repelled by the positive anode while being attracted to the negative cathode.

The size of the electrostatic force between two charges varies according to Coulomb's law. The bigger the charges, the stronger the force – the force is proportional to the size of the charges, Q. The greater the distance, d, between the two charges, the smaller the force – the force is inversely proportional to the distance squared.

$$\text{electrostatic force} \propto \frac{Q_1 \times Q_2}{d^2}$$

electrovalent bonding: see *ionic bonding*.

elements are chemically the simplest substances. All the atoms of an element have the same number of protons in the nucleus. The proton number (atomic number) identifies an element and fixes its position in the *periodic table*. When an atom turns into an ion by gaining or losing electrons it becomes a charged atom of the same element. The *isotopes* of an element have different numbers of neutrons in the nucleus but they have the same chemical properties because they have the same number of protons and therefore the same *electron configuration*.

elevation of boiling point: see *colligative properties*.

elimination reaction: a reaction that splits off a simple compound from a molecule to form a double bond.

Elimination of a *hydrogen halide* from a *halogenoalkane* produces an *alkene*. The elimination is favored if the halogen atom is in the middle of the carbon chain or at a branch in the chain. Favorable conditions involve heating the halogenoalkane with a solution of potassium hydroxide in ethanol. (Using ethanol as the solvent instead of water makes the alternative hydrolysis reaction less likely.)

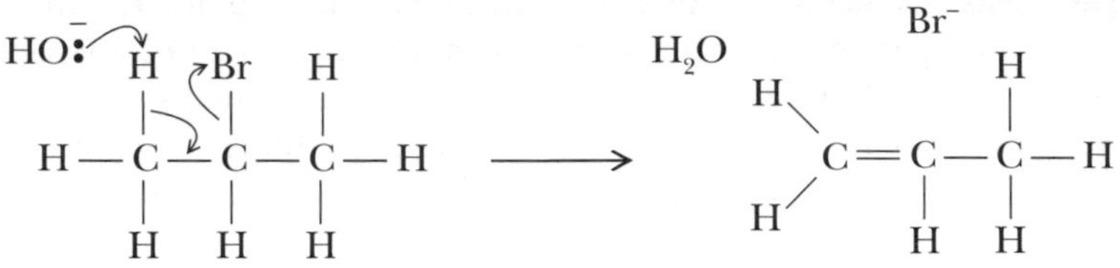

Elimination of hydrogen bromide from 2-bromopropane

Another example of an elimination reaction is the removal of water from an *alcohol* to form an alkene. This is a useful reaction in synthesis for introducing double bonds into molecules. The conditions for reaction are either to pass the vapor of the alcohol over a hot solid catalyst such as aluminum oxide. Alternatively the alcohol is dehydrated by heating with concentrated sulfuric acid.

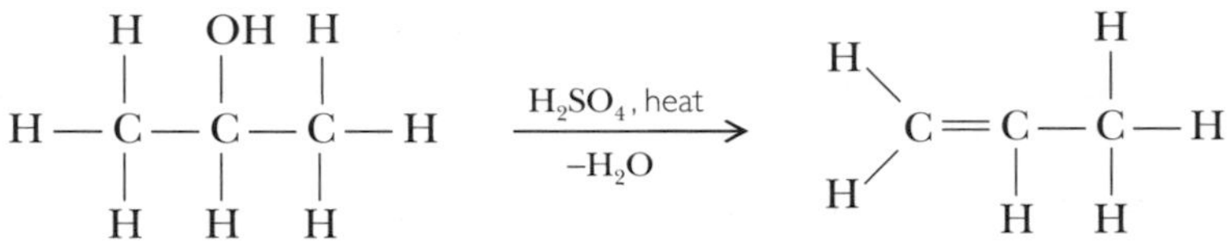

Formation of an alkene from an alcohol

Ellingham diagrams explain the conditions for *metal extraction* from oxide ores. The diagrams are graphs showing how the *free energy changes* of formation ($\Delta G^{\ominus}$) of oxides vary with temperature.

The more negative the value of $\Delta G^{\ominus}$, the greater the tendency for the element to combine with oxygen. So the lower the line in the diagram, the more stable the oxide. Up to 1300°C zinc has a stronger tendency to combine with oxygen than does carbon. Above this temperature carbon has the stronger affinity for oxygen and can reduce zinc oxide to zinc in a blast furnace.

Carbon cannot reduce aluminum oxide to aluminum in the temperature range shown on the graph. Industry uses electrolysis for *aluminum extraction.*

emf (electromotive force) measures the "voltage" of an electrochemical cell. The symbol for emf is E and the SI unit is the volt (V). The emf is the energy transferred in joules per coulomb of charge flowing through a circuit connected to a cell. The definition of the volt as a "joule per coulomb" makes it possible to calculate the *free energy change*, ΔG, for reactions from the values of the emf for *electrochemical cells, $E^{\ominus}_{cell}$.*

$$\Delta G^{\ominus} = -zFE^{\ominus}_{cell}$$

where z is the number of electrons transferred according to the equation for the reaction and F is the *Faraday constant.*

empirical formula: the formula of a compound found by calculation from the combining masses of elements. The empirical formula shows the simplest ratio of the

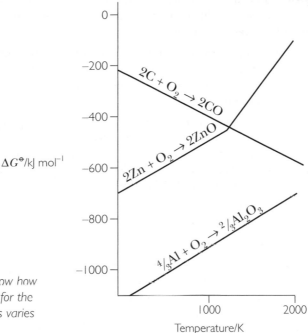

0
–200
–400
–600
–800
–1000
ΔG[⊖]/kJ mol⁻¹
2C + O2 → 2CO
2Zn + O2 → 2ZnO
4/3Al + O2 → 2/3Al2O3
1000
2000
Temperature/K

Ellingham diagram to show how the free energy changes for the formation of three oxides varies with temperature

amounts of elements in the compound; it therefore gives the ratio of the numbers of atoms.

For molecular compounds, the *relative molecular mass* shows whether or not the empirical formula is the same as the *molecular formula.*

Worked example:

Analysis of a sample of a salt shows that it consists of 1.30 g zinc combined with 0.24 g carbon and 0.96 g oxygen. What is the formula of the salt?

Notes on the method

Look up the molar masses of the elements in a book of data.

Recall that: amount of substance/mol $= \dfrac{\text{mass of substance/g}}{\text{molar mass/g mol}^{-1}}$

Answer

	zinc	**carbon**	**oxygen**
Combining masses	1.30 g	0.24 g	0.96 g
Molar masses of elements	65 g mol^{-1}	12 g mol^{-1}	16 g mol^{-1}
Amounts combined	$\dfrac{1.30\text{ g}}{65\text{ g mol}^{-1}}$	$\dfrac{0.24\text{ g}}{12\text{ g mol}^{-1}}$	$\dfrac{0.96\text{ g}}{16\text{ g mol}^{-1}}$
	= 0.02 mol	= 0.02 mol	= 0.06 mol
Simplest ratio of amounts	1	1	3

The formula is $ZnCO_3$.

emulsions consist of droplets of one liquid finely dispersed in another liquid. Emulsions are *colloids*. Milk is an emulsion of fat droplets in water. Salad cream is an emulsion of vegetable oil in vinegar.

An emulsion is often "thicker" (more viscous) than either liquid on its own. Many cosmetic and medical creams are emulsions. Foundation creams and brushless shaving creams are oil-in-water emulsions. Cold creams and cleansing creams are water-in-oil emulsions.

Just shaking two liquids together generally produces droplets that quickly separate back into two layers on standing. It is usually necessary to add an emulsifying agent to stabilize an emulsion. Salad dressing is an emulsion stabilized using mustard as the emulsifying agent. Mayonnaise is stabilized with egg yolk. Many creamy foods are emulsions and the lists of their ingredients include emulsifying agents such as lecithin and alginates.

Emulsifying agents are *surfactants*.

enantiomers: see *chiral compounds*.

enantiotropy: the existence of two *allotropes* of an element each of which can be stable over a range of conditions. Under atmospheric pressure, rhombic sulfur is the stable form of the element at room temperature and up to 95.5°C. Above this temperature the stable form is monoclinic sulfur. At the *transition temperature* the two allotropes are in equilibrium. Both forms consist of S_8 molecules.

Tin is another element that shows enantiotropy. The normal, malleable form of metallic tin is stable down to 13.2°C. Below this temperature the brittle, gray form is stable, giving rise to "tin plague" in samples stored for a time at low temperature. The change from the metallic crystal structure to diamond-like structure of the gray form is slow.

endothermic changes take in energy from their surroundings. Melting and evaporation are endothermic *changes of state*.

For an endothermic reaction the enthalpy change, ΔH, is positive. During an endothermic reaction more energy is taken up in breaking bonds in the reactants than is given out as new bonds form in the products.

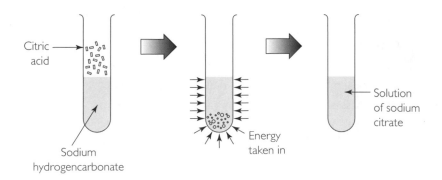

Diagrams to illustrate an endothermic reaction

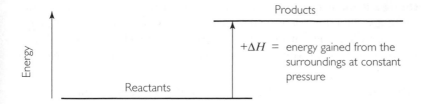

Energy level diagram *for an endothermic reaction*

The fact that there are *spontaneous* endothermic reactions shows that it is not safe to predict that a reaction will not happen just because the *enthalpy change*, ΔH, is positive. Even if ΔH is positive, the *free energy change* (ΔG) can be negative if the *entropy change* (ΔS_{system}) is large enough and positive.

end point: the point during a titration when a color change shows that enough of the solution in the burette has been added to react exactly with the amount of chemical in the flask. Ideally the end point corresponds with the *equivalence point*. In *acid–base titrations* it is common to use a colored *acid–base indicator* to detect the end point.

In some *redox titrations* the end point is shown by a permanent change in the color of the solution in the flask once a drop of excess reagent has been added. In *potassium manganate(VII)* titrations the solution in the flask becomes permanently pink with only a small excess of the purple-colored solution of manganate(VII) ions.

energy conservation is a consequence of the first law of *thermodynamics*. In the sciences, energy conservation helps to keep account of *energy transfers* because the total quantity of energy before and after any change is the same.

Public campaigns to "save energy" have a different meaning. They refer to the importance of conserving fuels and other useful sources of energy. Energy is conserved in the scientific sense when fuels burn but the energy is spread around at a relatively low temperature in the environment so it can no longer be used for heating and to drive engines.

energy density is the amount of energy available from a kilogram of fuel. This is especially important for fuels used for transport. The energy density of hexane (a hydrocarbon in gasoline) is 48 400 kJ kg^{-1}. Ethanol, an alternative fuel used on its own, or in gasohol, only has an energy density of 29 700 kJ kg^{-1}.

energy (enthalpy) level diagrams are a convenient way of displaying and comparing energy changes. The diagrams show the difference in energy between one state and another. Chemists use these diagrams to show the *energy levels* in atoms, and to summarize *exothermic* and *endothermic* processes.

energy levels in atoms are the energies of the electrons in the available *atomic orbitals*. According to *quantum theory* each electron in an atom has a definite energy. When atoms gain or lose energy the electrons jump from one energy level to another.

energy transfers from one *system* to another system, or between a system and its surroundings, happen in chemistry by heating, by the emission and absorption of radiation (such as light) or by the flow of electric charges.

enthalpy change is the exchange of energy between a reaction mixture (*system*) and its surroundings when the reaction takes place at constant *pressure*. The enthalpy change is calculated when the starting temperature of the reactants and final temperature of the products are the same. The symbol for an enthalpy change is ΔH and the units are kJ mol^{-1}.

The sign of ΔH is decided by noting what happens to the reaction mixture.

- If the reaction is *exothermic* the system loses energy to its surroundings and ΔH is negative
- If the reaction is *endothermic* the system gains energy from its surroundings and ΔH is positive.

Standard enthalpy changes for reactions are calculated for carefully specified conditions and for precise amounts of chemicals (in moles). The standard conditions for enthalpy changes are 298 K and 1 bar (= 100 kPa). The symbol for a standard enthalpy change is $\Delta H_{298}^{\ominus}$.

Books of data list standard enthalpy changes but it is often impossible to measure them directly under the stated conditions. Many values are determined indirectly using *Hess's law*. Values measured under nonstandard conditions are corrected to give the value under standard conditions.

Enthalpy changes for changes of state (*melting*, vaporizing or *sublimation*) are usually measured at the melting or boiling point.

enthalpy change of atomization is the *enthalpy change* to produce one mole of gaseous atoms from an element. The element at the start has to be in its *standard state* (normal, stable state) at 298 K and 1 bar *pressure*.

$$\text{element in its standard state} \xrightarrow{\Delta H_{at}^{\ominus}} \text{gaseous atoms} \atop \qquad\qquad\qquad\qquad\qquad\qquad\quad 1 \text{ mol}$$

Enthalpy of atomization

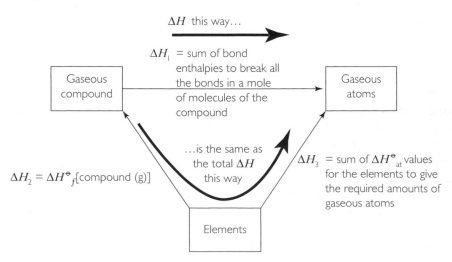

Thermochemical cycle to determine average bond enthalpies in methane, $\Delta H_1 = -\Delta H_2 + \Delta H_3$

Values for the standard enthalpy of atomization of elements are used in the *Born–Haber cycle* to determine *lattice energies*. They are also used to calculate *bond enthalpies*.

Like all thermochemical quantities, the precise definition is important. The standard enthalpy change of atomization of an element, $\Delta H^{\ominus}_{at, 298}$, is the enthalpy change when one mole of gaseous atoms forms from the element in its standard state under standard conditions.

enthalpy change of combustion is the *enthalpy change* when one mole of a compound burns completely in oxygen. The compound and the products of burning must be in their normal stable states. For a carbon compound complete combustion means that all the carbon burns to carbon dioxide and that there is no soot or carbon monoxide. When burning a compound containing hydrogen the water formed must end up as a liquid, not gas.

Values of enthalpies of combustion are much easier to measure than many other enthalpy changes. They can be calculated from measurements taken with a *bomb calorimeter*. The importance of these values is that, with the help of *Hess's law*, they can be used to calculate *enthalpy changes of formation*.

Like all thermochemical quantities, the precise definition of standard enthalpy of combustion is important.

The standard enthalpy change of combustion of a substance, $\Delta H^{\ominus}_{c, 298}$, is the enthalpy change when one mole of the substance completely burns in oxygen under standard conditions with the reactants and products in their standard states.

enthalpy change of formation is the *enthalpy change* when one mole of a compound forms from the elements in their normal stable states. The more stable state of an element is chosen where there are *allotropes*. For carbon, perhaps surprisingly, graphite turns out to be more stable thermochemically than diamond.

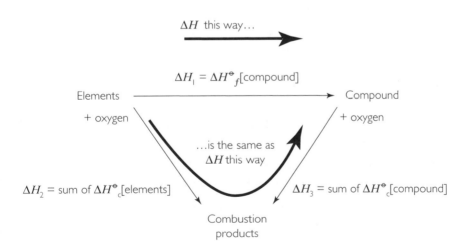

Outline of a thermochemical cycle for calculating standard enthalpies of formation from standard enthalpies of combustion, $\Delta H_1 = \Delta H_2 - \Delta H_3$

Tables of standard enthalpies of formation are very useful because, with a *Hess's law* cycle, they can be used to calculate the enthalpy changes for reactions.

Like all thermochemical quantities, the precise definition of standard enthalpy of formation is important.

The standard enthalpy change of formation of a compound, $\Delta H_{f,298}^{\ominus}$, is the enthalpy change when one mole of the compound forms from its elements under standard conditions with the elements and the compound in their standard states.

Worked example:

Calculate the enthalpy of formation of propane, C_3H_8, at 298 K given the standard enthalpies of combustion:

- propane, $\Delta H_c^{\ominus}(C_3H_8) = -2220$ kJ mol⁻¹
- carbon, $\Delta H_c^{\ominus}(C) = -393$ kJ mol⁻¹
- hydrogen, $\Delta H_c^{\ominus}(H_2) = -286$ kJ mol⁻¹.

Notes on the method

Draw up a thermochemical cycle. Use Hess's law to produce an equation for the enthalpy changes. All the enthalpy changes are given except $\Delta H_f^{\ominus}(C_3H_8)$.

Pay careful attention to the signs. Put the value and sign for a quantity in brackets when multiplying, adding or subtracting enthalpy values.

Answer

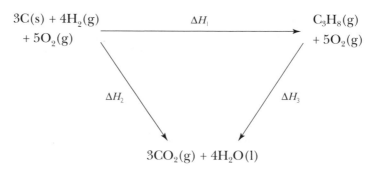

$$3C(s) + 4H_2(g) + 5O_2(g) \xrightarrow{\Delta H_1} C_3H_8(g) + 5O_2(g)$$

$$\Delta H_2 \searrow \qquad \swarrow \Delta H_3$$

$$3CO_2(g) + 4H_2O(l)$$

According to Hess's law $\Delta H_1 = \Delta H_2 - \Delta H_3$

$\Delta H_1 = \Delta H_f^{\ominus}(C_3H_8)$

$\Delta H_2 = 3 \times \Delta H_c^{\ominus}(C) + 4 \times \Delta H_c^{\ominus}(H_2) = 3 \times (-393\,\text{kJ mol}^{-1}) + 4 \times (-286\,\text{kJ mol}^{-1})$

$\qquad\qquad = -2323$ kJ mol⁻¹

$\Delta H_3 = \Delta H_c^{\ominus}(C_3H_8) = -2220$ kJ mol⁻¹

Hence $\Delta H_f^{\ominus}(C_3H_8) = (-2323\,\text{kJ mol}^{-1}) - (-2220\,\text{kJ mol}^{-1})$

$\qquad\qquad = -2323$ kJ mol⁻¹ $+ 2220$ kJ mol⁻¹

$\qquad\qquad = -103$ kJ mol⁻¹

---

enthalpy change of hydration is the *enthalpy change* when one mole of gaseous ions is hydrated under standard conditions to produce a solution in which the concentration of ions is 1 mol dm⁻³.

$$Na^+(g) + aq \longrightarrow Na^+(aq) \qquad\qquad \Delta H^{\ominus}_{hydration} = -390 \text{ kJ mol}^{-1}$$

In this equation "+ aq" is short for adding water.

enthalpy change of melting (fusion) is the *enthalpy change* when one mole of a solid turns to a liquid at its melting point.

Physicists generally use "specific latent heat" values when studying the energy changes when solids melt. Specific latent heats of melting are measured in joules per kilogram rather than joules per mole.

enthalpy change of neutralization is the *enthalpy change of reaction* when an acid and an alkali neutralize each other.

$$HCl(aq) + NaOH(aq) \longrightarrow NaCl(aq) + H_2O(l) \quad \Delta H_{neutralization} = -57.1 \text{ kJ mol}^{-1}$$

The enthalpy of neutralization for dilute solutions of *strong acid* with *strong base* is always close to 57.1 kJ mol⁻¹. The reason is that these acids and alkalis are fully ionized, so in every instance the reaction is the same:

$$H^+(aq) + OH^-(aq) \longrightarrow H_2O(l) \qquad\qquad \Delta H = -57.1 \text{ kJ mol}^{-1}$$

The enthalpy changes of neutralization for reactions involving weak acids and weak bases differ from this value because there are other energy changes, such as the energy needed to remove a proton from a weak acid.

Enthalpies of neutralization can be measured approximately by mixing solutions of acids and alkalis in a *calorimeter*.

enthalpy change of reaction is the *enthalpy change* when the amounts shown in the chemical equation react. The standard enthalpy change for reaction is defined at 298 K, 1 atmosphere pressure and with the reactants and products in their normal, stable states under these conditions. The concentration of any solution is 1 mol dm⁻³.

The enthalpy change for a reaction can easily be calculated from tabulated values for standard *enthalpy changes of formation* using *Hess's law*.

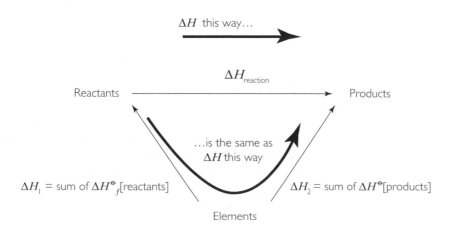

Outline of a thermochemical cycle for calculating standard enthalpies of reaction from standard enthalpies of formation

According to Hess's law:

$$\Delta H^{\ominus}_{reaction} = -\Delta H_1 + \Delta H_2$$

So $\Delta H^{\ominus}_{reaction} = \{sum\ of\ \Delta H^{\ominus}_f[products]\} - \{sum\ of\ \Delta H^{\ominus}_f[reactants]\}$

Worked example:

Calculate the enthalpy change for the reduction of iron(III) oxide by carbon monoxide.

$\Delta H^{\ominus}_f[Fe_2O_3] = -824\ kJ\ mol^{-1}$

$\Delta H^{\ominus}_f[CO] = -110\ kJ\ mol^{-1}$

$\Delta H^{\ominus}_f[CO_2] = -393\ kJ\ mol^{-1}$

Notes on the method

Write the balanced equation for the reaction.

All the enthalpy changes are given except $\Delta H^{\ominus}$ for the reaction.

Note that by definition $\Delta H^{\ominus}_f[element] = 0\ kJ\ mol^{-1}$

Pay careful attention to the signs. Put the value and sign for a quantity in brackets when multiplying, adding or subtracting enthalpy values.

Answer

$$Fe_2O_3(s) + 3CO(g) \longrightarrow 2Fe(s) + 3CO_2(g)$$

So $\Delta H^{\ominus}_{reaction} = \{sum\ of\ \Delta H^{\ominus}_f[products]\} - \{sum\ of\ \Delta H^{\ominus}_f[reactants]\}$

$\Delta H^{\ominus}_{reaction} = \{2 \times \Delta H^{\ominus}_f[Fe] + 3 \times \Delta H^{\ominus}_f[CO_2]\} - \{\Delta H^{\ominus}_f[Fe_2O_3] + 3 \times \Delta H^{\ominus}_f[CO]\}$

$= \{0 + 3 \times (-393\ kJ\ mol^{-1})\} - \{(-824\ kJ\ mol^{-1}) + 3 \times (-110\ kJ\ mol^{-1})\}$

$= (-1179\ kJ\ mol^{-1}) - (-1154\ kJ\ mol^{-1}) = -25\ kJ\ mol^{-1}$

---

enthalpy change of solution is the *enthalpy change* when one mole of a substance dissolves in a stated amount of water under standard conditions.

$$NaCl(s) + aq \longrightarrow Na^+(aq) + Cl^-(aq) \qquad \Delta H^{\ominus}_{solution} = -407\ kJ\ mol^{-1}$$

In this equation "+ aq" is short for adding water.

The enthalpy change of solution is the difference between the energy needed to separate the ions from the crystal lattice (– *lattice energy*) and the energy given out as the ions are hydrated (sum of the *hydration* enthalpies).

$$\Delta H^{\ominus}_{solution} = \Delta H^{\ominus}_{hydration\ cation} + \Delta H^{\ominus}_{hydration\ anion} - \Delta H^{\ominus}_{lattice}$$

Note that the enthalpy change of solution is a small difference between two large enthalpy changes. Also note that the lattice energy and the hydration enthalpies tend to be affected in the same way by changes in the sizes of the ions and their charges. The smaller the ions and the larger the charges, the greater the lattice energy but also the greater the hydration enthalpies. This means that it is not easy to make use of enthalpy cycles to account for trends in solubilities of ionic compounds down group 1 or group 2 in the periodic table.

Also note that an ionic salt may well dissolve in water even if $\Delta H^{\ominus}_{solution}$ is slightly positive. Dissolving makes a significant difference in the numbers of ways that particles and energy can be arranged. The *entropy* change of the system, $\Delta S^{\ominus}_{system}$, may be positive and large enough to outweigh a negative entropy change in the surroundings.

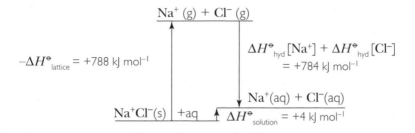

Energy level diagram for sodium chloride dissolving in water. Note that the enthalpy change for going from the crystal to the gaseous ions is −(lattice energy).

enthalpy change of vaporization is the *enthalpy change* when one mole of a liquid turns to a *vapor* at its boiling point. Evaporation separates the particles in a liquid so values for specific enthalpy of vaporization give a measure of the strength of the bonding between particles in liquids. Substances with strong ionic or metallic bonding have much higher boiling points and enthalpies of vaporization than substances consisting of molecules with weak *intermolecular forces*.

Physicists generally use specific latent heat values in studying the energy changes when liquids evaporate. Specific latent heats of vaporization are measured in joules per kilogram rather than joules per mole.

entity: a term that can refer to any distinct particle such as an atom, molecule, ion, electron or free radical. The term is used in precise definitions such as the definition of *amount of substance* in moles. It is important to be precise when specifying a particular entity. These, for example, are four distinct chemical entities: a hydrogen atom, H; a hydrogen molecule, H_2; a hydrogen ion, H^+; and a hydride ion, H^-.

entropy (S) is a thermochemical quantity that makes it possible to predict the direction of changes. Change happens in the direction that leads to a total increase in entropy. When considering chemical reactions it is convenient to calculate the total entropy change in two parts: the entropy change of the *system* and the entropy change of the surroundings.

$$\Delta S_{total} = \Delta S_{system} + \Delta S_{surroundings}$$

The entropy of a system measures the number of ways, W, of arranging the molecules and sharing out the energy between the molecules. Nothing seems to be happening to a closed flask of gas kept at a constant temperature. The *kinetic theory of gases* tells us, however, that the molecules are in rapid motion, colliding with each other and with the walls of the container. The gas stays the same while constantly rearranging its molecules and redistributing energy. The "number of ways," W, is large for a gas. Gases generally have higher entropies than liquids, which have higher entropies than solids. (The relationship between S and W was derived by Boltzman – see *thermochemistry*.)

The entropy change of the surroundings during a chemical reaction is determined by the size of the *enthalpy change*, ΔH, and the temperature, T. The relationship is:

$$\Delta S_{\text{surroundings}} = -\frac{\Delta H}{T}$$

The minus sign is included because the entropy change increases as the amount of energy transferred to the surroundings increases. For an exothermic reaction, which transfers energy to the surroundings, ΔH is negative, so $-\Delta H$ is positive.

For many exothermic reactions at about room temperature the value of $-\Delta H/T$ is much larger than ΔS_{system}, which means that ΔS_{total} is positive. This explains why exothermic reactions generally tend to proceed (see *feasibility*), but there are exceptions.

Chemists often find it more convenient to work with *free energy changes*, which can be regarded as "the total entropy changes in disguise."

environmental chemistry is the study of chemical changes in the environment. Chemists use a range of analytical methods to estimate the amounts of elements in the environment. They apply the theory of *reaction kinetics*, the *equilibrium law*, and *thermochemistry* to explain the changes they observe.

Environmental chemists use models to summarize their findings and to make predictions. The models show how the various elements cycle through the environment (see *carbon cycle* and *nitrogen cycle*). The models show the main reservoirs for an element and the size of the flows of an element from one reservoir to another.

Knowledge of the scale of natural changes shows whether or not human activity is likely to disturb natural changes locally, regionally or globally. So environmental chemistry helps scientists to assess the seriousness of various types of activity and the pollution it causes (see *steady state systems*, *ozone* and *greenhouse effect*).

environmental issues are of growing concern to chemists, the chemical industry and all who use chemicals, as scientists have shown the harm that some chemicals can do to living things. Analytical chemists have contributed greatly to our knowledge of what happens to chemicals in the environment by developing very sensitive analytical techniques, such as chromatography and spectroscopy, to measure minute traces of substances that were once undetectable.

A challenge for chemists in recent years has been to redesign chemical processes to reduce both the energy required and the waste by-products formed. This is both more profitable and less damaging to the environment.

enzymes are *protein* molecules that are the *catalysts* for biochemical reactions that would otherwise be very slow. Saliva contains the enzyme amylase, which aids digestion by speeding up the *hydrolysis* of starch to *sugar*. Catalase is an enzyme that protects living cells from a build-up of hydrogen peroxide by speeding up its decomposition to water and oxygen. Some washing powders contain proteases – enzymes that break down the proteins such as blood on dirty clothes.

Enzymes are highly specific. Each enzyme catalyzes a particular reaction. An enzyme has an *active site* that is just the right shape and size for the *substrate* molecules. Each enzyme works best at a particular temperature and pH, and is less effective under other conditions.

epoxy resins are used as adhesives. The *resin* is a sticky liquid *polymer* with relatively short chains.

Mixing the resin with a hardener starts a chemical reaction that cross-links the chains to make a hard, strong, glass-like polymer (see *cross-linking*). The higher the temperature, the faster the reaction.

epoxyethane is an important chemical intermediate used to manufacture *surfactants, solvents* and *lubricants*. Epoxyethane is made by mixing *ethene* with air or oxygen and passing the mixture at about 300°C under pressure over a *heterogeneous catalyst*. The catalyst is finely divided silver spread on the surface of an inert material such as alumina.

$$2\,CH_2{=}CH_2(g) \;+\; O_2(g) \;\longrightarrow\; 2CH_2\overset{O}{\underset{}{-}}CH_2(g)$$

Epoxyethane is a reactive and hazardous chemical so it is generally made and stored where it will be used.

Epoxyethane reacts vigorously with water, producing a range of products depending on the conditions.

$$n\,CH_2{-}CH_2 \;+\; H_2O \;\longrightarrow\; HO{+}CH_2CH_2O{+}_n H$$

Reaction of epoxyethane with water. When $n = 1$, the produce is ethane-1,2-diol, which is the main ingredient of antifreeze. When n is greater than 4 the poly(epoxyethane) may be useful as a solvent or as a nonionic surfactant.

equilibrium law is a quantitative law for predicting the amounts of reactants and products present when a *reversible reaction* reaches a state of *dynamic equilibrium*.

In general, for a reversible reaction at equilibrium:

$$aA + bB \;\rightleftharpoons\; cC + dD$$

$$K_c = \frac{[C]^c[D]^d}{[A]^a[B]^b}$$

This is the form for the equilibrium constant K_c when the *concentrations* of the reactants and products are measured in moles per liter. [A], [B] and so on are the equilibrium concentrations.

The concentrations of the chemicals on the right-hand side of the equation appear on the top line of the expression. The concentrations of reactants on the left appear on the bottom line. Each concentration term is raised to the power of the number in front of its formula in the equation.

For gas reactions it is often more convenient to use *partial pressures* as the measure of concentrations. The equilibrium constant is then K_p.

Equilibrium constants are constant for a particular temperature. The variation of K with temperature accounts for the *temperature effect on equilibria*.

Worked example:

Calculate the value of K_c for the reaction: $PCl_5(g) \rightleftharpoons PCl_3(g) + Cl_2(g)$ given that when 8.4 mol of $PCl_5(g)$ is mixed with 1.8 mol $PCl_3(g)$ and allowed to come to equilibrium in a 10 dm³ container the amount of $PCl_5(g)$ at equilibrium is 7.2 mol.

Notes on the method

Write down the equation. Underneath write first the initial amounts, then write the amounts at equilibrium. Use the equation to calculate the amounts not given.

Calculate the equilibrium concentrations given the volume of the container. Substitute in the expression for K_c.

Answer

Equation	$PCl_5(g)$	$\rightleftharpoons$	$PCl_3(g)$	+	$Cl_2(g)$
Initial amounts/mol	8.4		1.8		0
Equilibrium amounts/mol	7.2 (= 8.4 − 1.2)		1.8 + 1.2 = 3.0 mol		1.2 mol
Equilibrium concentrations/ mol dm⁻³	7.2 ÷ 10 = 0.72		3.0 ÷ 10 = 0.3		1.2 ÷ 10 = 0.12

$$K_c = \frac{[PCl_3(g)][Cl_2(g)]}{[PCl_5(g)]} = \frac{0.3 \text{ mol dm}^{-3} \times 0.12 \text{ mol dm}^{-3}}{0.72 \text{ mol dm}^{-3}} = 0.05 \text{ mol dm}^{-3}$$

equivalence point is the point during any *titration* when the amount in moles of one reactant added from a burette is just enough to react exactly with all of the measured amount of chemical in the flask as shown by the *balanced equation.*

In a well-planned titration the color change observed at the *end point* corresponds exactly with the equivalence point.

errors of measurement are the differences between measured values and the true values. Often the true value is not known so analysts have to assess the *confidence limits* for their results.

There are random errors that cause repeat measurements to vary and to scatter around a mean value. Averaging a number of readings helps to take care of random errors. The smaller the random errors, the more precise the data.

There are systematic errors that affect all measurements in the same way, making them all lower or higher than the true value. Systematic errors do not average out. Identifying and eliminating systematic errors is important for increasing the *accuracy of data.* Systematic errors can be reduced by using better equipment or improved practical technique.

esters are sweet-smelling compounds found in perfumes and fruit flavors. The ester 3-methylbutylethanoate gives pear drops their taste and smell. Ethyl butanoate has the odor of pineapples. Ripe fruits contain mixtures of esters.

The general formula for an ester is RCO_2R', where R and R' are *alkyl* or *aryl* groups. Ethyl ethanoate is only slightly soluble in water.

$$CH_3C\overset{O}{\underset{OCH_3}{\diagup}}$$

methyl ethanoate

$$CH_3C\overset{O}{\underset{OCH_2CH_3}{\diagup}}$$

ethyl ethanoate

$$\bigcirc\overset{O}{\underset{OCH_2CH_3}{C}}$$

ethyl benzoate

Names and structures of esters

An ester forms when a carboxylic acid reacts with an alcohol in the presence of a drop of concentrated sulfuric acid to act as a catalyst. The reaction is reversible. It takes an excess of the alcohol to convert most of the acid to ester.

$$CH_3C\overset{O}{\underset{OH}{\diagup}} + CH_3CH_2OH \underset{heat}{\overset{H^+}{\rightleftharpoons}} CH_3C\overset{O}{\underset{OCH_2CH_3}{\diagup}} + H_2O$$

Formation of ethyl ethanoate from ethanoic acid and ethanol

Another way to make an ester is to mix an alcohol with either an *acyl chloride* or an *acid anhydride*.

Hydrolysis splits an ester into an acid and an alcohol. Acids or bases can catalyze the hydrolysis. Base catalysis is generally more efficient because it is not reversible. The acid is produced as its negative ion, which does not react with the alcohol.

$$CH_3C\overset{O}{\underset{OCH_2CH_3}{\diagup}} + OH^- \underset{}{\overset{heat}{\rightleftharpoons}} CH_3C\overset{O}{\underset{O^-}{\diagup}} + CH_3CH_2OH$$

ester   salt

Base-catalyzed hydrolysis of ethyl ethanoate

Lithium tetrahydridoaluminate(III) (LiAlH$_4$) in dry ether reduces esters to alcohols more easily than it reduces carboxylic acids.

$$CH_3C\overset{O}{\underset{OCH_2CH_3}{\diagup}} \underset{dry\ ether}{\overset{LiAlH_4\ in}{\longrightarrow}} CH_3CH_2OH$$

Reduction of an ester to an alcohol by lithium tetrahydridoaluminate(III)

Compounds with more than one ester link include *triglycerides* in fats and oils as well as *polyester* fibers. Alkaline hydrolysis of fats and oils produces soaps.

Several compounds used in medicine are esters including *aspirin*, paracetamol and the local *anesthetics* novocaine and benzocaine. The insecticides malathion and pyrethrin are also esters.

ethene (CH$_2$=CH$_2$) is the simplest *alkene*. It is a reactive gas. The petrochemical industry makes ethene on a very large scale by *steam cracking* natural gas or naphtha from the *fractional distillation* of oil.

Ethene is the starting material for the manufacture of a vast range of petrochemicals. The main products are *addition polymers* such as polythene, pvc and polystyrene.

ethers are organic compounds with the general formula R — O — R', where R and R' are *alkyl* or *aryl* groups. The most familiar ether is ethoxyethane, which has a sweet smell and is an *anesthetic.*

$$CH_3—O—CH_3 \qquad CH_3CH_2—O—CH_2CH_3 \qquad CH_3—O—CH_2CH_3$$

methoxymethane   ethoxyethane   methoxyethane

Names and structures of ethers

Ethers are more *volatile* than alcohols because they have no hydrogen bonds. The vapor of ethoxyethane can be hazardous because it forms explosive mixtures in air.

Ethers are also much less soluble in water than alcohols. Ethoxyethane is a good solvent for covalent compounds but not for salts so it is one of the liquids used for *solvent extraction.*

Ethers are relatively unreactive because they do not have O — H bonds. They do not react with acids or alkalis, oxidizing agents, sodium or phosphorus pentachloride. This makes ethers such as ethoxyethane useful as nonaqueous solvents for reactions such as *lithium tetrahydridoaluminate*(III) (LiAlH$_4$) reductions and the formation and use of *Grignard reagents.*

eutectic mixture: the mixture with the lowest freezing point of all the possible mixtures of given substances. Metals can form eutectic mixtures, as can solutions of salts such as sodium nitrate in water.

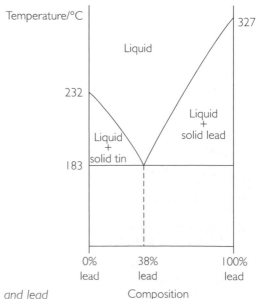

Phase diagram for mixtures of tin and lead

For pairs of metals, such as tin and lead, the eutectic mixture is the *alloy* with the low-est melting point of all the possible alloys. An alloy with the eutectic composition freezes (or melts) at one temperature like a pure metal. The melting point of the eutectic, however, is lower than the melting points of the pure metals.

The eutectic mixture of tin and lead melts at 183°C. This low temperature makes the eutectic useful as solder.

eutrophication happens when the water in rivers or lakes is enriched by fertilizers from farmland or by nutrients from sewage and this makes it possible for algae to multiply rapidly. Thick layers of algae block out the light from plants growing below the surface so that they cannot produce oxygen as fast as usual. Then bacteria start to break down the mass of algae using up the remaining oxygen in the water. Other organisms such as fish die because they are starved of oxygen.

evaporation happens at the surface of a liquid as it turns to a gas. This is an example of a *change of state*. As a liquid such as water evaporates, the faster-moving molecules near the surface escape from the pull of intermolecular forces and break away to become a vapor. Liquids tend to cool as they evaporate because the faster-moving molecules break away so that the average kinetic energy of the remaining molecules falls.

Evaporation is an *endothermic* process. Energy must enter from the surroundings to keep a substance at a constant temperature as it evaporates. So liquids feel cold as they evaporate on the skin.

excited state: the state of an atom or molecule when one or more of its electrons is raised to a higher energy above the stable *ground state*. Heating, electricity or elec-tromagnetic radiation can provide the energy to excite atoms or molecules. Energy is released back to the surroundings when the electrons fall back to the stable energy levels of the ground state. This happens during *flame tests*. Heat from a Bunsen flame excites the electrons in metal atoms from the sample. As the electrons drop back to the lower energy levels they give off radiation with a wavelength determined by the size of the energy jump (see *quantum theory*).

exothermic reactions give out energy to their surroundings. Freezing and condensing are exothermic *changes of state*.

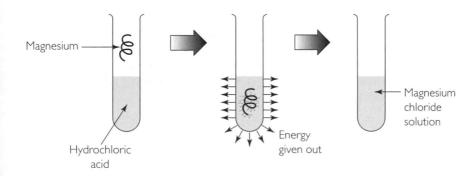

Magnesium

Hydrochloric acid

Energy given out

Magnesium chloride solution

Diagrams to illustrate an exothermic reaction

For an exothermic reaction the enthalpy change, ΔH, is negative. During an exothermic reaction more energy is given out as new bonds form in the products than is needed to break bonds in the reactants.

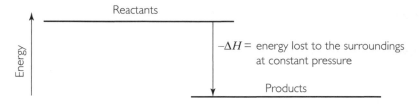

Energy level diagram *for an exothermic reaction*

Most *spontaneous reactions* are exothermic but there are exceptions so the *free energy change* (or total *entropy* change) must be examined to make reliable predictions about the direction and extent of change.

explosions are reactions that go with a bang. Gunpowder explodes if ignited in a confined space (see *fireworks*). The explosion is caused by the rapid build-up of pressure as the reaction produces a large volume of hot gas from a small volume of solid.

The "pop" during the test-tube test for hydrogen is a small explosion. This reaction explodes because it is a *free-radical chain reaction* with a step in which one radical reacts to produce two radicals, which can then both react. The branching chain reaction produces more and more reactive free radicals so the reaction goes faster and faster.

Explosives are compounds or mixtures of chemicals designed to produce explosions. Explosions are used in quarrying, mining and road building and to demolish old buildings. They are also used in warfare and as rocket propellants.

The Nobel prize was endowed with the wealth of the Swedish chemist Alfred Nobel (1833–1896) who discovered that the dangerous explosive nitroglycerine (propane-1,2,3-triol trinitrate) could be used safely if absorbed in the mineral kieselguhr. He sold this product as "dynamite." He also developed guncotton (cellulose nitrate) and gelignite (nitroglycerine in nitrocellulose).

High explosives only detonate if set off by a sudden shock, which is usually supplied by a detonator. Mercury fulminate can be used as a detonator because it explodes instantly when ignited.

extrusion is a process for shaping a metal, such as *aluminum*, or a *plastic*, such as pvc, by forcing it through a shaped nozzle (die). Cooks use extrusion in a similar way when decorating a cake with colored icing sugar or when mincing meat. A plastics extruder works by melting pellets of the polymer and then using a rotating screw to push the molten material through a die.

face-centered cubic structure is one of the two *close-packed* crystal structures of metals. Metals with the face-centered cubic structure are calcium, aluminum, cobalt, nickel and copper.

Fajan's rules are a guide that helps to predict the extent to which the bonding in a compound will be ionic, covalent or intermediate between ionic and covalent. Kasimir Fajan (1887–1975) was a physical chemist who noted that ionic bonding is favored if:

- the charges on the ions are small (1+ or 2+, 1– or 2–)
- the radius of the positive ion is large and the radius of the negative ion small.

The way to apply Fajan's rules is to start by picturing ionic bonding between two atoms and then to consider the extent to which the positive metal ion will polarize the neighboring negative ions, giving rise to some degree of electron sharing (that is a degree of covalent bonding).

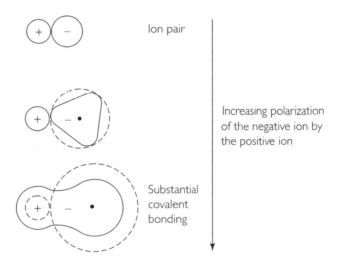

Ionic bonding with increasing degrees of electron sharing because the positive ion has polarized the neighboring negative ion. Dotted circles show the unpolarized ions.

The smaller a positive ion and the larger its charge, the greater the extent to which it tends to polarize a negative ion. So polarizing power increases along the series: Na^+, Mg^{2+}, Al^{3+}, Si^{4+}. Sodium chloride is an ionic, crystalline solid. The bonding in anhydrous *aluminum chloride* is largely covalent. Silicon chloride is a covalent, molecular liquid.

Ionic radii for metal ions in the third period

The larger the negative ion and the larger its charge, the more *polarizable* it becomes. So iodide ions are more polarizable than fluoride ions. Fluorine, which forms the small, single charge fluoride ion, forms more ionic compounds than any other nonmetal.

Fajan's rules help to account for the *diagonal relationship* between elements such as Li and Mg, Be and Al, B and Si.

Faraday constant (F) is the electric charge on one mole of electrons. The Faraday constant is used in calculations to determine the amount of change during *electrolysis*.

$$F = eL = 96\ 480\ C\ mol^{-1}$$

where e is the charge on one electron and L is the *Avogadro constant*. It is possible to measure F and e experimentally so this relationship can be used to arrive at a value for the Avogadro constant.

fats belong to the family of compounds call *lipids*. Fats are esters of propan-1,2,3-triol (*triglycerides*) that are solid at around room temperature (below 20°C) because they contain a high proportion of saturated *fatty acids*. Solid triglycerides are generally found in animals. The triglycerides from plants are mostly liquids at around room temperature; these are *vegetable oils*.

fatty acids are carboxylic acids with long hydrocarbon chains that are combined with propan-1,2,3-triol to make *triglycerides* in *fats* and *vegetable oils*. Saturated fatty acids do not have double bonds in the hydrocarbon chain. There is one or more double bond in an unsaturated fatty acid.

Fatty acid	Chemical name	Formula		Type
palmitic	hexadecanoic	$CH_3(CH_2)_{14}CO_2H$		saturated
stearic	octadecanoic	$CH_3(CH_2)_{16}CO_2H$		saturated
oleic	octadec-9-enoic	$CH_3(CH_2)_7CH = CH(CH_2)_7CO_2H$		unsaturated
linoleic	octadec-9,12-dienoic	$CH_3(CH_2)_4CH = CHCH_2CH = CH(CH_2)_7CO_2H$		unsaturated

Animal fats have a higher proportion of saturated fats in their triglycerides. In lard, for example, the main fatty acids are palmitic acid (28%), stearic acid (8%) and only 56% oleic acid. In olive oil the main fatty acids are oleic acid (80%) and linoleic acid (10%).

Polyunsaturated fats contain fatty acids with two or more double bonds in the chain.

Some fats or oils provide fatty acids that are essential to the human diet, including linoleic and linolenic acids.

f-block elements are the *lanthanide* and *actinide elements* in periods 6 and 7 of the periodic table. For these elements the last electron added to the atomic structure goes into one of the seven *f*-orbitals in the fourth or fifth shells. For convenience two rows of *f*-block elements are usually shown underneath the *periodic table* to cut down its overall width.

feasibility: a reaction is feasible if it tends to proceed – even if the reaction is very slow. In this sense the reaction between methane (in natural gas) and oxygen is feasible at room temperature but, because of a high *activation energy*, the reaction is so slow that it does not happen. Put a match to the mixture of air and gas and the reaction is rapid.

The test of feasibility is *free energy change* for the reaction. If ΔG is negative, the reaction tends to proceed.

For many chemical reactions, ΔG approximately equals ΔH, so chemists often use the sign of ΔH as a guide to feasibility. This can be misleading if the *entropy* change for the reaction system is large.

For *redox reactions, standard electrode potentials* offer an alternative way of deciding whether or not reactions tend to proceed. $\Delta G \propto -E_{cell}$, so if the cell emf is positive the redox reaction in the cell will tend to proceed.

For other reactions such as acid–base reactions, the easiest guide to the direction and extent of change is the equilibrium constant, K_c, where $\Delta G \propto -\ln K_c$.

What this shows is that ΔG, E_{cell} and K_c values can all answer the same questions for a reaction:

- Will the reaction proceed?
- How far will it go?

In practice chemists use the quantity that is most convenient to measure. Knowing the value of one of the three quantities, it is possible to calculate the other two because they are all related.

It is always important to bear in mind that even if a reaction is feasible it may be very slow.

feedstock is the raw material for a process in the *chemical industry*.

Fehling's solution is used to distinguish *aldehydes* from *ketones* and to identify *reducing sugars*. Aldehydes and reducing sugars give a positive result. Ketones and other sugars do not. The deep blue solution turns greenish and then loses its blue color as an orange-red precipitate of copper(I) oxide appears.

Fehling's reagent does not keep so it is made when required by mixing two solutions. One solution is copper(II) sulfate in water. The other solution is a solution of 2,3-dihydroxybutanedioate (tartrate) ions in strong alkali. The 2,3-dihydroxybutanedioate salt is included to form a complex with copper(II) ions so that they do not precipitate as copper(II) hydroxide with the alkali.

fermentation converts sugars to alcohol (ethanol) and carbon dioxide. Fermentation is an example of anaerobic *respiration*. Fermentation is catalyzed by a group of enzymes from yeast referred to as zymase. In brewing the aim is to produce alcohol in beer. In baking fermentation produces the gas bubbles that make the dough rise.

$$C_6H_{12}O_6(aq) \longrightarrow 2CO_2(g) + 2C_2H_5OH(aq)$$

glucose   carbon   ethanol
                     dioxide

ferrites are compounds such as the magnetic oxide of iron, Fe_3O_4, that can be used to make permanent magnets. They are ferromagnetic. Ferrites are *ceramics* so that they can be molded into complex shapes before being fired. They also have the great advantage that they do not conduct electricity.

ferromagnetism: the property of materials that can be used to make permanent magnets. The three ferromagnetic metals are iron, cobalt and nickel. Alnico is a magnetic alloy of these three metals.

fertilizers supply plants with the mineral salts they need for growth. Plants need three major nutrients: nitrogen, phosphorus and potassium, which must be available in the soil in a soluble form so that they can be taken up by roots.

Manure and compost are traditional fertilizers used in "organic farming." They release nutrients slowly as they rot down through the action of bacteria and fungi in the soil.

Intensive agriculture relies on fertilizers made from minerals and the air. "Straight fertilizers" contain one of the three elements nitrogen (N), phosphorus (P) or potassium (K). "Compound fertilizers" contain two or more of these elements.

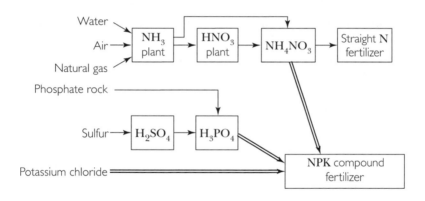

Flow diagram for manufacture of straight nitrogen and **NPK** *compound fertilizers*

Organic fertilizers, such as *urea*, have advantages over inorganic nitrates and ammonium salts. Organic fertilizers:

- release nitrogen more slowly by hydrolysis in the soil
- do not affect the pH of the soil to the same extent when spread on fields.

The use of manufactured fertilizers greatly increases crop yields. However, the use of large amounts of fertilizer increases the risk of nutrients leaching from the soil into rivers, lakes and groundwater. This can lead to *eutrophication.*

fiber reactive dyes are strongly bound to the fabrics they dye because they react with the molecules in the fibers, forming covalent bonds. They are fast *dyes* that do not fade during washing.

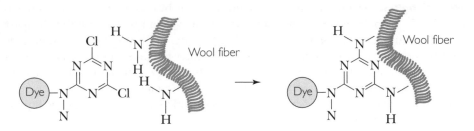

Structure of a fiber reactive dye that forms covalent bonds with amino groups in the protein molecules of wool

fibers are long thin threads that make up materials such as asbestos, wool and polyester fabrics. Most of the fibers used for textiles consist of natural or synthetic polymers. Wool, silk and hair are natural fibers made of *protein*. Cotton, linen and kapok are plant fibers made of the *carbohydrate* cellulose.

Semisynthetic fibers are made by modifying cellulose. Heating cellulose from wood with sodium hydroxide and then carbon disulfide produces a solution called "viscose." Forcing this solution through very small holes in a spinneret produces fine filaments. The filaments turn back into cellulose fibers as they flow though a tank of sulfuric acid. Cloth made from these fibers is known as rayon.

Treating cellulose from wood or cotton with ethanoic anhydride produces cellulose acetate. Cellulose acetate fibers are made by spinning a solution of the polymer in propanone. Fibers form as the solvent evaporates.

Examples of synthetic polymers used to make fibers are *polyester*, *polyamides* and the *addition polymer*, polypropylene. Synthetic polymers are spun into fibers by forcing the hot molten polymer through a spinneret. Fibers form as the liquid cools and solidifies.

Fibers of inorganic materials are increasingly important for making *composite* materials. Examples are the fibers of glass and graphite.

fillers are materials mixed with *plastics* or *rubbers* to modify their properties. Fillers can make plastics stronger, tougher, harder or easier to mold. Fillers are also used to cut costs by bulking out plastics with something cheaper.

filtration separates an insoluble solid from a liquid. The liquid that passes through the filter is the filtrate. The solid retained on the paper is the residue.

Filtering through a funnel with a filter paper folded into a cone can be very slow. For efficient filtration it is important that the paper is folded carefully and fitted accurately into the funnel. The paper is then wetted with water, or other solvent, before starting to filter. The funnel should never be filled to the top of the paper.

One way of filtering faster is to fold the circle of paper more times to produce a fluted filter paper so that the whole surface is available for filtration.

An even quicker method is to use a *Buchner flask and funnel*.

The use of a small plug of mineral wool or cotton wool in a small funnel cuts losses when filtering off a drying agent from an organic liquid before final distillation.

fire extinguishers put out fires by excluding air or by cooling to slow down burning. The choice of fire extinguisher depends on the type of fire. Water is the cheapest way to put out burning wood, paper or rubbish. Water cools the fire as it evaporates and produces steam, which helps to exclude air. Water is dangerous on electrical fires and useless on burning hydrocarbons or metals. Burning oils float on water and continues burning so water just spreads the fire. Burning metals react vigorously with water. Alternative fire extinguishers use carbon dioxide gas or nonflammable liquids such as halons and dry powders.

fireworks make *redox reactions* entertaining. The main active ingredient of any firework is gunpowder. Gunpowder is a mixture of two *fuels*, carbon and sulfur, with an *oxidant*, potassium nitrate. Gunpowder burns rapidly because the fuels are finely powdered and well mixed with the source of oxygen. Gunpowder explodes with a bang when confined because as the fuels burn they produce a large volume of the gases carbon dioxide and sulfur dioxide (see *explosions*). One cubic centimeter of gunpowder burns fast to make about 300 cm^3 of hot gas. The blue fuse that sets off fireworks is paper impregnated with potassium nitrate so that it will burn even when it is windy or damp.

The colors in fireworks come from tiny pellets of salts coated with gunpowder. The colors are the same as in *flame tests*: sodium for yellow, copper for blue-green and strontium for red.

first law of thermodynamics: see *thermodynmamics (laws of)*.

first-order reaction: a reaction is first order with respect to a reactant if the rate of reaction is proportional to the concentration of that reactant. The concentration term for this reactant is raised to the power one in the *rate equation*.

$$\text{Rate} = k\,[\mathbf{X}]^1 = k\,[\mathbf{X}].$$

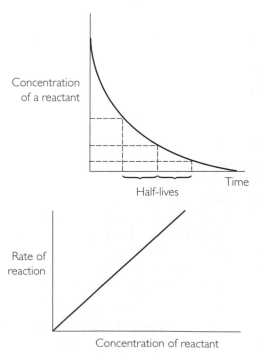

Variation of concentration of a reactant plotted against time for a first-order reaction: the gradient of this graph at any point measures the rate of reaction. The half-life for a first-order reaction is a constant so it is the same wherever it is read off the curve. It is independent of the initial concentration.

Concentration of a reactant

Half-lives — Time

Variation of reaction rate with concentration for a first-order reaction. The graph is a straight line through the origin showing that the rate is proportional to the concentration of the reactant.

Rate of reaction

Concentration of reactant

The rate of reaction of 2-bromo-2-dimethylpropane with hydroxide ions is first order with respect to the halogenoalkane but *zero order* with respect to hydroxide ions.

Rate $= k[(CH_3)_3CBr]$

fission means splitting. The word is used in two contexts in chemistry: bond breaking (*homolytic* and *heterolytic bond breaking*) and the splitting of atomic nuclei (nuclear fission).

flame tests help to detect some metal ions in salts. They are particularly useful in qualitative analysis to distinguish metal ions that otherwise behave in a similar way. Both magnesium and calcium ions, for example, are precipitated by sodium hydroxide to give white precipitates that are insoluble in excess of the alkali. Calcium compounds give an orange-red flame but magnesium compounds do not color a flame.

Metal ion	Color
lithium	bright red
sodium	bright yellow
potassium	pale mauve
calcium	orange-red
strontium	scarlet
barium	yellowish-green
copper(II)	blue-green

flammable substances are hazardous because they easily catch fire in air. Flammable substances are classified according to their degree of flammability:

- **flammable** – a liquid with a *flash point* equal to or below 55°C but above 21°C
- **extremely flammable** – a liquid with a flash point below 0°C and a boiling point less than or equal to 35°C.

Substances are labeled as **highly flammable** if they:

- may spontaneously catch fire in air
- are liquids with a flash point below 21°C but above 0°C
- are solids that may catch fire and keep burning after brief contact with a flame
- are gases that burn in air if ignited at normal pressure
- react to form flammable gases (such as hydrogen) in contact with water or water vapor.

flash point: the lowest temperature at which a small flame can ignite the *vapor* from a volatile liquid or solid.

float glass process: the industrial process for manufacturing large, uniform and smooth sheets of *glass*. Molten glass from a furnace at 1500°C pours onto a bath of molten tin where it stays liquid long enough for both surfaces to become flat and parallel. The glass cools and solidifies as it moves over the bath of tin. Once the glass is solid at about 600°C it can move onto rollers and gradually travel through an oven where it cools slowly to room temperature. This is *annealing*.

fluids are materials that flow. Liquids or gases are fluids because the atoms or molecules are not held in fixed positions but are free to move around.

fluorescent substances can absorb energy from ultraviolet (or other) radiation and immediately re-emit the energy as visible light. The inside surfaces of fluorescent lamps are coated with compounds such as magnesium tungstate and zinc silicate. These substances fluoresce when irradiated by the ultraviolet light from the mercury vapor in the lamp.

The optical brighteners in *detergents* are fluorescent. They absorb ultraviolet light from the Sun and re-emit the energy as blue light. This compensates for any yellowing of the fabric with age.

Fluorescence is an example of *luminescence.*

fluoridation involves adding traces of fluoride compounds to water supplies to prevent tooth decay. The benefits were discovered in areas where water supplies naturally contain fluoride ions. Adding fluoride ions to drinking water is controversial and opposed by people who think that any kind of enforced treatment is wrong. Others point to possible harmful effects because fluoride ions are *toxic* at higher concentrations.

fluorine (F) is a pale yellow gas made up of F_2 molecules. It is the most reactive of the halogens in *group 7* of the periodic table. Its *electron configuration* is [He] $3s^23p^5$.

Fluorine is the most electronegative of all elements (see *electronegativity*) so it forms ionic compounds with metals. Fluorine is the most powerful *oxidizing agent* and its oxidation state is −1 in all its compounds. It oxidizes other elements to their highest positive oxidation state. Sulfur, for example, forms SF_6.

Uses of fluorine include the manufacture of a wide range of compounds consisting of only carbon and fluorine (fluorocarbons). The most familiar of these is the very slippery, nonstick *addition polymer*, poly(tetrafluorethene), better known as Teflon.

Fluorocarbons are very *inert*, thermally stable and nonflammable. They are also non-toxic. They are electrical and thermal insulators. They are used during the manufacture and testing of electronic components, as refrigerants, coolants and lubricants. One fluorocarbon is a good solvent for oxygen and, in emergencies, can act as artificial blood.

fluorite structure: the cubic crystal structure of the ionic compound calcium

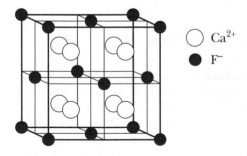

O Ca^{2+}

● F^-

Structure of calcium fluoride showing 8:4 coordination. The structure consists of a face-centered cubic array of positive ions with negative ions in the tetrahedral holes.

fluoride, CaF_2. Each positive ion is surrounded by eight nearest neighbors at the corners of a cube and each negative ion is surrounded by four positive ions. So the *coordination number*s are 8 for the positive ion and 4 for the negative ion.

Other compounds with this structure are the fluorides of Sr, Ba, Cd, Pb and Hg.

foams consist of gases finely dispersed in liquids or solids. Foams are *colloids*. The mass of bubbles in a liquid foam holds the liquid and gas in place. This is useful in foam fire extinguishers, which can blanket a fire with carbon dioxide held by the foam. It is also useful in shaving foam, which retains the liquid soap on the skin.

Solid foams can be rigid but have a low density. Expanded polystyrene and foamed polyurethanes are examples. These materials are excellent thermal insulators because they trap a large volume of gas and gases are very poor thermal conductors.

Foams improve the texture of food including bread, meringues and cakes. In bread the gas bubbles form by *fermentation*; in cakes they are produced by heating baking powder; and in meringues by whipping air into egg white before cooking.

food additives are natural or synthetic chemicals added to food, which can act as:
- colors to make food look more attractive
- preservatives to prevent the growth of microorganisms
- antioxidants to stop oxygen from the air making food unfit to eat – oxidation, for example, turns fats and oils rancid
- *emulsifiers* and stabilizers to control food texture
- sweeteners to improve the taste (see *sweetness*).

formula: used by chemists to represent the composition and structure of elements and compounds. (See *empirical formula, molecular formula, structural formula, skeletal formulas* and *displayed formula*.)

formula mass: see *formula unit*.

formula unit: the symbols used in equations and calculations to represent elements and compounds with *giant structures*. Examples are:
- sodium chloride, a giant structure of ions, formula unit NaCl
- silicon dioxide, a giant covalent structure, formula unit SiO_2.

The molar mass of a substance with a giant structure is the relative mass of its formula unit. For silicon dioxide (SiO_2) the molar mass = $[28 + (2 \times 16)]$ = 60 g mol^{-1}. This is sometimes called the formula mass.

fossil fuels are nonrenewable energy resources that we now burn to benefit from the Sun's energy, which was stored up millions of years ago by *photosynthesis*. The fossil fuels are coal, oil and natural gas.

fractional distillation is a method for separating mixtures of liquids with different boiling points. On a laboratory scale, the process takes place with a distillation apparatus fitted with a glass fractionating column fitted between the flask and the still-head. Separation is improved if the column is packed with inert glass beads or rings to increase the surface area where rising vapor can mix with condensed liquid running back to the flask. The column is hotter at the bottom and cooler at the top. The thermometer reads the boiling temperature of the compound passing over into the condenser.

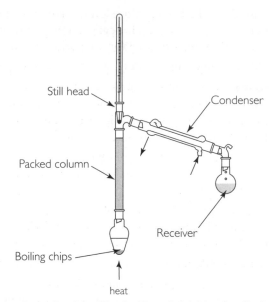

Apparatus for fractional distillation

Suppose the flask contains a mixture of two liquids. The boiling liquid in the flask produces a vapor that is richer in the more volatile of the liquids (the one with the lower boiling point).

Most of the vapor condenses in the column and runs back. As it does so it meets more of the rising vapor. Some of the vapor condenses. Some of the liquid evaporates. In this way the mixture repeatedly evaporates and condenses as it rises up the column. It is like carrying out a series of simple distillations. At each "stage" the vapor becomes richer in the more volatile component, thus improving separation.

fractional distillation of oil is a large-scale, *continuous process* for separating crude oil into fractions. A furnace heats the oil, which then flows into a fractionating tower containing about 40 "trays" pierced with small holes. Condensed vapor flows over the trays and runs down into the tray below. Rising vapor mixes with liquid on a tray as it bubbles up through the holes.

The column is hotter at the bottom and cooler at the top. Rising vapor condenses when it reaches the tray with liquid at a temperature below its boiling point. Condensing vapor releases energy, which heats the liquid in the tray and in turn evaporates the more volatile compounds in the mixture.

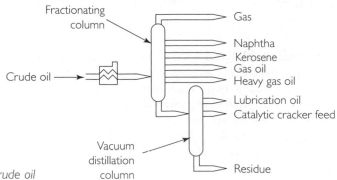

Fractional distillation of crude oil

With a series of trays the outcome is that the *hydrocarbons* with small molecules rise to the top of the column while larger molecules stay at the bottom. Fractions are drawn off from the column at various levels.

Some components of crude oil have boiling points too high for them to vaporize at atmospheric pressure. Lowering the pressure in a *vacuum distillation* column reduces the boiling points of the hydrocarbons and makes it possible to separate them.

fragmentation patterns: see *mass spectrometry*.

free energy change, ΔG: the thermochemical quantity used by chemists to decide whether a reaction tends to proceed and how far it will go. ΔG is the test for the *feasibility* of a reaction. If ΔG is negative, the reaction is feasible.

The advantage of ΔG values for chemists is that tables of standard free energies of formation can be used to calculate the standard free energy change for any reaction. The calculations follow exactly the same steps as the calculations to calculate standard *enthalpy changes of reactions* from standard *enthalpy changes of formation*.

The idea of *entropy* underlies the quantity "free energy." Any change tends to happen if the total entropy change is positive. Working with entropy values is generally less convenient because of the need to consider the entropy changes in the surroundings as well as in the reaction mixture. This was the reason why Willard Gibbs suggested the concept "free energy," which he defined by: $\Delta G = -T\Delta S_{total}$, where ΔS_{total} is the total entropy change:

$$\Delta S_{total} = \Delta S_{system} + \Delta S_{surroundings}$$

For a change at constant temperature and pressure:

$$\Delta S_{surroundings} = \frac{-\Delta H}{T}$$

and so: $\Delta S_{total} = \Delta S_{system} + \dfrac{-\Delta H}{T}$

Hence $-T\Delta S_{total} = -T\Delta S_{system} + \Delta H$

From Gibb's definition this becomes: $\Delta G = \Delta H - T\Delta S_{system}$

Often the $T\Delta S_{system}$ term is relatively small compared to the enthalpy change so that:

$$\Delta G \approx \Delta H$$

This is the reason that chemists often use ΔH values to decide whether or not a reaction will tend to proceed. The approximation becomes less justified at higher temperatures when T is bigger and so $T\Delta S_{system}$ is bigger.

free-radical chain reactions involve three stages:

- **initiation** – the step that produces free radicals
- **propagation** – steps giving products and more free radicals
- **termination** – steps that remove free radicals by turning them into molecules.

The reaction of an alkane with bromine in sunlight is a free-radical chain reaction. The main products are bromomethane and hydrogen bromide. The presence of some ethane in the mixture of products is evidence for the termination step.

Initiation: $Br \text{---} Br \longrightarrow Br\bullet + Br\bullet$

Propagation: $CH_4 + Br\bullet \longrightarrow CH_3\bullet + HBr$

$CH_3\bullet + Br_2 \longrightarrow CH_3Br + Br\bullet$

Termination: $CH_3\bullet + CH_3\bullet \longrightarrow CH_3CH_3$

$CH_3\bullet + Br\bullet \longrightarrow CH_3Br$

Free-radical chain reactions can also be used to make *addition polymers* from alkenes, and epoxy compounds.

free radicals are reactive particles with unpaired electrons. Free radicals form when covalent bonds break in a way that leaves one electron on each of the atoms joined by the bond. This is *homolytic bond breaking*. The symbol for a free radical generally shows the unpaired electron as a dot. Other paired electrons in the outer shells are generally not shown.

Formation of free radicals
$$Br\!:\!Br \longrightarrow Br\bullet + \bullet Br$$

Free radicals are *intermediates in reactions* taking place:

- in the gas phase at high temperature or in ultraviolet light
- in a nonpolar solvent, either when irradiated by ultraviolet light or with an initiator.

Examples of free-radical processes include the *cracking* of hydrocarbons, burning of *gasoline* in an engine cylinder and the formation and destruction of the *ozone* layer. (See also *free-radical chain reactions*.)

freezing point: the temperature at which a liquid turns to a solid. A pure liquid has a sharp freezing point, which is the same as its melting point. A *phase* diagram for the liquid shows how the freezing point varies with pressure.

Dissolving a solute in a liquid lowers its freezing point. Adding antifreeze to the water in an engine lowers the freezing point and so prevents the coolant freezing in winter. When there is a threat of ice, the highway authorities scatter salt on roads because a mixture of salt and water freezes at temperatures well below 0°C.

frequency of electromagnetic radiation: the number of complete waves passing any point per second. The SI unit of frequency, v, is the hertz (Hz). Frequencies of *electromagnetic radiation* vary from about 10^5 Hz for radio waves up to 10^{20} Hz for gamma rays.

All electromagnetic radiation travels at the same speed, c, in a vacuum. The frequency, *wavelength*, λ, and speed are related by: $c = v\lambda$.

Quantum theory shows that the higher the frequency, the higher the energy of the quanta (photons) of radiation.

Friedel–Crafts reaction: a method for forming $C \text{---} C$ bonds to build up a carbon skeleton by adding a side chain to *arenes* such as benzene. In a Friedel–Crafts reaction a *halogenoalkane* or an *acyl chloride* undergoes an *electrophilic substitution* reaction with an arene. The reaction takes place in the presence of a catalyst such as aluminum chloride (a *Lewis acid*).

One example is the substitution of a group with three carbon atoms to benzene using 2-chloropropane.

Friedel–Crafts reaction with a chloroalkane. Benzene reacting with 2-chloropropane

The reaction with an acyl chloride produces a *ketone.*

Friedel–Crafts reaction with an acyl chloride. Benzene reacting with ethanoyl chloride

This important type of reaction was discovered and developed jointly by the French organic chemist Charles Friedel (1832–1899) and the American, James Crafts (1839–1917). The reaction is used both on a laboratory and an industrial scale. A Friedel–Crafts reaction to make ethyl benzene is the first step in the production of the *addition polymer* poly(phenylethene), more often called polystyrene.

froth flotation is a process for separating valuable mineral from a rock made up of several minerals. The rock is finely crushed to separate the minerals and then stirred with a solution of *surfactants* as a stream of air bubbles rises up through the mixture. The surfactants are selected to make sure that the particles of metal *ore* are caught up by the bubbles and rise to the surface where they can be skimmed off. The unwanted minerals (or gangue) sink and flow away as a stream of waste.

fuel cell: an *electrochemical cell* that is continuously supplied with fuel and an oxidizing agent. A fuel cell produces electric power directly from a fuel without having to burn it and then use the energy to drive a turbine and spin a generator.

Hydrogen–oxygen fuel cells are used in the space shuttle. There are also fuel cell power plants operating on a much larger scale in some parts of the world, including Japan.

fuels burn in air or oxygen to release energy. Most power stations use *fossil fuels* to raise steam and generate electricity. Most of the fuels for transport are made from fractions produced by the *fractional distillation of crude oil.*

Gasoline is a blend of *hydrocarbons* based on the gasoline fraction (hydrocarbons with 5–10 carbon atoms). Jet fuel is produced from the kerosene fraction (hydrocarbons with 10–16 carbon atoms). Fuel for diesel engines is made from diesel oil (hydrocarbons with 13–25 carbon atoms).

Fuels have to be refined to remove components that would harm engines or cause air pollution when they burn. The proportion of *volatile* hydrocarbons added to gasoline is higher in winter to help cold starting but lower in summer to prevent vapor forming before the fuel gets to the carburetor. Oil refiners use *cracking, reforming* and *isomerization* to produce more of the branched hydrocarbons needed to make gasoline that will burn smoothly in engines. *Gasoline* additives include *alcohols* and *ethers* (such as MTBE), which raise the octane number and help to prevent *knocking*.

fullerenes are molecular *allotropes* of carbon. The best-known example is the "buckyball," *buckminsterfullerene*, C_{60}. Other fullerenes have formulas C_{28}, C_{32}, C_{50}, and C_{70}.

functional group: the atoms and bonding that give a series of organic compounds its characteristic properties and are responsible for most of the reactions. The hydrocarbon chain that makes up the rest of any organic molecule is generally inert to most common reagents such as acids and alkalis.

Examples of functional groups include the:

- two carbon atoms joined by a double bond in *alkenes*
- — Cl in chloroalkanes
- — OH in *alcohols*
- — NH_2 in *amines*
- — CO_2H in *carboxylic acids.*

fundamental particles are the particles that make up atoms. In chemistry the fundamental particles are protons, neutrons and electrons. Physicists with high-energy particle accelerators have shown that protons and neutrons are not fundamental but in turn made up of quarks.

fusion means either melting or joining. (See *enthalpy change of melting, melting* and *nuclear fusion.*)

G

gamma radiation (γ) is high-energy *electromagnetic radiation* given off during *radioactive decay*. The new nucleus formed when a radioactive atom emits an *alpha particle* or *beta particle* is often in an excited state; it gives off gamma rays as it loses energy. Emission of gamma rays does not cause a change in the structure of the nucleus.

The wavelengths of gamma rays are shorter than those of *X-rays*. Gamma radiation is *ionizing radiation* that is more penetrating than alpha or beta radiation and is stopped only by several centimeters of lead.

gas constant: the constant R in the *ideal gas* equation $PV = nRT$. The value of the constant depends on the units used for pressure and volume. If all quantities are in SI units with the pressure in N m^{-2} (pascals) and volume in cubic meters (m^3), then $R = 8.314\,\text{J K}^{-1}\,\text{mol}^{-1}$.

gas laws: the laws that describe the behavior of *ideal gases* and are summarized by the ideal gas equation. The gas laws include *Boyle's law*, *Charles's law* and *Avogadro's law*.

gas–liquid chromatography (glc) is a sensitive analytical technique for analyzing mixtures of liquids. In a modern gas–liquid apparatus, the stationary phase is a thin film of liquid adsorbed on the inside surface of a coiled capillary tube about 30 meters long inside an oven. A sample is injected into the hot column from a syringe. The mobile phase, which is a gas, carries the vapors through the column. The components in the mixture separate as they pass through the column. They are detected as they emerge and the signal from the detector is fed to a chart recorder.

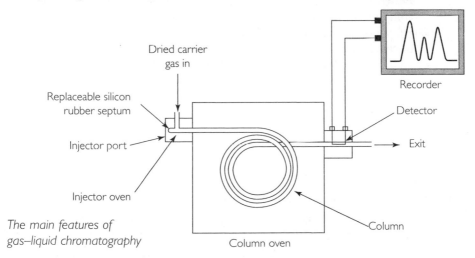

The main features of gas–liquid chromatography

The chart from the recorder shows how long it took each component of the mixture to pass through the column. This is the retention time. The areas under the peaks on the printout give a measure of the proportions of the components in a mixture.

A glc machine can be calibrated by injecting known amounts of compounds and recording their retention times.

Applications of glc include:

- tracking down the source of oil pollution from the pattern of peaks, which acts like a fingerprint for any batch of oil
- measuring the level of alcohol in urine or blood samples
- detecting and measuring pesticides in river water.

gasoline is the fuel for motor engines that consists mainly of a mixture of *hydrocarbons*. Gasoline has to be carefully blended if modern engines are to start reliably and run smoothly.

The starting point for making gasoline is the gasoline fraction from the *fractional distillation of oil*. Hydrocarbons in this fraction are mainly *alkanes* with 5 to 10 carbon atoms. Fractional distillation does not provide enough gasoline and produces more than enough of the heavier fractions, so oil refineries use *catalytic cracking* to make more hydrocarbons of the right size.

For smooth running the gasoline has to burn smoothly without *knocking*. The octane number of a fuel measures its performance. The higher the compression of fuel and air in the engine cylinders, the higher the octane number has to be to stop knocking.

The octane number scale was devised by Thomas Midgley (1889–1944) and he discovered antiknock additives based on lead, which were used for many years. Leaded fuel is now being phased out and the oil companies produce high-octane fuel by increasing the proportions of both branched alkanes and arenes plus blending in some oxygen compounds. The four main approaches are:

- *cracking*, which not only makes more small molecules but also forms hydrocarbons with branched chains
- *isomerization*, which turns straight-chain alkanes into branched-chain compounds by passing them over a platinum catalyst
- *reforming*, which turns cyclic alkanes into *arenes* such as benzene and methyl benzene
- **adding** *alcohols* **or** *ethers* such as MTBE (initials based on its older name methyl tertiary butyl ether; it is now called 2-methoxy-2-methylpropane).

Structure of the ether MTBE, which has an octane number of 120. Adding MTBE and other methods raise the octane number of gasoline from about 70 to 95 as required for unleaded premium gasoline.

$$CH_3 - \overset{\overset{\textstyle CH_3}{|}}{\underset{\underset{\textstyle CH_3}{|}}{C}} - O - CH_3$$

gas tests are used to identify gases produced during *qualitative analysis*.

Gas	Test	Observations
Hydrogen	Burning splint	Burns with a "pop"
Oxygen	Glowing splint	Splint bursts into flame (relights)
Carbon dioxide	Limewater (aqueous calcium hydroxide)	Turns milky white
Hydrogen chloride (hydrogen bromide	Smell Blue litmus	Pungent Turns red

and iodide react in the same way)	Ammonia vapor (from a drop of concentrated ammonia solution on a glass rod)	Thick white smoke
Chlorine	Color	Greenish-yellow
	Smell	Pungent – bleach-like
	Effect on moist blue litmus paper	Turns the paper red and then bleaches it
	Moist starch-iodide paper	Turns blue-black
Sulfur dioxide	Smell	Pungent
	Blue litmus	Turns red
	Acid dichromate(VI)	Turns green
Hydrogen sulfide	Smell	"Bad eggs"
	Burning splint	Gas burns – yellow deposit of sulfur
	Lead(II) ethanoate	Turns brown-black
Ammonia	Smell	Pungent
	Red litmus	Turns blue
Nitrogen dioxide	Color	Orange-brown
	Blue litmus	Turns red
Water vapor	Appearance	"Steams" in air
	Anhydrous cobalt(II) chloride paper	Turns from blue to pink

gas volume calculations use the gas laws and equations to calculate the volumes of gases involved in reactions. Gas volume calculations are straightforward when the reactants and products are all gases. Equal volumes of gases contain equal amounts in moles when measured under the same conditions – this is *Avogadro's law*. As a result the ratio of the gas volumes in a reaction must be the same as the ratio of the numbers of moles in the equation (see *Gay-Lussac's law of combining volumes*).

Worked example:

What volume of oxygen reacts with 60 cm³ methane and what volume of carbon dioxide forms if all gas volumes are measured under the same conditions?

Notes on the method
Write the balanced equation.

Note that below 100°C the water formed condenses to an insignificant volume of liquid.

Answer
The equation for the reaction is:

$$CH_4(g) + 2O_2(g) \longrightarrow CO_2(g) + 2H_2O(l)$$

1 mol   2 mol   1 mol

So 60 cm³ methane reacts with 120 cm³ oxygen to form 60 cm³ carbon dioxide.

The other approach to gas volume calculations is based on the fact that the volume of a gas, under given conditions, depends only on the amount of gas in moles. It does not matter which gas is involved so long as the gas is behaving (at least approximately) like an *ideal gas*.

volume of gas/cm^3 = amount of gas/mol × molar volume/cm^3 mol^{-1}

The molar volume for gases at *stp* (273 K and 101.3 kPa) is 22 400 cm^3.

For making estimates under laboratory conditions the molar volume of a gas is 24 000 cm^3 at room temperature and pressure. So under laboratory conditions the volume of gas formed in a reaction can be estimated from this relationship:

volume of gas/cm^3 = amount of gas/mol × 24 000 cm^3 mol^{-1}

Worked example:

What volume of hydrogen is produced under laboratory conditions when 1.95 g zinc reacts with excess acid?

Notes on the method

Start by writing the equation for the reaction. Convert the quantity of zinc to an *amount* in moles.

Answer

The equation for the reaction is:

$Zn(s) + 2HCl(aq) \longrightarrow ZnCl_2(aq) + H_2(g)$

The amount of zinc = 1.95 g ÷ 65 g mol^{-1} = 0.03 mol

1 mol zinc produces 1 mol hydrogen.

volume of hydrogen = 0.03 mol × 24 000 cm^3 mol^{-1} = 720 cm^3

Gay-Lussac's law of combining volumes states that when gases are involved in reactions, the ratios of the volumes of gases are simple whole numbers so long as all measurements are taken at the same temperature and pressure. For example, 50 cm^3 hydrogen react with 50 cm^3 chlorine to form 100 cm^3 of hydrogen chloride. The ratios are 1:1:2. The law is named after the French chemist Joseph Gay-Lussac (1778–1850).

Avogadro's law accounts for Gay-Lussac's observations. If equal volumes of gases contain equal numbers of molecules, under the same conditions, it follows that the ratios of the volumes are also the ratios of the number of molecules as the equation shows.

$H_2(g) + Cl_2(g) \longrightarrow 2HCl(g)$

gel: a *colloid* in which a liquid is finely dispersed in a solid. Table jelly is a typical gel with water loosely held in a network of large gelatine molecules. Warming or even shaking can break up the solid network so that the gel liquefies.

geometrical isomerism: molecules with the same molecular and structural formulas but different shapes (geometries). *Alkenes* and other compounds with C = C *double bonds* may have geometrical isomers because there is no rotation about the double bond. The isomers are labeled *cis* and *trans*. In the *cis* isomer, similar functional groups are on the same side of the double bond. In the *trans* isomer, similar functional groups are on opposite sides of the double bond.

Some inorganic *complexes* also have geometrical isomers.

Geometric isomers of but-2-ene. They are distinct compounds with different melting points, boiling points and densities.

cis-but-2-ene   trans-but-2-ene

The anticancer drug *cisplatin* is the *cis* isomer of a flat (planar) complex.

Cis and trans isomers of the octahedral complex $[Co(NH_3)_4Cl_2]^+$. The cis form is blue-violet. The trans form is green.

cis isomer   trans isomer

germanium (Ge) is an element with some metallic and some nonmetallic features. It is a metalloid: shiny like a metal but hard and brittle like a nonmetal. It is the element below silicon but above tin in *group 4* of the periodic table with the *electron configuration* $[Ar]3d^{10}4s^24p^2$. Germanium is a *semiconductor*.

giant structures: crystal structures in which all the atoms or ions are strongly linked by a network of bonds extending throughout the crystal. Substances with giant structures generally have high melting and boiling points.

All *metals* consist of giant structures of atoms held together by *metallic bonding*. Metal giant structures are good conductors of electricity because of the delocalized bonding electrons (see *delocalized electrons*). The layers of atoms in a metal can slide over each other so that metals are *malleable* and *ductile*.

Ionic compounds have giant structures held together by *ionic bonding*. Ionic compounds do not conduct electricity when solid but they do conduct when the ions are free to move on melting the compound or dissolving it in water.

A few *nonmetal* elements consist of giant structures of atoms held together by *covalent bonding*. Examples are carbon (as graphite or diamond) and silicon. Typically these elements do not conduct electricity because the electrons in covalent bonds are localized between pairs of atoms. Graphite is the exception with electrons delocalized over the layers of carbon atoms.

Some compounds of nonmetals with nonmetals, such as silicon dioxide and boron nitride, have giant structures with covalent bonding. These compounds are nonconductors because each bonding pair of electrons is localized between two atoms.

Many silicates are based on networks of silicon and oxygen atoms as in the *clay minerals*. Chains, sheets and three-dimensional arrays of silicate ions combined with metal ions give rise to many different minerals.

Gibbs free energy: see *free energy change*. The concept is named after the US physical chemist, Josiah Gibbs (1839–1903). Hence the symbol ΔG.

glass electrode: an electrode used in combination with a *reference electrode* to make a pH probe for a pH meter. A glass electrode has a thin walled bulb made of special glass that responds to changes in pH. A salt bridge connects the glass electrode to a reference electrode to make a complete electrochemical cell.

glasses are *ceramic* materials that are rigid like solids but which are not crystalline. Glass is made by melting one or more oxides in a furnace. The liquid glass is cooled until thick enough to mold and then shaped and cooled further until it sets solid.

It is possible to make glass from pure silicon dioxide (SiO_2) but it melts at 1700°C. Molten silicon dioxide is a thick, sticky liquid (*viscous*). As the liquid cools back to its melting point, the atoms cannot move freely enough to return to the ordered arrangement of crystalline silica. They become "frozen" into a disordered state.

Most glass is made from silica mixed with other oxides that melt at a lower temperature than pure silica. Windows, bottles and drinking glasses are made of soda lime glass. Lead glass is used for decorative cut glassware. *Borosilicate glass* is used to make ovenware and laboratory glassware.

Graham's law of diffusion says that the rate of *diffusion* of a gas is inversely proportional to the square root of its *molar mass* at constant temperature and pressure.

$$\text{rate of diffusion} \propto \frac{1}{\sqrt{M_r}}$$

This means that a gas with low molar mass such as hydrogen ($M_r = 2$) diffuses faster than a gas with a bigger molar mass such as oxygen ($M_r = 32$). According to Graham's law, hydrogen molecules diffuse four times faster than oxygen molecules. A balloon filled with hydrogen, H_2, deflates much more rapidly than a balloon filled with oxygen, O_2.

The *kinetic theory of gases* can account for Graham's law. The rate of diffusion of a gas depends on the average speed, c, of its molecules. According to the kinetic theory model the average kinetic energy ($\frac{1}{2}mc^2$) of the molecules (mass m) is the same for any gas at a particular temperature. So the value of c^2 is smaller for a gas with bigger m. Hence:

$$c \propto \frac{1}{\sqrt{M_r}}$$

graphical formulas: an alternative name for *displayed formulas*.

graphite is one of the *allotropes* of carbon, consisting of a giant structure of atoms. Carbon has by far the highest melting point (over 3800 K) of any element. Graphite has an almost ideal combination of physical properties for use as a high-temperature *ceramic* except that it has to be used in a nonoxidizing environment. Graphite bonded with clay is used to make crucibles for melting metals. Large blocks of graphite are used as *refractories* to line furnaces.

gravimetric analysis is a method of *quantitative analysis* for finding the composition and formulas of compounds based on accurate weighing of reactants and products. A familiar example is to find the formula of magnesium oxide by weighing a piece of magnesium in a crucible and then weighing the magnesium oxide produced after strong heating in air. Chemists have developed sophisticated and precise methods of gravimetric analysis, which include *combustion analysis* to find the formulas of organic compounds.

greenhouse effect: the effect of some gases in the air that keeps the surface of the Earth about 30°C warmer than it would be if there were no *atmosphere*. Without the greenhouse effect there would be no life on Earth.

When radiation from the Sun reaches the Earth's atmosphere about 30% is reflected into space, 20% is absorbed by gases in the air and about half reaches the surface of the Earth.

The warm surface radiates energy back into space but at longer, infrared wavelengths. Some of the infrared radiation is absorbed and warms up the atmosphere. This is the greenhouse effect.

The gases in the air that absorb infrared radiation are called greenhouse gases. Nitrogen and oxygen make up most of the air but they are not greenhouse gases. The main natural greenhouse gases are carbon dioxide, methane, dinitrogen oxide and water vapor.

The concentrations of greenhouse gases in the air are rising because of human activity such as burning *fossil fuels* and agriculture. This is enhancing the greenhouse effect. There is growing evidence that this is responsible for global warming.

Grignard reagents are reactive organic compounds containing magnesium atoms that are used to form C—C bonds in organic synthesis. They are examples of *organometallic compounds*. The reagents were discovered by the French organic chemist Victor Grignard (1871–1935).

Grignard showed that halogenoalkanes react with magnesium in dry ether (ethoxyethane).

$$RBr + Mg \longrightarrow RMgBr, \quad \text{where R represents an alkyl group.}$$

The C—Mg bond in a Grignard reagent is polarized with the metal atom at the positive end of the dipole and the carbon atom at the negative end. As a result, the carbon atom attached to magnesium is nucleophilic and C—C bonds form when Grignard reagents take part in nucleophilic substitution or addition reactions. This is what makes the reagents so useful in synthesis.

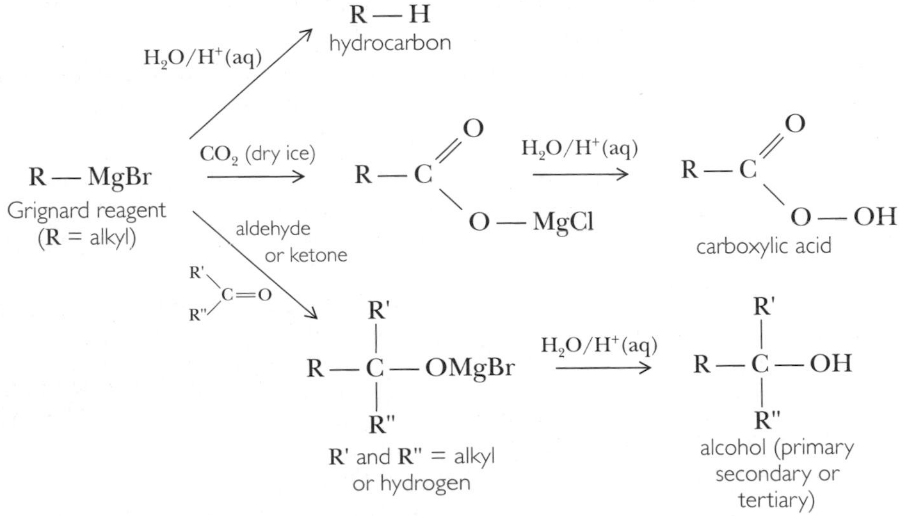

Summary of the reactions of Grignard reagents

ground state: the stable state of an atom or molecule with the electrons in the lowest available energy levels.

group: a vertical column of elements in the *periodic table*. Elements in the same group have similar chemical properties because they have the same outer *electron configuration*.

There are trends in properties down a group as the number of full inner electron shells increases and the atoms get larger. Generally the metallic characteristics of elements increase down a group. In *group 1* and *group 2* the metals get more reactive down the group.

Nonmetal characteristics decrease down a group. Down *group 7* the halogens get less reactive. *Group 4* shows a trend from nonmetals at the top to metals at the bottom with germanium, a *metalloid*, in the middle.

IUPAC now recommends that the groups should be numbered from 1 to 18. Groups 1 and 2 are the same as before. Groups 3 to 12 are the vertical families of *d-block elements*; the groups traditionally numbered 3 to 8 then become groups 13 to 18.

group 1 elements belong to the family of *alkali metals* with similar chemical properties because they all have one electron in an outer *s*-orbital (see *atomic orbitals*). These elements are more similar to each other than the elements in any other group. Even so, because of the increasing number of full, inner shells, there are trends in properties down the group from lithium to cesium. The element in period 7, francium, is very rare and all its isotopes are radioactive.

lithium, Li	$[He]2s^1$
sodium, Na	$[Ne]3s^1$
potassium, K	$[Ar]4s^1$
rubidium, Rb	$[Kr]5s^1$
cesium, Cs	$[Xe]6s^1$

The metals are powerful *reducing agents*. They react by losing the outer s electron to form M^+ ions. The first ionization energies decrease down the group as the increasing number of full shells means that the outer electron gets further away from the same effective nuclear charge (see *shielding*).

Atomic and ionic radii increase down the group. For each element the 1+ ion is smaller than the atom because of the loss of the outer shell of electrons. The tendency to react and form ions increases down the group.

The small size of the lithium ion means that it has a relatively high polarizing power and is heavily hydrated in solution. As a result lithium is in some ways not typical of the group as a whole. It resembles magnesium in some ways. This is an example of the *diagonal relationship*.

The metals are soft and easily cut with a knife. They are shiny when freshly cut but quickly dull in air as they react with moisture and oxygen. The metals are stored under oil.

All the metals burn brightly in oxygen on heating to form ionic oxides. Lithium forms a simple oxide, Li_2O. Sodium forms mainly the *peroxide*, Na_2O_2. The oxides are basic. They react with acids forming salts.

$$Li_2O(s) + 2HCl(aq) \longrightarrow 2LiCl(aq) + H_2O(l)$$

All the metals react with water to form hydroxides and hydrogen. The rate and violence of the reaction increases down the group. Lithium reacts steadily with cold water. Cesium reacts explosively.

All the metals react vigorously with chlorine to form colorless, ionic chlorides, M^+Cl^-, which are soluble in water. The crystal structures depend on the size of the metal ion (see *cesium chloride structure* and *sodium chloride structure*).

The hydroxides are:

- similar in that they all have the formula MOH, and are soluble in water, forming alkaline solutions (they are *strong bases*)
- different in that their solubility increases down the group.

The carbonates are similar in that they all have the formula M_2CO_3, and, with the exception of lithium, do not decompose on heating. The carbonates of sodium and potassium are soluble, forming alkaline solutions because the carbonate ion is a *base*.

The nitrates are:

- similar in that they all have the formula MNO_3, are colorless crystalline solids, are very soluble in water and decompose on heating
- different in that they become more difficult to decompose down the group. Lithium nitrate, like magnesium nitrate, decomposes on heating to the oxide, nitrogen dioxide and oxygen. The nitrates of sodium and potassium need strong heating to decompose and they form the nitrite:

$$2KNO_3(s) \longrightarrow 2KNO_2(s) + O_2(g)$$

group 2 elements belong to the family of *alkaline earth metals* with similar chemical properties because they all have two electrons in an outer *s*-orbital (see *atomic orbitals*).

beryllium, Be	$[He]2s^2$
magnesium, Mg	$[Ne]3s^2$
calcium, Ca	$[Ar]4s^2$
strontium, Sr	$[Kr]5s^2$
barium, Ba	$[Xe]6s^2$

The first member of the group, beryllium, is not a typical member of group 2. Because of the small size of the Be^{2+} ion, its chemistry is in many ways more like the chemistry of aluminum than of magnesium. This is an example of the *diagonal relationship*.

The following similarities and differences refer to the elements Mg, Ca, Sr and Ba. The symbol M is here used to represent any one of these elements.

The metals are *reducing agents* that react by losing their two *s* electrons to form M^{2+} ions. The first and second ionization energies decrease down the group as the increasing number of full shells means that the outer electrons get further away from the same effective nuclear charge (see *shielding*).

Atomic and ionic radii increase down the group. For each element the 2+ ion is smaller than the atom because of the loss of the outer shell of electrons. The tendency to react and form ions increases down the group.

The metals are harder and denser than group 1 metals and have higher melting points. In air the surface of the metals is covered with a layer of oxide.

All the metals burn brightly in oxygen on heating to form a white, ionic oxide, $M^{2+}O^{2-}$. The oxides are basic. They react with acids forming salts.

$$BaO(s) + 2HNO_3(aq) \longrightarrow Ba(NO_3)_2(aq) + H_2O(l)$$

All the metals react with water to form hydroxides and with hydrogen or acids to form salts and hydrogen. Magnesium reacts only slowly with hot water. Barium reacts quite fast even with cold water. Barium is so reactive with air and moisture that it is generally stored under oil like the alkali metals.

All the metals react vigorously with chlorine to form colorless, ionic chlorides, MCl_2. Unlike the group 1 chlorides, the chlorides of this group are usually hydrated. They are soluble in water.

The hydroxides are:
- similar in that they all have the formula $M(OH)_2$ and are to some degree soluble in water, forming alkaline solutions
- different in that their solubility increases down the group.

The carbonates are:
- similar in that they all have the formula MCO_3, are insoluble in water and decompose on heating, e.g.:
  $$CaCO_3(s) \longrightarrow CaO(s) + CO_2(g)$$
- different in that they become more difficult to decompose down the group (they become more thermally stable).

The nitrates are:
- similar in that they all have the formula $M(NO_3)_2$, are colorless crystalline solids, are very soluble in water and decompose to the oxide on heating:
  $$2Mg(NO_3)_2 \longrightarrow 2MgO(s) + 4NO_2(g) + O_2(g)$$
- different in that they become more difficult to decompose down the group.

The sulfates are:
- similar in that they are all colorless solids with the formula MSO_4
- different in that they become less soluble down the group.

group 4: a group of elements that shows a trend from *nonmetals* at the top to *metals* at the bottom. All these elements have four electrons in their outer shell. The characteristic oxidation states of the group are +4 and +2. The +2 state becomes more important down the group and is the more stable state of lead. This is an example of the *inert pair effect.*

carbon, C	$[He]2s^22p^2$
silicon, Si	$[Ne]3s^23p^2$
germanium, Ge	$[Ar]3d^{10}4s^23p^2$
tin, Sn	$[Kr]4d^{10}5s^23p^2$
lead, Pb	$[Xe]4d^{14}6s^23p^2$

The two common *allotropes* of carbon (diamond and graphite) consist of covalent giant structures. Silicon and germanium have diamond-like giant structures and are *semiconductors*.

The room-temperature allotrope of tin has a metallic structure. The low-temperature allotrope, gray tin, has the nonmetallic diamond structure. Lead has a metallic structure.

The two metals, tin and lead, have lower melting points than the nonmetals with giant structures.

The group 4 compounds in the +4 state generally behave more like the compounds of nonmetals:
- the +4 oxides (CO_2, SiO_2, SnO_2 and PbO_2) are acidic or, in the case of tin and lead, amphoteric with a bias toward *acidic oxide* behavior

- the +4 chlorides are molecular liquids that (with the exception of CCl_4) are rapidly hydrolyzed by water.

The compounds of tin and lead in the +2 state are more typical of metallic compounds:

- the +2 oxides (SnO and PbO) are *amphoteric* but with a bias toward *basic oxide* properties
- the +2 chlorides are white solids: $PbCl_2$ is an ionic solid.

The +4 state is more stable for tin, so that tin(II) compounds are reducing agents. Tin(II) chloride reduces iron(III) to iron(II), for example.

The +2 state is the more stable state for lead. So PbO_2 is a strong oxidizing agent. Lead(IV) oxide will oxidize chloride ions to chlorine gas.

group 7 elements belong to the family of *halogens* with similar chemical properties because they all have seven electrons in the outer shell – one less than the next noble gas in group 8. The element *astatine* in group 7 is very rare and highly radioactive. The halogens are all toxic.

fluorine, F $[He]2s^22p^5$

chlorine, Cl $[Ne]3s^23p^5$

bromine, Br $[Ar]3d^{10}4s^24p^5$

iodine, I $[Kr]4d^{10}5s^25p^5$

The symbol X is often used to represent a halogen.

The halogens all consist of diatomic molecules, X_2, linked by a single *covalent bond* and all are volatile. Intermolecular forces increase down the group as the numbers of electrons in the atoms increase, so melting points and boiling points rise down the group. Iodine atoms are the most polarizable. Fluorine and chlorine are gases at room temperature, bromine is a liquid and iodine a solid.

Halogen atoms are highly electronegative. They form ionic compounds or compounds with *polar covalent bonds. Electronegativity* decreases down the group. Bonding in aluminum fluoride is ionic, but anhydrous aluminum chloride is a covalent solid.

The halogens are powerful *oxidizing agents.* Fluorine is the strongest oxidizing agent and iodine the weakest in the group.

Hot iron burns in chlorine forming iron(III) chloride. The metal reacts much less vigorously with iodine forming iron(II) iodide. (See also *halide ions* and *hydrogen halides.*)

group 8 is a family of colorless, unreactive elements called the noble gases. The gases exist as single atoms. The *dispersion forces* between the atoms are very weak so at room temperature they behave very much like *ideal gases.* They have very low melting and boiling points. The strength of the forces between the atoms increases as the number of electron shells increases. The larger atoms are more *polarizable,* so melting points and boiling points rise down the group.

First ionization energies fall down the group as the outer electrons get further away from the nucleus. The ionization energies of the elements near the bottom of the group are low enough for them to be able to take part in chemical reactions and form compounds.

Helium, neon and *argon* do not form compounds with other elements. *Krypton* combines with fluorine. *Xenon* forms compounds with fluorine and oxygen.

Haber process: the process for *ammonia manufacture* developed by the German physical chemist Fritz Haber (1868–1934).

half-cell: an electrode dipping into a solution of ions. Two half-cells connected by a salt bridge make up an *electrochemical cell.*

half-equation: an *ionic equation* used to describe either the gain or the loss of electrons during a redox process. Half-equations help to show what is happening during a *redox reaction.* Two half-equations combine to give an overall balanced equation for a redox reaction.

Iron (III) ions can oxidize iodide ions to iodine. This can be shown as two half-equations:

electron gain (reduction): $Fe^{3+}(aq) + e^- \longrightarrow Fe^{2+}(aq)$

electron loss (oxidation): $2I^-(aq) \longrightarrow I_2(s) + 2e^-$

The number of electrons gained must equal the number lost. So the first half-equation must be doubled to arrive at the overall balanced equation:

$$2Fe^{3+}(aq) + 2e^- \longrightarrow 2Fe^{2+}(aq)$$
$$\underline{2I^-(aq) \longrightarrow I_2(s) + 2e^-}$$
$$2Fe^{3+}(aq) + 2I^-(aq) \longrightarrow 2Fe^{2+}(aq) + I_2(s)$$

half-life (chemical): the half-life of a chemical reaction is the time for the concentration of one of the reactants to fall by half. Half-lives help to identify first-order reactions. At a constant temperature, the half-life of a *first-order reaction* is the same wherever it is measured on a concentration/time graph. So the half-life is independent of the initial concentration.

half-life (radioactive): the time for half the atoms in a sample of a radioactive *isotope* to decay away. It is also the time for the count rate for alpha or beta particles from a sample to fall by half. Half-lives for radioactive isotopes can be as short as a fraction of a second or as long as millions of years. The half-lives of radioactive isotopes are unaffected by changes in temperature or pressure or the presence of catalysts. The half-life remains the same whether the atoms are in the elemental state or in one of its compounds.

halide ions are the ions of the halogen elements. They include the fluoride (F^-), chloride (Cl^-), bromide (Br^-) and iodide (I^-) ions.

Warming sodium chloride with concentrated sulfuric acid produces clouds of hydrogen chloride gas. This *acid–base reaction* can be used to make hydrogen chloride.

$$NaCl(s) + H_2SO_4(l) \longrightarrow HCl(g) + NaHSO_4(s)$$

Both sulfuric acid and hydrogen chloride are strong acids. The reaction goes from left to right because the hydrogen chloride is a gas and escapes from the reaction mixture, so the reverse reaction cannot happen.

This type of reaction cannot be used to make hydrogen bromide or hydrogen iodide, because bromide and iodide ions are strong enough reducing agents to reduce sulfur from the +6 state to lower *oxidation states.*

The reactions of halide ions with sulfuric acid show that there is a trend in the strength of the halide ions as *reducing agents*:

- chloride ions do not reduce sulfuric acid at all, so the only gaseous product is hydrogen chloride gas
- bromide ions turn to orange bromine molecules as they reduce H_2SO_4 to SO_2 (mixed with some hydrogen bromide gas)
- iodide ions are the strongest reducing agents; they turn into iodine molecules as they reduce H_2SO_4 to S and H_2S; scarcely any hydrogen iodide forms.

So the trend as reducing agents is: $I^- > Br^- > Cl^-$. In *group 7*, iodine is the weakest oxidizing agent so it has the least tendency to form negative ions. Conversely, iodide ions are the ones that most readily give up electrons and turn back into iodine molecules.

halogenation: see *chlorination, bromination* and *iodination.*

halogenoalkanes (or haloalkanes) are compounds formed by replacing one or more of the hydrogen atoms in *alkanes* with halogen atoms.

1-iodobutane
(primary)

2-bromobutane
(secondary)

2-chloro-2-methylpropane
(tertiary)

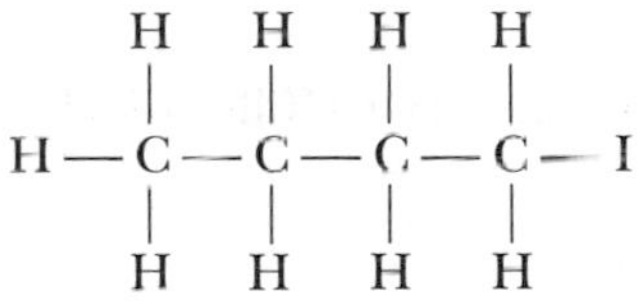

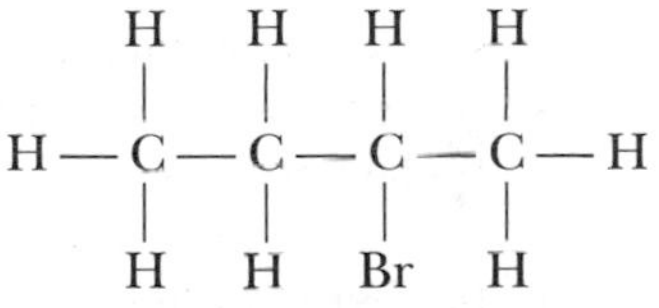

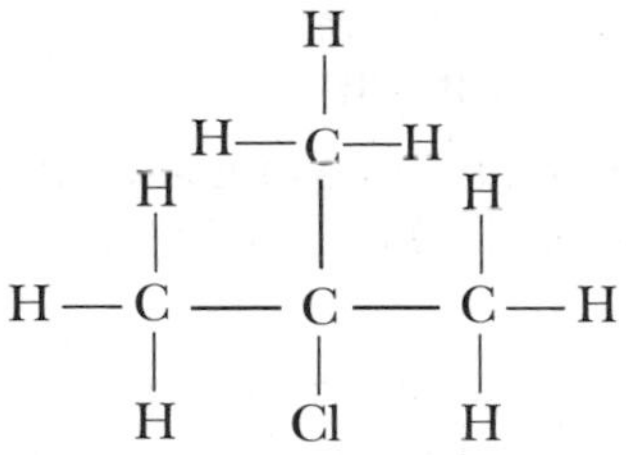

Names and structures of some halogenoalkanes. A primary halogenoalkane has the halogen atom at the end of the chain. A secondary compound has the halogen atom somewhere along the chain but not at the ends. A tertiary halogenoalkane has the halogen atom at a branch in the chain.

Chloromethane, bromomethane and chloroethane are gases at room temperature. Most other halogenoalkanes are colorless liquids that do not mix with water.

Halogen atoms are more electronegative than carbon atoms so a carbon—halogen bond is polar. The characteristic reactions of haloalkanes are *nucleophilic substitution* reactions.

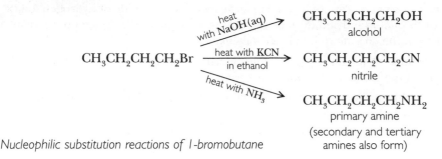

$$CH_3CH_2CH_2CH_2Br \xrightarrow{\substack{\text{heat} \\ \text{with NaOH (aq)}}} CH_3CH_2CH_2CH_2OH$$
alcohol

$$\xrightarrow{\substack{\text{heat with KCN} \\ \text{in ethanol}}} CH_3CH_2CH_2CH_2CN$$
nitrile

$$\xrightarrow{\text{heat with NH}_3} CH_3CH_2CH_2CH_2NH_2$$
primary amine
(secondary and tertiary amines also form)

Nucleophilic substitution reactions of 1-bromobutane

The rates of reaction of halogenoalkanes are in the order: RI > RBr > RCl, where R represents an alkyl group.

The C—I bond is the longest and the weakest (as measured by the mean *bond energy*). The C—Cl bond is the shortest and the strongest. Bond polarity does not appear to be a factor in determining the rates because chlorine is the most electronegative of the elements so the C—Cl bond is the most polar.

An *elimination reaction* happens on warming a halogenoalkane with a solution of potassium hydroxide in ethanol. The reaction goes more readily in compounds with a halogen atom at a branch in the carbon chain.

Halogenoalkanes are important intermediates in the manufacture of other chemicals. They are also used as:

- solvents (e.g. dichloromethane)
- refrigerants (e.g. hydrochlorofluorocarbons, such as $CHClF_2$, which are replacing *CFCs*)
- pesticides (e.g. bromomethane)
- fire extinguishers (e.g. CBr_2ClF).

There are growing restrictions on the uses of many halogenoalkanes because of concern about their hazards to health, their persistence in the environment and their effect on the *ozone* layer.

halogenoarenes are compounds formed by replacing one or more of the hydrogen atoms in an *arenes* with halogen atoms. An example is chlorobenzene, which is a colorless liquid at room temperature.

Structure of chlorobenzene

halogens is the family name of the *group 7* elements. The halogens are *fluorine, chlorine, bromine, iodine* and *astatine*. The name halogen means "salt-former" and is based on the fact that the elements combine with most metals to form salts (*halides*).

hardness is a property of materials that shows how easy they are to dent or scratch (see *Mohs scale*). The term is also used in the expression *hard water*.

hard water does not easily lather with *soap* but instead forms a greasy scum. Water is hard if it contains calcium or magnesium ions. Scum is a *precipitate* formed when soap mixes with water containing these ions.

$$Ca^{2+}(aq) + C_{17}H_{35}CO_2^-(aq) \longrightarrow Ca(C_{17}H_{35}CO_2)_2(s)$$

octadecanoate (stearate) ions in soap   insoluble precipitate (scum)

Water is temporarily hard if it contains the hydrogencarbonates of calcium or magnesium. This type of hardness is removed by boiling. Boiling reverses the reaction that produced the hard water as rain containing carbon dioxide trickled through limestone, chalk or dolomite.

$$Ca(HCO_3)_2(aq) \underset{\text{formation of hard water}}{\overset{\text{boiling}}{\rightleftharpoons}} CaCO_3(s) + H_2O(l) + CO_2(g)$$

The solid calcium carbonate precipitates as scale, which coats heating elements and gradually blocks the pipes in heating systems.

Permanent hardness is not removed by boiling. The mineral gypsum, $CaSO_4$, is slightly soluble in water and makes water permanently hard.

Ion exchange resin and other methods of *water treatment* soften water by removing calcium and magnesium ions.

heat exchangers are widely used in the chemical industry to transfer energy from a hot liquid or gas to a cooler liquid or gas.

A laboratory water condenser is a simple example of a heat exchanger. The water flowing in the jacket round the inner tube cools the hot vapor from a *distillation* column. The water flows in the opposite direction to the vapor.

An industrial heat exchanger is normally made of steel rather than glass and has many tubes carrying the hotter fluid through the surrounding container of cooler fluid.

Heat exchangers are important to the economics of industry. In *sulfuric acid manufacture* by the contact process the reaction of sulfur dioxide with oxygen to make sulfur trioxide is a highly *exothermic reaction*. The gases must be cooled after each pass through the *catalyst* to maximize the yield. Instead of letting the energy go to waste, the hot gases are cooled in heat exchangers in which water turns to steam. The steam is then used to generate electricity. Typically a sulfuric acid plant has no fuel bills because it can generate all the electricity it needs. This helps to make the process commercially viable.

heavy metals are metals such as cadmium, mercury and lead that have relatively high relative atomic masses. The term does not have a precise chemical meaning but is used in descriptions of pollution caused by toxic heavy metal ions.

heavy water is the common name for deuterium oxide, D_2O. This is water in which both the atoms linked to oxygen are the *deuterium* isotope of hydrogen.

helium (He) is the first member of the group of noble gases, *group 8*. Helium is the second most common element in the universe after hydrogen. The energy of stars such as the Sun comes from *nuclear fusion*, which turns hydrogen nuclei into helium nuclei. Helium was detected on the Sun by *spectroscopy* during a total eclipse in 1868 more than 20 years before it was isolated and identified on Earth.

On Earth one of the main sources of helium is *natural gas.* Some natural gas wells produce up to 7% helium. The gas boils at 4.2 K and is the coldest liquid available to study the properties of materials at low temperatures.

Helium is used to provide an inert atmosphere for welding and for growing crystals of pure *semiconductors* such as germanium and silicon.

Divers breathe a mixture of helium with oxygen. Helium is less soluble in blood than nitrogen and so this mixture reduces the risk of divers suffering from the "bends" (decompression sickness) when they come to the surface.

Helium is less dense than air under the same conditions of temperature and pressure. It is a much safer gas than hydrogen for filling airships and weather balloons.

Henderson–Hasselbalch equation: an equation that helps chemists to explain the behavior of *buffer solutions* and indicators. The equation is derived by rearranging the expression for the *acid dissociation constant* K_a of a weak acid and then putting both sides of the equation into logarithmic form. The advantage of taking logs is to produce an equation that can be easily used to calculate *pH* values, which are themselves logarithmic.

For a weak acid HA:

$$HA(aq) + H_2O(l) \rightleftharpoons H_3O^+(aq) + A^-(aq)$$

$$K_a = \frac{[H_3O^+(aq)][A^-(aq)]}{[HA(aq)]}$$

This rearranges to give:

$$[H_3O^+(aq)] = \frac{K_a[HA(aq)]}{[A^-(aq)]}$$

Taking logs and substituting pH for $-\lg[H_3O^+(aq)]$ and pK_a for $-\lg K_a$, gives:

$$pH = pK_a + \lg\frac{[A^-(aq)]}{[HA(aq)]} \quad \text{because} \quad -\lg\frac{[HA(aq)]}{[A^-(aq)]} = +\lg\frac{[A^-(aq)]}{[HA(aq)]}$$

In a mixture of a weak acid and its salt, the weak acid is only slightly ionized while the salt is fully ionized, so it is often accurate enough to assume that all the anions come from the salt present and all the un-ionized molecules from the acid.

Hence: $pH = pK_a + \lg\dfrac{[salt]}{[acid]}$, which is the Henderson–Hasselbalch equation.

So in a buffer solution with [acid] = [salt], $pH = pK_a + \lg 1 = pK_a$, since $\lg 1 = 0$.

Diluting a buffer solution does not change [salt]/[acid] so the pH does not change. The equation also shows why it takes a big change in the ratio [salt]:[acid] in a buffer solution to make a significant change in pH. Since $\log 1 = 0$, $\log 10 = 1$ and $\log 100 = 2$, the ratio has to change by a factor of ten to make the pH change by one unit.

The equation also explains why *acid–base indicators* change color roughly in the range $pH = pK_{in} \pm 1$. When $pH = pK_a$, $[HIn] = [In^-]$ and the two different colors of the indicator are present in equal amounts the indicator is midway through its color change.

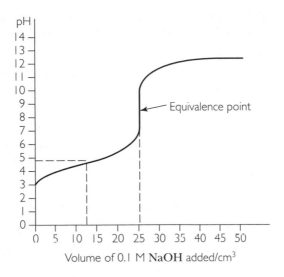

Curve showing the change of **pH** when a 25 cm³ 0.1 mol dm⁻³ ethanoic acid, a weak acid, is titrated with a strong base. Halfway to the end point half the acid has been converted to its salt, so [acid] = [salt] and **pH** = pK_a = 4.8.

Add a few drops of acid and the pH falls. The characteristic acid color of the indicator is distinct when [HIn] ≈ 10 × [In⁻]. At this point pH = pK_a + log 0.1 = pK_a − 1, since log 0.1 = −1.

Add a few drops of alkali and the pH rises. The characteristic alkaline color of the indicator is distinct when [In⁻] ≈ 10 × [HIn]. At this point pH = pK_a + log 10 = pK_a + 1, since log 10 = +1.

Henry's law describes the effect of changing the pressure on the solubility of a gas in a liquid. The law applies only to gases that are slightly soluble. It does not apply to the solubility in water of gases such as ammonia or hydrogen chloride that react as they dissolve.

The law states that the mass of gas that dissolves in a certain volume of a liquid at constant temperature varies with the *partial pressure* of the gas above the liquid.

The law applies to the solubility of gases such as nitrogen, oxygen and *helium* in water and can be used to explain the dangers faced by divers breathing gas mixtures under pressure.

Henry's law is a special case of the *equilibrium law* and can be described in the following form since the partial pressure of a gas is a measure of its concentration:

$$\frac{\text{concentration of gas in solution at equilibrium}}{\text{concentration of gas above the liquid}} = K \text{ (a constant)}$$

Hess's law makes it possible to calculate *enthalpy changes* that cannot be measured. The law states that the enthalpy change for a reaction is the same whether it takes place in one step or a series of steps. So long as the reactants and the products are the same, the overall enthalpy change will be the same whether the reactants are converted to products directly or through two or more intermediate reactions.

Hess's law is used to calculate:

- *enthalpy changes of formation* from *enthalpy changes of combustion*
- *enthalpy changes of reaction* from enthalpy changes of formation
- lattice energies in the *Born–Haber cycle.*

heterocyclic compounds are compounds with rings made of carbon atoms with atoms of at least one other element such as nitrogen, sulfur or oxygen. The bases in *DNA* are heterocyclic compounds. *Adenine* is an example. Many *alkaloids* are also heterocyclic compounds.

The structure of the heterocyclic compound nicotine or 3-(1-methyl-2-pyrrolidyl)pyridine. Nicotine is present in the leaves of tobacco plants. Pure nicotine, a colorless liquid, is highly toxic. Nicotine from tobacco plants is used as an insecticide but the compound is better known as the addictive drug in tobacco smoke.

nicotine

heterogeneous catalyst: a *catalyst* that is in a different *phase* from the reactants. Generally a heterogeneous catalyst is a solid while the reactants are gases or in solution in a solvent.

The advantage of a heterogeneous catalyst is that it can be held in a reaction vessel as the reactants flow in and the products flow out. There no difficulty in separating the products from the catalyst.

Heterogeneous catalysts are used in large-scale *continuous processes.* In the Haber process for *ammonia manufacture* the nitrogen and hydrogen gases flow through a reactor containing small lumps of iron.

Platinum metal alloyed with other metals such as rhodium is an important catalyst. It is used to oxidize ammonia during *nitric acid manufacture.* It is also used in *catalytic converters.* In a catalytic converter the expensive catalyst is finely divided and supported on the surface of a ceramic to increase the surface area in contact with the exhaust gases. Similarly, the expensive silver catalyst used to manufacture *epoxyethane* is finely spread over the surface of alumina.

Impurities in the reactants can "poison" catalysts so that they become less effective. Carbon monoxide poisons the iron catalyst used in the Haber process. Lead compounds in the exhaust from an automobile engine poison catalytic converters so lead-free gasoline must be used.

Heterogeneous catalysts work by adsorbing reactants at *active sites* on the surface of the solid. Nickel acts as a catalyst for the addition of hydrogen to $C = C$ in *unsaturated compounds* by adsorbing hydrogen molecules, which probably split up into single atoms held on the surface of the metal crystals.

If a metal is to be a good catalyst for a *hydrogenation* reaction it must not adsorb the hydrogen so strongly that the hydrogen atoms become unreactive. This happens with tungsten. Equally, if adsorption is too weak there will not be enough adsorbed atoms for the reaction to proceed at a useful rate, as is the case with silver. The

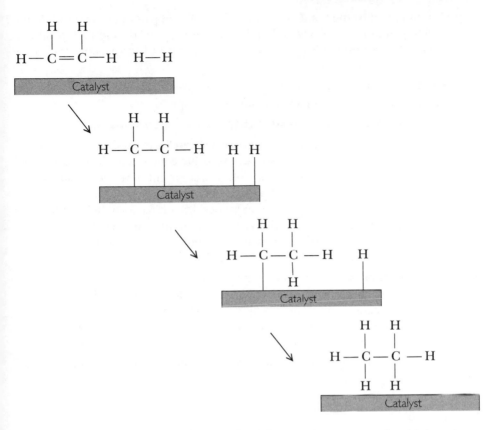

Possible mechanism for the hydrogenation of an alkene in the presence of a nickel catalyst

strength of adsorption must have a suitable intermediate value. Suitable metals for hydrogenation are nickel, platinum and palladium.

heterogeneous equilibrium: an equilibrium system in which the substances involved are not all in the same *phase*. An example is the equilibrium state involving two solids and a gas, formed on heating calcium carbonate in a closed container.

$$CaCO_3(s) \rightleftharpoons CaO(s) + CO_2(g)$$

The concentrations of solids do not appear in the expression for the equilibrium constant. Pure solids have a constant "concentration."

$$K_c = [CO_2(g)] \text{ or } K_p = p_{CO_2}$$

The same applies to the equilibrium between a solid and its saturated solution in water (see *solubility product constants*).

heterolytic bond breaking (fission): the type of bond breaking that produces ionic *intermediates in reactions*. In heterolytic fission, a *covalent bond* breaks so that one

$$H{:}Br \longrightarrow H^+ \quad {:}Br^-$$

Heterolytic bond breaking

$$H{-}Br \longrightarrow H^+ + Br^-$$

of the atoms joined by the bond takes both of the shared pair of electrons while the other is left with none. This type of bond breaking happens during *electrophilic* and *nucleophilic substitution* and *addition reactions* and is favored when reactions take place in *polar solvents* such as water.

hexadentate ligand: a molecule or ion that forms six *coordinate* (dative) *bonds* with the central metal ion in a complex. A common example is *edta*.

hexagonal close-packed structure (hcp): see *close-packed structures*.

high-performance liquid chromatography (hplc) is a sophisticated version of *liquid chromatography*. The technique is able to separate components in a mixture that are very similar to each other. The mobile phase is a solvent of very high purity. The stationary phase consists of very small particles of a solid such a silica packed into a long steel tube. The use of fine particles increases the surface area, helping to make the separation efficient. A pump provides the very high pressure needed to force the solvent through the tightly packed column. One application of hplc is to study what happens to drugs as they are metabolized in the body.

Hofmann degradation is a reaction that turns an *amide* into a primary *amine* while removing a carbon atom from the molecule. The reaction shortens the carbon chain, hence the term "degradation." The reaction was discovered by August von Hofmann (1818–1892). He was a pioneering German organic chemist who was head of the Royal College of Chemistry in London, England, for 20 years from 1845.

Amides react in this way when treated with bromine and concentrated sodium hydroxide solution.

$$CH_3CH_2CH_2\overset{\displaystyle O}{\underset{NH_2}{C}} \xrightarrow[\text{warm}]{Br_2/KOH} CH_3CH_2CH_2NH_2$$

amide   amine

Equation for the Hofmann degradation of an amide to a primary amine with one less carbon atom

homogeneous catalyst: a *catalyst* that is in the same phase as the reactants. Typically the reactants and the catalyst are dissolved in the same solution.

Transition metal ions can be effective homogeneous catalysts because they can gain and lose electrons as they change from one *oxidation state* to another. The oxidation of iodide ions by persulfate ions, for example, is very slow.

$$S_2O_8^{2-}(aq) + 2I^-(aq) \longrightarrow 2SO_4^{2-}(aq) + I_2(aq)$$

The reaction is catalyzed by iron(III) ions in the solution. A possible mechanism is that iron(III) is reduced to iron(II) as it oxidizes iodide ions to iodine. The $S_2O_8^{2-}(aq)$ ions oxidize the iron(II) back to iron(III), ready to oxidize some more of the iodide ions, and so on.

Acid catalysis and *base catalysis* are other examples of homogeneous catalysis.

homogeneous equilibrium: an equilibrium in which all the substances involved are in the same *phase*.

homologous series: a series of closely related organic compounds. The compounds in a homologous series have the same functional group and can be described by a general formula. The formula of one member of the series differs from the next member by CH_2. Primary *alcohols* are an example of a homologous series with the general formula $C_nH_{(2n+2)}O$. Physical properties, such as the boiling point, show a steady trend in values along a homologous series.

homolytic bond breaking (fission): the type of bond breaking that produces *free radicals* with unpaired electrons. In homolytic fission, a *covalent bond* breaks so that the atoms joined by the bond separate, each taking one of the shared pair of electrons.

$$:Br\overset{\times\times}{\underset{\times\times}{\cdot}}Br\overset{\times}{\times} \longrightarrow :\overset{\cdot\cdot}{Br}\cdot \quad \overset{\times\times}{\underset{\times\times}{\times}}Br\overset{\times}{\times}$$

Homolytic bond breaking

$$Br\frown Br \longrightarrow Br^{\bullet} + {\bullet}Br$$

hormones are chemical messengers carried round the body in the bloodstream. Hormones produce a response from particular target cells. Hormones are produced by glands and pass directly into the blood. Examples of hormones are *insulin* from the islet cells in the pancreas, adrenaline from the adrenal glands near the kidneys and sex hormones produced by the testes in men and the ovaries or other organs in women.

Hund's rule is one of the rules that help to predict electron configurations of atoms (see *aufbau principle*). The rule states that the most stable arrangement of electrons in an atom is the one with as many unpaired electrons as possible, all with parallel *spins*. For example, in a nitrogen atom, the three *p*-electrons have parallel spins and each occupy a separate *p*-energy level.

Electron configuration of a nitrogen atom

N 1s ⇅ 2s ⇅ 2p ↑ ↑ ↑

hydration takes places when water molecules bond to ions or add to molecules. Water molecules are *polar* and so they are attracted to both positive and negative ions.

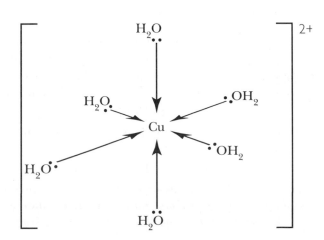

Hydrated copper (II) ion. Here coordinate (dative covalent) bonds hold the water molecules to the metal ions.

It is hard to see why the charged ions in a crystal of sodium chloride separate and go into solution in water with only a small energy change. Where does the energy come from to overcome the attraction between the ions? The explanation is that the ions are so strongly hydrated by the polar water molecules that the sum of the *enthalpy changes of hydration* nearly balances the *lattice energy*.

Some metal ions are hydrated in crystals as well as solution. In many hydrated salts the metal is present as a complex ion. This is true of copper(II) ions in blue copper sulfate. Cobalt(II) ions also bond to water molecules when blue (anhydrous) cobalt(II) chloride turns pink with water.

Hydrogen ions are hydrated in solution. They do not float around freely, but bond to water molecules forming *oxonium ions*.

The term hydration is also used to describe the addition of water to molecules such as *alkenes*. Ethene, for example, is hydrated when mixed with steam and passed over a phosphoric acid catalyst.

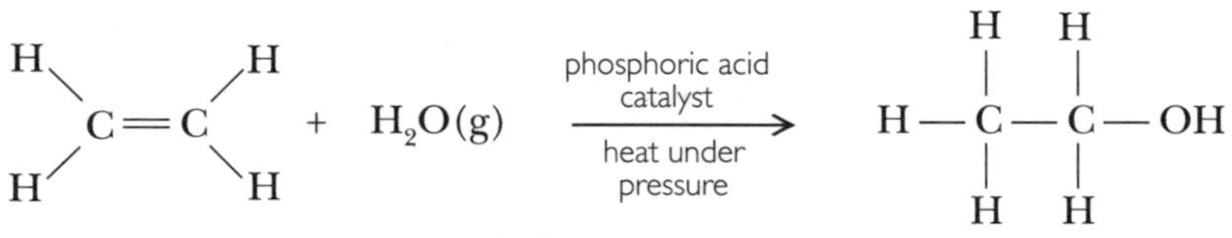

Equation for the hydration of ethene

hydrazine (N_2H_4) is a colorless fuming liquid that is manufactured by oxidizing ammonia with sodium chlorate(I) in the presence of gelatin. Hydrazine, like ammonia, is a base and a reducing agent. It has a *lone pair of electrons* on each nitrogen atom.

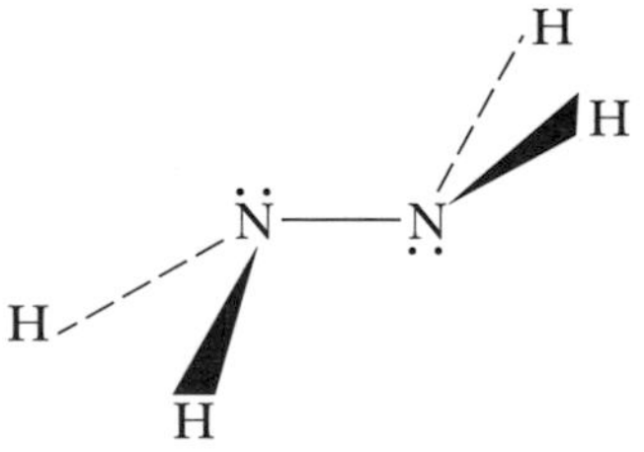

Structure and shape of a hydrazine molecule

Hydrazine with one hydrogen replaced by a methyl group can be used as a rocket fuel in space; it catches fire on contact with liquid N_2O_4.

hydrides are compounds of elements with hydrogen. The hydrides of the group 1 and 2 metals are ionic and contain the hydride ion, H^-.

$$2Na(s) + H_2(g) \longrightarrow 2Na^+H^-(s)$$

Ionic hydrides are ionic crystals. They are rapidly hydrolyzed by water because the hydride ion is a strong base.

$$H^-(s) + H_2O(l) \longrightarrow H_2(g) + OH^-(aq)$$

The hydrides of nonmetals are covalently bonded molecular liquids and gases. They include the *hydrogen halides*, *water*, hydrogen sulfide and *ammonia*. There are very many hydrides of carbon including the *alkanes*, *alkenes* and *arenes*.

The properties of the hydrides of the three highly *electronegative* elements nitrogen, oxygen and fluorine are affected by *hydrogen bonding*.

Hydrogen also forms *interstitial hydrides* with some *d-block elements*.

hydrocarbons are compounds that consist of just carbon and hydrogen. Important classes of hydrocarbons are the *alkanes, alkenes, alkynes* and *arenes*.

hydrochloric acid is a solution of hydrogen chloride gas in water. Hydrogen chloride is a strong acid so the solution in water is fully ionized into aqueous hydrogen ions (*oxonium ions*) and chloride ions. The concentration of commercial concentrated hydrochloric acid is about 12 mol dm^{-3}. Dilute hydrochloric acid (about 2 mol dm^{-3}) is commonly used as a laboratory reagent. Hydrochloric acid has the advantage of being cheaper and safer to dilute than sulfuric acid. It is a nonoxidizing acid, unlike dilute nitric acid.

hydrogen is the commonest element in the universe. Stars, like the Sun, consist mainly of hydrogen and get their energy from *nuclear fusion*, which turns hydrogen into *helium*.

Hydrogen atoms are the smallest of all atoms, consisting, normally, of one proton and one electron in the 1s-orbital (see *atomic orbitals*). There are two other *isotopes*: *deuterium* and *tritium*.

Life on Earth depends on hydrogen. Most *organic compounds* contain hydrogen and life requires water – hydrogen oxide.

Hydrogen is an important industrial chemical. It is produced from steam and natural gas for *ammonia manufacture*. It is also one of the products of the *electrolysis of brine*. Hydrogen is used to *hydrogenate* vegetable oils for margarine and similar spreads.

Hydrogen forms a wide range of *hydrides* with other elements.

hydrogen bonding is a type of attraction between molecules that is much stronger than other types of *intermolecular force*, but much weaker than covalent bonding.

Hydrogen bonding affects molecules in which hydrogen is covalently bonded to one of the three highly *electronegative* elements nitrogen, oxygen and fluorine.

The hydrogen atoms lie between two highly electronegative atoms. They are hydrogen bonded to one of them and covalently bonded to the other. The *covalent bond* is highly polar. The small hydrogen atom ($\delta+$) can get close to the other electronegative atom ($\delta-$) to which it is strongly attracted.

The three atoms associated with a hydrogen bond are always in a straight line.

Hydrogen bonding in hydrogen fluoride

Hydrogen bonding accounts for:

- the relatively high boiling points of ammonia, water and hydrogen fluoride, which are out of line for the trends in the properties of the other hydrides in groups 5, 6 and 7

- the open structure of *ice*
- the tertiary structure of *proteins*
- the pairing of bases in a *DNA* double helix
- the pairing up (*dimerization*) of carboxylic acids in a nonaqueous solvent.

hydrogen electrode: a *half-cell* of great theoretical importance but of limited practical significance. By definition the *standard electrode potential* of the hydrogen electrode is zero, $E^{\ominus}(\frac{1}{2}H_2| H^+) = 0.00$ V.

A standard hydrogen electrode sets up an equilibrium between hydrogen ions in solution (1 mol dm^{-3}) and hydrogen gas (at 1 bar pressure), all at 298 K on the surface of a platinum electrode coated with platinum black.

By convention, when a standard hydrogen electrode is the left-hand electrode in an electrochemical cell, the cell emf is the electrode potential of the right-hand electrode.

$$Pt[H_2(g)] \mid 2H^+(aq) \mathrel{\vdots} Zn^{2+}(aq) \mid Zn(s)$$

Conventional diagram to represent the cell that defines the standard electrode potential of the $Zn^{2+}(aq)|Zn(s)$ electrode

hydrogen emission spectrum: the spectrum of radiation from excited hydrogen gas. There is a bluish glow when a high voltage is applied across the electrodes at each end of a glass tube containing hydrogen at low pressure. A spectroscope produces a line spectrum that can be recorded photographically.

Each line in the emission spectrum corresponds to electrons dropping from a higher energy level to a lower level. The series of lines are named after the people who first discovered or studied them.

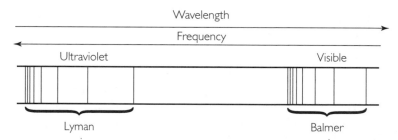

The series of lines in the hydrogen emission spectrum

The pattern of energy levels in a hydrogen atom with just one electron is simpler than in other atoms with more than one electron. In a hydrogen atom all the orbitals in the same shell have the same energy. So the energy levels correspond to the main shells.

The lines of the Balmer series are in the visible region. The lines of the Lyman series are in the ultraviolet. The bigger the energy jumps, the higher the *frequency of electromagnetic radiation* emitted.

The energy gaps between energy levels get smaller as electrons recede from the nucleus. As a result, in each series, the differences between the energy jumps get smaller and smaller until they converge. They converge at the high-frequency end. The biggest jump in the Lyman series is for an electron dropping back from the very edge of an atom to the lowest energy level. The size of this jump is the *ionization energy* for a hydrogen atom. So the ionization energy of hydrogen can be calculated from the frequency of the convergence limit of the Lyman series since (according to *quantum theory*) $\Delta E = h\nu$.

hydrogen halides are compounds of hydrogen with the *halogens*. They are all colorless, molecular compounds with the formula HX, where X stands for F, Cl, Br or I.

The bonds between hydrogen and the halogens are *polar*. The H—F bond is so polar that the properties of the compound are affected by *hydrogen bonding*.

Hydrogen chloride, hydrogen bromide and hydrogen iodide are similar in that they are:

- colorless gases at room temperature that fume in moist air
- very soluble in water, forming acid solutions (hydrochloric, hydrobromic and hydriodic acids)
- *strong acids* so they ionize completely in water.

Hydrogen chloride, hydrogen bromide and hydrogen iodide show some trends down *group 7* in that they:

- become less thermally stable – heating does not decompose hydrogen chloride but a hot wire will decompose hydrogen iodide into hydrogen and iodine
- become easier to oxidize to the halogen – hydrogen iodide is a strong *reducing agent.*

Hydrogen fluoride is rather different from the other hydrogen halides:

- it is a liquid at room temperature (boiling point 19.9°C) because of hydrogen bonding
- it is a *weak acid*
- its solution in water (hydrofluoric acid) reacts with glass and can be used for etching.

hydrogen ions (H⁺) are hydrogen atoms that have lost an electron. Since a hydrogen atom consists of one proton and one electron this means that a hydrogen ion is just a *proton*. In water, hydrogen ions do not float around freely; they become attached to water molecules, forming oxonium ions, H_3O^+. A lone pair on the oxygen atom forms a dative bond with the hydrogen ion (see *coordinate bond*).

Bonding in an oxonium ion

Hydrogen ions (protons) transfer from an acid to a base during an *acid–base reaction.* This gives rise to the definition of an acid as a proton donor and a base as a proton acceptor.

hydrogen peroxide (H_2O_2), when pure, is a pale blue liquid. Like water it is a *hydride* of oxygen and it is a *hydrogen bonded,* molecular liquid.

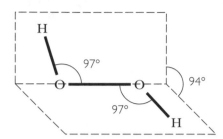

Bonding and shape of a molecule of hydrogen peroxide

Hydrogen peroxide is usually supplied in solution in water. Solutions are sometimes labeled with the "volume strength." For example, "20 volume" hydrogen peroxide decomposes to give 20 cm³ oxygen from 1 cm³ of solution (measured at 0°C and 1 atmosphere pressure, *stp*).

Only in peroxides does oxygen have the oxidation state −1, in between 0 and −2. So hydrogen peroxide can act as both an *oxidizing agent* and as a *reducing agent.*

Hydrogen peroxide decomposes slowly on standing in the dark, but much more rapidly in the present of a catalyst such a powdered manganese(IV) oxide or the *enzyme* catalase. This is a *disproportionation reaction* with oxygen starting in the −1 state and ending up in the −2 and 0 states. Hydrogen peroxide, as it were, oxidizes and reduces itself.

$$2H_2O_2(aq) \longrightarrow 2H_2O(l) + O_2(g)$$

$$
\begin{array}{lll}
0 & O_2 & \\
-1 & H_2O_2 & O_2{}^{2-} \\
-2 & H_2O & O^{2-}
\end{array}
$$

Oxidation states of oxygen

As an oxidizing agent, hydrogen peroxide is used as a bleach. It is used to bleach paper and textiles and to manufacture bleaches used in washing powders. In water treatment it destroys microorganisms. The great advantage of hydrogen peroxide as a bleach is that it turns into water when it reacts, avoiding contamination or pollution.

$$H_2O_2(aq) + 2H^+(aq) + 2e^- \longrightarrow 2H_2O(l)$$

Hydrogen peroxide is not a powerful reducing agent but it will decolorize an acid solution of manganate(VII) ions. A *potassium manganate(VII)* titration is one way of determining the concentration of a solution of hydrogen peroxide.

$$H_2O_2(aq) \longrightarrow O_2(g) + 2H^+(aq) + 2e^-$$

hydrogenation is a reaction that adds hydrogen to a compound. Hydrogenation converts liquid vegetable oils to the solid fats used as ingredients of margarine. In these reactions hydrogen adds to double bonds in the hydrocarbon chains of unsaturated *fatty acids.* Hydrogen adds to C $=$ C double bonds at room temperature in the presence of a platinum or palladium catalyst or on heating in the presence of a nickel catalyst. (See also *heterogeneous catalyst*.)

hydrolysis: a reaction in which a compound is split apart in a reaction involving water. Hydrolysis reactions are often catalyzed by acids or alkalis.

$$CH_3C\overset{O}{\underset{OC_2H_5}{<}} \quad + \quad OH^-(aq) \quad \xrightarrow[\text{aqueous alkali}]{\text{heat with}} \quad CH_3C\overset{O}{\underset{O^-}{<}} \quad + \quad C_2H_5OH$$

ester 　　　　　　　　　　　　　　　　　　　　 salt of 　　　　　　　 ethanol
　　　　　　　　　　　　　　　　　　　　 ethanoic acid

Hydrolysis of the ester ethyl ethanoate catalyzed by alkali

Hydrolysis is used to make *soap* from fats and oils. This is an example of *ester* hydrolysis.

Other examples of hydrolysis in organic chemistry convert:

- *halogenoalkanes* to *alcohols*
- *acyl chlorides*, *acid anhydrides*, and *nitriles* to carboxylic acids.

hydrolysis of salts changes the pH of a solution of a salt by altering the concentrations of H_3O^+ and OH^- ions.

Solutions of aluminum salts and iron(III) salts are acidic because of hydrolysis. The hydrated *aluminum(III) ion*, for example, is an acid. Al^{3+}, because of its polarizing power, draws electrons toward itself, so that the water molecules can give away protons more easily than free water molecules.

$$[Al(H_2O)_6]^{3+}(aq) + H_2O(l) \longrightarrow [Al(H_2O)_5OH]^{2+}(aq) + H_3O^+(aq)$$

Solutions of the salts of weak bases are acidic. This includes the salts of ammonia and amines. The NH_4^+ ion in an ammonium salt is an acid because ammonia (the weak base) does not have a strong hold on the protons it accepts.

$$NH_4^+(aq) + H_2O(l) \rightleftharpoons NH_3(aq) + H_3O^+(aq)$$

Solutions of the salts of weak acids are alkaline. This includes the salts of:

- carbonic acid (carbonates)
- sulfurous acid (sulfites)
- ethanoic acid (ethanoates)
- hydrogen sulfide (sulfides).

The negative ions from weak acids are strong bases; they take hydrogen ions from water molecules and turn back into the acid.

$$CH_3CO_2^-(aq) + H_2O(l) \rightleftharpoons CH_3CO_2H(aq) + OH^-(aq)$$

hydrosphere: the watery part of the Earth's surface. This includes the oceans, rivers, lakes, groundwater and glaciers. Over 80% of the hydrosphere is in the oceans and shallow seas. Almost all the rest of the water is trapped in sediments.

The oceans are linked to the rest of the hydrosphere by the *water cycle*: water evaporates from the sea into the atmosphere, falls as rain or snow onto land and then returns to the oceans via rivers and lakes.

hygroscopic substances absorb water from the air. The chemicals used as drying agents in *desiccators* are hygroscopic; they include anhydrous calcium chloride and calcium oxide. It is difficult to weigh hygroscopic substances accurately, which makes them unsuitable as *primary standards* for titrations.

ice: the solid state of water, which is remarkable because, at the freezing point, it is less dense than liquid water and so floats. Ice owes its open cagelike structure to *hydrogen bonding*. Each water molecule is hydrogen bonded to four others. The hydrogen bonds are 0.177 nm long, which is much longer than the length of a covalent O — H bond (0.094 nm). The distance between the oxygen atoms is equal to the sum of the lengths of a hydrogen bond and a normal O — H bond. Note that in every instance the three atoms O — H ⋯⋯ O are in a straight line.

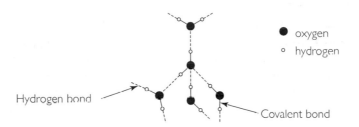

● oxygen
○ hydrogen

Hydrogen bond

Covalent bond

Structure of ice

The view from some angles shows the oxygen atoms in ice arranged in puckered hexagons – a pattern that is reflected in the hexagonal shapes of snowflakes.

When ice melts the open structure partly collapses as some of the hydrogen bonds break, so at 0°C the liquid is denser than the solid.

ideal gases: gases that obey the ideal gas equation $pV = nRT$, where p is the pressure in N m^{-2} (pascals), V is the volume in m^3, T is the temperature on the *kelvin* scale in K, n the *amount* in moles and R the *gas constant*. It is important to convert all the quantities to *SI units* before substituting values in the equation.

The ideal gas equation incorporates all the *gas laws*. For example, with a fixed amount of gas n is constant, so at constant temperature pV = constant, which is *Boyle's law*.

In practice *real gases* deviate from ideal gas behavior. Under laboratory conditions the gases that are close to behaving like ideal gases are the ones that are well above their boiling points such as the *noble gases*, nitrogen, oxygen and hydrogen. For these gases at room temperature and pressure the assumptions of *kinetic theory* are nearly true. The attractive forces between these nonpolar molecules are small enough to be ignored and the volume of the molecules is insignificant compared to the total volume of gas.

The ideal gas equation can be used to determine the *molar mass* of gases and of other substances that evaporate easily.

ideal mixture: a mixture of liquids that obeys *Raoult's law*. Only very similar compounds form ideal mixtures, such as the two *alkanes* hexane and heptane or the two *alcohols*, propan-1-ol and propan-2-ol.

A mixture of two liquids A and B is only ideal if the *intermolecular forces* in pure A, in pure B and in the mixture of A and B are all the same strength. A mixture of liquids deviates from Raoult's law if the intermolecular forces in the mixture are stronger or weaker than in the pure liquids.

ignition temperature: the lowest temperature at which a substance will spontaneously catch fire in air. There is no need for a flame to ignite a gas or *vapor* at or above its ignition point. Examples of ignition temperatures in air are: hexane, 487°C, and ethanol, 558°C.

immiscible liquids are liquids that do not mix. As a rule, *nonpolar* liquids such as hexane and other hydrocarbons do not mix with polar liquids such as water.

Oily hydrocarbon liquids are usually less dense than water so they form a separate, colorless layer on top of water. Liquid organic halogen compounds such as dichloromethane are often denser than water so that they give rise to a separate liquid layer underneath water.

Liquids that are immiscible are useful in *solvent extraction.*

immobilized enzymes are *enzymes* bound to a solid so that they can be easily recovered from a reaction mixture by filtering or centrifuging. Alternatively the solid holding the enzyme can be contained in a column and the raw material (*substrate*) passed through the column, turning into products in the presence of the trapped enzyme *catalyst.* Three methods of linking an enzyme to a solid support are:

- ionic bonding between charged amino side-chains on the protein molecules of the enzyme and charged groups on the support
- trapping the enzyme in a tangle of polymer molecules
- using covalent bonds to attach the enzyme to the insoluble solid.

Immobilized enzymes are used to convert starch from corn into glucose and then to convert much of the glucose to fructose, which is sweeter than glucose or sucrose (see *sweetness*). Using immobilized enzymes has meant a big fall in the cost of high fructose syrup used to make colas and other soft drinks.

indicators are used to detect the end point during titrations. *Acid–base indicators* change color over a range of pH values. Starch is used as an indicator in *iodine-thiosulfate* redox titrations. Other indicators are available for redox titrations and for *complex-forming titrations.*

inductive effect: a term to describe the extent to which electrons are pulled away from, or pushed toward, a carbon atom by the atoms or groups to which it is bonded. The word is sometimes used in accounts of reaction mechanisms.

More electronegative atoms pull electrons away from a carbon atom, so the carbon carries a slight positive charge. This means that the carbon atom is open to attack by nucleophiles, which happens when carbon is bonded to oxygen, chlorine or bromine.

Other groups, especially *alkyl groups*, have a slight tendency to push electrons toward the carbon atom to which they are bonded. One of the effects of this kind of inductive effect is that a secondary *carbocation* is more stable than a primary carbocation. This helps to account for the products formed during *electrophilic addition* of compounds such as HBr to unsymmetrical alkenes (see *Markovnikov rule*).

inert chemicals: a chemical is inert if it has no tendency to react under given circumstances. The lighter *noble gases*, helium and neon, live up to the original name for *group 8*. They are inert toward all other reagents.

Nitrogen is a relatively unreactive gas that can be used to create an "inert atmosphere" free of oxygen, which is much more reactive. Nitrogen is not inert in all circumstances. It reacts, for example, with hydrogen in the *Haber process* and with oxygen at high temperatures to form *nitrogen oxides.*

Sometimes there is no tendency for a reaction to proceed because the reactants are stable. This is so if the *free energy change* for the reaction is positive.

Sometimes there is no reaction even though thermochemistry suggests that it should proceed. The free energy change is negative so the change is feasible (see *feasibility*). A high activation energy means that the rate of reaction is very slow. Methane, for example, does not burn in oxygen at room temperature even though it would be energetically favorable for it to do so. This is an example of a substance being kinetically inert. The term "kinetic stability" is sometimes used but it helps to make a clear distinction between "thermochemical stability" and "kinetic inertness."

inert gases: the older name for the group of *noble gases*, which was used until the discovery of compounds formed by xenon.

inert pair effect: describes the observation that, for *groups* 3, 4 and 5 of the periodic table, the *oxidation state* that is 2 below the highest state becomes increasingly stable down the group. In group 4, for example, the main oxidation state for carbon and silicon is +4. The +2 oxidation state becomes important in the chemistry of tin and lead. In the chemistry of lead the +2 state is even more stable relative to the +4 state than it is in the chemistry of tin. What this means is that two of the four electrons in the outer shell become less available for bonding down the group, hence the term "inert pair effect." This effect is best regarded as a reminder of a trend rather than an explanation.

infrared (IR) spectroscopy is an analytical technique used to identify functional groups in organic molecules. Most compounds absorb IR radiation. The wavelengths they absorb correspond to the natural frequencies at which vibrating bonds in the molecules bend and stretch. It is *polar covalent bonds* such as $O-H$, $C-O$ and $C=O$ that absorb strongly as they vibrate.

Bonds vibrate in particular ways and absorb radiation at specific wavelengths. This means that it is possible to look at an IR spectrum and identify particular functional groups.

Molecules with several atoms can vibrate in many ways because the vibrations of one bond affect others close to it. Complex patterns of vibrations can be used as a "fingerprint" to be matched against the recorded IR spectrum in a database. Comparing the IR spectrum of a product of synthesis with the spectrum of the pure compound can be used to check that the product is pure.

inhibitor: a chemical that stops or slows down a specific chemical reaction. Inhibitors are sometimes called negative *catalysts*. Liquid *monomers* such as phenyl (ethene) are often supplied with a dissolved inhibitor to prevent polymerization in the bottle.

Enzyme inhibitors are very important in the control of metabolism. Competitive inhibition reduces the rate of a reaction catalyzed by an enzyme in the presence of a molecule with a similar shape to the normal *substrate.* The inhibitor binds to the *active site* of the enzyme and stays there unchanged, stopping normal enzyme activity.

initial rate method: a method for finding the order of a chemical reaction and the form of its *rate equation*. This method is used for reactions with several terms in the rate equation, which makes other methods hard to use.

The method is based on finding the rate immediately after the start of a reaction. This is the one point when all the concentrations are known.

The procedure is to make up a series of mixtures in which all the initial concentrations are the same except one. A suitable method is used to measure the change of concentration with time for each mixture (see *rates of reaction*). The results are used to plot concentration/time graphs. The initial rate for each mixture is then found by drawing tangents to the curve at the start and calculating their gradients.

Worked example:

The initial rate method was used to study the reaction $A + 2B \longrightarrow C + D$. The initial rate was calculated from five graphs plotted to show how the concentration of B varied with time for different initial concentrations of reactants.

Experiment	Initial concentration of A/mol dm^{-3}	Initial concentration of B/mol dm^{-3}	Initial rate of reaction/mol dm^{-3} s^{-1}
1	0.10	0.05	2×10^{-4}
2	0.20	0.05	8×10^{-4}
3	0.30	0.05	18×10^{-4}
4	0.20	0.10	8×10^{-4}
5	0.20	0.20	8×10^{-4}

What is:

- the rate equation for the reaction?
- the value of the rate constant?

Notes on the method

Recall that the rate equation cannot be worked out from the balanced equation for the reaction.

First study the experiments in which the concentration of A varies but the concentration of B stays the same. How does doubling or tripling the concentration of A affect the rate?

Next study the experiments in which the concentration of B varies but the concentration of A stays the same. How does doubling the concentration of B affect the rate?

Substitute values for any one experiment in the rate equation to find the value of the rate constant, k. Take care with the units.

Answer

From experiments 1, 2 and 3: doubling $[A]_{initial}$ increases the rate by a factor of 4 (2^2). Tripling $[A]_{initial}$ increases the rate by a factor of 9 (3^2). So rate $\propto [A]^2$.

From experiments **2, 4 and 5**: doubling $[B]_{initial}$ does not change the rate. So rate $\propto [B]^0 = 1$.

The reaction is second order with respect to A and zero order with respect to B. The rate equation is:

rate $= k\,[A]^2$

Rearranging this equation, and substituting values from experiment 2:

$$k = \frac{rate}{[A]^2} = \frac{8 \times 10^{-4} \text{ mol dm}^{-3} \text{ s}^{-1}}{(0.2 \text{ mol dm}^{-3})^2}$$

$k = 0.02 \text{ mol}^{-1} \text{ dm}^3 \text{ s}^{-1}$

---

inorganic chemistry is the study of the chemical elements and their compounds. Inorganic chemistry includes the chemistry of the element carbon and a few of its compounds such as carbon monoxide, carbon dioxide, tetrachloromethane and the carbonates. The chemistry of most other carbon compounds belongs to *organic chemistry*.

Most of the reactions of inorganic chemicals belong to one of these four types:

- *acid–base*
- *redox*
- *ionic precipitation*
- *complex forming* (or *ligand* exchange).

insulin is the *hormone*, produced by special cells in the pancreas, that helps to control the level of glucose in the blood. Digestion of food after a meal raises the level of glucose in blood. In response the pancreas secretes insulin, which circulates round the body and speeds up the rate at which cells take up glucose.

Insulin is a *protein* consisting of two folded chains of amino acids that are *cross-linked* by disulfide links.

interhalogen compound: a compound formed when one halogen combines with another. For example, passing a stream of chlorine gas over solid iodine produces a red-brown liquid, iodine monochloride, ICl. With excess chlorine this turns to a yellow solid, iodine trichloride, ICl_3, which is unstable and easily decomposes back to ICl.

intermediate bonding is bonding that is neither purely ionic nor purely covalent. In most compounds the bonding between the atoms of different elements is to some extent intermediate between the two extremes.

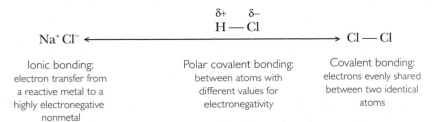

A spectrum from purely ionic to purely covalent bonding

The *electronegativity* values for two elements are a guide to the extent to which the bonds between them will be covalent, ionic or intermediate between the two. Electronegativity values are particularly useful for discussing *polar covalent bonds.*

Where the bonding is largely ionic, *Fajan's rules* are a guide to the extent to which the metal (positive) ion will distort neighboring negative ions, giving rise to a degree of electron sharing.

intermediates in reactions are atoms, molecules, ions or *free radicals* that do not appear in the balanced equation but are formed during one step of a reaction, then used up in the next step. Chemists can use spectroscopy to detect intermediates that exist only for a short time during a reaction.

Examples of reaction intermediates are the free radicals formed during a *free-radical chain reaction* or the *carbocations* formed during *nucleophilic substitution* by the S_N1 mechanism and during *electrophilic addition* to alkenes.

Energy changes in the course of a reaction. Note the energy dip as the intermediate forms. The dip is not deep enough for the intermediate to exist as a stable product. Contrast this with the energy profile for a reaction with just a transition state between reactants and products.

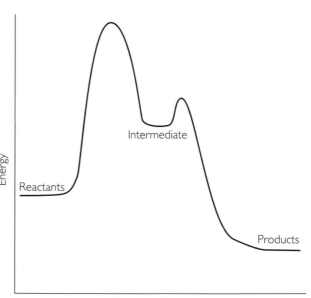

intermolecular forces are weak attractive forces between molecules. Without intermolecular forces there could be no molecular liquids or solids. Also *real gases* would behave more like *ideal gases.*

Weak intermolecular forces arise from electrostatic attractions between *dipoles*, including attractions between:

- molecules with permanent dipoles such as hydrogen chloride molecules
- a permanent dipole in one molecule and a dipole induced in a neighboring molecule, such as the attraction between hydrogen bromide and an ethene molecule
- instantaneous dipoles created fleetingly in nonpolar atoms or molecules (see *dispersion forces*).

Generally intermolecular forces get bigger as molecules get longer and there is a larger area of contact over which intermolecular forces can operate. This accounts for the rise in melting and boiling points as the number of carbon atoms increases in the series of straight-chain *alkanes*. The strength of *thermoplastic polymers* depends on the total strength of intermolecular forces between tangled long-chain molecules.

Weak intermolecular forces, due to attractions between temporary and permanent dipoles, are often called *van der Waals forces*. Forces of this kind are roughly a hundred times weaker than covalent bonds.

The properties of some molecular compounds are affected by stronger intermolecular forces called *hydrogen bonding*. Hydrogen bonds are about ten times stronger than van der Waals forces.

interstitial hydrides are compounds formed by *d-block elements* with hydrogen. The hydrogen atoms fit into the spaces between the atoms in the metal crystal. The holes are the interstices of the crystal, hence the name.

The amounts of hydrogen in the lattice vary with the temperature and pressure. The compounds do not have a definite composition. The hydride of titanium has the variable formula TiH_x, where x is less than 2.

Palladium reacts particularly well with hydrogen and can absorb nearly a thousand times its own volume of the gas at room temperature.

Interstitial hydrides release hydrogen gas on heating so they have been investigated as a possible safe way of storing hydrogen.

intramolecular forces are the strong *covalent bonds* between atoms in a molecule. They are about one hundred times stronger than the weak *intermolecular* forces between molecules. Substances consisting of small molecules melt and boil at relatively low temperatures because of the weakness of the forces between the molecules. The strong intramolecular forces in small molecules do not normally break during melting and boiling.

iodination is a reaction in which an iodine atom replaces a hydrogen atom in an organic molecule. One example is the iodination of propanone – a reaction that appears in the study of reaction rates. The reaction is *acid catalyzed*.

$$CH_3COCH_3(aq) + I_2(aq) \longrightarrow CH_2ICOCH_3(aq) + H^+(aq) + I^-(aq)$$

iodine (I) is a lustrous gray-black solid at room temperature, formula I_2, which sublimes when gently warmed to give a purple vapor (see *sublimation*). Iodine is a *halogen*, the fourth element in *group 7*, with the *electron configuration* $[Kr]4d^{10}5s^25p^5$.

Iodine consists of diatomic molecules with pairs of atoms held together by single *covalent bonds*. The molecules are nonpolar so the *intermolecular forces* are relatively weak, but stronger than in bromine because the atoms are larger and have more electrons. This makes iodine molecules more *polarizable* than bromine molecules.

Iodine, like the other halogens, is an *oxidizing agent* but a less powerful oxidizing agent than bromine.

Iodine reacts with metals to form iodides. Because of the polarizability of the large iodide ion, the iodides formed with small cations or highly charged cations are essentially covalent (see *Fajan's rules*). Examples are lithium iodide, magnesium iodide and aluminum iodide.

Iron(III) iodide and copper(II) iodide do not exist because iodide ions reduce the metal ions to their lower oxidation state. The only iodides of these metals are iron(II) iodide and copper(I) iodide.

Iodine oxidizes hydrogen on heating, forming hydrogen iodide. Unlike the reactions of chlorine and bromine, this is a reversible reaction that has been studied in detail to establish the *equilibrium law.*

$$H_2(g) + I_2(g) \rightleftharpoons 2HI(g)$$

Hydrogen iodide is a fuming, acidic gas. Like the other *hydrogen halides* it is very soluble in water and a strong acid.

Iodine is only very slightly soluble in water. It is much more soluble in a solution of potassium iodide because of the formation of the *tri-iodide ion.* Iodine solution in aqueous potassium iodide is a brownish-yellow color. Iodine dissolves freely in nonpolar solvents such as hexane, forming a solution with the same color as iodine vapor.

As a weaker oxidizing agent, iodine converts thiosulfate ions to tetrathionate ions. This is a quantitative reaction used in *iodine–thiosulfate titrations.*

Iodine and its compounds are used to make pharmaceuticals, photographic chemicals and dyes. Iodine is needed in the diet so that the thyroid gland in the neck can make the *hormone* thyroxine, which regulates growth and metabolism. In many regions sodium iodide is added to table salt to supplement the iodine in the diet and drinking water and so prevent goiter.

iodine number: a measure of the degree of *unsaturation* of a *fat* or oil. Some *fatty acids* in fats and oils are fully *saturated*, having no double bonds. Other fatty acids are unsaturated; they have double bonds. The iodine number is found by measuring how much iodine will add to double bonds per 100 g oil. The higher the iodine number, the more unsaturated the fat or oil. Values range from 25–30 g per 100 g for butter, which is high in saturated fats, to 80–140 g per 100 g for a vegetable oil such as soya oil, which is high in unsaturated fats.

iodine–thiosulfate titrations: a useful analytical method for measuring *amounts* of *oxidizing agents.* The method is based on the fact that oxidizing agents convert iodide ions to iodine quantitatively. Among the oxidizing agents that do this are iron(III) ions, copper(II) ions, chlorate(I) ions, dichromate(VI) ions in acid, iodate(V) ions in acid and manganate(VII) ions in acid.

$$2I^-(aq) \longrightarrow I_2(aq) + 2e^-$$

The iodine stays in solution in excess potassium iodide, turning a yellow-brown (see *tri-iodide ion*).

The iodine produced is then titrated with a *standard solution* of sodium thiosulfate, which reduces iodine molecules back to iodide ions. This too happens quantitatively exactly as in the equation.

$$I_2(aq) + 2S_2O_3^{2-}(aq) \longrightarrow 2I^-(aq) + S_4O_6^{2-}(aq)$$

The greater the amount of oxidizing agent added, the more the iodine formed and so the more thiosulfate needed to react with it. When thiosulfate is added from a burette the color of the iodine gets paler. Near the end point the solution is a very pale yellow. Adding a little soluble starch solution as an indicator near the end point gives a sharp color change from blue-black to colorless.

Worked example:

Calculate the concentration of a solution of sodium thiosulfate standardized by this method. A 0.0642 g sample of potassium iodate(V), KIO_3, was dissolved in water in a conical flask. Excess of potassium iodide was dissolved in the solution, which was then acidified with dilute sulfuric acid. The iodine formed was titrated with the solution of sodium thiosulfate from a burette. The volume of sodium thiosulfate solution needed to decolorize the blue iodine–starch color at the end point was 24.50 cm³.

Notes on the method

Write the equations and calculate the amount in moles of $S_2O_3^{2-}$ equivalent to 1 mol IO_3^-.

There is then no need to consider the amounts of iodine in the calculations.

Look up the *molar mass* of potassium iodate: $M_r(KIO_3) = 214.0$ g mol⁻¹

Only use your calculator at the last step of the calculation to avoid repeated rounding errors.

Answer

The equations for producing iodine:

$$IO_3^-(aq) + 5I^-(aq) + 6H^+(aq) \longrightarrow 3I_2(aq) + 3H_2O$$

The equation for the reaction during the titration:

$$I_2(aq) + 2S_2O_3^{2-}(aq) \longrightarrow 2I^-(aq) + S_4O_6^{2-}(aq)$$

So 1 mol IO_3^- produces 3 mol I_2, which then reacts with 6 mol $S_2O_3^{2-}$.

The amount of KIO_3 at the start $= \dfrac{0.0642\ g}{214.0\ g\ mol^{-1}}$

6 mol $S_2O_3^{2-}$ react with the iodine formed by 1 mol IO_3^-.

So the amount of thiosulfate in 24.5 cm³ (= 0.0245 dm³) solution

$$= 6 \times \frac{0.0642\ g}{214.0\ g\ mol^{-1}}$$

So the concentration of the sodium thiosulfate solution

$$= 6 \times \frac{0.0642\ g}{214.0\ g\ mol^{-1}} \times \frac{1}{0.0245\ dm^3}$$

$$= 0.0735\ mol\ dm^{-3}$$

iodoform reaction: see *tri-iodomethane reaction.*

ion exchange is a process for exchanging ions in a solution and is used to soften and deionize water. An ion exchange resin consists of small beads of a *polymer* that has been modified so that along the chains there are ionic groups. In a cation exchange resin the polymer has negatively charged groups, which attract positive ions.

A water softener contains a cation exchanger in which all the negatively charged sites are attracting sodium ions. As hard water flows over the resin beads the calcium ions in the *hard water* change places with the sodium ions. The softened water can then be used for washing without forming insoluble precipitates with *soaps* and other *detergents.*

Ion exchange is a reversible process. Once all the sodium ions in a bed of resin have been used up it can be recharged by running a concentrated solution of sodium chloride through it to replace calcium ions with sodium ions, ready to soften more water. The salt added to a dishwasher is needed to make sure that the water softener in the machine is regenerated in this way.

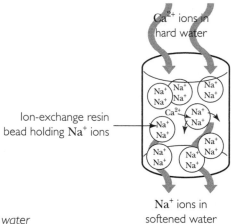

Ion-exchange resin bead holding Na⁺ ions

Ca^{2+} ions in hard water

Na^+ ions in softened water

Using ion exchange to soften water

It takes two ion exchange resins to deionize water: a cation resin holding hydrogen ions and an anion resin with hydroxide ions. As water runs through the two resins the cation exchanger holds onto positive metal ions and replaces them with hydrogen ions. The anion exchanger holds onto the negative ions and replaces them with hydroxide ions. Then H^+ (aq) + OH^-(aq) $\longrightarrow$ H_2O(l), so no ions are left in solution.

ionic bonding is one of three types of strong chemical bonding. Ionic bonding occurs in compounds of metals with nonmetals. Ionic compounds form particularly when the reactive *s-block* metals combine with the halogens of group 7 or oxygen in group 6. The *crystal structures of ionic compounds* are three-dimensional lattices of ions.

Ionic bonding is the result of *electrostatic forces* of attraction between positive metal ions and negative nonmetal ions. The larger the charges on the ions, the bigger the attractive force. The smaller the ions, the closer the charges get to each other and the stronger the force of attraction.

Electron *dot and cross diagrams* provide a balance sheet for keeping track of the electrons when ionic compounds form. These diagrams do not describe the *mechanisms of the reactions.*

$$Na^{\bullet} \quad + \quad {}_{\times}^{\times\times}Cl{}_{\times}^{\times} \quad \longrightarrow \quad Na^+ \quad + \quad {}_{\times\times}^{\times\times}Cl{}_{\times}^{\times} \, {}^-$$

sodium atom   chlorine atom   sodium ion   chloride ion
(2.8.1)   (2.8.7)   (2.8)   (2.8.8)

$$Ca{}_{\bullet}^{\bullet} \quad + \quad {}_{\times\times}^{\times\times}F{}_{\times}^{\times} \, {}_{\times\times}^{\times\times}F{}_{\times}^{\times} \quad \longrightarrow \quad Ca^{2+} \quad + \quad {}_{\times\times}^{\times\times}F{}_{\times}^{\times} \, {}^- \, {}_{\times\times}^{\times\times}F{}_{\times}^{\times} \, {}^-$$

calcium atom   two fluorine atoms   calcium ion   two fluoride ions
(2.8.8.2)   (2.7)   (2.8.8)   (2.8)

Dot and cross diagrams for the formation of sodium chloride and calcium fluoride

Energy is needed to remove electrons from metal ions (see *ionization energy*). The energy changes on adding electrons to nonmetal atoms are quite small (see *electron affinity*). Ionic crystals are stable because of the large release of energy as the ions form a crystal lattice (see *lattice energy*). The *Born–Haber cycle* helps to analyze the stability of ionic crystals. This energy cycle also helps to explain why it is generally true that the atoms of *s*- and *p-block elements* gain or lose electrons to attain the electron configuration of the nearest *noble gas*.

ionic character of bonds: a phrase used to describe the extent to which bonds between the atoms of two different elements are polar. The greater the difference in electronegativity between the elements, the more ionic the bonding. (See also *ionic bonding, polar covalent bonds, intermediate bonding* and *Fajan's rules*.)

ionic equations describe chemical changes by showing only the reacting ions in solution. These equations leave out the *spectator ions*, which remain in solution unchanged. For example, an ionic equation shows that the use of a barium salt to test for sulfate ions is essentially the same reaction whether the reagent is barium chloride or barium nitrate and whatever the source of the sulfate ions.

$$Ba^{2+}(aq) + SO_4^{2-}(aq) \longrightarrow BaSO_4(s)$$

Note that ionic equations are balanced both for atoms and charges.

An ionic equation also shows that the neutralization of any fully ionized *strong acid* by a fully ionized *strong base* is essentially the same process:

$$H^+(aq) + OH^-(aq) \longrightarrow H_2O(l)$$

ionic precipitation is a reaction that produces a solid precipitate on mixing two solutions. This type of reaction can be used to make an insoluble salt from two soluble salts. Silver bromide forms as a precipitate on mixing solutions of silver nitrate and potassium bromide. This is best represented by an *ionic equation* leaving out the *spectator ions*.

$$Ag^+(aq) + Br^-(aq \longrightarrow AgBr(s)$$

This is the reaction used to make silver bromide for *photography*. Silver metal is dissolved in nitric acid to make silver nitrate, $Ag^+NO_3^-$. Then the solution of silver nitrate is mixed with potassium bromide (K^+Br^-) in a solution of gelatin. This produces a very fine precipitate of silver bromide (AgBr) suitable for making a photographic film.

Ionic precipitation reactions play a big part in *anion tests* and *cation tests*.

ionic product of water, K_w: a constant for the equilibrium produced by the ionization of water. There are *oxonium ions* and hydroxide ions even in pure water because of a transfer of hydrogen ions between water molecules. This only happens to a very slight extent. At equilibrium in pure water: $[H_3O^+(aq)] = 10^{-7}$ mol dm^{-3}

$$H_2O(l) + H_2O(l) \rightleftharpoons H_3O^+(aq) + OH^-(aq)$$

The equilibrium constant $K_c = \dfrac{[H_3O^+(aq)]\,[OH^-(aq)]}{[H_2O(l)]^2}$

There is such a large excess of water that $[H_2O(l)]$ is a constant, so the relationship simplifies to: $K_w = [H_3O^+(aq)][OH^-(aq)]$

where K_w is the ionic product of water.

In pure water $[H_3O^+(aq)] = [OH^-(aq)] = 10^{-7}$ mol dm^{-3}

Hence $K_w = 10^{-14}$ mol^2 dm^{-6}

K_w is a constant in all aqueous solutions at 298 K. This makes it possible to calculate the pH of alkalis.

Worked example:

What is the pH of a 0.02 mol dm^{-3} solution of sodium hydroxide?

Notes on the method

Sodium hydroxide is fully ionized in solution. So in this solution

$[OH^-(aq)] = 0.02$ mol dm^{-3}

$pH = -lg\,[H_3O^+(aq)]$

Answer

For this solution:

$K_w = [H_3O^+(aq)] \times 0.02$ mol dm$^{-3} = 10^{-14}$ mol^2 dm^{-6}

So $[H_3O^+(aq)] = \dfrac{10^{-14} \text{ mol}^2 \text{ dm}^{-6}}{0.02 \text{ mol dm}^{-3}} = 5 \times 10^{-13}$ mol dm^{-3}

Hence $pH = -lg\,(5 \times 10^{-13}) = 12.3$

---

ionic radius is the radius of an ion in a crystal. Ionic radii are determined by X-ray diffraction methods. The radius of the positive ion of an element is smaller than its atomic radius. The radius of the negative ion of an element is larger than its atomic radius.

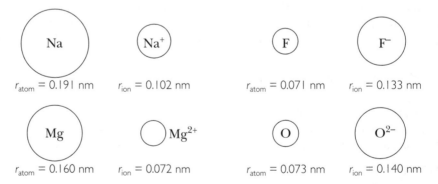

Na	Na$^+$	F	F$^-$
$r_{atom} = 0.191$ nm	$r_{ion} = 0.102$ nm	$r_{atom} = 0.071$ nm	$r_{ion} = 0.133$ nm
Mg	Mg^{2+}	O	O^{2-}
$r_{atom} = 0.160$ nm	$r_{ion} = 0.072$ nm	$r_{atom} = 0.073$ nm	$r_{ion} = 0.140$ nm

Comparison of the radii of atoms and ions

Trends in ionic radius help to account for patterns of bonding and properties in the *periodic table.*

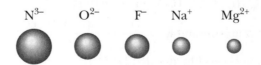

$$N^{3-} \qquad O^{2-} \qquad F^- \qquad Na^+ \qquad Mg^{2+}$$

Ionic radii for selected elements. All the ions shown have the same electron configuration. They are isoelectronic.

Note these patterns:

- down any group the ionic radii increase as the number of inner full shells increases
- across a period, the radii of ions with the same electron configuration decrease as the nuclear charge increases.

Ions in solution are hydrated (see *hydration*). The radius of the ion plus the hydrating water molecules is larger than the ion in a crystal. A smaller ion is likely to be more heavily hydrated than a larger ion with the same charge.

Ion	Radius in a crystal/nm	Radius when hydrated/nm
Li^+	0.074	1.00
Na^+	0.102	0.79

ionization energy: a measure of the energy needed to remove an electron from a gaseous atom or ion. Ionization energies give evidence for the arrangement of electrons in atoms in shells and subshells. Ionization energies can help to explain which ions an element can form. Values for ionization energies are used in energy cycles, such as the *Born–Haber cycle*, to investigate bonding in compounds.

The first ionization energy for an element is the energy needed to remove one mole of electrons from one mole of gaseous atoms. Successive ionization energies for the same element measure the energy needed to remove a second, third, fourth electron, and so on.

Ionization energies can be measured by *mass spectrometry* or by studying the emission spectra of atoms (see *hydrogen emission spectrum*). In these ways it is possible to measure energy changes involving ions that do not normally appear in chemical reactions.

$$Na(g) \longrightarrow Na^+(g) + e^-$$ first ionization energy = 496 kJ mol^{-1}

$$Na^+(g) \longrightarrow Na^{2+}(g) + e^-$$ second ionization energy = 4563 kJ mol^{-1}

$$Na^{2+}(g) \longrightarrow Na^{3+}(g) + e^-$$ third ionization energy = 6913 kJ mol^{-1}

There are 11 electrons in a sodium atom so there are 11 successive ionization energies for this element. The *electron configuration* of the element is $1s^2 2s^2 2p^6 3s^1$. There is 1 electron in the outer shell, which is furthest from the nucleus and shielded by ten inner electrons. There are eight electrons in the second shell and these are closer to the nucleus and only have two inner *shielding* electrons. The two inner electrons feel the full attraction of the nuclear charge and are closest to the nucleus. They are hardest to remove.

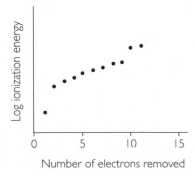

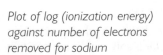

Plot of log (ionization energy) against number of electrons removed for sodium

So the successive ionization energies for an element rise and there are big jumps in value each time electrons start to be removed from the next shell in toward the nucleus.

In the *periodic table*, ionization energies tend to rise from left to right across a period because from one element to the next the added electron goes into the same main shell as the charge on the nucleus increases by one. The rise in values is not smooth but shows a 2–3–3 pattern, corresponding to the way that the *s*- and *p*-orbitals fill up (see *atomic orbitals*).

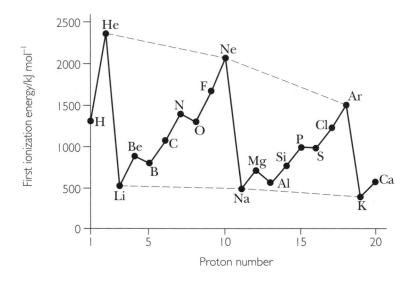

Plot of first ionization energy against proton number for the elements H to Ca

The 2*s* orbital is full at Be, there is then a slight dip as the next electron goes into a *p*-orbital with a slightly higher energy. The three *p*-orbitals each have one electron in a nitrogen atom. The dip at oxygen happens as the next electron has to pair up with another electron. Nevertheless, the main factor is the charge on the nucleus, which increases steadily across the period. This pattern repeats from Na to Ar.

Ionization energies decrease down a group. Down a group the number of full shells increases. The increased shielding effect balances out the increasing charge on the nucleus. The outer electrons get further and further away from the same effective nuclear charge, so they are easier to remove.

ionization of water: see *ionic product of water.*

ionizing radiation includes all the types of radiation with enough energy per photon to ionize atoms. Ionizing radiation includes *alpha* and *beta particles, gamma radiation* and *X-rays*. Living cells are very sensitive to ionizing radiation. High doses of ionizing radiation can kill living cells and even small doses can cause mutation. Exposure to ionizing radiation can, in time, give rise to cancer.

iron (Fe) is a *d-block* metal that shows the characteristic behavior of the *transition metals*. Its *electron configuration* is: $[Ar]3d^64s^2$. The pure metal is soft and easily worked.

It is strongly *ferromagnetic*. In most of its uses iron is mixed with other elements to make *steel*. Iron is so widely used that *corrosion of the metal* is a serious economic problem.

Iron can exist in more than one *oxidation state*. Iron dissolves in dilute acids to form iron(II) salts. The aqueous iron(II) ion is pale green. Oxidizing agents including oxygen in the air, chlorine or potassium manganate(VII) all oxidize iron(II) to iron(III). The aqueous iron(III) ion is yellow.

$$Fe^{2+}(aq) \longrightarrow Fe^{3+}(aq) + e^-$$

Iron ions form *complexes* in both the +2 and the +3 states. The hexacyanoferrate(II) ion, $Fe(CN)_6^{4-}$, gives a deep blue precipitate with $Fe^{3+}(aq)$ ions. The hexacyanoferrate(III) ion, $Fe(CN)_6^{3-}$, gives a deep blue precipitate with $Fe^{2+}(aq)$ ions. This is one way to distinguish iron(II) and iron(III) ions in solution.

A very sensitive test for iron(III) is to add a dilute solution of thiocyanate ions, SCN^-. A blood-red precipitate forms due to the formation of iron complexes such as: $[Fe(SCN)(H_2O)_5]^{2+}$.

Iron and its compounds act as *homogeneous* and *heterogeneous catalysts*.

iron extraction produces the metal from its oxide ores in large blast furnaces.

Coke burning in air heats the furnace.

$$C(s) + O_2(g) \longrightarrow CO_2(g)$$

Coke also produces the *reducing agent* by reacting with carbon dioxide further up the furnace to make carbon monoxide.

$$C(s) + CO_2(g) \longrightarrow 2CO(g)$$

The carbon monoxide reduces the oxide ore to iron,

$$Fe_2O_3(s) + 3CO(g) \longrightarrow 2Fe(l) + 3CO_2(g)$$

Where the furnace is hot enough, carbon too can act as the reducing agent.

Limestone ($CaCO_3$) decomposes to calcium oxide (CaO), which combines with silicon dioxide and other impurities to make a liquid *slag*. For example:

$$CaO(s) + SiO_2(s) \longrightarrow CaSiO_3(l)$$

The molten metal and slag run to the bottom of the furnace where the slag floats on the metal so that it can be tapped off separately.

irritant chemicals do not destroy tissues, so they are less than corrosive. However, skin or eyes may become inflamed or affected by sores if exposed to the chemical. This may happen quite quickly or after extended or repeated contact with the chemical.

isoelectric point: the pH at which the overall charge on an *amino acid* or *protein* is zero. At this pH amino acids or proteins do not move toward one or other of the electrodes during *electrophoresis*.

At low pH an amino acid has a positive charge because there is an extra hydrogen ion on the basic amino group. At high pH an amino acid is negatively charged because the carboxylic acid group has given away a hydrogen ion. At the pH of the isoelectric point the amino acid is present in solution as a *zwitterion* and the total charge is zero.

Isoelectric points vary from one amino acid to another because of differences in their side chains.

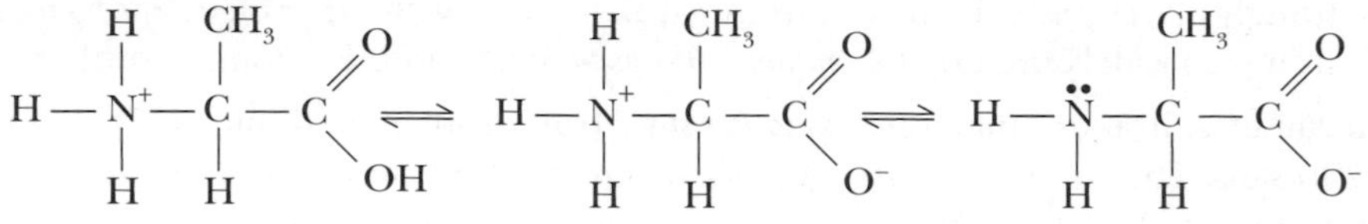

in acid solution | zwitterion | in alkaline solution

The charges on alanine at different pH values

A large protein molecule is at its least soluble in water at its isoelectric point when it is uncharged.

isoelectronic atoms and ions have the same number and arrangement of electrons. The following particles are all isoelectronic: N^{3-}, O^{2-}, Fe^-, Ne, Na^+, Mg^{2+} and Al^{3+}. They all have the *electron configuration* $1s^2 2s^2 2p^6$.

Methane and the ammonium ion are isoelectronic. Both have ten electrons, two in the first shell of the central atom and eight forming four covalent bonds with hydrogen atoms. They both have the same shape (see *shapes of molecules*).

isolated system: see *system.*

isomerization is a process used in oil refining to convert straight-chain *alkanes*, such as pentane, into branched *isomers*, such as 2-methylbutane. The value of the process is that branched alkanes increase the octane number of *gasoline*. Isomerization happens when the hot hydrocarbon vapor passes over a *catalyst.*

isomers are compounds with the same molecular formula but different structures. Structural isomerism may arise because:

- the hydrocarbon chain is branched in different ways

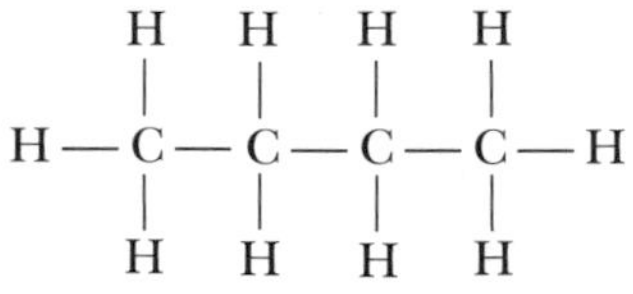

butane

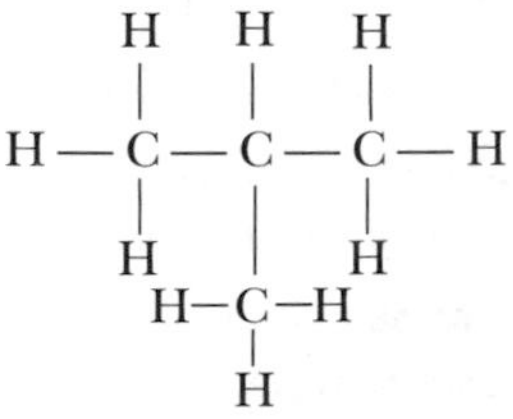

2-methylpropane

Isomers of C_4H_{10}

- the functional group is in a different position

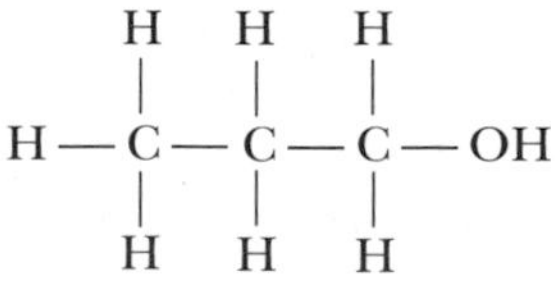

propan-1-ol

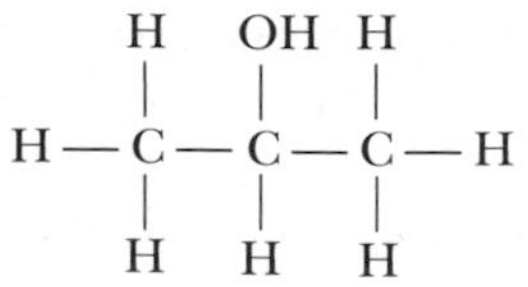

propan-2-ol

Isomers of C_3H_8O

- the functional groups are different.

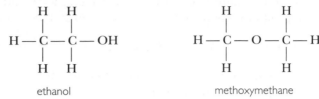

Isomers of C_2H_6O

ethanol   methoxymethane

(See also *geometrical isomerism* and *optical isomers*.)

isomorphous compounds have the same type of chemical formula and crystallize with the same shape and structure. *Alums* are isomorphous. They form octahedral crystals.

isotactic polymer: an *addition polymer* with a regular structure. In isotactic poly(propene), for example, all the methyl side chains are on the same side of the carbon chain. The molecules coil into a regular helical shape and pack together to form a highly crystalline polymer that is very strong. This form of the polymer is useful for hardwearing fibers, tough moldings in motor vehicles and containers that can hold boiling water.

Structure of isotactic poly(propene) with all the methyl groups on the same side of the carbon chain

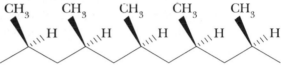

isotopes are atoms of the same element that have the same number of protons in the nucleus but a different number of neutrons. In other words the atoms of isotopes have the same *proton* (atomic) *number* but different *nucleon* (mass) *numbers*. The isotopes have the same chemical properties because they have the same number and arrangement of electrons (*electron configuration*).

The three isotopes of carbon: carbon-12, carbon-13 and carbon-14. The first two are not radioactive, but carbon-14 is a beta emitter.

Symbol:	$^{12}_6C$	$^{13}_6C$	$^{14}_6C$
Neutrons:	6	7	8
Protons:	6	6	6

The isotopes of an element can be separated and detected by *mass spectrometry*. Peaks in a mass spectrum are often multiple because of the existence of isotopes.

Mass spectrum of chlorine

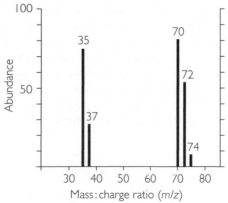

isotopic abundance: the proportions of the different *isotopes* of an element. Chlorine, for example, has two isotopes: chlorine-35 and chlorine-37. Naturally occurring chlorine contains 75% of chlorine-35 and 25% of chlorine-37.

$$\text{So the mean } \textit{relative atomic mass } = \frac{(3 \times 35) + 37}{4} = 35.5$$

Most relative atomic mass values are not whole numbers because most elements have several naturally occurring isotopes.

isotopic labeling uses *isotopes* as markers to trace the movement of chemicals or to investigate what happens to particular atoms during chemical changes (see also *tracers*). Atoms of the normally abundant isotope of an element in a molecule are replaced by a different isotope.

Isotopes have the same chemical properties so it is possible to use them to follow what happens during a change without altering the normal course of the process. Radioactive isotopes can be tracked by detecting their radiation. The fate of nonradioactive isotopes can be followed by analyzing samples using *mass spectrometry*.

Isotopic labeling has been used to investigate the mechanism of *ester* hydrolysis. Using water labeled with oxygen-18 (instead of the normal isotope oxygen-16) it was shown that it is the C — O bond in the ester that breaks and not the O — C_2H_5 bond. Mass spectrometry showed that the heavier oxygen atoms end up in the acid and not in the alcohol.

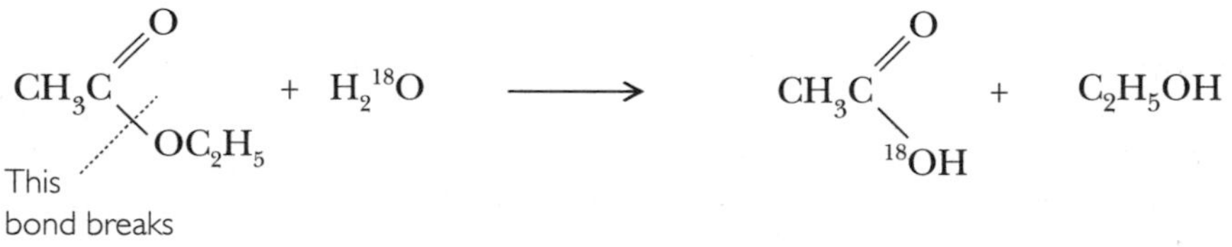

Use of labeling to investigate bond breaking during ester hydrolysis

isotropic solids have properties that are the same in all directions. Crystals of sodium chloride are isotropic because the ions are spherical and the crystal structure is cubic. Most substances are more or less *anisotropic*.

IUPAC (International Union of Pure and Applied Chemistry): the recognized authority for the names of chemical compounds, for chemical symbols and terms and the values of data such as relative atomic masses. IUPAC names are systematic names based on a set of rules that make it possible to determine the chemical structure of a compound from its name. Chemists increasingly use approved IUPAC names for simpler compounds but stick to traditional names when the systematic name is complex. The systematic name 2-hydroxypropane-1,2,3-tricarboxylic acid describes the structure but is cumbersome compared to the traditional name citric acid based on its occurrence in citrus fruits.

J

joule (symbol J) is the *SI unit* of energy. The quantities of energy transferred during chemical reactions are relatively large, so chemists generally measure energy changes in kilojoules (kJ). 1 kJ = 1000 J.

K_c is the symbol for an equilibrium constant with the concentrations measured in moles per liter (see *equilibrium law*).

K_p is the symbol for an equilibrium constant for an equilibrium involving gases with the concentrations measured by *partial pressures*.

Equilibrium	K_p	Units of K_p (using the SI unit of pressure, Pa)
$H_2(g) + I_2(g) \rightleftharpoons 2HI(g)$	$K_p = \dfrac{(p_{NH_3})^2}{(p_{H_2})(p_{I_2})}$	no units
$N_2(g) + 3H_2(g) \rightleftharpoons 2NH_3(g)$	$K_p = \dfrac{(p_{NH_3})^2}{(p_{N_2})(p_{H_2})^3}$	Pa^{-2}
$N_2O_4(g) \rightleftharpoons 2NO_2(g)$	$K_p = \dfrac{(p_{NO_2})^2}{(p_{N_2O_4})}$	Pa

Kekulé structure: a ring structure for *benzene* proposed by the German chemist Friedrich Kekulé in 1865. According to Kekulé the idea of a ring structure came to him while he was day dreaming in front of a fire.

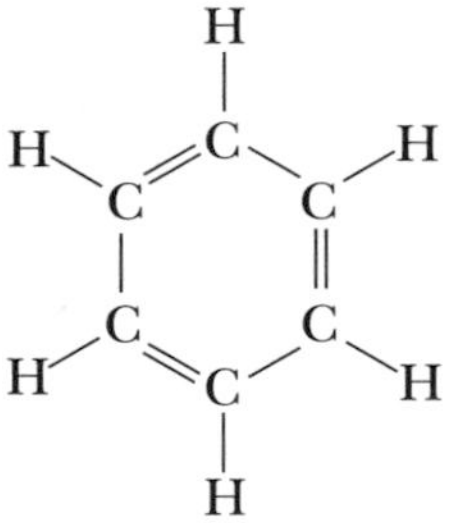

Representations of the Kekulé structure for benzene

The problem with this structure is that it suggests that there should be two isomers of 1,2-dichlorobenzene.

Isomers of 1,2-dichlorobenzene suggested by the Kekulé structure. Isomers with this formula have never been separated. There is only one form of the compound.

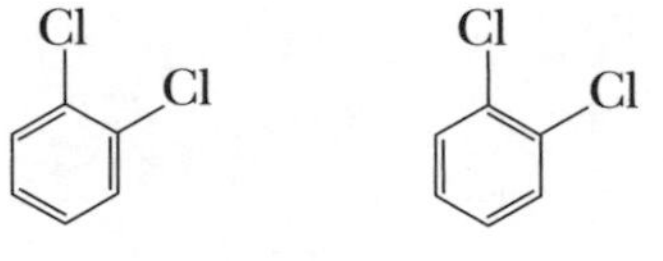

In practice it has never been possible to separate isomers of disubstituted benzenes. To get around this problem Kekulé suggested that benzene molecules rapidly alternate between the two possible structures. This is not the modern explanation. Today, chemists use the idea of *delocalized electrons* to account for the benzene structure.

kelvin (symbol K) is the *SI unit* of temperature. Temperatures above *absolute zero* are measured in kelvins. Temperatures on the Celsius scale use the same size units but zero is set at the freezing point of water (273.15 K). Temperature differences measured on either scale are the same and given as kelvins (K).

kerosene is a mixture of hydrocarbons produced by the *fractional distillation of oil*. Part of the kerosene fraction is refined for use as a domestic fuel, while some is cracked to make *gasoline*. Most of the kerosene fraction, however, is purified for use as the fuel for jet engines in aircraft.

ketones are *carbonyl compounds* in which the carbonyl group is attached to two *alkyl groups*. The carbonyl group is the *functional group* that gives ketones (and *aldehydes*) their characteristic properties. Ketones are named after the alkane with the same carbon skeleton by changing the ending "e" to "one." Where necessary a number in the name shows the position of the carbonyl group.

Oxidation of secondary alcohols with acidified potassium dichromate(VI) produces ketones, which, unlike aldehydes, are not easily oxidized further.

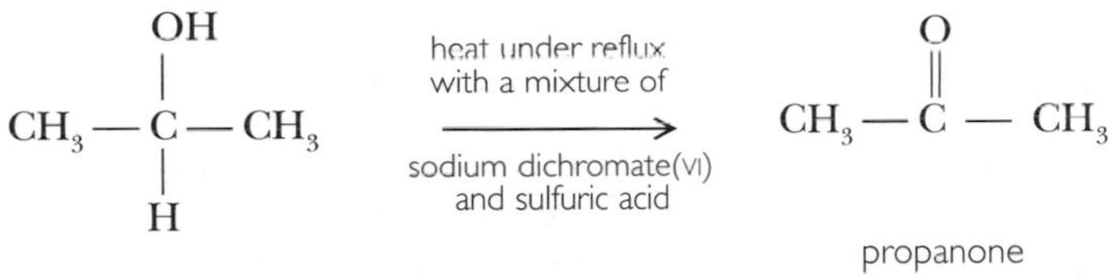

Oxidation of propan-2-ol to propanone

Fehling's solution and *Tollens reagent* cannot oxidize ketones. There is no change when testing ketones with these reagents.

Sodium tetrahydridoborate(III) reduces ketones to secondary alcohols.

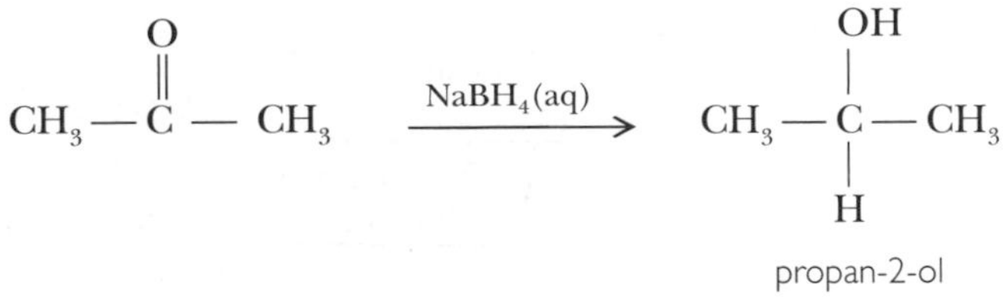

Reduction of propanone to propan-2-ol

Ketones, like aldehydes, undergo addition. These are *nucleophilic addition reactions*.

Sometimes addition is immediately followed by elimination of water in *addition–elimination reactions*.

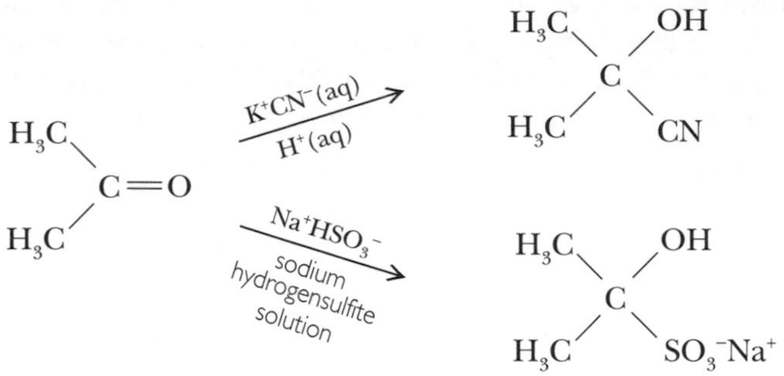

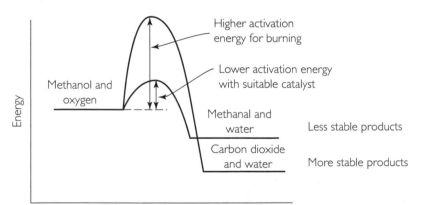

H_3C \ $C=O$ / H_3C

$\xrightarrow[\text{H}^+(aq)]{\text{K}^+\text{CN}^-(aq)}$

H_3C \ OH / C \ H_3C / CN

$\xrightarrow[\substack{\text{sodium} \\ \text{hydrogensulfite} \\ \text{solution}}]{\text{Na}^+\text{HSO}_3^-}$

H_3C \ OH / C \ H_3C / $SO_3^-Na^+$

Addition reactions of propanone

kilogram (symbol kg) is the *SI unit* of mass. 1 kg = 1000 g.

kinetic control: a term used when the product of a reaction is the one that forms faster, rather than an alternative product that is more *stable* but forms more slowly.

The production of methanal from methanol and oxygen is an example of kinetic control.

$$2CH_3OH(g) + O_2(g) \longrightarrow 2HCHO(g) + 2H_2O(l)$$

This reaction is fast in the presence of a suitable catalyst at a temperature at which the alternative reaction cannot take place. The alternative is burning to carbon dioxide and water. Combustion is more exothermic but has a higher activation energy.

$$2CH_3OH(g) + O_2(g) \longrightarrow 2CO_2(g) + 4H_2O(l)$$

Reaction profiles for alternative reactions illustrating kinetic and thermodynamic control

In the absence of a catalyst, and at a higher temperature, methanol burns to produce the products that are thermodynamically more stable. In these circumstances the system is under *thermodynamic control.*

kinetic inertness is the property of a reaction that does not proceed even though the reaction appears to be feasible (see *feasibility*). The reaction tends to go according to the equilibrium constant, or the *standard electrode potentials*, or the *free energy change*, yet nothing happens. There is no change because the rate of reaction is too slow to be noticeable. There is a barrier preventing change – usually a high *activation energy*. The compound or mixture is inert.

Examples of kinetic inertness are:

- a mixture of methane (natural gas) and oxygen at room temperature
- a solution of *hydrogen peroxide* in the absence of a catalyst
- *aluminum* metal in dilute hydrochloric acid.

Kinetic stability is a term often used for kinetic inertness. It helps, however, to make a sharp distinction between two quite different types of explanation. For clarity, chemists refer to:

- systems with no tendency to react as "stable"
- systems that should react but do not do so for a rate (kinetic) reason as "inert."

kinetics of reactions: see *reaction kinetics*.

kinetic theory of gases: an explanation of why gases obey the *gas laws*. The theory is based on a model of an *ideal gas*. The assumptions are that:

- a gas consists of molecules in rapid, random motion
- the volume of the molecules can be neglected in comparison with the total volume of gas
- the molecules do not attract each other (no *intermolecular forces*)
- the collisions with the walls of any container are perfectly elastic.

By applying Newton's laws of motion and then assuming that the average kinetic energy of molecules is proportional to temperature, it is possible to derive the ideal gas equation from this model.

The model helps to explain why *real gases* deviate from ideal gas behavior.

The model of gas molecules in rapid random motion underlies the theories of *reaction kinetics* and chemical equilibrium.

knocking is a noise from a *gasoline* engine heard when the mixture of fuel and air ignites too early while still being compressed by the piston. This is preignition.

Compression heats up the mixture of fuel and air. Preignition means that the fuel starts burning before being ignited by a spark from the spark plug. Internal combustion engines run powerfully if the fuel starts to burn when the piston is at the right point in the cylinder so that the expanding gases force the piston down smoothly. Knocking is a sign that a fuel with a higher octane number is needed. Prolonged knocking damages an engine.

krypton (Kr) is a *noble gas* that makes up less than 0.1% of *air*. The gas is separated from the other gases in the air by *fractional distillation* and used to fill fluorescent lights and flashbulbs.

L

labile complexes: a term used to describe *complex ions* in which it is easy to replace the *ligands*. Ligand exchange is difficult or impossible with inert complexes.

Chromium(III) and cobalt(III) complexes are *kinetically inert*. Most other complexes are labile.

lanthanide elements: the series of 14 elements between lanthanum and hafnium in the sixth period of the *periodic table*. Across this series of elements the electrons fill the 4*f* energy levels. These elements were once called the "rare earths" but, apart from promethium, they are not rare. Cerium is five times as abundant as lead. The elements all have very similar chemical properties. They can be separated by *ion exchange* or *chromatography*. The main source of these elements is the ore monazite.

lattice: a term used to describe a network of atoms or ions in a crystal.

lattice energy: the standard *enthalpy change* when one mole of an ionic compound forms from free gaseous ions.

$$Na^+(g) + Cl^-(g) \longrightarrow NaCl(s) \qquad \Delta H_{lattice} = -787 \text{ kJ mol}^{-1}$$

Note the difference between the lattice energy and the standard *enthalpy change of formation* of sodium chloride, which refers to the formation of a compound from its elements, $\Delta H_f^{\ominus}[NaCl(s)] = -411 \text{ kJ mol}^{-1}$.

Lattice energy is one of the thermochemical quantities that cannot be measured directly. Lattice energies are calculated indirectly with the help of the *Born–Haber cycle*.

Lattice energies give a measure of the strength of the ionic bonding in a crystal. Ionic bonding is the result of the *electrostatic forces* between the oppositely charged ions. So, for a given crystal structure, the lattice energy increases if:

- the charge on the ions increases
- the ions get smaller (and so closer together).

Lattice energies are used in thermochemical cycles to explore the factors that determine the *enthalpy change of solution* of ionic salts.

layer lattice: a crystal lattice in which there is strong bonding within layers of atoms but relatively weak bonding between the layers. It is often easy to cleave materials with a layer lattice along planes parallel to the layers. Examples of substances with layer lattices are graphite, mica and molybdenum sulfide. Graphite and molybdenum sulfide are used as *lubricants* because of the ease with which layers of atoms slide over each other.

Le Chatelier's principle is a qualitative guide to the effect of changes in concentration, pressure or temperature on a system at equilibrium. The principle was suggested as a general rule by the French physical chemist Henri Le Chatelier (1850–1936).

The principle states that when the conditions of a system at equilibrium change, the position of equilibrium shifts in the direction that tends to counteract the change.

The principle can be used to discuss the conditions chosen for *ammonia manufacture*. The equilibrium system involved is:

$$N_2(g) + 3H_2(g) \rightleftharpoons 2NH_3(g) \qquad \Delta H = -92.4 \text{ kJ mol}^{-1}$$

There are four moles of gases on the left side of the equation but only two moles on the right. Le Chatelier's principle predicts that raising the pressure will make the equilibrium shift from left to right. This reduces the number of molecules and so tends to reduce the pressure. So increasing the pressure increases the proportion of ammonia at equilibrium.

The reaction is *exothermic* from left to right and so *endothermic* from right to left. Le Chatelier's principle predicts that raising the temperature will make the position of equilibrium shift in the direction that takes in energy (tending to cool the mixture). So raising the temperature lowers the proportion of ammonia at equilibrium.

Le Chatelier's principle can be misleading, especially when predicting the effects of changes in concentration or pressure. It is generally better to use the *equilibrium law* and the values of K_c or K_p to predict the effect of changes in concentration or pressure.

leaching is a process for separating a material from an insoluble solid using a suitable solvent. Leaching is one of the methods used to extract metals from low-grade ores. Copper is obtained in this way from waste dumps at old mines. These dumps contain ores that have been oxidized by weathering. The finely divided ore is treated with sulfuric acid in a leach tank stirred by a flow of air.

$$Cu_2(OH)_2CO_3(s) + 4H^+(aq) \longrightarrow 2Cu^{2+}(aq) + 3H_2O(l) + CO_2(g)$$

Leaching also describes the extraction of nitrates and other fertilizers from soil by rainwater. Water draining through the soil can carry away soluble nitrate ions into lakes and streams, causing *eutrophication*.

lead (Pb) is a grayish metal often used on roofs of buildings because it resists corrosion and is malleable so that it can be bent to fit the shape and create a waterproof flashing where roof tiles meet walls. Lead is a dense metal and is an effective shield to stop X-rays and other radiations. Lead melts at a relatively low temperature for a metal and, when alloyed with tin, produces solder with an even lower melting point (see *eutectic mixture*).

Lead comes below tin in *group 4* of the periodic table. It forms compounds in two *oxidation states*: +2 and +4. The +2 state is more stable so that compounds in the +4 state are oxidizing agents.

Lead forms two soluble lead(II) compounds: the nitrate and the ethanoate. Lead ions are colorless in solution. Adding alkali to a solution of lead(II) ions gives a white precipitate of $Pb(OH)_2$ that dissolves in excess, showing this hydroxide is *amphoteric*.

The pigment chrome yellow consists of lead chromate, which precipitates on mixing a solution of lead(II) ions with a solution of chromate(VI) ions.

Large amounts of lead are still used to produce the gasoline additive lead tetraethyl, $Pb(C_2H_5)_4$. Burning leaded gasoline has greatly increased the concentrations of lead in the environment. Many countries have decided to phase out leaded gasoline because lead compounds are toxic and can cause brain damage, especially in children.

lead–acid cell: an *electrochemical cell* that is rechargeable because the chemical changes at the electrodes are reversible. The working of the cells involves lead in three *oxidation states* as Pb(0), Pb(II) and Pb(IV).

In a fully charged lead–acid cell the negative electrode consists of lead metal. The positive electrode consists of lead coated with lead(IV) oxide. The electrodes dip into a solution of sulfuric acid. These are the electrode processes as current flows:

- at the negative electrode:

$$Pb(s) + SO_4^{2-}(aq) \longrightarrow PbSO_4(s) + 2e^-$$

- at the positive electrode:

$$PbO_2(s) + SO_4^{2-}(aq) + 4H^+(aq) + 2e^- \longrightarrow PbSO_4(s) + 2H_2O(l)$$

The equations help to explain why the cell is rechargeable. The changes that happen as a current flows from the cell both produce an insoluble solid, lead sulfate. This traps the lead(II) ions beside the electrode instead of dissolving in the electrolyte. So when the current is reversed to charge up the cell, the two reactions can be reversed, turning lead(II) back to lead metal at one electrode and back to PbO_2 at the other.

A 12-volt automobile battery usually consists of six 2 V lead–acid cells connected in series. Banks of lead–acid cells can be used to provide emergency standby power for lighting wherever a mains power cut could be serious. Lead–acid cells have the great advantage that they can be recharged many times and last for a long time.

leaving group: an atom or group of atoms that breaks away from a molecule during a *substitution reaction*.

Nucleophilic substitution *of a hydroxide ion for a bromide ion from 1-bromobutane. The bromide ion is the leaving group.*

Some groups are better at leaving than others. A water molecule is a better leaving group than a hydroxide ion. This explains why the substitution reactions of *alcohols* go faster in acid conditions.

Nucleophilic substitution *of a bromide ion for a hydroxide ion in propan-2-ol. The reaction goes faster under acid conditions. The* — OH *group in the alcohol is protonated, so the leaving group is a water molecule.*

Lewis acid/base theory: a theory that gives a very broad definition of acids and bases in terms of electron pairs. A Lewis acid is a molecule or ion that can form a bond by accepting a pair of electrons. A Lewis base is a molecule or ion that can form a bond by donating a pair of electrons.

The formation of an *oxonium ion* is a Lewis acid–base reaction between the proton (a Lewis acid) and a water molecule (a Lewis base). So, in this theory, it is the proton rather than the proton donor, that is an acid.

Formation of an oxonium ion as the Lewis base, water, forms a dative covalent bond with a proton

$$H^+ \quad \overset{H}{\underset{\underset{\text{Lewis}}{\text{base}}}{:O{-}H}} \longrightarrow \underset{\underset{\text{}}{}}{H{-}\overset{H}{\underset{\bullet\bullet}{O}}{-}H}{}^+$$

Lewis acid   Lewis base

This much wider definition of acids and bases describes the formation of a *complex ion* as a reaction between a metal ion (a Lewis acid) and *ligands* (Lewis bases).

Complex formation as a Lewis acid–base reaction

$$\underset{\underset{\text{acid}}{\text{Lewis}}}{Ni^{2+}} \quad + \quad \underset{\underset{\text{base}}{\text{Lewis}}}{6\,{:}NH_3} \quad \longrightarrow \quad \underset{\text{Complex ion}}{[Ni(NH_3)_6]^{2+}}$$

Aluminum chloride ($AlCl_3$) is a Lewis acid. This accounts for its use as a catalyst in a *Friedel–Crafts reaction.*

$$\underset{\text{Lewis acid}}{\overset{\text{Cl}}{\underset{\text{Cl}}{Cl{-}Al}}} \quad \underset{\text{Lewis base}}{Cl{-}Cl} \longrightarrow \left[\overset{\text{Cl}}{\underset{\text{Cl}}{Cl{-}Al{-}Cl}}\right]^- \quad + \quad \underset{\underset{\text{in benzene}}{\text{for substitution}}}{\underset{\text{Electrophile}}{Cl^+}}$$

Aluminum chloride acting as a Lewis acid

Chemists normally use the *Brønsted–Lowry theory*. When they use the terms acid and base they mean "proton donor" and "proton acceptor." To signal that they are using the wider Lewis definition they refer to "Lewis acids" and "Lewis bases."

ligands are the molecules or ions bound to the central metal ion in a *complex ion*. Examples of molecules that can act as ligands are water and ammonia. Examples of ions that act as ligands are hydroxide ions, chloride ions and cyanide ions. Ligands have one or more *lone pairs of electrons* that can form *coordinate bonds* to the metal ion (see *bidentate ligands, hexadentate ligands* and *edta*).

Reactions involving complex ions in solution often involve exchanging one ligand for another. They are ligand exchange reactions and are often reversible.

$$[Cu(H_2O)_6]^{2+}(aq) \; + \; 4NH_3(aq) \; \rightleftharpoons \; [Cu(NH_3)_4(H_2O)_2]^{2+}(aq) \; + \; 4H_2O(l)$$

Reversible ligand exchange reaction of copper(II) ions

limiting reactant: the chemical in a reaction mixture that is present in an amount that limits the theoretical yield (see *yield calculations*). Often in a chemical synthesis some of the reactants are added in excess to make sure that the most valuable chemical is converted as far as possible to the required product. The limiting reactant is the one that is not in excess and so is used up (if the reaction goes to completion).

lipids: a broad class of biological compounds that are soluble in organic solvents (such as ethanol) but insoluble in water. Lipids are very varied and include *fatty acids, fats, vegetable oils,* phospholipids and *steroids.*

liquid chromatography was the first type of *chromatography* developed. The Russian botanist Michel Tswett developed the technique to separate plant pigments. In 1903 he separated leaf colors (chlorophylls, carotenes and xanthophylls) by dissolving a leaf extract in a hydrocarbon solvent. He added the extract to the top of a column of powdered chalk and then passed more pure solvent through the column to complete the separation. Running solvent through the column to separate the mixture is called elution and the liquid that flows out of the bottom is the eluate.

This is an example of *adsorption* chromatography. Each compound in the mixture has its own equilibrium between adsorption on the solid and solution in the solvent. Compounds that are strongly adsorbed by the stationary phase move slower; compounds that are more soluble in the solvent move faster.

The liquid leaving the bottom of the column is collected in a series of tubes. Tubes containing parts of the mixture can be detected by their color or some other method such as their appearance in UV light. Components of the mixture can be recovered by evaporating the solvent from these tubes.

liquid crystal: a state of matter that is more ordered than a liquid but less ordered than a solid. Although the liquid crystal state was first noticed as long ago as 1888, it is only since the early 1970s that such crystals have been developed for use in digital watches, calculators and portable computer screens. Much of the pioneering work was done in the United Kingdom by a team lead by George Gray.

liquids flow to take the shape of their container. The atoms, molecules or ions in a liquid are free to move about but with nothing like the freedom of the molecules of a gas. The particles of a liquid are generally slightly more widely spaced than in a solid but the density of packing is only slightly less. Liquids lack the order of crystalline solids. Liquids, like solids, are hard to compress. Unlike gases, they have a definite volume.

liter (symbol l) is a unit of *volume* equal to 1000 cm^3. A liter is the same as a decimeter cubed (dm^3). $1 \text{ dm}^3 = 10 \text{ cm} \times 10 \text{ cm} \times 10 \text{ cm} = 1000 \text{ cm}^3$. Chemists use the dm^3 when calculating because the units can then be worked through consistently. While the m^3 is the *SI unit* of volume, dm^3 is accepted as convenient, and is preferred to the liter.

lithium (Li) is a soft, shiny metal that turns dark gray in air. It is the first member of *group 1* with the *electron configuration* $[He]2s^1$.

Like other group 1 metals, lithium:

- is stored in oil
- floats on water and reacts, but quite slowly, forming hydrogen and LiOH, which is soluble and strongly alkaline

- burns in air with a colored flame (bright red) forming an oxide (Li_2O)
- forms an ionic, crystalline chloride.

The small size of the lithium ion means that some features of lithium chemistry are not typical of the group as a whole:

- hydration – the Li^+ ion is heavily hydrated in water and lithium has the most negative hydration energy in group 1; as a result the *standard electrode potential* for $Li^+(aq)|Li(s)$ is most negative for the group
- solubilities – lithium carbonate and lithium fluoride are only slightly soluble while most other simple compounds of group 1 metals are soluble
- thermal stability – lithium carbonate decomposes on heating while all the other group 1 carbonates are stable; lithium nitrate decomposes to the oxide on heating, unlike the nitrates of sodium and potassium
- covalent bonding – lithium forms a wide range of covalent molecular compounds such as ethyl lithium, C_2H_5Li.

lithium aluminum hydride: see *lithium tetrahydridoaluminate(III)*.

lithium tetrahydridoaluminate(III) (LiAlH$_4$) is a powerful reducing agent used to reduce *aldehydes, ketones, esters* and *carboxylic acids* to alcohols. Many chemists still use the older name, lithium aluminum hydride.

In its reactions the tetrahydridoaluminate(III) ion can be regarded as a source of hydride ions (H^-). The reagent is rapidly hydrolyzed by water so it has to be used in an anhydrous solvent such as dry ether. Where possible *sodium tetrahydridoborate(III)* is preferred because it is easier and safer to use.

lithosphere: the rocks, weathered rocks and soils of the Earth's crust, which make up less than 0.0001% of the volume of the planet. The crust consists largely of oxygen (46.6% by mass) mainly combined with silicon (27.7%) in *silicate* minerals. Only a few other elements are abundant: aluminum (8.1%), iron (5%), calcium (3.6%), sodium (2.8%), potassium (2.6%) and magnesium (2.1%). All other elements together make up the remaining 1.4%.

localized electrons: electron pairs forming covalent bonds between two atoms. Localized electrons are not free to move through a structure, so giant structures with normal covalent bonds, such as diamond and silicon dioxide, do not conduct electricity, unlike giant structures with *delocalized electrons* such as metals and graphite.

logarithms in chemistry are of two kinds, logarithms to base 10 (lg) and natural logarithms to base e (ln).

Chemists use logarithms to base 10 to handle values that range over several orders of magnitude. Logs to base 10 are defined such that:

- lg 1000 = 3
- lg 100 = 2
- lg 10 = 1
- lg 1 = 0
- lg 0.1 = −1
- lg 0.01 = −2

In general lg $10^x = x$.

The hydrogen ion concentration in aqueous solutions typically ranges from 1 to 10^{-14} mol dm^{-3}. The definition of pH ($-\lg [H^+(aq)]$) covers this range in a scale running from 0 to 14.

Also by definition: $\lg xy = \lg x + \lg y$ and $\lg x^n = n \lg x$

so $\lg 1/x = \lg x^{-1} = -\lg x$.

Natural logarithms appear in relationships in thermochemistry and chemical kinetics. They follow similar mathematical rules as logarithms to base 10. In general $\ln e^x = x$.

lone pair of electrons: a pair of electrons in the outer shell of one of the atoms in a molecule or ion that is not involved in bonding.

$$H-\overset{\displaystyle H}{\underset{\displaystyle \bullet\bullet}{|}}\ddot{O}\!: \qquad H-\overset{\displaystyle H}{\underset{\displaystyle \bullet\bullet}{|}}N-H \qquad H-\ddot{\underset{\bullet\bullet}{O}}\!:^{-} \qquad :\overset{\bullet\bullet}{\underset{\bullet\bullet}{Br}}\!:^{-}$$

Examples of molecules and ions with lone pairs of electrons

Lone pairs of electrons:

- affect the *shapes of molecules*
- form *coordinate* (dative covalent) *bonds*
- are important in the chemical reactions of compounds such as *water* and *ammonia*
- are important in *nucleophilic addition* and *nucleophilic substitution* reactions.

(See also *Lewis acids and bases.*)

lubricants are used to reduce friction wherever one surface slides over another. Lubricating oils for engines are usually based on oil fractions with molecules in the size range C_{20} to C_{34}. Synthetic lubricants for specialist purposes include *silicones*, esters and polymers made from *epoxyethane*.

luminescence is a term that includes all the examples of substances emitting light at low temperatures, in contrast to incandescence, which is the emission of light by objects when they are hot, such as the filament of an electric lamp.

Examples of luminescence are:

- **fluorescence** – the immediate emission of light by a material exposed to other radiation such as UV radiation, X-rays or an electron beam
- **phosphorescence** – delayed and slow emission of light from a material after exposure to other forms of radiation
- **chemiluminescence** – light given out during chemical changes (such as from light sticks, fireflies or glow-worms)
- **triboluminescence** – light given out when crushing or breaking a material (such as the flashes of light seen in a darkened room when crushing sugar or opening a self-adhesive envelope).

macromolecular substances are materials made up of very large molecules. They are usually called *polymers*. Macromolecules, like small molecules, have strong *covalent bonds* holding the atoms together within the molecules (*intramolecular forces*) but relatively weak attractions between the molecules (*intermolecular forces*).

Unfortunately the term macromolecule is also used by some writers to describe covalent *giant structures* such as diamond and silica. The argument is that a crystal of a covalent giant structure is like a vast single molecule. This use of the term can be confusing and is best avoided.

magnesium (Mg) is a reactive metallic element in *group 2* of the periodic table. Its *electron configuration* is [Ne]$3s^2$. Samples of the silvery-white metal usually look gray because they are covered with a layer of magnesium oxide.

The source of magnesium metal is electrolysis of molten magnesium chloride obtained either from seawater or salt deposits. The low density of the metal helps to make light alloys, especially with aluminum. These alloys, which are strong for their weight, are especially valuable for automobiles and aircraft. The reactivity of aluminum makes it suitable as the "sacrificial" metal in *anodes* used to protect pipelines and ships from *corrosion* (see *cathodic protection*).

Magnesium burns very brightly in air with an intense white flame forming the white solid magnesium oxide (MgO). It is used in *fireworks* and flares.

Magnesium reacts very slowly with cold water but much more rapidly on heating in steam.

$$Mg(s) + H_2O(g) \longrightarrow MgO(s) + H_2(g)$$

Magnesium forms ionic compounds with nonmetals in which the metal is in the +2 oxidation state as Mg^{2+}. Mg^{2+} is the central metal ion in a chlorophyll molecule.

Magnesium oxide is a white solid made by heating magnesium carbonate. It is a *basic oxide*. In water it turns to magnesium hydroxide, which is slightly soluble. The *antacid* milk of magnesia is a suspension of magnesium hydroxide in water. Magnesium oxide has a high melting point and is used as a *refractory* ceramic to line furnaces.

Epsom salts, a laxative, consist of hydrated magnesium sulfate ($MgSO_4.7H_2O$).

main group elements: a term used by some chemists to describe the elements in the *s-block* and *p-block* of the *periodic table* but excluding the transition elements in the *d-block* and *f-block*.

malleability: metals are malleable if they can be hammered into shape without breaking. It is possible to make very thin sheets of a malleable metal such as gold by hammering.

manganese (Mn) is a hard, gray brittle *d-block* metal with the *electron configuration* [Ar]$3d^54s^2$.

The main oxidation states of manganese are:

- **+7, MnO_4^-** – the purple manganate(VII) ion, which is a strong oxidizing agent especially in acid solution
- **+4, MnO_2** – an insoluble, black compound that is an oxidizing agent in acid solution
- **+2, Mn^{2+}** – the pink manganese(II) ion in salts such as manganese(II) sulfate.

Under special conditions it is also possible to produce solutions with red manganese(III) ions or green manganate(VI) ions. Manganate(VI) is stable in alkaline solution but *disproportionates* to manganate(VI) and manganese(IV) oxide on adding acid. (See also *potassium manganate(VII)*.)

manometer: an instrument for measuring *pressure*. A manometer consists of a U-tube containing a liquid such as water or mercury.

Typically one arm of a manometer is open to the atmosphere, so the instrument measures the extent to which the pressure inside the apparatus is higher or lower than atmospheric pressure.

Markovnikov rule: a rule that predicts the main product when a compound HX (such as H—Br, H—OSO_3H or H—OH) adds to an unsymmetrical *alkene* (such as propene). The rule is that the hydrogen atom adds to the carbon atom that already has more hydrogen atoms attached to it. This pattern was first reported by the Russian chemist Vladimir Markovnikov who studied a great many alkene *addition reactions* during the 1860s.

Markovnikov rule

The mechanism for electrophilic addition helps to account for this rule. When HBr is added to propene there are two possible intermediate *carbocations*. The secondary carbocation is preferred because it is slightly more stable than the primary carbocation. The secondary ion has two alkyl groups pushing electrons toward the positively charged carbon atom (see *inductive effect*). This helps to stabilize the ion by "spreading" the charge over the ion (see figure).

mass (symbol *m*) is a fundamental physical quantity. The *SI unit* of mass is the kilogram (kg). 1 kg = 1000 g.

Mass can be determined by measuring the pull of gravity on a specimen. This is how chemists usually measure the masses of chemicals with a chemical balance.

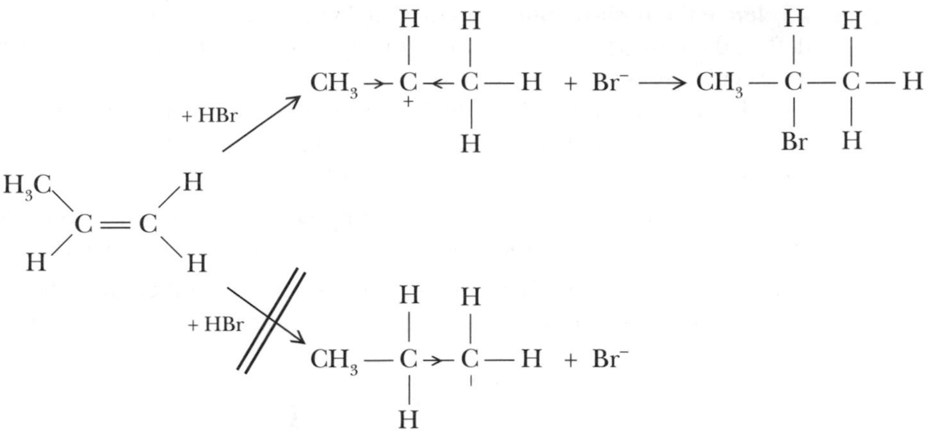

$$CH_3 \rightarrow \overset{\overset{\displaystyle H}{|}}{\underset{\underset{\displaystyle H}{|}}{\overset{+}{C}}} \leftarrow \overset{\overset{\displaystyle H}{|}}{\underset{}{C}} - H \;+\; Br^- \longrightarrow CH_3 - \overset{\overset{\displaystyle H}{|}}{\underset{\underset{\displaystyle Br}{|}}{C}} - \overset{\overset{\displaystyle H}{|}}{\underset{\underset{\displaystyle H}{|}}{C}} - H$$

+ HBr

$$\underset{\underset{\displaystyle H}{|}}{\overset{\overset{\displaystyle H_3C}{\diagdown}}{}} C = C \underset{\underset{\displaystyle H}{\diagdown}}{\overset{\diagup H}{}}$$

+ HBr

$$CH_3 - \overset{\overset{\displaystyle H}{|}}{\underset{\underset{\displaystyle H}{|}}{C}} \rightarrow \overset{\overset{\displaystyle H}{|}}{\underset{}{C}} - H \;+\; Br^-$$

Markovnikov rule: an explanation

Alternatively masses can be found by seeing how much an object accelerates when a force acts on it. This is how chemists measure the masses of ionized atoms and molecules in *mass spectrometry*.

mass number: see *nucleon number*.

mass spectrometry: an accurate instrumental technique for determining *relative atomic masses* and *relative molecular masses*. Mass spectrometry can also help to determine molecular structures and to identify unknown compounds.

Inside a mass spectrometer there is a high vacuum so that it is possible to produce and study ionized atoms and molecules including fragments of molecules that do not otherwise exist.

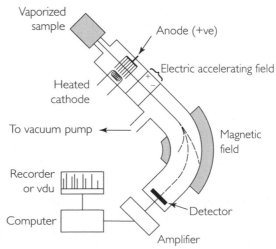

Diagram of a mass spectrometer

The stages in producing a mass spectrum are as follows:

- inject a small sample into the instrument, where it vaporizes
- bombard the sample with a beam of high-energy electrons, which turns the atoms or molecules into positive ions by knocking out electrons

223

- accelerate the positive ions in an electric field
- deflect the moving stream of ions with a magnetic field to focus ions with a particular mass onto the detector
- feed the signal from the detector to a computer, which prints out a mass spectrum as the magnetic field steadily changes over a range of values to focus the series of ions with different masses one by one onto the detector.

The instrument is calibrated using a reference compound with a known structure and molecular mass so that the computer can print a scale on the mass spectrum.

The mass spectrum for an element shows the relative abundance of different *isotopes* of the element. This makes it possible to calculate the relative atomic mass for the element.

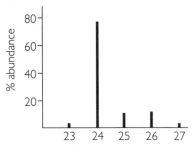

Mass spectrum of magnesium

Mass of the positive ions detected

When molecular compounds are being analyzed, the peak of the ion with the highest mass is usually the whole molecule ionized. So the mass of this "parent ion" is the relative molecular mass of the compound.

Bombarding molecules with high-energy electrons splits them into fragments so the mass spectrum is a "fragmentation pattern." The computer has a database of mass spectra so it can identify an unknown compound by matching its spectrum with one in its database.

A chemist who synthesizes new compounds can study their fragmentation patterns to identify the fragments from their masses and then piece together likely structures with the help of evidence from other methods of analysis such as *infrared spectroscopy* and *nuclear magnetic resonance spectroscopy.*

The combination of *gas–liquid chromatography* (glc) with mass spectrometry is of great importance in modern chemical analysis. First glc separates the chemicals in an unknown mixture, such as a sample of polluted water; then mass spectrometry detects and identifies the components.

matches use phosphorus compounds to make a flame. In a match that will strike anywhere, the head contains phosphorus sulfide (P_4S_3) and potassium chlorate(v) as an oxidizing agent. The head contains the fuel and the oxidant and needs only friction to heat the match and start a fire.

Safety matches have sulfur and potassium chlorate(v) in the head and red phosphorus in the striking strip on the side of the box.

Maxwell–Boltzmann distribution: the distribution of molecular kinetic energies for a gas at a particular temperature.

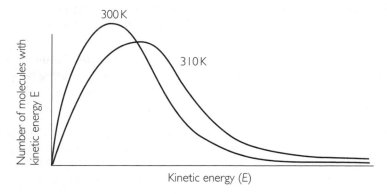

Boltzman distribution of molecular kinetic energies in a gas at two temperatures. The modal speed gets higher as the temperature rises. The area under the curve gives the total number of molecules. This does not change as the temperature rises so the peak height falls as the curve widens.

The Boltzman distribution is important in the *collision theory* of reaction rates and helps to account for the effects of temperature changes and *catalysts* on *rates of reaction*.

mechanism of a reaction: a description of how a reaction takes place, showing step by step the bonds that break and the new bonds that form. Some mechanisms involve *homolytic bond breaking* with *free-radical* intermediates. Other mechanisms involve *heterolytic bond breaking* and ionic intermediates.

Mechanisms with ionic intermediates can be classified according to the type of attacking molecules or ions involved. *Nucleophiles* attack atoms at the δ+ end of *polar covalent bonds. Electrophiles* attack regions that are electron rich, especially double bonds and the *delocalized electrons* in arenes.

Evidence used to support a proposed mechanism include the:

- *rate equation* for the reaction
- identification of *intermediates* using *spectroscopy* or other methods
- use of *isotopic labeling* to track what happens to particular atoms during a reaction.

medicine: a substance or mixture of substances used to treat a disease or to give relief from the symptoms of disease. A medicine normally contains one or more active *drugs* dissolved in water or mixed with an inert solid. Mixing the active ingredient with an inert material makes it easier to give an accurate dose.

For a medicine taken by mouth, added flavoring may make the medicine more palatable and coloring can help to identify a drug. Other drugs are taken by injection or drawn into the lungs by a deep breath.

The pharmaceutical industry employs many chemists in *drug development* for medicine.

melting is a change of state from a solid to a liquid. Another word for melting is fusion. The melting point for a pure substance is the temperature at which the solid and liquid are in equilibrium. It is the same temperature as the *freezing point*. Melting points vary with pressure but only very slightly.

Pure compounds have sharp melting points. Measuring melting points is a way of checking the purity and identity of compounds. This technique is especially important in *organic chemistry*.

Molecular substances melt at relatively low temperatures because the intermolecular forces between molecules are weak. *Giant structures*, with strong bonding between the atoms, have high melting points. Energy is needed to overcome the bonds between particles as a substance melts (see *enthalpy change of melting*).

meniscus: the curved surface of a liquid in a tube. Water forms a concave meniscus in a glass tube because water molecules can form *hydrogen bonds* with oxygen atoms at a clean glass surface. This allows water to wet the glass (see *wetting*). Mercury atoms bond strongly with themselves but not with atoms in glass, so mercury has no tendency to wet glass and forms a convex meniscus.

Chemists have to allow for the shape of the meniscus when calibrating and reading graduated glassware such as pipettes and graduated flasks. The correct procedure is to adjust the level until the bottom of the meniscus just touches the mark as seen from eyes on a level with the mark.

mercury (Hg) is the only liquid metal at room temperature. As a dense liquid, mercury (density 13.6 g cm^{-3}) has long been used to measure pressure in *manometers* and barometers. A *pressure* of 1 atmosphere is the pressure at the bottom of a column of mercury 760 mm high.

Mercury forms *amalgams* with metals. In the chlor-alkali industry, a mercury cell for the electrolysis of sodium chloride (brine) has a flowing mercury cathode (see *electrolysis of brine*). The product of electrolysis at the cathode is an amalgam of sodium in mercury. The amalgam flows to a separate vessel where the sodium in the amalgam reacts with water to make sodium hydroxide and hydrogen. This process produces very pure sodium hydroxide but it is being phased out because of the pollution problems caused by the traces of mercury that escape into the environment. Mercury vapor and mercury compounds are very toxic.

metabolism consists of all the chemical changes in living things, most of which are catalyzed by *enzymes*. Some metabolic reactions (catabolism) break down larger molecules into smaller ones, such as the *hydrolysis* and *oxidation* of food. Other metabolic processes (anabolism) produce more complex molecules from simpler molecules, such as *proteins* from *amino acids*.

metal extraction involves two main types of process to reduce metal compounds to metals:

- **pyrometallurgy** – reactions at high temperature often above 1000°C;
  - electrolysis of a molten compound (for example, *aluminum extraction*)
  - chemical reduction by coke in a blast furnace (for example, *iron extraction*)
  - chemical reduction by a more reactive metal (for example, *chromium and titanium extraction*)
- **hydrometallurgy** – reactions at low temperature in solution in water;
  - electrowinning using *electrolysis* of an aqueous solution (for example, *zinc extraction*)

– cementation using a *displacement reaction* (for example, using iron to displace copper from a solution of copper(II) sulfate).

metallic bonds: the strong bonding between atoms in metal crystals. Each metal atom in a metal crystal contributes electrons from its outer shell to a "sea" of *delocalized electrons*. Only elements with relatively low first *ionization energies* form metallic crystals.

By losing electrons the metal atoms become positively charged. So a metal crystal consists of positively charged metal atoms held together by a "sea" of shared electrons.

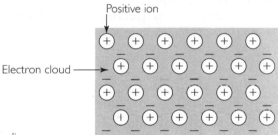

Simplified picture of metallic bonding

Metals conduct because the shared bonding electrons can drift through the crystal structure from atom to atom when there is an electric potential difference.

Metals can bend without breaking because metallic bonding is not highly directional. Lines or layers of metal atoms can shift their position in a crystal without the bonds breaking.

metalloid: an element with properties in between those of metals and non-metals. One example of such intermediate behavior is that metalloids are *semiconductors*. Their electrical conductivities are between those of metals and non-metal insulators.

In *group 4*, the metalloid germanium comes between two nonmetals at the top of the group and two metals at the bottom. Other examples of metalloids are *arsenic*, antimony and tellurium. Some chemists also classify silicon and boron as metalloids.

metals are elements on the left-hand side of the *periodic table* with one, two or three electrons in the outer shell that take part in bonding and chemical reactions.

Physically, metals are :

- shiny when freshly polished and free of corrosion
- good conductors of electricity and thermal energy
- *malleable* and *ductile*
- (usually) solids with high melting and boiling points (only six metals melt below 100°C – mercury, which is a liquid, gallium and four group 1 metals: sodium, potassium, rubidium and cesium).

Chemically, metals tend to:

- lose electrons forming positive ions (they are *reducing agents*)

- form *basic* or *amphoteric oxides* and hydroxides (which are *alkalis* if soluble in water)
- form solid, ionic chlorides.

The more an element shows these properties, the greater its "metallic character."

methylated spirit: ethanol (alcohol) mixed with about 5% methanol. Industrial methylated spirit is used as a *solvent* commercially and in laboratories. Surgical spirit is industrial methylated spirit with other additives including castor oil.

The methylated spirit sold in hardware stores as a solvent and fuel may be additionally dyed blue.

micelle: a cluster of *surfactant* molecules in a solution. A micelle has the "water-hating" (hydrophobic) hydrocarbon chains tangled together inside with the "water-loving" (hydrophilic) ends of the molecules on the outside.

Cross section of a spherical micelle formed when a surfactant dissolves in water. A micelle is likely to consist of about 50 to 100 molecules. The diameter of a micelle is in the range 5 to 50 nm.

The inside of a micelle is nonpolar. Unlike water, a solution of a surfactant in water can dissolve oil and grease. The molecules of oily dirt diffuse to the inside of the micelles.

microwaves: *electromagnetic radiation* with wavelengths in the range 1 mm to 30 cm and frequencies in the range 10^8 to 10^9 Hz. A polar molecule can absorb microwave radiation. The quanta of microwave radiation correspond to the energy jumps when molecules gain energy and rotate faster (see *quantum theory*).

A microwave oven is "tuned" so that the radiation is absorbed by water molecules to make them spin. The microwaves can pass through food where they are absorbed by liquid water molecules. As the water molecules gain energy they bump into neighboring molecules and the energy spreads through the food as the molecules spin, vibrate and move around more, so the food gets hotter.

milliliter (symbol ml) is a unit of *volume* often used on chemical glassware, in medicine and domestically. A milliliter is one thousandth of a *liter*.

$$1000 \text{ ml} = 1000 \text{ cm}^3 = 1 \text{ dm}^3 = 1 \text{ liter}$$

minerals are the naturally occurring elements and compounds in the crust of the Earth. Most rocks are mixtures of minerals. There are round about 3000 minerals, of which 300 or so are important to the mineral and chemical industries.

Many *ores* contain only a small percentage of the useful minerals. The purpose of mineral processing is to separate the valuable mineral from the waste rock ("gangue").

Processing generally starts by crushing and grinding the ore to break it up and separate the mineral grains. The methods used to separate the minerals include:

- mechanical separation, often based on differences in *density*
- *froth flotation*
- chemical extraction by *leaching.*

mirror-image molecules: see *chiral compounds.*

miscible liquids are liquids that mix with each other. The general rule is that "like dissolves like." This means that:

- nonpolar liquids mix freely with other nonpolar liquids (for example, *hydrocarbons* mix freely, as they do in *gasoline*)
- polar liquids mix with polar liquids (for example, ethanol mixes with water)
- but polar and nonpolar liquids do not mix (gasoline floats on water).

mixed oxides are oxides that consist of a lattice of oxide ions (O^{2-}) with two or more types of metal ions, M^{n+}, in the spaces between the negative ions. So they are not mixtures of oxides but a distinct compound with a mixture of metal ions.

Examples of mixed oxides are:

- **red lead** (Pb_3O_4), which has a crystal lattice made up of ions in the proportions $2Pb^{2+}: Pb^{4+}: 4O^{2-}$
- **magnetite** (Fe_3O_4), the magnetic ore of iron originally called lodestone, which contains $2Fe^{3+}$ ions for each Fe^{2+} ion in the lattice, and other magnetic *ferrites* such as $CaFe_2O_4$ in which Ca^{2+} ions take the place of Fe^{2+}
- **spinel** ($MgAl_2O_4$), made by heating aluminum oxide with magnesium oxide. Replacing some Al_2O_3 with 1% Cr_2O_3 produces a ruby-like gemstone.

mixtures are many and varied but all consist of two or more substances mixed up together. Unlike compounds, which have a definite formula, the composition of mixtures can vary widely.

The study of mixtures is very important because chemists have to know how to:

- separate mixtures – by *chromatography, distillation, filtration, froth flotation,* and *solvent extraction*
- formulate new mixtures for special purposes – when making *medicines, paints, detergents, dyes, pesticides, fertilizers* and many other products.

mobile phase: the liquid or gas that moves over the stationary *phase* during *chromatography.*

Mohs scale of hardness: a scale for comparing the *hardness* of materials and minerals. The scale is based on scratching one substance with another. A harder material scratches a less hard material. The scale ranges from 1 for talc, which is very soft, to 10 for diamond, which is very hard.

molar concentration: see *concentration of solutions.* In some books you will see the term "molarity" used for the molar concentration. Chemists still sometimes write 2.0 M to describe a solution with a molar concentration of 2.0 mol dm^{-3}.

molarity: see *molar concentration.*

molar mass: the mass per mole of a chemical (see *amount of substance*). The symbol for the molar mass is M. The unit is g mol^{-1}. As always with molar amounts the chemical *entity* must be specified. The molar mass of hydrogen atoms $M(H) = 1$ g mol^{-1}. The molar mass of hydrogen molecules $M(H_2) = 2$ g mol^{-1}.

The molar mass for the atoms of an element is numerically equal to the *relative atomic mass* of the element. The relative atomic mass of carbon is 12. The molar mass of carbon atoms = 12 g mol^{-1}.

The molar mass of a substance is calculated by adding up the molar masses of the atoms in the formula.

$$M_r(H_2O) = [(2 \times 1 \text{ g mol}^{-1}) + 16 \text{ g mol}^{-1}] = 18 \text{ g mol}^{-1}$$
$$M_r(CuSO_4) = [63.5 \text{ g mol}^{-1} + 32 \text{ g mol}^{-1} + (4 \times 16 \text{ g mol}^{-1})] = 159.5 \text{ g mol}^{-1}$$
$$M_r(CuSO_4.5H_2O) = [159.5 \text{ g mol}^{-1} + (5 \times 18 \text{ g mol}^{-1})]$$
$$= 249.5 \text{ g mol}^{-1}$$

Molar masses can be measured experimentally by *mass spectrometry*.

Another method for measuring molar masses applies to gases and to liquids that are easy to vaporize. The procedure is to inject a weighed sample of liquid into a syringe heated in an oven. Measurements taken include the *volume* of vapor, the temperature of the vapor and its *pressure* (the *atmospheric pressure*). Measurements are converted to *SI units* and then substituted in the *ideal gas* equation to find the amount in moles, n.

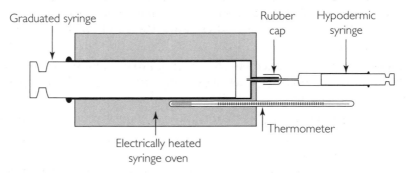

Syringe method for determining molar masses of volatile liquids

---

Worked example:

A 0.124 g sample of a liquid evaporated to give 45 cm^3 vapor at 100°C and a pressure of 1 atmosphere. What is the molar mass of the liquid?

Notes on the method

Convert all units to SI units.

Substitute in the equation $PV = nRT$ to find n (the amount in moles).

Answer

Pressure $= 101.3 \times 10^3$ Nm^{-2}

Volume $= 45 \times 10^{-6}$ m^3

Temperature $= 373$ K

The gas constant $= 8.31 \, \text{J} \, \text{mol}^{-1} \, \text{K}^{-1}$

$$n = \frac{PV}{RT} = \frac{101.3 \times 10^3 \, \text{Nm}^{-2} \times 15 \times 10^{-6} \, \text{m}^3}{8.31 \, \text{J} \, \text{mol}^{-1} \, \text{K}^{-1} \times 373 \, \text{K}} = 1.47 \times 10^{-3} \, \text{mol}$$

$$\text{molar mass} = \frac{\text{mass of sample}}{\text{amount in moles}} = \frac{0.124 \, \text{g}}{1.47 \times 10^{-3} \, \text{mol}} = 84 \, \text{g} \, \text{mol}^{-1}$$

molar volume: the volume of a one mole *amount of substance*. The molar volume of any gas is the same under given conditions of temperature and pressure. This follows from *Avogadro's law* or from the *ideal gas* equation.

Rearranging the ideal gas equation, $PV = nRT$, gives: $V = \dfrac{nRT}{P}$

This shows that, for one mole of gas ($n = 1$), the volume (the molar volume) depends only on the temperature and pressure since R is a constant. The molar volume of an ideal gas at stp (273 K and $101.3 \times 10^{-3} \, \text{N} \, \text{m}^{-2}$) $= 22\,400 \, \text{cm}^3$.

mole: the chemist's term for an amount of a substance containing a particular number of atoms, molecules ions or any other type of particles. The word entered the language of chemistry at the end of the nineteenth century based on the Latin word for a heap or pile.

The mole is the *SI unit* for *amount of substance*. One mole is the amount of substance that contains as many specified *entities* (atoms, molecules, ions, electrons and so on) as there are atoms in exactly 12 g of the carbon-12 *isotope*. The number of entities per mole is the *Avogadro constant*.

mole fraction: a way of measuring the proportion of a substance in a mixture where it is the amount in moles that is important and not the chemical nature of the components.

In a mixture of n_A moles of A with n_B moles of B and n_C moles of C, the mole fractions (symbol X) are given by the following:

$$X_A = \frac{n_A}{n_A + n_B + n_C} \qquad X_B = \frac{n_B}{n_A + n_B + n_C} \qquad X_C = \frac{n_C}{n_A + n_B + n_C}$$

So the mole fraction of B is the fraction of all the moles that are moles of B.

The sum of all the mole fractions is 1, so $X_A + X_B + X_C = 1$.

Mole fractions are used by chemists when studying:

- gas mixtures (see *partial pressures*)
- the vapor pressure of solutions and mixtures of liquids (see *Raoult's law*).

molecular formula: a formula that shows the number of atoms of each element in a molecule. The molecular formula of chlorine is Cl_2, that of ammonia is NH_3 and that of ethanol is C_2H_5OH. The term molecular formula applies only to substances that consist of *molecules*.

A molecular formula is always a simple multiple of the *empirical formula*. Analysis shows that the empirical formula of hexane is C_3H_7. The mass spectrum shows that the relative molecular mass of hexane is 86. The relative mass of the empirical formula $M_r(C_3H_7) = (3 \times 12) + (7 \times 1) = 43$. So the molecular formula is twice the empirical formula. The molecular formula of hexane is C_6H_{14}.

molecular models: physical and computer models used to show the atoms in molecules, the bonding between them and the shapes of molecules in three dimensions. In many physical models there is an agreed color code: C – black, H – white, O – red, N – blue and Cl – green. Computer-generated models often use different colors. (See *ball and stick models* and *space-filling models*.)

molecular orbitals are the orbitals in molecules that form as *atomic orbitals* overlap and interact when atoms bond together. Molecular orbitals fill with electrons according to the same rules as atomic orbitals. Molecular orbitals show the relative energies of the electrons in molecules. Their shapes also show the regions in space where there is a high probability of finding electrons. (See *sigma bond* and *pi bonds*.)

molecular sieve: a solid with very fine pores that can separate molecules according to size. Small molecules can fit into the holes or channels in the crystal structure while larger molecules cannot. (See *zeolites*.)

molecularity of reaction steps: the number of reacting particles taking place in one step in the *mechanism of a reaction*. Often the term refers specifically to the rate-determining step in the mechanism. The S_N1 mechanism for *nucleophilic substitution* is unimolecular. The S_N2 mechanism is bimolecular.

molecule: a group of atoms held together by covalent bonding. Most nonmetals are molecular, such as H_2, N_2, P_4, S_8, Cl_2, Br_2 and I_2. Most compounds of nonmetals with other nonmetals are also molecular, such as H_2O, CO_2, CH_4, NH_3, HBr, $SiCl_4$, PCl_3.

The covalent bonds in molecules are strong (*intramolecular forces*). The forces between molecules (*intermolecular forces*) are weak. Molecular substances have low melting and boiling points because of the weakness of intermolecular forces.

monochromatic radiation is radiation with a single wavelength. Spectrometers contain a diffraction grating or prism to provide monochromatic radiation. Rotating the grating or prism allows the instrument to scan across the range of wavelengths provided by the source of radiation.

A filter in a colorimeter is a cheap way of selecting a narrow range of wavelengths typically with a band width of 20 to 50 nm. The disadvantage of a filter is that the operator has to change the filter to change from one band of wavelengths to another.

Monochromatic light is also important when measuring the rotation of *polarized light* by optically active compounds.

monodentate ligands are *ligands* that use a single *lone pair of electrons* to form one bond with the central metal atom in a *complex ion*. Examples of monodentate ligands are ammonia molecules, water molecules, chloride ions and cyanide ions.

monomers are the small molecules that join together in long chains to make *polymers*.

monoprotic acid: an *acid* that can give away (donate) only one *proton* per molecule. Examples of monoprotic acids are: hydrogen chloride, HCl; ethanoic acid, CH_3CO_2H; and nitric acid, HNO_3.

monosaccharide: see *carbohydrates*.

monotropy: a type of allotropy in which there is a one-way tendency for a less stable *allotrope* to change to the more stable allotrope. The rate of change may be imperceptibly slow. Carbon and phosphorus both show monotropy. Graphite is thermodynamically stable relative to diamond. The red allotrope of phosphorus is stable relative to the white form. (Compare with *enantiotropy*.)

mordant: a chemical that fixes a dye to the fibers of a textile. Alums and other aluminum salts are used as mordants. *Coordinate bonds* form both between — OH groups of cotton and aluminum ions and between oxygen atoms on the dye and aluminum ions.

Fiber

Aluminum ions acting as a mordant for the dye alizarin

Alizarin is a natural red dye once extracted from the roots of the madder plant but now made synthetically. Alizarin only sticks fast to cloth in the presence of a mordant and the color of the dye varies depending on the metal ions in the mordant.

multiple bonds are *double bonds* or *triple bonds* between atoms in molecules. In a double bond there are two shared pairs of electrons. In a triple bond there are three shared pairs.

mutagens are agents that cause mutations. A mutation is a change in the genetic material of living cells. Some chemicals are mutagenic and so are the forms of *ionizing radiation*.

names of carbon compounds: modern *IUPAC* names make it possible to determine the name from the formula and the formula from the name.

The name of an organic compound is based on the longest straight chain or main ring of carbon atoms in the skeleton of carbon atoms. If the main part is a straight chain the name is based on the corresponding *alkane.* For ring compounds the name is based on the corresponding *alicyclic* compound or *arene.*

Numbering the carbon atoms identifies the positions of side chains and *functional groups*, with the number repeated if there are two side groups on the same carbon atom. At all times chains are numbered from the end that gives the lowest possible numbers in the name. Numbers are omitted when there is no doubt about the position of the side chains or functional groups, as in ethanol.

Prefixes (in front of) and suffixes (following) the hydrocarbon name identify the side chains and functional groups.

Where there are two or more of the same side chain or functional group the number is stated as di, tri, tetra and so on.

Prefixes are used for:

- *alkyl groups*, such as 2,3-dimethylbutane or 1,3,5-trimethylbenzene
- *halogenoalkanes*, such as 2-iodopropane or tetrachloromethane.

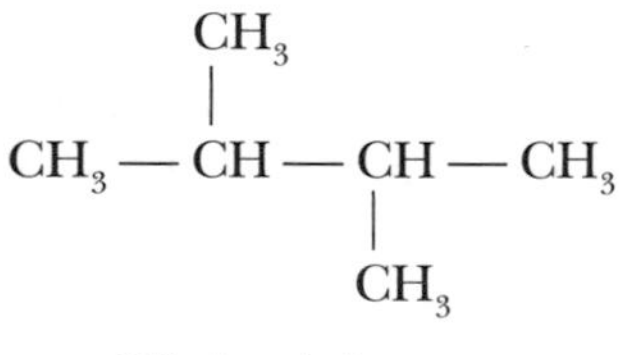

2,3-dimethylbutane

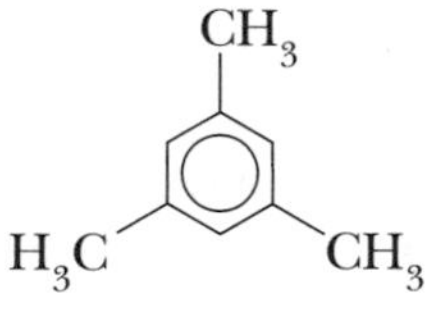

1,3,5-trimethylbenzene

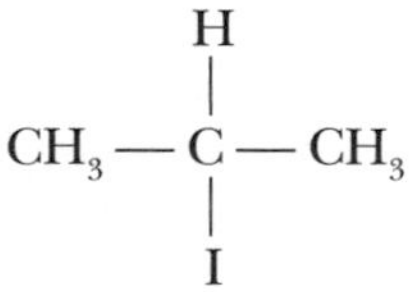

2-iodopropane

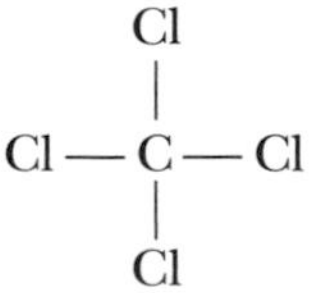

tetrachloromethane

Structures of the examples

Suffixes are used for:

- double bonds in *alkenes*, such as but-2-ene (with a double bond between the second and third carbon atoms)

- *alcohols*, such as propan-1,2,3-triol
- *aldehydes*, such as propanal
- *ketones*, such as pentan-3-one
- *carboxylic acids*, such as hexanoic acid and ethanedioic acid
- *amines*, such as ethylamine and *phenylamine*.

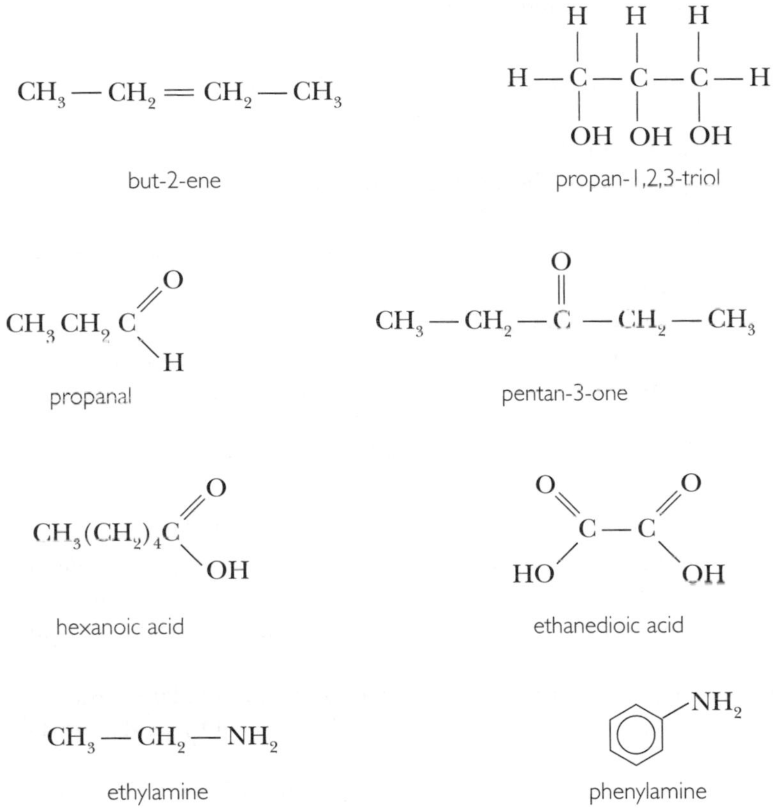

$$CH_3 — CH_2 = CH_2 — CH_3$$

but-2-ene

$$H—C—C—C—H$$ with OH OH OH

propan-1,2,3-triol

$$CH_3 CH_2 C \big\langle{}^O_H$$

propanal

$$CH_3 — CH_2 — \overset{O}{\overset{\|}{C}} — CH_2 — CH_3$$

pentan-3-one

$$CH_3(CH_2)_4 C \big\langle{}^O_{OH}$$

hexanoic acid

$$HO \diagdown \overset{O}{C} — \overset{O}{C} \diagdown OH$$

ethanedioic acid

$$CH_3 — CH_2 — NH_2$$

ethylamine

phenylamine

Structures of the examples

The systematic names of complex molecules can be hard to pronounce and cumbersome. Chemists sometimes still use older, traditional names, which were often based on the Latin name for the source of the compound or where it was discovered. The organic acid 2,3-dihydroxybutanedioic acid, for example, occurs in grape juice. The traditional name is tartaric acid from "tartar," the name of the recrystallized deposits of tartaric acid salts collected from inside wine containers.

names of complex ions: the systematic names of complex ions show:

- first the number of *ligands*, "di," "tri," "tetra," "penta," "hexa"
- then the type of ligands (in alphabetical order if there is more than one type of ligand), such as "aqua" for water molecules, "ammine" for ammonia, "chloro" for chloride ions and "cyano" for cyanide ions

- next the identity of the central metal atom in a form that shows whether or not the ion is a cation or an anion:
  - for cations (and uncharged complexes) the metal name is normal, such as silver, iron or copper
  - for anions the metal name ends in "ate" and often has an old-fashioned style such as argentate for silver, ferrate for iron and cuprate for copper
- finally the oxidation number of the metal.

Examples:

- $[Ag(NH_3)_2]^+$ is the diamminesilver(I) ion
- $[Cu(H_2O)_6]^{2+}$ is the hexaaquacopper(II) ion
- $[CuCl_4]^{2-}$ is the tetrachlorocuprate(II) ion
- $[Fe(CN)_6]^{4-}$ is the hexacyanoferrate(II) ion
- $[Fe(CN)_6]^{3-}$ is the hexacyanoferrate(III) ion.

Note that the overall charge on the complex ion is the sum of the charges on the metal ion and the ligands.

names of inorganic compounds are becoming increasingly systematic but chemists still use a mixture of names. Most chemists prefer to call $CuSO_4.5H_2O$ hydrated copper(II) sulfate, or perhaps copper(II) sulfate-5-water but not the fully systematic name tetraaquocopper(II) tetraoxosulfate(VI)-1-water. The systematic name has much more to say about the arrangement of atoms, molecules and ions in the blue crystals but it is too cumbersome for normal use.

These are some of the basic rules for common inorganic names:

- the ending "ide" shows that a compound contains just two elements mentioned in the name. The more *electronegative* element comes second, for example, sodium sulfide (Na_2S), carbon dioxide (CO_2) and phosphorus trichloride (PCl_3)
- the small Roman numerals in names are the oxidation numbers of the elements, for example iron(II) sulfate ($FeSO_4$) and iron(III) sulfate $Fe_2(SO_4)_3$
- the names of *oxoacids* end "ic" or "ous" as in sulfuric (H_2SO_4) and sulfurous (H_2SO_3) acids and nitric (HNO_3) and nitrous (HNO_2) acids, where the "ic" ending is for the acid in which the central atom has the higher oxidation number
- the corresponding endings for the salts of oxoacids are "ate" and "ite" as in sulfate (SO_4^{2-}) and sulfite (SO_3^{2-}) and in nitrate (NO_3^-) and nitrite (NO_2^-).

To avoid misunderstandings chemists give the name and formula. If necessary they may also give two names: the systematic name and the traditional name.

nanometer: the unit of length used for the sizes of atoms, molecules and ions. One nanometer (1 nm) is one thousand millionths of a meter (10^{-9} m). So there are one million nanometers in a millimeter (1000 nm = 1 mm). One nanometer is roughly five times the diameter of a hydrogen atom.

naphtha is a mixture of hydrocarbons from the *fractional distillation of oil*. The naphtha fraction is an important feedstock for the *petrochemical industry*. Naphtha contains *hydrocarbons* with 6 to 10 carbon atoms in their molecules.

narcotics are powerful painkillers (analgesics) that also lessen anxiety and give a feeling of wellbeing. Regular use of narcotic analgesics can lead to drug dependence. Morphine is the oldest and most well-known narcotic; it is obtained from the dried juice of opium poppies (so it is an opiate). Morphine is used medically to treat patients in severe pain.

Diamorphine, otherwise known as heroin, is made from morphine. It is an even more powerful analgesic than morphine. It is also highly addictive so its medical use is limited mainly to the treatment of pain in patients who are going to die.

Codeine is another opiate. It is a much less powerful painkiller than morphine but it does not cause dependence. Unlike morphine, codeine can be taken by mouth. Codeine is an ingredient of some cough medicines because it helps to stop people coughing.

natural gas is a *fossil fuel* used for domestic heating, for raising steam in power stations and as a feedstock for the *petrochemical industry*. The composition of natural gas varies from one gas field to the next. It consists mainly of methane mixed with other *hydrocarbons* such as ethane, propane and butane together with variable amounts of carbon dioxide, nitrogen, helium and hydrogen sulfide.

Natural gas is processed before being supplied to homes. Hydrocarbons other than methane are separated for use in the petrochemical industry. Sulfur compounds are removed and a trace of a smelly chemical is added so that people notice gas leaks.

natural product chemistry is the study of chemicals produced by living things. Natural products include *carbohydrates, proteins, nucleic acids* and *lipids*. Before the start of the modern organic chemical industry, natural products from plants were the important ingredients of perfumes, dyes, oils, food flavors and drugs.

Plants may become important again as a large-scale source of chemicals now that genetic engineering makes it possible to transfer genes from one species to another.

neon (Ne) is the second member of the family of *noble gases,* coming below helium, with the *electron configuration* $[He]2s^22p^6$. Neon is best known for the red glow of neon lamps and tubes. It is separated from air as the other gases are liquefied. Neon boils at 27 K so it does not condense at the temperatures used to liquefy oxygen, nitrogen and argon.

neutralization reaction: a reaction in which an acid reacts with a base to form a *salt.*

$$HCl(aq) + NaOH(aq) \longrightarrow NaCl(aq) + H_2O(l)$$

Mixing equal amounts (in moles) of hydrochloric acid with sodium hydroxide produces a *neutral solution* of sodium chloride.

Strong acids, such as hydrochloric acid, and *strong bases,* such as sodium hydroxide, are fully ionized in solution, as is the salt formed, sodium chloride. Writing ionic equations for these examples shows that neutralization is essentially a reaction between aqueous hydrogen ions and hydroxide ions. This is supported by the values for the *enthalpy changes of neutralization.*

$$H_3O^+(aq) + OH^-(aq) \longrightarrow 2H_2O(l)$$

The surprise is that neutralization reactions do not always produce neutral solutions. Neutralizing a weak acid such as ethanoic acid with an equal amount in moles of a strong base sodium hydroxide produces a solution of sodium ethanoate, which is alkaline.

Neutralizing a weak base, such as ammonia, with an equal amount of the strong acid hydrochloric acid produces a solution of ammonium chloride, which is acidic.

Where a salt has either a "parent acid" or a "parent base" that is weak it dissolves to give a solution that is not neutral (see *hydrolysis of salts*). The "strong parent" in the partnership "wins":

- weak acid/strong base – the salt is alkaline in solution
- strong acid/weak base – the salt is acidic in solution.

neutral oxides are nonmetal oxides that do not react with water to form acids. The common examples are carbon monoxide (CO), nitrogen monoxide (NO) and dinitrogen oxide (N_2O). All three of these oxides are insoluble in water.

neutral solution: a solution with pH 7. Since pH = $-\lg [H_3O^+]$, this means that the concentration of aqueous hydrogen ions in a neutral solution is 10^{-7} mol dm^{-3} at 298 K.

neutrons are the uncharged particles in the nuclei of *atoms*. The number of neutrons in an atom can vary without changing its chemical properties. This accounts for the existence of *isotopes*.

nickel (Ni) is a hard, grayish but shiny *d-block* metal with the *electron configuration* $[Ar]3d^84s^2$. Nickel is relatively unreactive so it is used to make spatulas and crucibles. Nickel is a constituent of many alloys including some alloy *steels* and the ferromagnetic alloy Alnico in permanent magnets.

The common oxidation state of nickel is +2. Nickel(II) salts, such as the sulfate $NiSO_4$, are green.

Finely divided nickel metal is a good catalyst for *hydrogenation* reactions. It is a *heterogeneous catalyst*. It is used to "harden" unsaturated *vegetable oils* by adding hydrogen across the double bonds.

After extraction from its ores, nickel is purified by *electrolysis*. An older process for purifying nickel took advantage of the fact that the metal forms a volatile, neutral complex with carbon monoxide. The oxidation state of the metal is zero, so the complex is called tetracarbonylnickel(0). The impure metal reacts with carbon monoxide at 50°C. The complex evaporates leaving the impurities behind. The vapor of the complex passes to a second vessel where it decomposes at about 200°C.

$$Ni(s) + 4CO(g) \rightleftharpoons [Ni(CO)_4](l)$$

This was an effective but hazardous process because both carbon monoxide and the nickel complex are highly toxic.

nickel–cadmium cells are now widely used as rechargeable "NiCad" cells. As in a *lead–acid cells*, when a current flows the products formed at the electrodes are insoluble solids that stay put instead of dissolving in the electrolyte. This means that the electrode processes can be reversed as the cell is recharged. The electrode processes as a NiCad cell supplies a current are:

anode (oxidation): $Cd(s) + 2OH^-(aq) \longrightarrow Cd(OH)_2(s) + 2e^-$

cathode (reduction): $NiO(OH)(s) + H_2O(l) + e^- \longrightarrow Ni(OH)_2(s) + OH^-(aq)$

Unlike lead–acid cells, NiCad cells must be regularly discharged fully and then recharged if they are to retain their full capacity.

nitrates are *salts* of nitric acid (HNO_3) that all contain the nitrate ion (NO_3^-). Nitrates are common in laboratory chemistry because they are all soluble in water. Since nitric acid is a *strong acid*, the nitrate ion is a very weak base and does not change the pH when dissolved in water.

The reason that the nitrate ion is a weak base is that the negative charge is *delocalized* over the planar ion. Delocalization stabilizes the ion (see *oxoacids*).

Heating decomposes nitrates. Hydrated nitrates first give off steam, then the usual products are the metal oxide, oxygen and the brown gas nitrogen dioxide.

$$2Mg(NO_3)_2(s) \longrightarrow 2MgO(s) + O_2(g) + NO_2(g)$$

The exceptions are the nitrates of sodium and potassium, which are hard to decompose and give only the nitrite and oxygen.

$$2NaNO_3(s) \longrightarrow 2NaNO_2(s) + O_2(g)$$

Nitrates are *oxidizing agents*. In alkaline conditions they are reduced to ammonia by aluminum metal on heating. This reaction is used as a test for nitrates since the basic ammonia gas can be detected by turning litmus paper blue (see *anion tests*). More effective than aluminum is an alloy of aluminum, zinc and copper.

$$NO_3^-(aq) + 6H_2O(l) + 8e^- \longrightarrow NH_3(g) + 9OH^-(aq)$$

Plants take up nitrogen from the soil in the form of nitrate ions. So a diet rich in vegetables is rich in nitrate too. Nitrates have had a bad press because they are associated with the environmental problem *eutrophication*.

nitration of benzene is an *electrophilic substitution* reaction that takes place in the presence of a nitrating mixture of concentrated nitric and sulfuric acids. The product is nitrobenzene.

The purpose of the concentrated sulfuric acid is to produce the nitronium ion NO_2^+, which is an *electrophile*.

Mechanism for the nitration of benzene

Nitration of arenes is important because it produces a range of useful products including the explosive tnt (trinitrotoluene, or 1-methyl-2,3,5-trinitrobenzene). Nitro compounds are also intermediates in the synthesis of chemicals used to make *polyurethanes*. Nitro groups are easily reduced to amine groups. Aryl amines, such as *phenylamine*, are important intermediates in the production of dyes, such as *azo dyes*.

nitric acid (HNO_3): pure nitric acid is a colorless, fuming liquid but it gradually turns yellow as it decomposes, forming nitrogen dioxide. It is a highly corrosive but important chemical reagent because it can act as a:

- **strong acid** – nitric acid ionizes fully as it dissolves in water:
  $$HNO_3(l) + H_2O(l) \longrightarrow H_3O^+(aq) + NO_3^-(aq)$$
  Dilute nitric acid neutralizes bases producing soluble salts called *nitrates*.
- **powerful oxidizing agent** – in this role nitric acid oxidizes:
  - most metals including metals such as copper that do not react with nonoxidizing acids
  - nonmetals, forming oxides in the highest oxidation state of the element, giving I_2O_5 with iodine, for example
  - ions in solution such as iodide ions to iodine and iron(II) ions to iron(III)
- **nitrating agent** – in this role it is used for the *nitration of benzene* and other arenes.

nitric acid manufacture: a process for converting ammonia to nitric acid in two stages:

- oxidation of ammonia by oxygen on the surface of a catalyst gauze made of an alloy of platinum and rhodium:
  $$4NH_3(g) + 5O_2 \rightleftharpoons 4NO(g) + 6H_2O(g) \qquad \Delta H = -909 \text{ kJ mol}^{-1}$$
- absorption in water in the presence of oxygen to make nitric acid:
  $$2NO(g) + O_2(g) \rightleftharpoons 2NO_2(g)$$
  $$4NO_2(g) + O_2(g) + 2H_2O(l) \longrightarrow 4HNO_3(g)$$

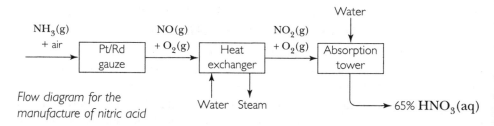

Flow diagram for the manufacture of nitric acid

Nitric acid is used in the production of ammonium nitrate. Ammonium nitrate is largely used as a nitrogen *fertilizer*. Ammonium nitrate is also widely used as part of most *explosives* for mining and quarrying. Nitric acid is used to make other explosives such as nitrocellulose and nitroglycerine.

Nitric acid is an important reagent in the production of intermediates for making *plastics*, especially nylon and *polyurethanes*.

nitriles: are organic compounds with the functional group $-C\equiv N$. Their general formula is $R-CN$ where R is an *alkyl* or an *aryl group*.

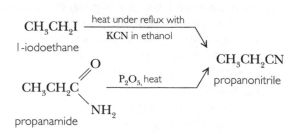

Two ways of making nitriles

Hydrolysis converts a nitrile to a *carboxylic acid*. Acids or alkalis can catalyze this reaction. Reduction with *lithium tetrahydridoaluminate(III)* converts nitriles to amines.

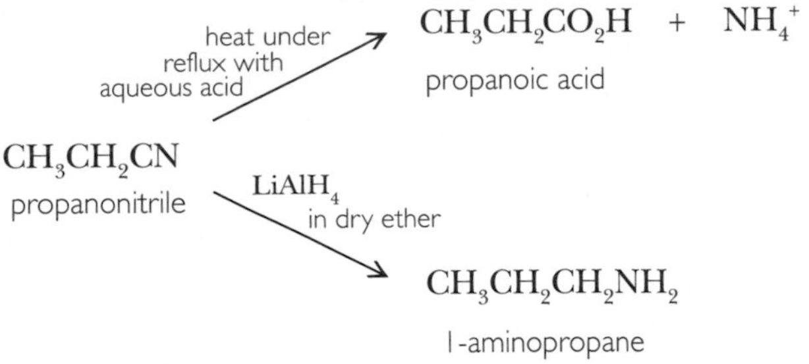

$$CH_3CH_2CO_2H \ + \ NH_4^+$$

propanoic acid

heat under
reflux with
aqueous acid

$$CH_3CH_2CN$$
propanonitrile

$LiAlH_4$
in dry ether

$$CH_3CH_2CH_2NH_2$$
1-aminopropane

Reactions of nitriles

Nitriles are useful intermediates in organic synthesis, especially when there is a need to add to the carbon skeleton of the molecule.

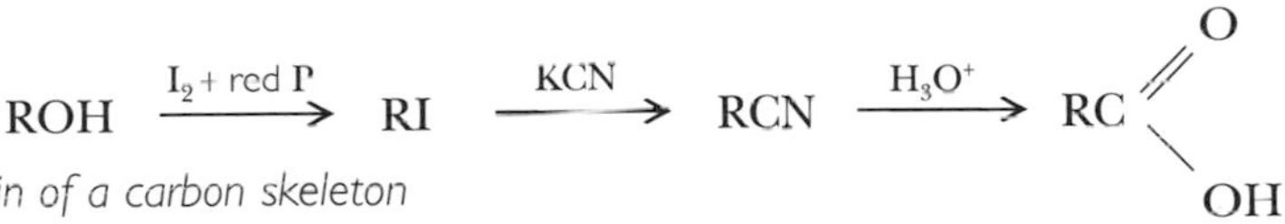

$$ROH \ \xrightarrow{I_2 + \text{red P}} \ RI \ \xrightarrow{KCN} \ RCN \ \xrightarrow{H_3O^+} \ RC\overset{\displaystyle O}{\underset{\displaystyle OH}{\big\backslash}}$$

Lengthening the chain of a carbon skeleton

nitrites are salts of *nitrous acid*. The two common examples are sodium nitrite ($NaNO_2$) and potassium nitrite (KNO_2). Sodium nitrite and potassium nitrite are preservatives and curing agents used in cooked meats and sausages.

nitrogen (N_2) is an element that is chemically quite *inert* but which plays a vital part in the environment and forms many compounds of natural and economic importance. Nitrogen is the first element in group 5 of the *periodic table* with the *electron configuration* $[He]2s^2 2p^3$. Nitrogen gas (N_2) is unreactive because the atoms are joined by a very strong triple bond and the molecule is nonpolar.

The bonding in a nitrogen molecule. The bond energy for the triple bond is 945 kJ mol^{-1}.

$$:N:::N: \qquad N{\equiv}N$$

The inertness of nitrogen makes it useful wherever oxygen must be excluded, as in food packaging, the *float glass process*, some chemical processing and the production of *semiconductor* chips.

Nitrogen makes up 79% of the air and can be separated by *fractional distillation* of liquid *air*. Alternatively, when only nitrogen is needed, the gas can be separated using:

- *selectively permeable membranes*, which let though all the gases except nitrogen, which is retained
- molecular sieves (*zeolites*) that absorb oxygen but let nitrogen pass through.

nitrogen cycle: the ways by which the element nitrogen circulates through the environment. The nitrogen cycle is chemically complex because nitrogen occurs in the environment in a range of oxidation states. Some of the nitrogen is inorganic as

NH_3 and NH_4^+, N_2, N_2O, NO_2^- or NO_3^-. Some of it is organic as *amino acids, proteins* and *nucleic acids* in living things or their remains.

There are three main reservoirs of nitrogen:

- the air (about 3×10^{20} mol N)
- the crust of the Earth (about 2×10^{16} mol N)
- the oceans (about 6×10^{16} mol N).

The main types of chemical change in the cycle are:

- **nitrogen fixation** – converting nitrogen from the air into inorganic and then organic nitrogen
- **denitrification** – converting inorganic nitrogen in the soil or oceans to nitrogen gas in the air
- **assimilation** – converting inorganic nitrates to organic nitrogen compounds
- **mineralization** – converting organic nitrogen in living things into inorganic nitrites and nitrates.

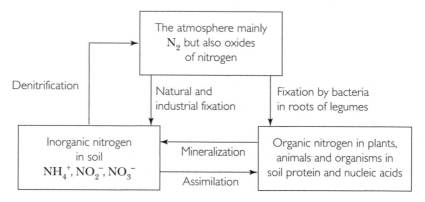

Diagram of the nitrogen cycle. Note that this version of the cycle leaves out the oceans, which are major reservoirs of nitrogen compounds.

nitrogen fixation: any process that converts *nitrogen* gas in the *air* to nitrogen compounds, which can be taken up by plants and converted to amino acids, proteins and nucleic acids. Nitrogen fixation happens naturally:

- during thunderstorms the energy in lightning allows nitrogen and oxygen to combine to form oxides of nitrogen, which are washed into the soil by rain and taken up by plants as nitrates
- some soil bacteria have an enzyme nitrogenase that can harness the energy of *ATP* to convert nitrogen from the air into ammonium compounds
- bacteria in the nodules of leguminous plants such as peas, beans and clover can also make ammonium salts from nitrogen.

As agriculture became more intensive the demand for nitrogen by crops outstripped the rate it could be produced by natural processes. Manures could not meet the demand either, so the challenge for chemists was to find a practicable and economic way to fix nitrogen industrially. This is the problem that was solved by Fritz Haber, leading to *ammonia manufacture* by the Haber process. Some of the ammonia is used for *nitric acid manufacture* and the two chemicals combine to make nitrogen *fertilizers*.

nitrogen oxides: there are six compounds of nitrogen with oxygen. All the oxides have positive enthalpies of formation. They are unstable relative to the elements and are easily decomposed by heating. Two of the oxides, N_2O_3 and N_2O_5, are particularly unstable and of little practical importance. Oxides of nitrogen contribute to air pollution. NO_x is a general formula used in accounts of air pollution to stand for any of the various nitrogen oxides when fuels burn at high temperatures in engines and furnaces. NO_x contributes to *acid rain* and the formation of *photochemical smog*.

Oxidation state	Formula	Name	Type	ΔH_f / kJ mol^{-1}	Notes
+4	$2NO_2$ N_2O_4	nitrogen dioxide and dinitrogen tetroxide	acidic	+33.2 (for NO_2)	NO_2 is the brown gas formed on heating nitrates. It is used as an oxidant in rocket fuels. Lowering the temperature makes the gas paler as the equilibrium favors the colorless N_2O_4
+2	NO	nitrogen monoxide	neutral	+90.2	Colorless but reacts with oxygen in the air to make NO_2; an intermediate in the manufacture of nitric acid from ammonia
+1	N_2O	nitrous oxide	neutral	+82.0	Colorless; also called laughing gas

Laughing gas is the traditional name for dinitrogen oxide (N_2O). The gas can be used as an *anesthetic* for dentistry and minor surgery. Dinitrogen oxide is soluble in fats. It is tasteless and nontoxic, and is used as the foaming agent and propellant in cans of whipped cream.

nitrous acid (HNO_2) is an unstable, *weak acid* that is an important reagent for producing the *diazonium salts* needed to make *azo dyes*. Nitrous acid is too unstable to be stored so it is made in solution when needed by adding a strong acid, such as hydrochloric acid, to a solution of sodium nitrite:

$$NO_2^-(aq) + H_3O^+(aq) \longrightarrow HNO_2(aq) + H_2O(l)$$

The solution of the acid is blue. It starts to decompose at room temperature, giving off nitrogen monoxide (NO), which turns brown as it meets the air and turns into nitrogen dioxide (NO_2).

The systematic name of the acid is dioxonitric(III) acid, which is sometimes abbreviated to nitric(III) acid. This shows that nitrogen is in the +3 oxidation state. When it decomposes it *disproportionates* to the +5 and the +2 states.

$$3HNO_2(aq) \longrightarrow HNO_3(aq) + 2NO(g) + H_2O(l)$$

$$ +3 +5 +2$$

Oxidation states of nitrogen

nmr: see *nuclear magnetic resonance spectroscopy.*

NO$_x$: see *nitrogen oxides.*

noble gases: the unreactive gases in *group 8* of the periodic table. They were called the "inert gases" until the discovery that *krypton* and *xenon* can form compounds. Even so, the gases keep apart from most chemical changes and react only with highly reactive chemicals such as fluorine and oxygen.

The term "noble" has been used for a long time to describe metals such as gold and silver. These metals were *inert* to the reagents used by alchemists and early chemists.

nomenclature: see *names of carbon compounds, names of complex ions* and *names of inorganic compounds.*

nonaqueous solvent: any *solvent* other than water. A nonaqueous solvent has to be used if the *solute* will not dissolve in water. For this reason turpentine (a *hydrocarbon* solvent) is used to make oil paint while other organic solvents are used as nail-varnish removers, stain removers and dry-cleaning fluids. A nonaqueous dry-cleaning fluid removes dirt without causing shrinkage or other damage to fabrics harmed by water.

A nonaqueous solvent has to be used for a reaction in solution if one of the reactants or products is rapidly hydrolyzed by water. For this reason *lithium tetrahydridoaluminate(III)* reductions take place in ether solution.

The choice of solvent can affect the outcome of a reaction. A solution of potassium hydroxide or sodium hydroxide in water hydrolyzes *halogenoalkanes* to alcohols. If the solvent is ethanol it is much more likely that an *elimination* reaction will happen and the product will be an alkene.

nonmetals are the elements toward the right-hand side of the *periodic table* that do not show the characteristic properties of metals. In general nonmetals:

- consist of small molecules with the atoms linked by *covalent bonding* (H_2, S_8, P_4 and Cl_2); the exceptions include carbon, silicon and red phosphorus in which covalent bonding is continuous throughout the *giant structure* of atoms
- are mostly gases at room temperature because of the weak *intermolecular forces* (for example, hydrogen, oxygen, nitrogen, chlorine and all the noble gases)
- if solid, are not shiny like metals; they are brittle rather than bendable and do not normally conduct electricity or thermal energy
- tend to form negative ions by gaining electrons when they react with metals
- form *acidic oxides* that react with water to produce *oxoacids*
- form covalent molecular chlorides that are liquids and usually rapidly hydrolyzed by water, such as PCl_3 and $SiCl_4$
- form covalent molecular hydrides that are gases at room temperature, such as CH_4, SiH_4, NH_3, HCl, HBr and HI – the notable exception is water, which is a liquid because of *hydrogen bonding.*

nonpolar solvent: a solvent in which the molecules are not *polar*. Examples of non-polar solvents are the many liquid *hydrocarbons* and the mixtures of hydrocarbons obtained by refining crude oil. These are also *nonaqueous solvents*.

Following the general rule that "like dissolves like," nonpolar solvents dissolve many compounds that consist of small molecules. Chlorine, bromine and iodine, for example, dissolve freely in hexane. The stain removers and dry-cleaning fluids intended to remove oily grease from clothes consist of nonpolar solvents.

Nonpolar solvents do not dissolve ionic crystals. The interaction between nonpolar molecules and ions is much too weak to surround ions and pull them away from the crystal against the *electrostatic forces* between ions with the opposite charge.

nonstoichiometric compounds are compounds with formulas that do not have simple whole-number ratios of atoms. The formulas of nonstoichiometric compounds vary. Many oxides and sulfides of *d-block elements* have variable formulas; for instance, iron(II) sulfide ($Fe_{1.1}S$ to $FeS_{1.1}$) and iron(II) oxide ($Fe_{1.06-1.19}O$). This variation is a result of variable oxidation states and irregularities in the crystal lattice. Other examples are the *interstitial hydrides* of *d*-block elements such as vanadium hydride, $VH_{0.6}$.

nuclear fusion is the process that produces the energy of the Sun and other stars. It is also the process that accounts for the origin of all the elements.

In the Sun, at a temperature of ten million degrees or so, hydrogen atoms fuse to make helium atoms, releasing about 10^9 kJ per mole of helium formed.

$$4\,{}^1_1H \longrightarrow {}^4_2He + 2 \text{ positrons}$$

The pressure and temperature at the center of very large stars is high enough for helium nuclei to fuse to make heavier elements such as carbon, silicon and iron. Since helium has an even number of *nucleons*, it turns out that elements with even *proton numbers* are more abundant than other elements.

Iron is the final product of the series of *exothermic* fusion reactions. Energy is needed to make heavier elements. Heavier elements form during the highly energetic explosion when massive stars run out of nuclear fuel and start to collapse and then burst apart. The massive explosion is a supernova, which scatters dust and gas through the universe where it mixes with hydrogen and helium.

In time the remains of "dead" stars start to coalesce into new stars and the process starts all over again. The Sun is an example of a second-generation star; it and the planets of the solar system formed from the remains of supernovas. This explains the variety of elements on Earth in a Universe where over 90% of all atoms are hydrogen.

nuclear magnetic resonance spectroscopy (nmr): a powerful analytical technique for finding the structures of carbon compounds. The technique is used to identify unknown compounds, to check for impurities and to study the shapes of molecules.

In medicine, magnetic resonance imaging uses nmr to detect the hydrogen nuclei in the human body, especially in water and lipids. A computer translates the information from a body scan into 3-D images of the soft tissue and internal organs, which are normally transparent to X-rays.

The name of the technique summarizes its key features:

- **nuclear** – the technique detects nuclei of atoms such as hydrogen-1 (protons)
- **magnetic** – the nuclei detected by the technique are the ones that act like tiny magnets that can line up either in the same direction or in the opposite direction to an external magnetic field
- **resonance** – the absorption of energy is from radiowaves with the frequency corresponding to the size of the energy jump as the nuclei flip from one alignment in a magnetic field to the other.

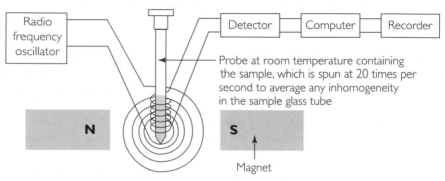

Diagram of an nmr spectrometer

Samples for analysis are dissolved in a solvent with no hydrogen-1 atoms. Also in the solution is some tetramethyl silane (TMS), which is a standard reference compound that produces an absorption peak well away from the sample peaks.

The tube with the sample is supported in a strong magnetic field. The operator turns on an oscillator that produces radiation at radio frequencies (rf). The rf detector records the intensity of the signal as the oscillator scans across a range of wavelengths.

The recorder prints out a spectrum with peaks wherever the sample absorbs radiation strongly. The zero on the scale is fixed by the absorption of hydrogen atoms in the reference chemical TMS. The distances of the sample peaks from zero are called their "chemical shifts" (δ).

Each peak corresponds to a hydrogen nucleus in a different chemical situation. The area under a peak is proportional to the number of nuclei in each situation. In

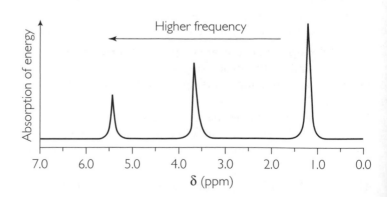

NMR spectrum for ethanol at low resolution

ethanol (CH_3CH_2OH) there are hydrogen nuclei in three environments that have different chemical shifts.

At high resolution it is possible to produce nmr spectra with more detail and which provide even more information about molecular structures.

nuclear reactions: changes affecting the nuclei of atoms. Nuclear reactions are brought about by bombarding materials with high-energy particles in particle accelerators or with beams of neutrons from nuclear reactors.

Nuclear reactions can be used to make elements that do not occur naturally, with higher proton numbers than uranium. Bombarding uranium-238 with neutrons produces uranium-239, which decays by beta decay to neptunium. Neptunium in turn decays to plutonium.

$$^{238}_{92}U \; + \; ^{1}_{0}n \; \longrightarrow \; ^{239}_{92}U \; \xrightarrow{\text{decay}} \; ^{239}_{93}Np \; + \; ^{0}_{-1}e$$
$$\text{neutron} \qquad\qquad\qquad\qquad\qquad \beta\text{-particle}$$

$$\text{decay} \;\bigg\downarrow$$

$$\longrightarrow \; ^{239}_{94}Pu \; + \; ^{0}_{-1}e$$
$$\beta\text{-particle}$$

Nuclear reactions producing the transuranium elements neptunium and plutonium. Note that the nucleon numbers and proton numbers balance.

Nuclear reactions are used to make radioactive isotopes for use as tracers.

nucleic acids are the molecules that carry genetic information and control protein synthesis in cells. There are two main types of nucleic acid, *DNA* and *RNA*. Nucleic acids are polynucleotides formed as *nucleotides* link together in long chains.

nucleon: a particle in the nucleus of an atom – either a *proton* or a *neutron*.

nucleon number: the nucleon number for an atom is an alternative term to mass number. The nucleon number is the total number of protons and neutrons in the nucleus. Isotopes have the same *proton number* but different nucleon numbers.

nucleophiles are molecules or ions with a *lone pair of electrons* that can form a new covalent bond. Nucleophiles are reagents that attack molecules where there is a partial positive charge, $\delta+$. So they seek out positive charges – they are "nucleus-loving."

$H-\ddot{\underset{\displaystyle ..}{O}}{:}^{-}$	hydroxide ion	$H-\underset{\displaystyle ..}{\overset{\displaystyle H \atop \mid}{O}}{:}$ water molecule
$:C\equiv N$	cyanide ion	$H-\underset{\displaystyle ..}{\overset{\displaystyle H \atop \mid}{N}}-H$ ammonia molecule
$:\!\overset{\displaystyle ..}{\underset{\displaystyle ..}{Br}}\!:^{-}$	bromide ion	$CH_3CH_2-\overset{\displaystyle ..}{\underset{\displaystyle ..}{O}}{:}^{-}$ ethoxide ion

Examples of nucleophiles

Nucleophiles take part in *nucleophilic addition* and *nucleophilic substitution reactions*.

nucleophilic addition reaction: the attack of a nucleophile on a *carbonyl compound* leading to an *addition reaction*. The *electronegative* oxygen draws electrons away from carbon so that the $C=O$ bond in the aldehyde or ketone is *polar*. The incoming nucleophile uses its lone pair to form a new bond with the carbon atom. This displaces one pair of electrons in the double bond onto oxygen. Oxygen has thus gained one electron from carbon and now has a negative charge.

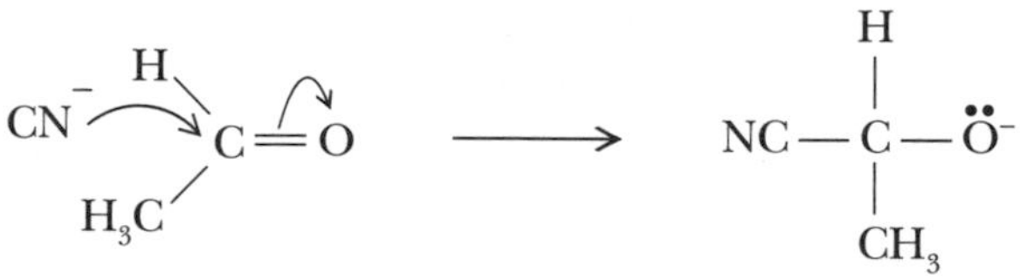

intermediate

First step of nucleophilic addition of hydrogen cyanide to ethanal

To complete the reaction, the negatively charged oxygen acts as a *base* and gains a proton.

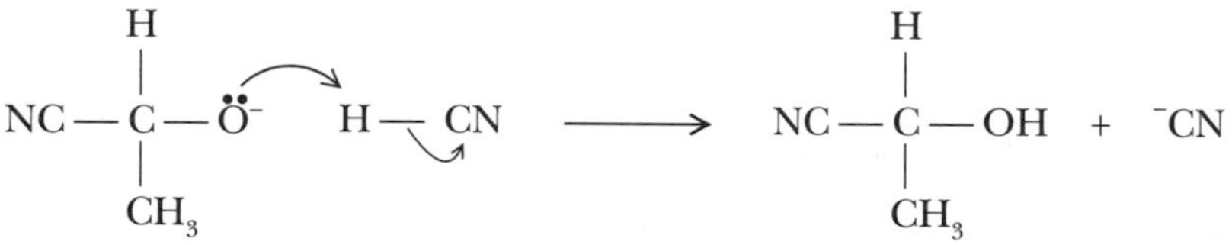

intermediate

Second step of nucleophilic addition of hydrogen cyanide to ethanal

nucleophilic substitution in derivatives of carboxylic acids: nucleophilic attack on the carbon atom of the $C=O$ bond in the functional group, which leads to a *substitution reaction*. The first step is similar to *nucleophilic addition*.

The *electronegative* oxygen draws electrons away from carbon so that the $C=O$ bond in the aldehyde or ketone is *polar*. The incoming nucleophile uses its lone pair to form a new bond with the carbon atom. This displaces one pair of electrons in the double bond onto oxygen. Oxygen has thus gained one electron from carbon and now has a negative charge.

The first step in the attack of a nucleophile on a derivative of a carboxylic acid. If X = OC_2H_5 the compound is an ethyl ester, if X = Cl it is an acyl chloride, if X = NH_2 it is an amide.

At this point the negative oxygen does not gain a proton; instead it uses a pair of electrons to reform the double bond and displace X.

Nucleophiles that react with esters, acyl chlorides and amides in this way are hydroxide ions and hydride ions from the tetrahydridolithium(I) ion.

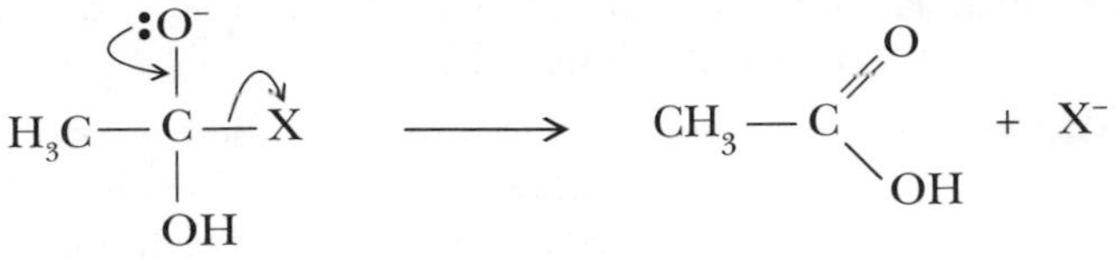

The second step eliminates X as an X⁻ ion.

nucleophilic substitution in halogenoalkanes: nucleophilic attack on the carbon atom of the C—X bond in a *halogenoalkane*, RX, which leads to a *substitution reaction*, where X = Cl, Br or I. Study of the *rate equations* suggests that there are two different mechanisms.

Hydrolysis of *primary* halogenoalkanes such as bromobutane is overall second order. The rate equation has the form: rate = $k[C_4H_9Br][OH^-]$.

The suggested mechanism shows the C—Br bond breaking as the nucleophile, OH⁻, forms a new bond with carbon.

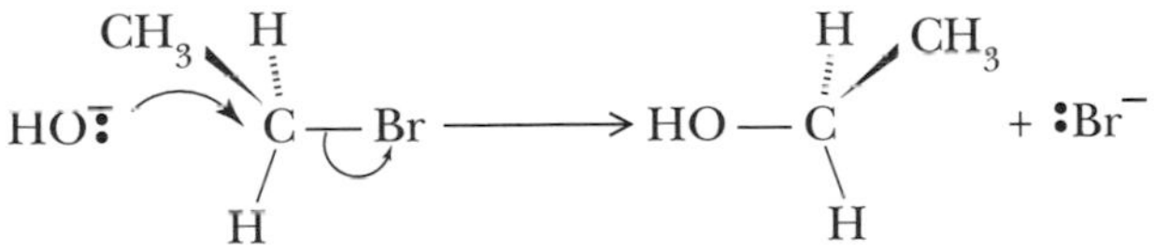

The S_N2 mechanism. Substitution–Nucleophilic–2 (for bimolecular – that is, two molecules or ions involved in the rate-determining step)

Hydrolysis of *tertiary* halogenoalkanes such as 2-bromo-2-methylpropane is first order. The rate equation has the form: rate = $k[C_4H_9Br]$.

The suggested mechanism shows the C—Br bond breaking first to form a *carbocation intermediate*. Then the nucleophile OH⁻ forms a new bond with carbon.

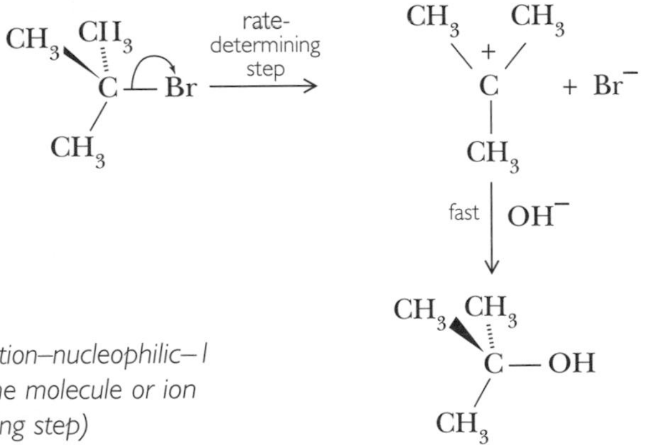

The S_N1 mechanism. Substitution–nucleophilic–I (for unimolecular – that is, one molecule or ion involved in the rate-determining step)

nucleotide: the *monomer* that polymerizes to make *nucleic acids, DNA* and *RNA*. A nucleotide consists of three parts:

- **a five-carbon sugar** – ribose in RNA and deoxyribose in DNA
- **a phosphate group**
- **a nucleotide base** – there are five different bases, *adenine*, cytosine, guanine, thymine and uracil, often abbreviated as A, C, G, T and U.

In the nucleotides that make up DNA the base is one of A, C, G or T. In RNA, thymine, T, is replaced by uracil, U.

nuclide: an atom of an element with a specified *nucleon* (mass) *number*. The *isotopes* of chlorine are the two nuclides ^{35}Cl and ^{37}Cl. The term nuclide is frequently used in the study of radioactive atoms, hence the term "radionuclide" for atoms that are *radioactive*.

octet rule: this was first suggested as a guide by the US chemist Gilbert Lewis in 1916. The rule says that atoms tend to gain, lose or share electrons when they combine with other atoms to acquire a stable octet of electrons. The "stable octet" is the eight $s^2 p^6$ electrons, corresponding to the outer *electron configuration* of the nearest noble gas in the periodic table.

Dot and cross diagrams for molecules and ions showing outer shells with eight electrons as in the nearest noble gas

There are many exceptions to the octet rule, so it is not a safe guide. The rule works pretty well for the elements Li to F in period 2 because there are only four *s*- and *p*-orbitals in the second shell (see *atomic orbitals*). The octet rule also works for ionic compounds of *s-block elements* with the halogens, oxygen and sulfur. Exceptions arise in period 3 and beyond, because *d-orbitals* in the third shell can become involved in bonding.

Born–Haber cycles can help to account for the octet rule in ionic compounds. When magnesium, for example, forms ionic compounds with the Mg^{2+} ion the extra *ionization energy* needed to remove two rather than one electron from the outer shell is more than compensated for by the big increase in *lattice energy*. An Mg^{2+} ion is much smaller than an Mg^+ ion because of the loss of the outer shell and the greater charge.

Removing a third electron from a magnesium atom needs much more energy because it involves taking an electron from the next shell where the electrons are more strongly held by the nucleus. If it could form, an Mg^{3+} ion would be little smaller than an Mg^{2+} ion so the increased lattice energy is not enough to compensate for the very large third ionization energy.

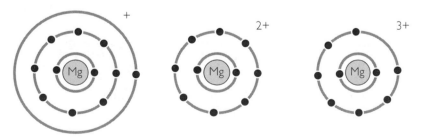

Electron configurations of Mg^+, Mg^{2+} and Mg^{3+} ions

odd-electron compounds: stable compounds with an odd number of electrons in an outer shell. Examples are two *nitrogen oxides*: nitrogen oxide and nitrogen dioxide. Both are exceptions to the *octet rule*.

Dot and cross diagrams showing the odd-electrons in molecules

optical isomers: *isomers* that have opposite effects on *polarized light*. One isomer rotates the plane of polarized light clockwise (the + isomer). The other isomer rotates the plane of polarized light in the opposite direction (the − isomer). Rotations are measured in an instrument called a polarimeter. Optical activity is characteristic of *chiral compounds*.

Optical isomerism is shown by molecules with the same structure but different three-dimensional shapes, so it is a type of *steroisomerism*.

orbitals: see *atomic orbitals* and *molecular orbitals*.

order of reaction: see *rate equations*.

ore: a *mineral* mass that can be profitably mined and processed to produce a metal. Prospectors seek ore bodies, which are local concentrations of ores. After mining or quarrying the first stages of processing separate the valuable minerals from waste rock.

The work of the mineral industry would be impossible if minerals were evenly distributed throughout the *lithosphere*. Fortunately, natural processes have produced concentrations of valuable minerals with much higher percentages of rare metals than in the Earth's crust.

organic acids: see *carboxylic acids*.

organic analysis consists of chemical methods for *qualitative* and *quantitative analysis* to identify organic compounds and work out their composition and structure.

In a modern laboratory organic analysis is based on a range of automated and instrumental techniques including *combustion analysis, mass spectrometry, infrared spectroscopy, ultraviolet spectroscopy* and *nuclear magnetic resonance spectroscopy*.

Melting points and boiling points also provide a check on the identity and purity of compounds.

Traditionally, chemical tests helped to identify *functional groups* in organic molecules. Preliminary tests typically involve observing:

- the state and appearance of the compound
- its solubility in water and the pH of any solution
- the type of flame when a small sample burns.

Functional group	Test	Observations
$\diagdown$ $\diagup$ $C = C$ $\diagup$ $\diagdown$ in an *alkene*	• Shake with a dilute solution of bromine • Shake with a very dilute, acidic solution of potassium manganate(VII)	• Orange color of the solution decolorized • Purple color fades and the solution turns colorless
$\mid$ $- C - X$ $\mid$ where X = Cl, Br or I	• Warm with a solution of sodium hydroxide, cool, acidify with nitric acid, then add silver nitrate solution	• Precipitate is white from a chloro compound, creamy yellow from a bromo compound and yellow from an iodo compound (*hydrolysis* produces ions from the covalent molecules)
$\mid$ $- C - OH$ $\mid$ in a *primary* *alcohol*	• Add a solution of sodium carbonate • Add a very small piece of sodium to the anhydrous compound • Warm with an acidic solution of potassium dichromate(VI)	• No reaction: unlike acids, alcohols do not react with carbonates • Colorless gas forms (hydrogen) • Orange solution turns green and gives a fruity smelling vapor; alcohols are oxidized by dichromate(VI) but not by *Fehling's solution*
$\diagdown$ $C = O$ $\diagup$ in *aldehydes* and *ketones*	• Add 2,4-dinitrophenyl-hydrazine solution • Warm with fresh *Fehling's solution* • Warm with fresh *Tollens reagent*	• Aldehydes and ketones both give yellow or red precipitates • Solution turns greenish and then an orange-red precipitate forms with aldehydes, but not ketones • Silver mirror forms with aldehydes but not with ketones
$- CO_2H$ in *carboxylic acids*	• Measure the pH of a solution • Add a solution of sodium carbonate • Add a neutral solution of iron(III) chloride	• Acidic solution with pH about 3–4 • Mixture fizzes, giving carbon dioxide • Methanoic and ethanoic acids give a red color

organic chemistry is the study of carbon compounds (except the very simplest such as the oxides and carbonates). There are more carbon compounds than the compounds of any other element because carbon atoms have a remarkable ability to join up in stable chains, branched chains and rings. Organic chemists have devised ways to organize the mass of information about millions of compounds and reactions so that it makes sense.

One approach is to group compounds into series each with a distinctive *functional group*. Examples are the *alkanes, alkenes, arenes, carbonyl compounds* and *carboxylic acids*.

Another way of making sense of carbon chemistry is to classify reactions. One classi-fication describes what happens to the molecules: *addition reactions, substitution reactions, elimination reactions* and *rearrangement reactions*. An alternative classification of reactions is based on the *mechanisms of the reaction* showing the types of reagents, the method of bond breaking and the nature of any *intermediates*. This includes:

- *homolytic bond breaking* with *free-radical intermediates*
- *heterolytic bond breaking* with *electrophiles* and *nucleophiles* as the attacking reagents leading to ionic intermediates.

Biochemistry and *polymer chemistry* are specialist aspects of organic chemistry.

Organic chemists have proved their understanding of organic structures and reactions by devising ways to synthesize increasingly complex molecules.

organic preparations take place in four main stages to make pure organic compounds.

Stage	Activities	Commonly used techniques
Planning	• Deciding on the reaction • Calculating reacting quantities from the equation • Deciding on the conditions for reaction	• Consulting reference books • *Risk* analysis
Carrying out the reaction	• Measuring out the reactants • Mixing them in a suitable apparatus • Controlling the temperature	• Heating in a flask with a *reflux condenser* • Shaking immiscible reactants in a stoppered container
Separating the product from the reaction mixture	• "Working up" the reaction mixture to obtain a crude product	• *Distillation* • *Steam distillation* • Vacuum filtration
Purifying the product and testing for purity	• Purifying liquids by shaking with reagents to extract impurities in a separating funnel, followed by drying and distillation • Purifying solids by recrystallization and filtration • Using tests to check on the identity and purity of the product • Calculating the percentage yield (see *yield calculations*)	• *Fractional distillation* and measuring boiling point*s* • *Solvent extraction* • *Recrystallization* • Measuring melting points • *Thin-layer chromatography* • *Infrared spectroscopy* • *Organic analysis*

organic routes: pathways from reactants to the required product in one or several steps. Organic chemists often start by examining the "target molecule" and then work back through a series of steps to find suitable starting chemicals that are cheap enough and available. In recent years chemists have developed computer programs to help with the process of working back from the target molecule to a range of possible starting points in a systematic way.

organometallic compounds: organic compounds that contain a metal atom. *Grignard reagents* are organometallic compounds formed with magnesium.

osmosis is the movement of a solvent by diffusion through a *selectively permeable membrane.* The membrane allows small solvent molecules through but not larger dissolved molecules or ions.

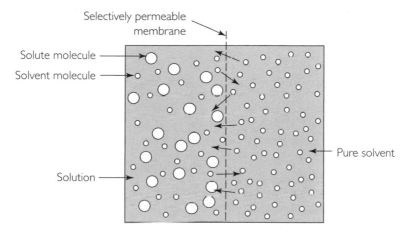

Solute molecule

Solvent molecule

Selectively permeable membrane

Solution

Pure solvent

Osmosis at a molecular level. The concentration of solvent molecules is higher in the pure solvent than in the solution. Solvent molecules diffuse in both directions but overall they move from the solvent into the solution.

The membranes that surround living cells are selectively permeable. This makes osmosis important in biology. Solutions for medical treatment of the eyes and other delicate parts of the body are formulated to have the same osmotic potential as body fluids, as are isotonic drinks.

osmotic pressure: the pressure needed to stop *osmosis* when the solution is separated from pure solvent by a selectively permeable membrane. Osmotic pressure depends on the concentration of solute particles and not on their chemical nature. There is a formula relating osmotic pressure to concentration at a given temperature. With the help of this formula osmotic pressure measurements can be used to determine the *molar masses* of large molecules such as *proteins* and *polymers.*

If the pressure applied to the solution is greater than the osmotic pressure, the direction of net flow reverses and pure solvent moves out of the solution. This is reverse osmosis, which can make drinking water from salty water.

oxidant: an alternative term to *oxidizing agent,* which is convenient when describing *half-equations* for *redox reactions* and *standard electrode potentials.* By convention, when electrode potential values are being assigned the half-equation takes the form:

$$\text{oxidant} + ne^- \rightleftharpoons \text{reductant}$$

Every half-equation involves an oxidant and a reductant.

oxidation: originally this meant combination with oxygen but the term now covers all reactions in which atoms, molecules or ions lose electrons. The definition is further extended to cover molecules as well as ions by defining oxidation as a change that makes the *oxidation number* of an element more positive, or less negative.

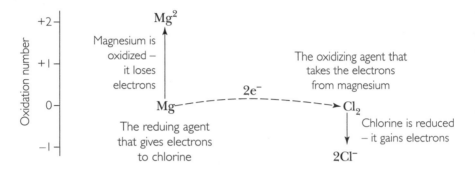

Chlorine oxidizes magnesium by taking two electrons from each magnesium atom.

Oxidation and reduction always go together in *redox reactions.*

Oxidation number rules apply in principle in organic chemistry but it is often easier to use the older definitions. Oxidation is either addition of oxygen to a molecule or removal of hydrogen.

$$
\underset{\text{primary alcohol}}{CH_3 - \overset{\displaystyle H}{\underset{\displaystyle H}{C}} - OH}
\xrightarrow{\text{oxidation}}
\underset{\text{aldehyde}}{CH_3 - C\overset{\displaystyle O}{\underset{\displaystyle H}{\big\|}}}
\xrightarrow{\text{oxidation}}
\underset{\text{carboxylic acid}}{CH_3 - C\overset{\displaystyle O}{\underset{\displaystyle OH}{\big\|}}}
$$

Two-stage oxidation of a primary alcohol, first to an aldehyde and then to a carboxylic acid

oxidation numbers are used by chemists to define *oxidation* and *reduction* and to identify *redox reactions.* The advantage of oxidation numbers is that they apply to molecules and complex ions as well as to simple atoms and ions. The sum of the oxidation numbers in an uncharged compound is zero.

Chemists have agreed a set of rules for deciding on the oxidation numbers of elements:

- the oxidation numbers of uncombined elements are zero
- in a simple ion the oxidation number is the charge on the ion
- the sum of oxidation numbers in an uncharged compound is zero

- the sum of the oxidation numbers in an ion made of several atoms is equal to the charge on the ion
- some elements have fixed oxidation numbers (see table).

Metals		Nonmetals	
group 1 (Li, Na, K)	+1	hydrogen	+1
group 2 (Mg, Ca, Ba)	+2	(except in metal hydrides)	
group 3 (Al)	+3	fluorine	−1
		oxygen	−2
		(except in peroxides and compounds with fluorine)	
		chlorine	−1
		(except in compounds with fluorine and oxygen)	

Oxidation numbers appear in the *names of inorganic compounds* and the *names of complex ions*. They also help with writing balanced redox equations.

$$MgO \qquad NH_4^+ \qquad CCl_4 \qquad MnO_4^-$$
$$+2 \ -2 \qquad -3 \ +1 \qquad +4 \ -2 \qquad +7 \ -2$$

$$Al_2O_3 \qquad SO_4^{2-} \qquad H_2SO_4 \qquad Cr_2O_7^{2-}$$
$$+3 \ -2 \qquad +6 \ -2 \qquad +1 \ +6 \ -2 \qquad +6 \ -2$$

Examples of the application of oxidation number rules. Note that each element in a compound is assigned an oxidation number.

oxidation states: the states of oxidation or reduction shown by an element in its chemistry. The states are labeled with the oxidation numbers of the element in each state.

Describing the chemistry of an element according to oxidation state is a useful way of making sense of a large number of compounds and reactions. See for example the entries for *chlorine, manganese, hydrogen peroxide* and *nitrogen oxides*.

oxides are compounds of elements with oxygen. The compounds of *metals* with oxygen are *basic oxides* or *amphoteric oxides*. The compounds of *nonmetals* with oxygen are either *acidic oxides* or *neutral oxides*.

oxidizing agents are chemical reagents that can oxidize other atoms, molecules or ions by taking away electrons from them. Common oxidizing agents are *oxygen, chlorine, bromine, hydrogen peroxide*, the manganate(VII) ion, in *potassium manganate(VII)*, and the dichromate(VI) ion.

Some reagents change color when they are oxidized, which makes them useful for detecting oxidizing agents. In particular, a colorless solution of iodide ions is oxidized to iodine, which turns the solution to a yellow-brown color.

$$2I^-(aq) \longrightarrow I_2(aq) + \ 2e^-$$

electrons taken by the oxidizing agent

This can be a very sensitive test if *starch* is also present because starch forms an intense blue-black color with iodine. Moistened starch–iodide paper is a version of this test that can detect oxidizing gases such as chlorine and bromine.

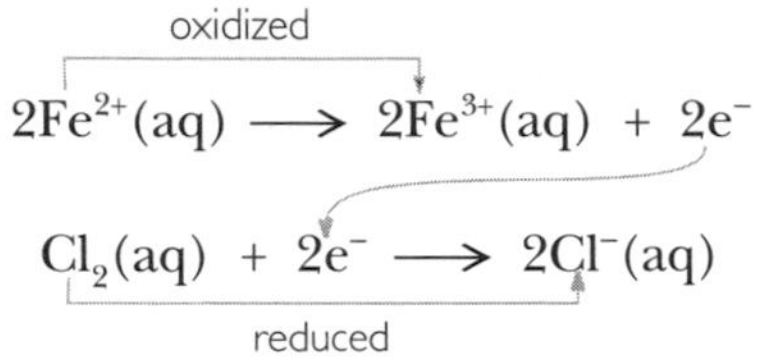

$$\text{oxidized}$$
$$2Fe^{2+}(aq) \longrightarrow 2Fe^{3+}(aq) + 2e^-$$

$$Cl_2(aq) + 2e^- \longrightarrow 2Cl^-(aq)$$
$$\text{reduced}$$

Chlorine acting as an oxidizing agent by taking electrons from iron(II) ions. An oxidizing agent is itself reduced when it reacts. Oxidation and reduction always go together; hence the term redox reactions.

oxidizing substances: substances that are hazardous if they come into contact with materials that burn – especially if they are flammable liquids. The danger is that oxidizing substances will start a fire in contact with materials that can burn.

oximes are compounds formed by an *addition–elimination reaction* between a carbonyl compound and hydroxylamine. The reaction takes place in three stages:

- nucleophilic addition
- gain and loss of hydrogen ions
- elimination of water.

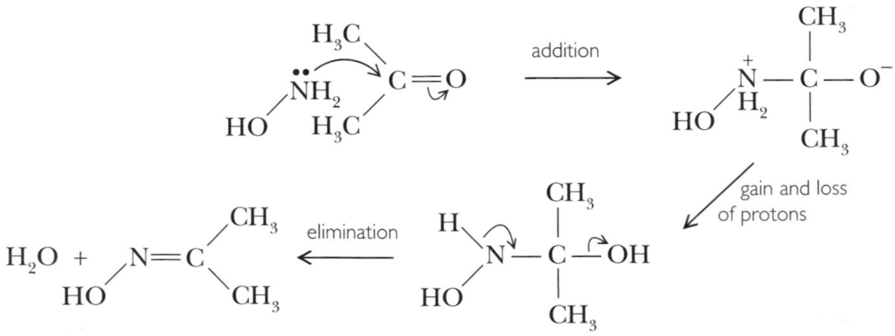

Addition–elimination reaction of hydroxylamine with propanone

Oximes are crystalline compounds. They can be made as intermediates in the laboratory synthesis of compounds with carbon–nitrogen bonds.

oxoacids are acids that form when acidic nonmetal *oxides* react with water.

Oxoacid	Structure	Oxoanion	Formula
sulfuric acid, H_2SO_4	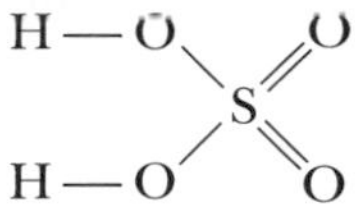 H—O, O, S, H—O, O	sulfate ion hydrogensulfate ion	SO_4^{2-} HSO_4^-
sulfurous acid, H_2SO_3	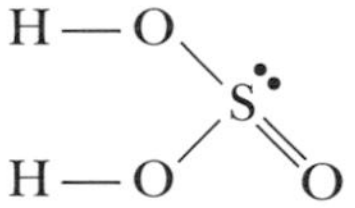 H—O, S, H—O, O	sulfite ion	SO_3^{2-}
nitric acid, HNO_3	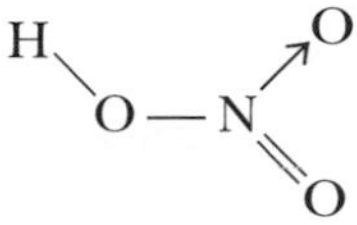 H, O—N, O, O	nitrate ion	NO_3^-
nitrous acid, HNO_2	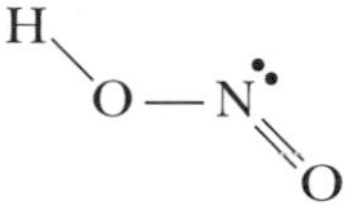 H, O—N, O	nitrite ion	NO_2^-

The systematic names for oxoacids are not widely used but they make it possible to determine the formulas from the names. The systematic name for sulfuric acid is tetraoxosulfuric(VI) acid.

Oxoacids ionize in solution by giving hydrogen ions to water molecules.

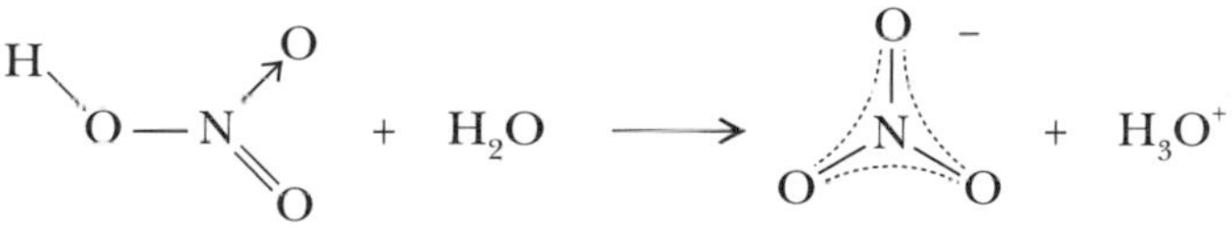

Ionization of nitric acid in water showing delocalization of the charge on the nitrate ion

Delocalization spreads the charge on the oxoanion, thus stabilizing the ion and favoring ionization. The more oxygen atoms doubly bonded to the central atom, the stronger the acid. As a result, sulfuric acid is a stronger acid than sulfurous acid and nitric acid is a stronger acid than nitrous acid. So where an element forms two oxoacids, the one with the element in the higher oxidation state is the stronger.

oxonium ions are aqueous hydrogen ions or hydrated *protons* formed when an *acid* dissolves in water. A *lone pair of electrons* on a water molecule forms a *coordinate bond* (or dative covalent bond) with a hydrogen ion from an acid.

The formula of the oxonium ion is H_3O^+. It is often convenient to write $H^+(aq)$ instead, but remember that the hydrogen ion is *hydrated*.

(Alternative names for the oxonium ion used by some authors are hydroxonium ion and hydronium ion.)

oxygen (O) is a colorless, odorless and highly reactive gas that makes up about a fifth of the *air* by volume and is essential to life. It is the first element in group 6 with the *electron configuration* $[He]2s^22p^4$. Most oxygen occurs in the form of O_2 molecules but *ozone*, O_3, is a second *allotrope*.

All living organisms need oxygen for respiration. Green plants produce oxygen by *photosynthesis* in sunlight. Many biochemical molecules include oxygen atoms, for example *carbohydrates*, *fats*, *proteins* and *nucleic acids*.

Oxygen is the most abundant element in the *lithosphere*, mainly in the silicon–oxygen *giant structures* of *silicates*.

Oxygen combines with most other elements to form *oxides*. Particularly important is *water*, the oxide of hydrogen.

Air separation plants use *fractional distillation* to separate oxygen and other gases. Alternatively, where only oxygen is required, the nitrogen from the air can be absorbed in a bed of a molecular sieve such as a *zeolite*.

Oxygen is used industrially in making *steel*. The manufacture of chemicals is another major use. Smaller quantities are used with a fuel for high-temperature metal cutting and welding. Oxygen is required medically by people with lung disease and is also used for *water treatment* to improve the quality of water contaminated with organic pollutants.

ozone (O_3): a colorless, reactive and unstable gas that is an *allotrope* of oxygen.

Ozone is an *oxidizing agent* and, like oxidizing bleaches, it will destroy micro-organisms. Ozone is increasingly used to treat drinking water and swimming pools as an alternative to chlorine.

Ozone often features in stories about *environmental issues*. The ozone layer in the upper *atmosphere* is a "good thing." The ozone high in the stratosphere protects living things by absorbing harmful UV radiation from the Sun. *CFCs* and other pollutants, such as the pesticide methyl bromide, tend to destroy the protective ozone layer.

In the lower atmosphere ozone is a "bad thing" because it is harmful to living things and helps to cause *photochemical smog*. Ozone attacks and splits $C = C$ bonds. This is ozonolysis, which can damage and destroy materials such as natural rubber.

P

paint is a product formulated to protect and decorate surfaces. A paint has three ingredients:

- pigments, which scatter and absorb light so that the paint covers up the surface underneath and decorates it with color
- *polymers*, which hold the pigment to the surface by forming a smooth plastic film as the paint dries and sets – in gloss paints the film-forming polymers are alkyd resins (see *polyesters*); in emulsion paints they are a latex polymer
- a vehicle that is a liquid in which the other ingredients are dissolved or dispersed – in gloss paint the vehicle is traditionally a *hydrocarbon* solvent; in emulsion paints it is water.

paper chromatography: a type of *chromatography* in which the stationary phase is water in the fibers of paper and the moving phase is another solvent such as ethanol or propanone. The technique is used to analyze mixtures such as inks, food colors, dyes and amino acids.

During paper chromatography the chemicals in a mixture *partition* themselves between two solvents: water and the moving solvent. Each component has a different equilibrium constant (partition constant), which decides whether it has a greater tendency to dissolve in the stationary phase or in the mobile phase. As a result the mixture separates as the chemicals move at different speeds.

If the conditions are kept the same, each chemical in a mixture will move a fixed fraction of the distance moved by the solvent. The R_f *value* for the substance is a measure of this fraction.

If the chemicals in a mixture are colorless they are invisible on the paper. If so, the analyst has to "develop" the plates with a suitable "locating agent." After chromatography of amino acids, for example, the paper can be sprayed with ninhydrin solution and warmed. The amino acids then show up as purple spots.

paramagnetism: a type of magnetism shown by substances with unpaired electrons. Paramagnetic substances are weakly attracted into a magnetic field. The effect is very much weaker than the *ferromagnetism* of iron. Most compounds have orbitals filled by pairs of electrons with opposite *spins* so that their magnetic properties cancel out. These substances are very weakly repelled by a magnetic field. This is diamagnetism.

Chemists measure paramagnetism to detect unpaired electrons in the *d-orbitals* of *transition metal* compounds.

partial pressures are a useful alternative to concentrations when studying mixtures of gases and gas reactions. In a mixture of gases A, B and C the sum of the three partial pressures equals the total pressure.

$$p_{total} = p_A + p_B + p_B$$

According to the *ideal gas* equation $pV = nRT$ and this equation is obeyed pretty well by real gases. In a mixture of gases the gas molecules move around independently. It is the number of molecules that matters and not their chemical nature. So the partial pressure for each gas is the pressure it would exert if it was the only gas in the container under the same conditions; thus:

$$p_A = \frac{n_A RT}{V}, \quad p_B = \frac{n_B RT}{V} \quad \text{and} \quad p_C = \frac{n_C RT}{V}$$

Since R is a constant, these equations show that at constant temperature:

$$p_A \propto \frac{n_A}{V}, \quad p_B \propto \frac{n_B}{V} \quad \text{and} \quad p_C \propto \frac{n_C}{V}$$

So the partial pressures are proportional to the concentrations of the gases, since $n \div V$ is the concentration in moles per unit volume. This is the justification for working in partial pressures when applying the equilibrium law to gas reactions (see K_p).

The total pressure in a mixture can be "shared out" between the gases according to their *mole fractions, X*. So:

$$p_A = X_A n_A, \quad p_B = X_B n_B \quad \text{and} \quad p_C = X_C n_C$$

Worked example:

An experimental study of the equilibrium mixture of $N_2O_4(g)$ and $NO_2(g)$ found that one equilibrium mixture contained 9.01×10^{-3} mol of $N_2O_4(g)$ and 7.16×10^{-3} mol of $NO_2(g)$ at 298 K and 3.99×10^4 Pa pressure. Calculate the partial pressures of the two gases.

Notes on the method
First calculate the mole fractions of the two gases.

Multiply the total pressure by the mole fractions to get the partial pressures.

Check that the sum of the partial pressures equals the total pressure.

Answer
Total number of moles $= 9.01 \times 10^{-3}$ mol $+ 7.16 \times 10^{-3}$ mol $= 16.17 \times 10^{-3}$ mol

$$\text{Mole fraction of } N_2O_4(g) = \frac{9.01 \times 10^{-3} \text{ mol}}{16.17 \times 10^{-3} \text{ mol}} = 0.557$$

$$\text{Mole fraction of } NO_2(g) = \frac{7.16 \times 10^{-3} \text{ mol}}{16.17 \times 10^{-3} \text{ mol}} = 0.443$$

Partial pressure of $N_2O_4(g) = 0.557 \times 3.99 \times 10^4$ Pa $= 2.22 \times 10^4$ Pa

Partial pressure of $NO_2(g) = 0.443 \times 3.99 \times 10^4$ Pa $= 1.77 \times 10^4$ Pa

---

particles are extremely small pieces of matter ranging from protons to grains of sand. Chemists use the term "particle" in several ways. At the smallest end of the scale they refer to protons, neutrons and electrons as *fundamental particles*. But they also use the term as a general word to cover atoms, molecules and ions when discussing the movements of particles in solids, liquids and gases. In addition, chemists use the term particle when describing much larger solid specks of matter finely dispersed in *colloids* such as paint, muddy water and smoke.

particulates are solid particles suspended in the air. In rural areas the main sources of particulates are natural. They include soil and sand swept up by winds, as well as volcanic dust and salt from sea spray.

In urban areas pollution comes mainly from the incomplete combustion of fuels in engines and power stations. The solid particles consist of carbon and unburnt hydrocarbons. Diesel engines are prone to producing particulates in their exhausts. These harmful particulates can damage health, causing problems such as asthma and eye irritation.

partition: the distribution of a dissolved substance between two *solvents* that do not mix (they are *immiscible*). Partition is the basis for *solvent extraction* and *paper chromatography*.

Shaking a solid with two immiscible solvents produces an equilibrium system to which the *equilibrium law* applies. The ratio of the concentrations in the two layers is a constant, at a given temperature:

$$K = \frac{[X]_{\text{solvent 1}}}{[X]_{\text{solvent 2}}}$$

This special case of an equilibrium constant is called the partition constant or partition coefficient. (Some writers prefer the term "distribution constant.")

Note that partition obeys the equilibrium law only so long as the dissolved chemical has the same molecular structure in both solvents.

parts per million, ppm: a unit of *concentration* often used for low concentrations of pollutants in water. The density of water is 1 g cm^{-3} and dilute solutions have almost the same density. So the mass of 1 dm^3 ($= 1000 \text{ cm}^3$) of water is 1000 g. For dilute solutions:

   1 ppm = 1 mg substance dissolved in 1 dm^3 water

Pauli exclusion principle: the fundamental principle that states that no two electrons in an atom can have the same value for all four *quantum numbers*. This rule accounts for the fact that no orbital can hold more than two electrons. The two electrons have opposite *spins*.

p-block elements are the elements in groups 3, 4, 5, 6, 7 and 8 in the *periodic table*. For these elements the last electron added to the atomic structure goes into one of the three *p*-orbitals in the outer shell (see *atomic orbitals*).

PCBs (polychlorinated biphenyls) are a group of compounds formed from two linked benzene rings. They are liquids with valuable properties that mean that they have been widely used in transformers, in hydraulic equipment, as *plasticizers* and lubricants. PCBs are suited to these applications because they are very stable, nonflammable, involatile and particularly suited for use in some electrical equipment (because they have high dielectric constants). Some PCBs are also toxic pesticides.

Structure of a PCB

The problem with PCBs is that they escape into the environment where they are very persistent. PCBs can be a hazard too if they are mixed with waste burnt in an incinerator at too low a temperature. The danger is that incomplete combustion produces highly toxic polychlorobenzodioxins and polychlorobenzofurans. Modern incinerators are designed to operate at a high enough temperature to break $C-Cl$ bonds and destroy PCBs.

peptides are compounds made up of chains of *amino acids*. The simplest example is a dipeptide with just two amino acids linked. For chemists this is an example of an *amide* bond but the tradition in biochemistry is to call it a "peptide bond." The formation of a peptide bond is an example of a *condensation reaction*.

Formation of a peptide bond between two amino acids

Polypeptides are long-chain peptides. There is no precise dividing line between a peptide and a polypeptide. A *protein* molecules consists of one or more polypeptide chains.

Note that some writers make a distinction between polypeptides and the longer amino acid chains in proteins. They restrict the definition of polypeptides to chains with 10 to 50 or so amino acids.

percentage composition: the percentage by mass of each of the elements in a compound. Percentage composition is one way of expressing the results of chemical analysis, such as *combustion analysis*. The *empirical formula* of the compound can be calculated from these results.

Worked example:

What is the empirical formula of copper pyrites, which has the analysis 34.6% copper, 30.5% iron and 34.9% sulfur?

Notes on the method

Follow the procedure in the worked example for finding an *empirical formula*.

The percentages show the combining masses in a 100 g sample.

Answer

	copper	iron	sulfur
Combining masses	34.6 g	30.5 g	34.9 g
Molar masses of elements	64 g mol^{-1}	56 g mol^{-1}	32 g mol^{-1}
Amounts combined	$\dfrac{34.6 \text{ g}}{64 \text{ g mol}^{-1}}$	$\dfrac{30.5 \text{ g}}{56 \text{ g mol}^{-1}}$	$\dfrac{34.9 \text{ g}}{32 \text{ g mol}^{-1}}$
	= 0.54 mol	= 0.54 mol	= 1.09 mol
Simplest ratio of amounts	1	1	2

The formula is $CuFeS_2$.

The percentage composition of a compound can be worked out from its chemical formula. This is a guide to people who formulate products such as fertilizers, medicines and cleaning agents.

Worked example:

Two common nitrogen fertilizers are urea $(H_2N)_2CO$, and ammonium nitrate, NH_4NO_3. Compare the percentage of nitrogen in the two compounds.

Notes on the method

Look up the relative atomic masses of the elements and use them to determine the two *relative formula masses*. (Note that when part of a formula is in brackets the number outside refers to all the atoms in the bracket.)

Answer

Relative formula mass of urea $= 2 \times (2 + 14) + 12 + 16 = 60$
of which $(2 \times 14) = 28$ is nitrogen

Percentage of nitrogen in urea $= \dfrac{28}{60} \times 100\% = 46.7\%$

Relative formula mass of ammonium nitrate $= 14 + 4 + 14 + (3 \times 16) = 80$
of which $(2 \times 14) = 28$ is nitrogen

Percentage of nitrogen in ammonium nitrate $= \dfrac{28}{80} \times 100\% = 35\%$

Urea contains the higher percentage of nitrogen.

percentage yield: see *yield calculations*.

perfumes: fragrant chemicals used not only for expensive cosmetics but also to give a smell to everyday household products. Many natural perfumes are essential oils separated from plants by *steam distillation* or *solvent extraction*. Increasingly, however, perfumes now contain synthetic chemicals, some of which are identical to those extracted from natural sources.

Experts use an analogy with music to describe the odors from complex perfumes. "Top notes" are the most volatile chemicals, the main effect depends on the "middle notes" and the most long lasting are the "end notes." So a perfume chemist has to understand the volatility of perfume chemicals.

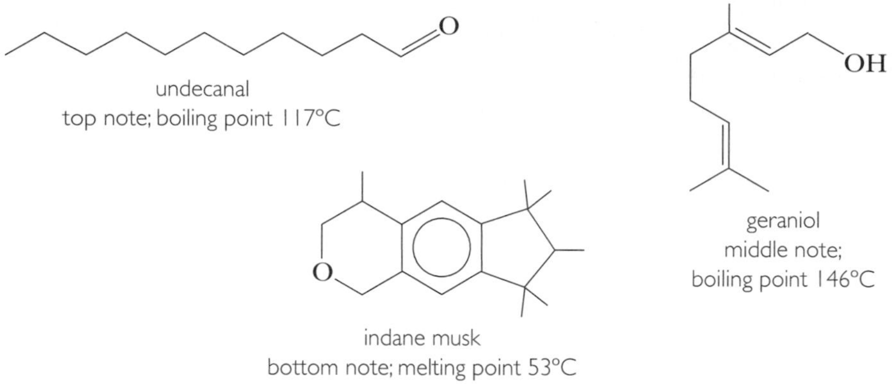

O
undecanal
top note; boiling point 117°C
OH
geraniol
middle note;
boiling point 146°C
O
indane musk
bottom note; melting point 53°C

Skeletal formulas *of some perfume chemicals showing top, middle and end notes*

The connection between odor and chemical structure is little understood so there is no easy way to predict smells by examining molecular models.

periodic table: a table of the elements arranged in order of *proton number* (atomic number). Periods are the horizontal rows in the table. Each period ends with a *noble gas.* The vertical columns are *groups* arranged in blocks – the *s-block, p-block, d-block* and *f-block* based on the *electron configurations* of the elements.

1 2
3 4 5 6 7
8
s-block
d-block
p-block
f-block

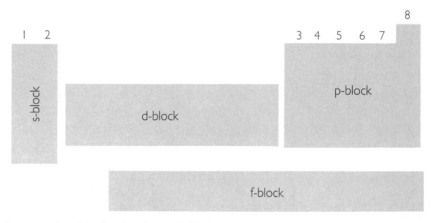

Outline periodic table showing the main blocks

The periodic table was a triumph for nineteenth-century chemistry. In 1869 Dmitri Mendeleev published a version of the table on which all later versions have been based. He succeeded thanks to his insight that at that time there were still many undiscovered elements.

Mendeleev based his table according to his periodic law that when elements are arranged in order of atomic mass, similar properties recur at intervals. He left gaps in his table for undiscovered elements and predicted their properties. His success with these predictions helped to persuade other scientists of the merits of his ideas when the missing elements were discovered in the few years following his predictions.

periodicity is a pattern that repeats itself. The most obvious repetition in the periodic table is from *metals* on the left of each period to *nonmetals* on the right.

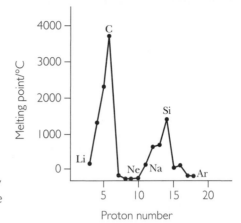

A plot of melting point against proton number for periods 2 and 3. Note the repeating pattern. This is an example of periodicity. A plot of first ionization energy against proton number is another example of a periodic pattern.

The properties of structures of the elements in periods 2 and 3 show repeated patterns:

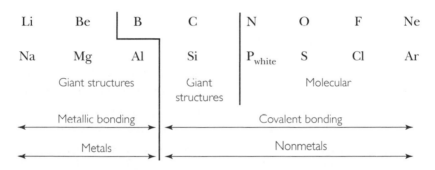

Periodicity: structure and properties of elements in periods 2 and 3

The *oxides* of reactive metals are ionic and basic. The oxides of nonmetals are covalently bonded and acidic with *amphoteric oxides* in between.

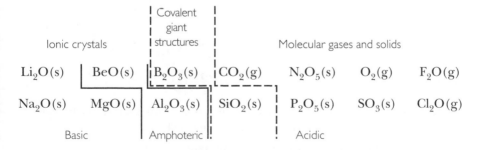

Periodicity: formulas, structures, bonding and acid–base character of oxides in periods 2 and 3, showing the oxide with the element in its highest oxidation states where there is more than one oxide

The chlorides of reactive metals are ionic. They dissolve in water to give neutral solutions. The chlorides of nonmetals consist of covalent molecules and they are normally hydrolyzed by water.

Ionic crystals	Polar covalent giant structures		Molecular gases and solids			
$LiCl(s)$	$BeCl_2(s)$	$BCl_3(g)$	$CCl_4(l)$	$NCl_3(s)$	$Cl_2O(g)$	$ClF(g)$
$NaCl(s)$	$MgCl_2(s)$	$AlCl_3(s)$	$SiCl_4(s)$	$PCl_3(l)$	$S_2Cl_2(s)$	$Cl_2(g)$

| Dissolve in water giving a neutral solution | Partially hydrolyzed to give an acidic solution | Hydrolyzed by water giving an acidic soloution (unless inert as is CCl_4) |

Periodicity: formulas, structures, bonding and behavior in water of chlorides in periods 2 and 3

permanent dipole: see *polar molecules* and *intermolecular forces*.

peroxides are compounds related to *hydrogen peroxide*, H_2O_2. The inorganic peroxides of *s-block elements* are ionic and contain the O_2^{2-} ion. When sodium burns in air it forms sodium peroxide, Na_2O_2. Barium similarly produces barium peroxide, BaO_2.

Inorganic peroxides are powerful *oxidizing agents*. The peroxide ion is a *strong base* so inorganic peroxides react with water and dilute acids to make hydrogen peroxide.

Organic peroxides can act as a source of *free radicals* to initiate *addition polymerization* of unsaturated compounds.

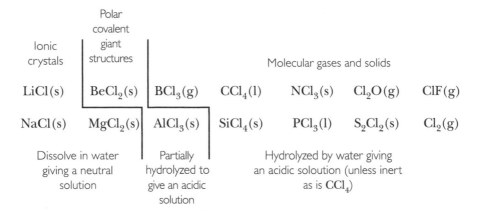

A benzoyl peroxide molecule splitting to form two free radicals. The O—O bond is relatively weak.

pesticides are *agrochemicals* that kill the living organisms that cause damage to crops, food, wood, fabrics and other materials. They include:

- herbicides such as paraquat and glyphosate
- insecticides including organochlorines such as DDT, organophosphorus compounds such as malathion, and pyrethroids
- fungicides.

Research chemists make and test many new compounds in search of pesticides that are:

- fast-acting
- specific so that they kill only the pests without harming other organisms
- effective at low doses
- biodegradable so that they quickly break down in the environment.

petrochemical industry: the part of the *chemical industry* based on crude oil and natural gas. The industry has developed and expanded massively since the late 1930s.

petroleum: a name for crude oil that is also used for some products from the *fractional distillation* and refining of oil. The *naphtha* fraction is an important feedstock for the chemical industry and is sometimes called the "light petroleum fraction."

Petroleum ether is a laboratory solvent that does not contain *ether*. Petroleum ether, which distills in the range 40–60°C, consists mainly of C_5 *hydrocarbons*. The solvent boiling in the 60–80°C range contains mainly C_6 hydrocarbons.

pH changes during acid–base titrations: the variation of pH as a solution of a base flows from a burette into a flask containing a measured volume of acid. Plotting a graph of pH against volume of alkali added gives a shape determined by the nature of the acid and the base.

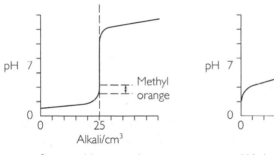

Strong acid – strong base   Weak acid – strong base

Graphs to show the pH change on adding 0.1 mol dm⁻³ of the named alkali to 25 cm³ of a 0.1 mol dm⁻³ of the named acid. Note the sharp change of pH around the equivalence point. The graphs show the pH range for the color change of an acid–base indicator *for detecting the* end point *of the titration.*

The indicator chosen to detect the end point must change color completely in the pH range of the near vertical part of the curve. Note that at the equivalence point, when exactly equal amounts of acid and base have been added, the pH is not always neutral. (See also *neutralization reaction.*)

pH scale: a logarithmic scale for measuring the concentration of aqueous hydrogen ions in solutions.

$$pH = -\lg [H_3O^+(aq)]$$

pH	0	1	2	3	4	5	6	7	8	9	10	11	12	13	14
$[H_3O^+(aq)]$/mol dm⁻³	10^0	10^{-1}	10^{-2}	10^{-3}	10^{-4}	10^{-5}	10^{-6}	10^{-7}	10^{-8}	10^{-9}	10^{-10}	10^{-11}	10^{-12}	10^{-13}	10^{-14}

increasingly acidic ⟵   neutral   ⟶ increasingly alkaline

Worked example:

What is the pH of 0.02 mol dm^{-3} hydrochloric acid?

Notes on the method

Hydrochloric acid is a strong acid so it is fully ionized. Note that 1 mol HCl gives 1 mol $H_3O^+(aq)$.

Enter the value of $[H_3O^+(aq)]$ in your calculator, then press the log button, finally press +/– to reverse the sign.

Answer

$[H_3O^+(aq)] = 0.02$ mol dm^{-3}

pH $= -\log(0.02) = 1.7$

Worked example:

What is the aqueous hydrogen ion concentration in a cola drink with pH 2.3?

Notes on the method

pH $= -\log[H_3O^+(aq)]$

From the definition of *logarithms* this rearranges to $[H_3O^+(aq)] = 10^{-pH}$.

Enter the pH value in your calculator, press +/– to reverse the sign and then the inverse log button (10^x). (The order of pressing the buttons matters.)

Answer

pH $= 2.3$

$[H_3O^+(aq)] = 10^{-2.3} = 5 \times 10^{-3}$ mol dm^{-3}

pharmaceutical industry: that part of the *chemical industry* that makes drugs and *medicines*.

phase: the three states of matter – solid, liquid or gas. A phase diagram is a map showing the states of a compound over a range of temperatures and pressures.

The "liquid" area on the phase diagram for water shows all the conditions of temperature and pressure when water is a liquid. Similarly the "solid" area shows the conditions for water to be solid. The "vapor" region shows the conditions under which water is a gas.

The lines show the conditions when two phases can be together in equilibrium. At 1 atmosphere pressure, ice and liquid water are in equilibrium at the melting point, 0°C; while liquid water and steam are in equilibrium at the boiling point, 100°C.

Chemical systems often have more than one phase. Each phase is distinct but needs not be pure:

- a solid in equilibrium with its saturated solution is a two-phase system
- in the reactor for *ammonia manufacture* the mixture of nitrogen, hydrogen and ammonia gases is one phase, with the iron catalyst being a separate solid phase
- *chromatography* separates mixtures by letting the components in a mixture come to equilibrium between two phases – the stationary phase and the mobile phase.

The same material broken up into little pieces still counts as one phase. In a *colloid* one phases is finely dispersed as specks, droplets or bubbles in a continuous phase.

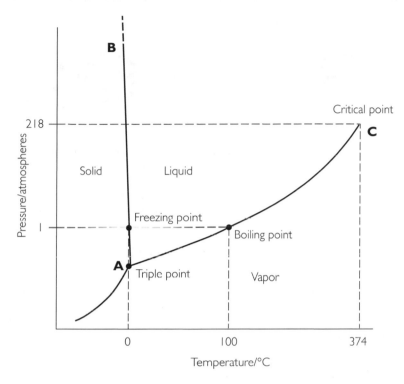

Phase diagram for water. Line AB shows how the melting point of ice varies with pressure. Line AC shows how the boiling point varies with pressure. Point A is the triple point, which defines the only conditions of temperature and pressure at which ice, water and water vapor can be in equilibrium.

phenols: a series of compounds with one or more — OH groups directly attached to a benzene ring. The simplest example is phenol, C_6H_5 — OH.

Structure of phenol and other phenols

The main uses of phenol are to make:

- *thermosetting polymers*
- *epoxy resins* for adhesives
- *intermediates* for the manufacture of nylon.

The hydroxyl group and the benzene ring in phenol interact. The benzene ring makes the hydroxyl group more acidic in phenol than it is in *alcohols*. Phenol is acidic enough to form salts with alkalis. So phenol dissolves easily in a solution of sodium hydroxide.

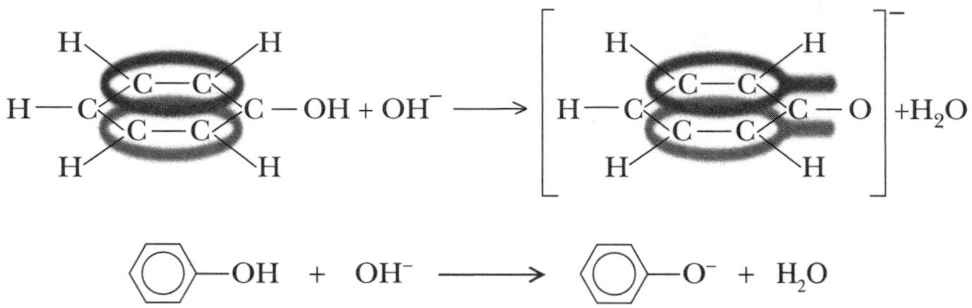

Phenol reacting with alkali. Note that the phenoxide ion is stabilized because the negative charge can be spread by delocalization over the whole molecule. This cannot happen in alcohols.

Phenol is not as acidic as *carboxylic acids*. It does not ionize significantly in water and does not react with carbonates to produce carbon dioxide.

The hydroxyl group makes the benzene ring more reactive. *Electrophilic substitution* takes place under much milder conditions with phenol than with benzene. Adding aqueous bromine to a solution of phenol produces an immediate white precipitate of 2,4,6-tribromophenol as the bromine color fades.

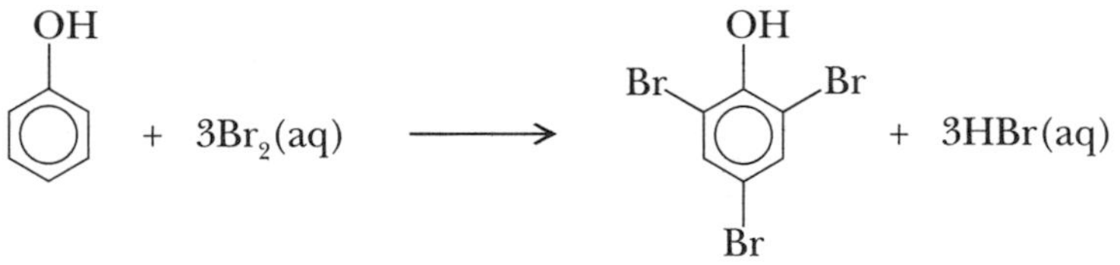

Reaction of phenol with bromine. The reaction is rapid at room temperature and there is no need for a catalyst.

Halogenated phenols are used as *disinfectants*.

phenyl group: the group C_6H_5 —, which is present in many compounds where one of the hydrogen atoms in benzene has been replaced by another atom or group.

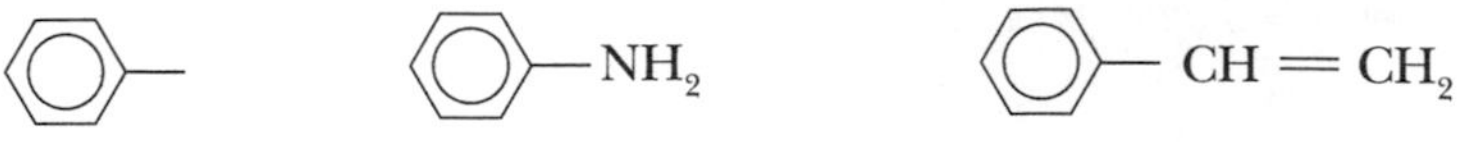

phenyl group   phenylamine   phenylethene (styrene)

Structure of the phenyl group and compounds derived from benzene

The use of phenyl in this way dates back to the first studies of benzene when "phene" was suggested as an alternative name for the compound, based on a Greek word for "giving light." Benzene was found in the tar formed on heating coal to produce gas for lighting.

Note that "benzyl" refers to aryl compounds with a carbon atom attached directly to the benzene ring.

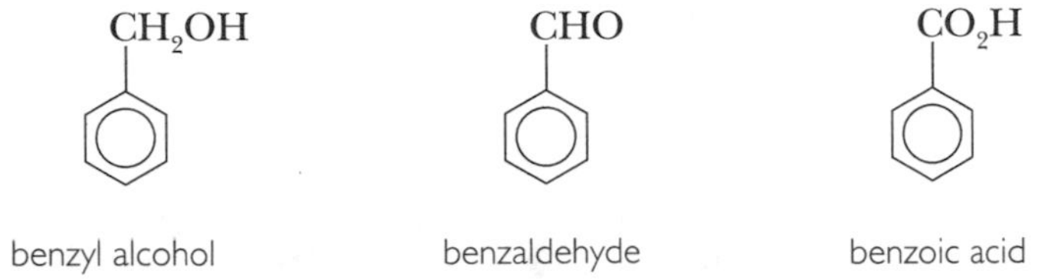

benzyl alcohol   benzaldehyde   benzoic acid

Benzyl alcohol and other compounds related to $C_6H_5.CH_2$—

phenylamine is a primary *amine* with an —NH_2 group attached to a benzene ring. There is a two-step laboratory route from benzene to aniline. First *nitration* then reduction.

The chemical industry makes phenylamine from phenol and ammonia with an alumina catalyst. Phenylamine and other arylamines are important intermediates in the manufacture of *azo dyes*. This is because they react with nitrous acid below 10°C to produce *diazonium salts*.

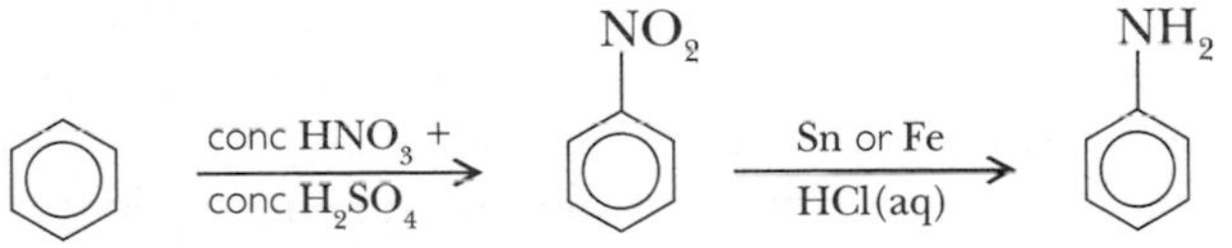

Formation of phenylamine from benzene

phosphorescence: see *luminescence*.

phosphoric(v) acid (H_3PO_4) is manufactured on a large scale from phosphate rock to make *fertilizers*, *detergent* phosphates and phosphates for food and drink. The pH of a typical cola drink is 2.3 because it contains 0.05% phosphoric acid. Another use of phosphoric acid is to make iron more resistant to corrosion.

phosphorus (P) is a highly reactive element and important *nonmetal*. It is the second element in group 5 of the *periodic table*, with *electron configuration* $[Ne]3s^22p^3$.

There are two common *allotropes*:

- **white phosphorus**, which is molecular (P_4) and has to be stored under water otherwise it catches fire in air
- **red phosphorus**, which is made up of long chains of P_4 units, is more stable and does not catch fire in air at room temperature.

There is also a black allotrope.

White phosphorus condenses when phosphorus vapor cools. This happens in the manufacture of phosphorus from phosphate rock (fluorapatite). The red form is more stable and, at 540 K, white phosphorus changes rapidly to the red form without a catalyst.

Phosphorus forms two oxides. They are both molecular and both *acidic oxides.* The more important oxide is P_4O_{10}, which forms as a white solid when white phosphorus burns in excess air (see *phosphoric acid*).

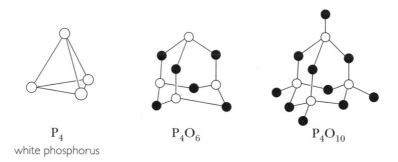

P_4
white phosphorus

P_4O_6

P_4O_{10}

Structures of white phosphorus, phosphorus(III) oxide, P_4O_6 and phosphorus(V) oxide, P_4O_{10}

As a laboratory reagent P_4O_{10} is used as a drying and dehydrating agent. It dehydrates *amides* to *nitriles*.

Phosphorus also forms two chlorides. Phosphorus trichloride (PCl_3) is made commercially from white phosphorus and chlorine. It is an important intermediate in the manufacture of medical drugs, insecticides and flame retardants. PCl_3 is a molecular compound. At room temperature it is a colorless fuming liquid that is rapidly hydrolyzed by water.

Phosphorus pentachloride (PCl_5) forms when PCl_3 reacts with excess chlorine. It is a volatile solid. It too is rapidly hydrolyzed by water and is a laboratory reagent for replacing hydroxyl groups with chlorine atoms in alcohols and carboxylic acids.

photochemical smog is produced by sunlight and the pollutants from the exhaust gases of motor vehicles. This type of *smog* forms on still, sunny days when there is no wind to blow away the gases. It is severe in cities such as Los Angeles where weather conditions and the local geography tend to trap pollutants in the city.

The primary pollutants are *nitrogen oxides* and unburnt *hydrocarbons* that are emitted in large amounts during the morning rush hour in a city. Bright sunlight during the middle of the day sets off photochemical reactions involving oxygen in the air. The products are the secondary pollutants that create smog.

The level of *ozone* in the air rises and oxidizing *free radicals* form. The unburnt hydrocarbons are then oxidized to *aldehydes, ketones* and other chemicals such as organic nitrates, which irritate the eyes and lungs.

Catalytic converters are designed to lessen this kind of pollution.

photochemistry: the study of reactions caused by light or other forms of *electromagnetic radiation*. Photons of ultraviolet light have enough energy to break covalent bonds and form *free radicals*. These reactive intermediates can then start *free-radical chain reactions*. Photochemistry is important in the environment as well as in the laboratory (see *ozone* and *photochemical smog*).

photography uses chemical reactions to form images. Photography is based on the chemistry of silver and shows that, like other *d-block elements*, silver can act as a *catalyst*, form *complex ions* and take part in *redox reactions*. Photographic film consists of tiny silver bromide crystals in a film of gelatin on a strip of transparent plastic (see *ionic precipitation*). The stages of photography are as follows.

1 **Exposure** – in both black and white and color photography the first step is a photochemical reaction. Light produces a few atoms of silver on the surface of exposed silver bromide crystals:

$$2AgBr(s) \longrightarrow 2Ag(s) + Br_2(l)$$

At this stage there is no visible image.

2 **Development** – the atoms of silver are the catalyst for the next stage when the film is taken out of the camera and treated with a solution of the developer. In black and white photography the developer is a *reducing agent* that turns many more of the silver ions in exposed crystals to silver. Exposed parts of the film turn black. In color photography the developer is oxidized to an intermediate, which then reacts with other chemicals in the gelatin layers of the film to produce colored dyes.

3 **Fixation** – this removes unexposed and undeveloped silver bromide to stop the whole film turning black when it is brought out into the light. The fixer is a solution of sodium thiosulfate. Thiosulfate ions form a complex with silver ions, turning insoluble silver bromide into a soluble complex:

$$AgBr(s) + 2S_2O_3^{2-}(aq) \longrightarrow [Ag(S_2O_3)_2]^{3-}(aq) + Br^-(aq)$$

4 **Bleaching** – this is needed only in color photography. In black and white photography the grains of silver formed by the developer stay to form the black areas of the negatives and prints. In color photography the silver has done its job once it has helped to make the colored dyes. So the silver is removed by treatment with a solution of iron(III) ions. The silver ions are thus removed from the film.

$$Ag(s) + Fe^{3+}(aq) \longrightarrow Ag^+(aq) + Fe^{2+}(aq)$$

photon: a quantum of light energy (see *quantum theory* and *electromagnetic radiation*).

photosynthesis is the process by which plants use energy from the Sun to convert carbon dioxide and water to *carbohydrates* and oxygen. It is the starting point for the synthesis of all the organic molecules in plants, including *proteins*, *lipids* and *nucleic acids*. The nitrogen, phosphorus and other elements that plants need are taken in from the soil as soluble salts.

Chlorophyll, the green pigment in plants, absorbs light and transfers the energy to electrons. With the help of other molecules the energy is used to split water into hydrogen and oxygen and to make *ATP*. All the oxygen released into the air during photosynthesis comes from water.

Through a series of biochemical steps, the hydrogen atoms from water produce a reducing agent which, with ATP, converts carbon dioxide to the basic building block for carbohydrates and other chemicals. So all the carbon and oxygen in carbohydrates comes from carbon dioxide.

physical chemistry: the branch of chemistry that provides the theories that help to make sense of inorganic and organic chemistry. Physical chemistry explores the states of matter and uses *kinetic theory* to explain the properties of solids, liquids and gases. Physical chemistry also investigates the interactions between *electromagnetic radiation* and matter to explain structures and bonding. Physical chemists use the full range of the electromagnetic spectrum in the various types of *spectroscopy*.

The methods and theories of physical chemistry help to answer four important questions about all sorts of chemical reactions:

- How much? – measuring *amounts* of chemicals makes it possible to find the formulas of compounds and the *balanced equations* for reactions, which in turn makes it possible to calculate the quantities of reactants and products involved in reactions.
- How far and in which direction? – the *equilibrium law, enthalpy changes, free energy changes* and *entropy changes* as well as *electrode potentials* help chemists to predict the direction and likely extent of chemical change.
- How fast? – the study of *rates of reaction* explores the factors that determine the speed of chemical change.
- How? – *rate equations*, the use of *isotopes* as *tracers* and the various types of spectroscopy help chemists to understand the *mechanisms of reactions*.

physical properties: properties that describe how a substance behaves when it is chemically unchanged. Examples include:

- appearance (color, transparency)
- mechanical properties (*strength, hardness, ductility*)
- electrical properties (*electrical conductivity*)
- thermal properties (*melting* and *boiling* points, thermal conductivity, *specific heat capacity* and latent heats of melting and vaporization).

pi (π) bonds: the type of bond found in molecules with double and triple bonds. The bonding electrons in a π-orbital are formed by sideways overlap of two atomic *p*-orbitals. In a π-bond the electron density is concentrated on either side of the line between the nuclei of the two atoms joined by the bond.

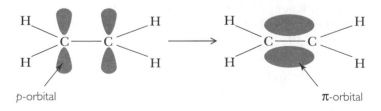

π-bond in ethene

Pi bonds prevent rotation about the double bond, and give rise to *geometrical isomerism.* Electrons in π-bonds are *delocalized* in molecules with alternating double and single bonds (*conjugated systems*).

pipettes are used to measure small volumes of liquid accurately. A volumetric pipette usually has a bulb for the main volume of the solution and then a single calibration line in the narrow tube above the bulb. This type of pipette can be used to deliver the same fixed volume of a solution again and again during titrations.

pK: the logarithmic form of an equilibrium constant, which is particularly useful for *pH* calculations. Taking *logarithms* produces a convenient small scale of values.

Examples:

- $pK_a = -\lg K_a$
- $pK_b = -\lg K_b$
- $pK_w = -\lg K_w$

The *Henderson–Hasselbalch equation* is one illustration of the advantage of working with pK_a instead of K_a. Another is the use of pK_w (the logarithmic version of the *ionic product of water*).

$$K_w - [H_3O^+][OH^-] = 10^{-14} \text{ at } 298 \text{ K}$$

Taking logarithms gives: $\lg K_w = \lg [H_3O^+] + \lg[OH^-] = \lg 10^{-14} = -14$

Multiplying through by -1 reverses the signs:

$$-\lg K_w = -\log [H_3O^+] - \lg[OH^-] = 14$$

Hence: $pK_w = pH + pOH = 14$, where pOH is defined as $-\log[OH^-]$ by analogy with pH.

So: $pH = 14 - pOH$, which makes it easy to calculate the pH of alkaline solutions.

Worked example:

What is the pH of a 0.02 mol dm^{-3} solution of sodium hydroxide?

Notes on the method

Sodium hydroxide (NaOH) is a *strong base* so it is fully ionized.

Find the values of logarithms by entering the value in a calculator and then pressing the lg button.

Answer

$[OH^-] = 0.02$ mol dm^{-3}

$pOH = -\lg 0.02 = 1.7$

$pH = 14 - pOH = 14 - 1.7 = 12.3$

Planck's constant: see *quantum theory.*

plaster of Paris is the main ingredient of building plasters and much is used to make plasterboard. The white powder is made by heating the mineral gypsum in kilns to remove most of the water of crystallization.

$$CaSO_4.2H_2O(s) \longrightarrow CaSO_4.\tfrac{1}{2}H_2O(s) + \tfrac{3}{2}H_2O(g)$$

Stirring plaster of Paris with water produces a paste that soon sets as it turns back into interlocking grains of gypsum. Plaster makes good molds because it expands slightly as it sets so that it fills every crevice.

plastic materials are materials that can be molded by gentle pressure. Examples are potter's clay and wax. Once molded, a plastic material keeps its new shape, unlike an *elastomer*, which tends to spring back to its original shape.

plasticizers are additives mixed with *polymer* materials to make them more flexible. A plasticizer is usually a liquid with a high boiling point, such as large *ester* molecules. The molecules of the plasticizer get between the polymer chains and reduce the intermolecular forces between the chains so that they can slide past each other. Rigid uPVC (unplasticized) is suitable for window frames and guttering. Adding a plasticizer to PVC changes the polymer to a material suitable for squeeze bottles, hose pipes and the insulation on electric cables.

plastics: materials made of long-chain molecules that at some stage can be easily molded into shape. *Thermoplastics* become *plastic materials* when they are hot and harden on cooling. Some thermoplastics are rigid and brittle at room temperature such as polystyrene and uPVC; others, such as polythene, are flexible.

platinum (Pt) is a valuable metal that is the most abundant of the group of so-called "platinum metals" that occur together in sulfide ores. The platinum metals are the *d-block elements* ruthenium and osmium, rhodium and iridium plus palladium and platinum.

Platinum is about as abundant as gold. It is mined in South Africa where the yield of metal is about 30 g from 10 tonnes of rock.

Platinum is an attractive metal and it is very unreactive so it does not tarnish. The main use of platinum is for jewelry. As well as being expensive, it is a *malleable* and *ductile* metal so it can be worked into shape.

Chemists take advantage of the inertness of the metal in electrochemistry. Platinum electrodes are required to measure *standard electrode potentials*. The conductor in a standard *hydrogen electrode* is platinum covered with a thin layer of finely divided metal (platinum black) deposited by electrolysis.

Platinum is an effective *catalyst*. Its catalytic activity is enhanced by alloying with rhodium. The second main use of platinum is to make *catalytic converters* for automobiles. Platinum–rhodium gauzes catalyze the oxidation of ammonia in *nitric acid manufacture*. Another use for a platinum–rhodium catalyst is "platforming," which is **plat**inum catalyzed *reforming* in oil refining.

Platinum forms a range of *complex ions* some of which, like *cisplatin*, are used to treat cancer.

polar covalent bonds are covalent bonds formed between atoms of different elements so that the shared electrons are drawn toward the more *electronegative* atom.

Examples of molecules with polar bonds

$$
\begin{array}{c}
H \\
| \quad \delta+ \quad \delta- \\
H - C - Br \\
| \\
H
\end{array}
\qquad
\begin{array}{c}
H_3C \diagdown \; \delta+ \quad \delta- \\
\qquad C = O \\
H_3C \diagup
\end{array}
$$

One end of the bond has a slight excess of negative charge ($\delta-$). The other end of the bond has a slight deficit of electrons so that the charge cloud of electrons does not cancel the positive charge on the nucleus ($\delta+$).

Molecules with polar bonds are generally more reactive than nonpolar molecules, especially with ionic reagents such as acids, alkalis and oxidizing agents. The presence of polar bonds makes molecules open to attack by *electrophiles* and *nucleophiles*.

polar molecules have polar bonds that do not cancel each other out, so that the whole molecule is polar.

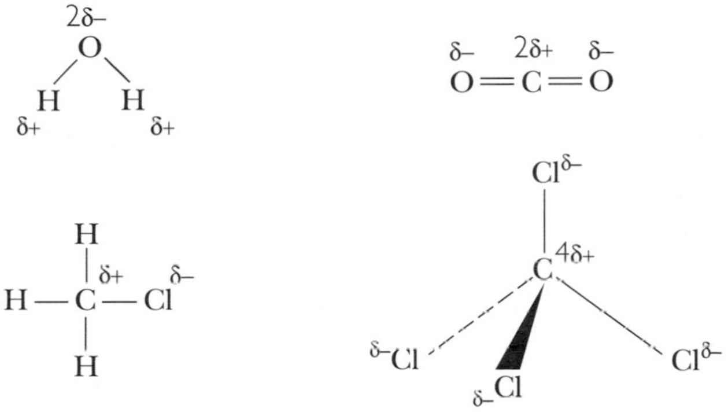

Overall polar   Overall nonpolar

Molecules with polar bonds. Note that in the examples on the left the net effect of all the bonds is a polar molecule. In the examples on the right the overall effect is a nonpolar molecule.

Polar molecules are little electrical dipoles (they have a positive pole and a negative pole). Dipoles tend to line up in an electric field. The bigger the dipole, the bigger the twisting effect (dipole moment). By making measurements with a polar substance between two electrodes it is possible to calculate dipole moments. The units are Debye units, named after the physical chemist Peter Debye (1884–1966).

The *intermolecular forces* are stronger between molecules with permanent dipoles.

Molecule	Dipole moment (in debye units)
HCl	1.08
H_2O	1.94
CH_3Cl	1.86
$CHCl_3$	1.02
CCl_4	0
CO_2	0

Measuring dipole moments can distinguish geometrical isomers.

Polarity of geometric isomers   Overall polar   Overall nonpolar

polar solvents are *solvents* made of *polar molecules*. Highly polar solvents such as water are needed to dissolve ionic compounds (see *hydration*). In organic chemistry the use of polar solvents favors *heterolytic bond breaking* and reactions with ionic intermediates.

polarizability: an indication of the extent to which the electron cloud in a molecule or ion is distorted by a nearby electric charge.

Larger molecules with more electrons are generally more polarizable. The *dispersion forces* that account for weak intermolecular forces between nonpolar molecules are stronger between molecules that are more polarizable.

Fajan's rules are a guide to the degree of polarization of negative ions by neighboring positive ions.

polarized light: a light beam in which all the waves are vibrating in the same plane.

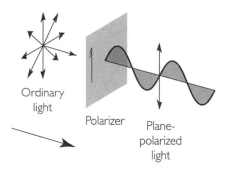

Ordinary
light

Polarizer

Plane-
polarized
light

Ordinary light and polarized light

Light is plane-polarized after passing through a sheet of Polaroid. *Optical isomers* rotate the plane of polarized light.

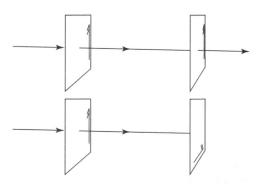

Effect of passing a light beam through two sheets of Polaroid. After the first sheet the light is polarized. The beam passes through the second sheet if it is aligned the same as the first. No light gets through if the second sheet is rotated through 90°.

polyamides are *polymers* in which the monomer molecules are linked by amide bonds. The first important polyamides were formed by *condensation polymerization* between diamines and dicarboxylic acids.

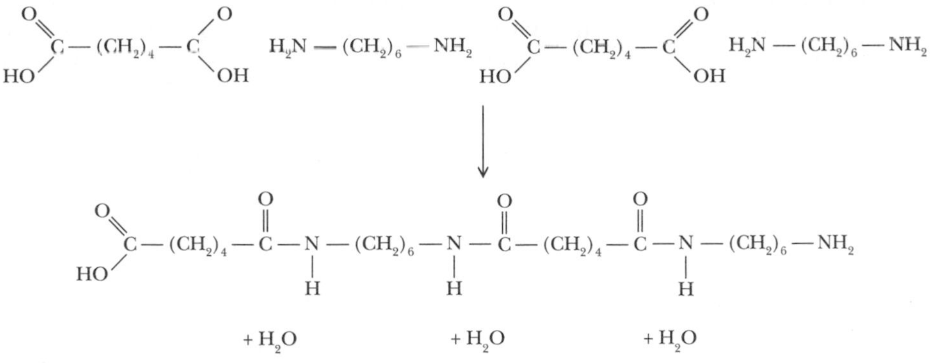

$$\underset{HO}{\overset{O}{\underset{}{\parallel}}}C-(CH_2)_4-C\overset{O}{\underset{OH}{}} \quad H_2N-(CH_2)_6-NH_2 \quad \underset{HO}{\overset{O}{\underset{}{\parallel}}}C-(CH_2)_4-C\overset{O}{\underset{OH}{}} \quad H_2N-(CH_2)_6-NH_2$$

$$\underset{HO}{\overset{O}{\parallel}}C-(CH_2)_4-\overset{O}{\overset{\parallel}{C}}-\underset{H}{N}-(CH_2)_6-\underset{H}{N}-\overset{O}{\overset{\parallel}{C}}-(CH_2)_4-\overset{O}{\overset{\parallel}{C}}-\underset{H}{N}-(CH_2)_6-NH_2$$

$$+\,H_2O \qquad\qquad +\,H_2O \qquad\qquad +\,H_2O$$

Condensation polymerization to make Nylon-6,6. The numbers in the name indicate the numbers of carbon atoms in the two monomers.

polyesters are *polymers* formed by *condensation polymerization* between acids with two carboxylic acid groups and alcohols with two or more hydroxyl groups. Units in the polymer chains are linked by a series of *ester* bonds.

The monomers for making polyester fibers are benzene-1,4-dicarboxylic acid and ethan-1,2-diol.

Alkyd *resins*, ingredients of gloss paint, also consist of long chains linked by ester bonds. The polymer chains have *unsaturated hydrocarbon* side chains. When exposed to air, the *double bonds* in the side chains of neighboring polymer molecules react so that the chains become *cross-linked*. As a result the resin hardens to a smooth film as the paint dries and sets.

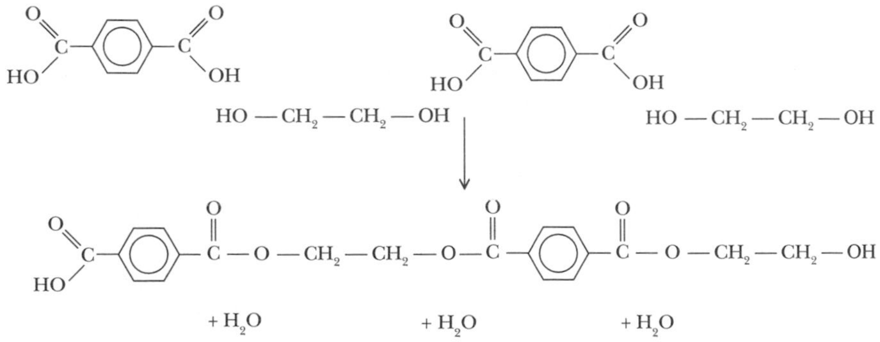

Condensation polymerization to produce polyester

polymer chemistry is the study of the synthesis, structure and properties of *polymers*. It is a branch of chemistry that developed in the twentieth century. Leo Baekland developed *Bakelite* in 1905 with little help from theory. The first *thermosetting polymers* were discovered before chemists understood the structure of big molecules.

In 1922 the German chemist Hermann Staudinger published his theory that natural rubber, cellulose and related substances consist of long-chain molecules. He had to fight hard to persuade other chemists to accept his theory, which is now taken for granted.

One of the people who was convinced by the new theory was the American industrial chemist Wallace Carothers. He wrote an article in 1931 in which he introduced the terms *addition polymerization* and *condensation polymerization*. His team at Du Pont invented the synthetic *rubber*, Neoprene. They also discovered the first completely synthetic polymer (nylon), which went into production in 1939.

The 1930s were probably the most important years in the development of the plastics industry. It was the time when the addition polymers polythene, pvc and polystyrene were all developed commercially. The high-pressure process for making polythene was discovered and developed in the mid-1930s as an unexpected offshoot of the study of high-pressure gas reactions by Eric Fawcett and Reginald Gibson working for the UK chemical company ICI.

Also in the 1930s, Otto Bayer was pursuing his interests in isocyanates in the laboratories of the IG Farben Industries in Germany. He too faced opposition in his pursuit of new polymeric materials. His breakthrough came in 1941 when he and his team discovered the possibility of producing *polyurethane* foams. It took ten more years of development work before large-scale manufacturing could begin.

It was in the early 1950s that Karl Ziegler in Germany discovered how to polymerize ethene at low temperatures using a new kind of catalyst. At the same time Giulio Natta in Italy discovered the benefits of producing *isotactic polymers* (see *Ziegler–Natta catalysts*).

Research and development since the 1950s has produced many new specialized polymer materials including the biodegradable polymers.

polymerization: a process in which many small molecules (*monomers*) join up in long chains (see *addition polymerization* and *condensation polymerization*).

polymers are long-chain molecules. Natural polymers include *proteins*, polysaccharides (see *carbohydrates*) and *nucleic acids*. Synthetic polymers include *polyesters*, *polyamides* and the many polymers formed by the *addition polymerization* of compounds with $C = C$ bonds.

The properties of polymers are very varied. Polymeric materials include *plastics*, *elastomers* and *fibers*.

As polymer science has developed, chemists and materials scientists have learnt how to develop new materials with particular properties. Some of the ways of modifying polymeric materials include:

- altering the average length of the polymer chains
- changing the structure of the monomer, perhaps by adding side groups that increase *intermolecular forces*
- varying the degree of *cross-linking* between chains
- *copolymerization*
- controlling the three-dimensional shape of the polymer (see *isotactic polymer*)

- changing the alignment of the polymer chains, for example by spinning the polymer into fibers and then stretching the fibers
- adding fillers, pigments and *plasticizers*
- making *composites.*

polymorphism: the existence of two or more crystalline forms of a substance. Some ionic compounds are polymorphic. Zinc sulfide, for example, can crystallize either with the *zinc blende structure* or with the alternative *wurtzite structure.* Polymorphism in solid elements is an example of *allotropy.*

polyols are compounds with more than one hydroxyl group. They include diols, such as ethan-1,2-diol and triols such as propan-1,2,3-triol (better known as glycerine or glycerol). Polyols are used to make *polyurethanes.*

polysaccharides: see *carbohydrates.*

polyurethanes are a varied range of cross-linked polymers made from two liquids – a *polyol* and an isocyanate. Polymerization is exothermic and happens at room temperature. Adding a chemical to make a gas means that the polymer forms as a plastic foam. By choosing different isocyanates and polyols, manufacturers can vary the properties of the polyurethane. The products range through flexible foam for bedding and upholstery, rigid foam for wall panels and refrigerators, hard-wearing but bendable soles for shoes and ingredients for paints and adhesives.

One of the great advantages of polyurethanes is that they can be made where they are needed without any complex machinery. A furniture manufacturer, for example, can buy the two liquid ingredients and then mix them in a mold so that the polymer takes up the required shape for a chair as it forms.

p-orbitals: see *atomic orbitals.*

potassium (K): is a very soft, shiny metal that rapidly tarnishes in moist air. It is the third member of *group 1* with the *electron configuration* $[Ar]4s^1$.

Like other group 1 metals, potassium:

- is stored in oil
- floats on water, melts and reacts violently, forming hydrogen, which catches fire, and KOH, which is soluble and strongly alkaline
- forms an ionic, crystalline chloride, K^+Cl^-.

Unlike lithium and sodium, potassium produces a *superoxide* (KO_2) when it burns in air. This is an ionic compound with the O_2^- ion. One of the main uses of potassium is to make this oxide for use in emergency breathing apparatus. The oxide removes carbon dioxide from moist breathed-out air and replaces it with oxygen.

$$4KO_2(s) + 4CO_2(g) + 2H_2O(l) \longrightarrow 4KHCO_3(s) + 3O_2(g)$$

Potassium, as potassium ions, is an essential nutrient for plants and an ingredient of NPK *fertilizers.*

potassium manganate(VII) (KMnO$_4$) consists of grayish-black crystals that dissolve in water to give a deep purple solution. It is used as a powerful *oxidizing agent.*

Potassium manganate(VII) is an important reagent in *redox titrations* because it will oxidize many reducing agents in acid conditions. The reactions go according to their equations, which makes them suitable for quantitative work.

$$MnO_4^-(aq) + 8H^+(aq) + 5e^- \longrightarrow Mn^{2+}(aq) + 4H_2O(l)$$

No indicator is required for a manganate(VII) titration. When the solution is added from a burette the manganate(VII) rapidly changes from purple to colorless (because the color of the Mn^{2+} ion is so pale). At the end point it takes only the slightest excess of manganate(VII) to give a permanent red-purple color.

In organic chemistry potassium manganate(VII) is a reagent used to oxidize the side chains of *arenes*.

precipitation: a reaction that produces an insoluble product from soluble chemicals in solution. A common example is the formation of an insoluble salt on mixing solutions of two soluble salts (see *ionic precipitation*).

Ionic precipitation is the basis of many *anion tests* and *cation tests*.

In *organic analysis* the 2,4-dinitrophenylhydrazine reagent for aldehydes and ketones forms a precipitate by an *addition–elimination reaction*. The *Fehling's solution* or *Tollens reagent* tests, used to distinguish aldehydes from ketones, both make precipitates by redox reactions.

precision of data: data is precise if repeat measurements have values that are close to each other. Precise measurements have a small random *error*.

Precise measurements may or may not be accurate. As a result of a systematic error a series of precise measurements may give values that are almost the same but are not the true value.

pressure is defined as force per unit area. The *SI unit* of pressure is the pascal (Pa), which is a pressure of one newton per square meter (1 N m^{-2}). The pascal is a very small unit so pressures are often quoted in kilopascals (kPa).

When gases are being studied the standard pressure is *atmospheric pressure*, which is:

$$101.3 \times 10^3 \text{ N m}^{-2} = 101.3 \text{ kPa}.$$

In accounts of chemical processes, multiples of atmospheric pressure give an indication of the extent to which gases are compressed (see for example *ammonia manufacture*).

The standard pressure for definitions in thermodynamics is now 1 bar, which is:

$$100\,000 \text{ N m}^{-2} = 100 \text{ kPa}$$

The *partial pressure* of a gas is a measure of its concentration in a mixture of gases.

primary, secondary and tertiary organic compounds are labels that distinguish different chemical situations for functional groups in *alcohols, halogenoalkanes, amines* and *carbocations*.

The labels have the same meaning for alcohols, halogenoalkanes and carbocations but a different meaning for amines.

primary standard: a chemical that can be weighed out accurately to make up a *standard solution* for *volumetric analysis*. A primary standard must:

- be very pure
- not gain or lose mass when exposed to the air (so it must not be *hygroscopic* or *deliquescent*)
- be soluble in water
- have a relatively high molar mass so weighing errors are minimized
- react exactly as described by the chemical equation.

A convenient primary standard for *acid–base titrations* is anhydrous sodium carbonate.

Primary standards for *redox titrations* include potassium dichromate(VI) and potassium iodate(V).

promoters are chemicals that make catalysts more effective. The iron catalyst in the Haber process for *ammonia manufacture* contains potassium hydroxide as a promoter. The vanadium(V) oxide catalyst used in *sulfuric acid manufacture* has potassium sulfate on a silica support to act as a promoter.

propagation is a step in a *free-radical chain reaction.*

propanone (acetone) is the simplest *ketone*, CH_3COCH_3, which is widely used as a solvent. Three to four million tonnes of propanone are manufactured worldwide each year. Propanone is also used to make monomers for the manufacture of *polymers*, including acrylics, polycarbonates and *epoxy resins*. Most propanone is made in the cumene process, which also produces *phenol.*

proportionality: a description of any relationship that takes the form:

$$y \propto x \text{ or } y = \text{constant} \times x$$

The volume of a fixed amount of an ideal gas, for example, is proportional to the temperature on the *kelvin* scale at constant pressure. The rate of a *first-order reaction* is proportional to the concentration of the reactant in the rate equation.

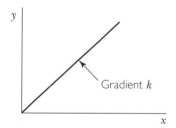

A graph showing that y is proportional to x. A straight line through the origin. $y = kx$. The gradient of the line gives the value of the constant k.

protecting group: a group introduced into an organic molecule during a synthesis to stop an unwanted reaction. Once the reaction is complete the protecting group is removed.

proteins consist of long chains of *amino acids* joined by *peptide* bonds. Some fibrous proteins are vital to the structure of animals, including the proteins in muscles, ligaments, tendons, skin and hair. Other proteins coil up into a globular shape and dissolve in body fluids where they act as oxygen carriers, *enzymes* and *hormones*.

Biochemists describe the structure of proteins at a series of levels:

- **the primary structure** is the sequence of amino acids in the polymer chains
- **the secondary structure** is the way in which the chains are arranged and held in place by *hydrogen bonding* within and between chains – this includes the coiling of chains into an α-helix in proteins such as keratin and the formation of layers of parallel chains as in the β-pleated sheets of silk
- **the tertiary structure** describes the three-dimensional folding of protein chains that gives some proteins, such as enzymes, a definite three-dimensional shape held in place by hydrogen bonding, disulfide "bridges" and interactions between amino acid side chains with surrounding water molecules
- **the quaternary structure** describes the linking of two or more amino acid chains as in the hormone *insulin*, which consists of two chains linked by disulfide bonds, or in antibodies consisting of four chains.

protium ($_1^1$H) is the abundant isotope of hydrogen. It is sometimes called protium to distinguish it from deuterium, $_1^2$H, and tritium, $_1^3$H.

proton: one of the two types of particle that make up the nucleus of an atom. The relative mass of a proton is 1 and its charge is +1. The number of protons in the nucleus of an atom is the *proton number*.

A hydrogen atom, H, normally consists of one proton in the nucleus and one electron in the first shell. So a hydrogen ion, H^+, is simply a proton. Chemists often use the terms "hydrogen ion" and "proton" interchangeably, especially when describing *acid–base reactions* as *proton transfer* reactions.

proton magnetic resonance spectroscopy: *nuclear magnetic resonance spectroscopy* (nmr) when the nuclei involved are hydrogen nuclei (or protons).

proton number: the number of protons in the nucleus of an atom. (Formerly known as the atomic number.)

proton transfer describes the movement of a hydrogen ion (or *proton*) from an acid to a base during an *acid–base reaction*. According to the *Brønsted–Lowry theory* an acid is a proton donor and a base a proton acceptor.

purification: a process used by chemists to remove impurities from the products of reaction. Common methods of purification include:

- *distillation* or *fractional distillation* for liquids
- *steam distillation* to obtain a liquid with a high boiling point that does not mix with water
- *recrystallization* to separate solids from solid impurities
- *solvent extraction* for liquids or solids.

Some types of *chromatography* are also used not only for analysis but also to separate pure products.

Chemists use a range of techniques to test for purity. A chemical is pure if it:

- melts exactly at its melting point
- boils at its boiling point
- gives only one spot or peak when analyzed by chromatography
- gives a printout that matches the spectrum of a known pure sample when analyzed by *infrared spectroscopy*.

qualitative analysis is any method for identifying chemicals in a sample. Examples of qualitative analysis include:

- *gas tests* such as the use of limewater to detect carbon dioxide
- *anion tests* such as the use of silver nitrate solution to detect and distinguish chlorides, bromides and iodides
- the separation and identification of amino acids by *paper chromatography*
- the identifying of *functional groups* in an organic compound using *infrared spectroscopy*.

quantitative analysis: any method for determining the amount of a chemical in a sample. Examples of quantitative analysis include:

- an *acid–base titration* to determine the concentration of a solution of hydrochloric acid
- the use of a *colorimeter* to determine the concentration of a colored *complex ion*
- testing the blood-alcohol concentration by *infrared spectroscopy*
- finding the relative abundances of the *isotopes* of chlorine by *mass spectrometry*.

quantum numbers identify the *energy level* or *atomic orbital* occupied by an electron in an atom. Theory shows that four quantum numbers uniquely identify each electron in an atom:

- the principal quantum number indicates the distance of the electron from the nucleus
- the second quantum number identifies the type of atomic orbital, s, p, d or f
- the third quantum number shows the direction in space of the orbital, p_x, p_y or p_z
- the fourth quantum number states the alignment of the *spin*, spin up or spin down.

The principal quantum number identifies the main *shell* occupied by an electron. The first shell ($n = 1$) can hold 2 electrons, the second shell ($n = 2$) up to eight electrons and the third shell ($n = 3$) up to 18 electrons. Thus the maximum number of electrons in a shell is given by $2n^2$.

quantum theory states that radiation is emitted or absorbed in discrete amounts called energy quanta. Max Planck, the German physicist, put forward the theory in a paper published in 1900. Quanta have energy $E = h\nu$ where h is Planck's constant and ν is the frequency of the radiation.

The Danish physicist Niels Bohr took up quantum theory in 1913 to explain the lines in hydrogen's *atomic emission spectra*. Bohr's theory could account very well for the frequencies of the lines in the spectrum of the hydrogen atom by making these assumptions:

- electrons in a hydrogen atom can only be at certain definite *energy levels*
- a photon of light is emitted or absorbed when an electron jumps from one energy level to another
- the energy of the photon, *E*, equals the difference between the two energy levels
- the frequency of the radiation emitted or absorbed is related to the energy of the photon by $E = h\nu$.

quartz is a crystalline form of *silica* (silicon dioxide). Quartz has a high melting point because it consists of a covalently bonded *giant structure* in which each silicon atom is linked to four oxygen atoms and each oxygen atom to two silicon atoms.

quaternary ammonium cations are the cations formed when all the hydrogen atoms in an ammonium ion are replaced by *alkyl groups*.

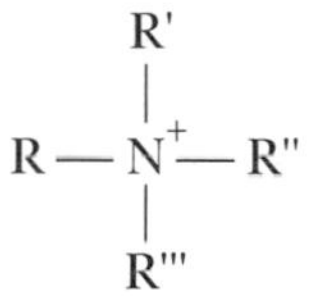

$$R-\overset{\overset{\displaystyle R'}{|}}{\underset{\underset{\displaystyle R'''}{|}}{N^+}}-R''$$

General structure of a quarternary ammonium cation

Cationic *surfactants* used in fabric and hair conditioners are quaternary ammonium salts such as dodecyltrimethylammonium bromide, $CH_3(CH_2)_{11}N^+(CH_3)_3Br^-$.

quenching: the rapid cooling of a hot metal sample during heat treatment by plunging it into cold oil or water. Quenching a hot metal produces a different structure to slow cooling.

Similarly, chemists "quench" reactions by sudden cooling. This effectively stops (or "freezes") the reaction. In this way it is possible to find the composition of an equilibrium mixture or measure the concentration of a reactant or product during a study of rate of reaction.

racemic mixture: a mixture of equal amounts of the two mirror-image forms of a *chiral compound*. The mixture does not rotate *polarized light* because the two *optical isomers* have equal and opposite effects so they cancel each other out.

Lactic acid (2-hydroxypropanoic acid) from muscles is optically active because it consists of the (+) isomer. Lactic acid from sour milk is not optically active because it is a 50:50 racemic mixture of the two mirror-image forms. Laboratory synthesis of lactic acid also produces the racemic mixture because there is an equal chance of the two isomers forming.

radioactive decay: the decay of a radioactive nucleus to form the nucleus of another element by *alpha decay* or beta decay. *Gamma rays* may also be emitted.

radioactive *nuclide* $\longrightarrow$ daughter nuclide + alpha or beta radiation

Many radioactive nuclides (or radioactive *isotopes*) are part of a *decay series*.

Radioactive decay is a *first-order reaction*. The rate of decay is proportional to the number of radioactive atoms. This means that each radionuclide decays with a constant *half-life*.

Radionuclides with a short half-life decay more quickly and tend to give off more intense radiation. The unit of radioactivity is the *becquerel* (symbol Bq).

Half-lives for radioactive decay are unaffected by changes in temperature, pressure or chemical state. This is the principle of the technique used to find the age of the remains of living things or of rocks. Knowing the half-lives it is possible to estimate ages by measuring the proportions of different nuclides in a sample.

Raoult's law: a law that predicts the *vapor pressure* of mixtures of liquids and solutions. The law states that in a mixture of two liquids A and B:

$$\frac{\text{vapor pressure of A}}{\text{over the mixture}} = \textit{mole fraction} \text{ of A} \times \text{vapor pressure of pure A}$$

$$\frac{\text{vapor pressure of B}}{\text{over the mixture}} = \textit{mole fraction} \text{ of B} \times \text{vapor pressure of pure B}$$

The total vapor pressure of the mixture is the sum of the vapor pressures of A and B over the mixture.

Only *ideal mixtures* obey the law. These are mixtures of very similar liquids so that the *intermolecular forces* between molecules of A and B in the mixture are closely similar to the intermolecular forces in pure A and pure B.

If the intermolecular forces between A and B are overall stronger than in the pure liquids, then the mixture is less volatile than Raoult's law predicts and has a lower vapor pressure. This leads to a negative deviation from the law.

If the intermolecular forces between A and B are overall weaker than in the pure liquids, then the mixture is more volatile than Raoult's law predicts and has a higher vapor pressure. This leads to a positive deviation from the law.

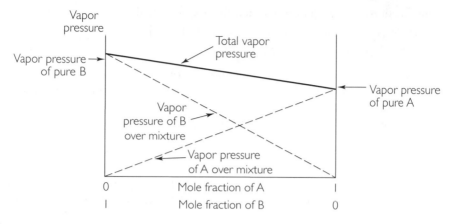

Graph to illustrate the meaning of Raoult's law

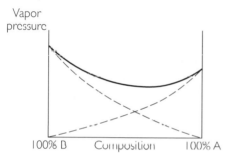

Negative deviation from Raoult's law because of stronger forces between the molecules in the mixture

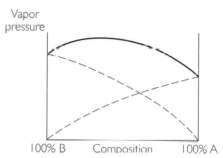

Positive deviation from Raoult's law because of overall weaker forces between the molecules in the mixture than in the pure liquids

rare earths: the traditional name of the *lanthanide elements*.

rate constant: see *Arrhenius equation* and *rate equations*.

rate-determining step: the slowest step in the mechanism of a reaction, which therefore controls the overall rate of reaction. It is generally the molecules or ions involved (directly or indirectly) in the rate-determining step that appear in the rate equation for the reaction.

Nucleophilic substitution in halogenoalkanes such as 2-bromo-2-methylpropane involves a two-step mechanism. The first step, which is the bond-breaking step in this S_N1 mechanism, is the rate-determining step. It involves only halogenoalkane molecules. Hydroxide ions are not involved. So the hydroxide ion concentration does not appear in the rate equation, which has the form:

$$\text{rate} = k[C_4H_9Br].$$

The rate-determining step in a multistep reaction is the one with the highest activation energy.

rate equations are equations that show how changes in concentration, temperature and catalysts affect the rate of a reaction.

For the reaction of hydrogen peroxide with hydriodic acid:

$$H_2O_2(aq) + 2I^-(aq) + 2H^+(aq) \longrightarrow 2H_2O(l) + I_2(aq)$$

$$\text{Rate} = k[H_2O_2(aq)][I^-(aq)]$$

Note that the rate equation cannot be deduced from the balanced equation; it has to be found by experiment. The equation shows that this reaction is *first order* with respect to each reactant. Overall it is a *second-order reaction*.

Methods for finding the order of reaction include:

- the *half-life* method
- the *initial rate method.*

The rate constant, k, is constant only for a particular temperature. The value of k varies with temperature. A rise in temperature of 10 K doubles the value of k and so doubles the rate of reaction if the *activation energy* is about 50 kJ mol^{-1}. Adding a *catalyst* lowers the activation energy and so increases the value of k and hence the rate of reaction.

The *Arrhenius equation* is the relationship between the rate constant, the activation energy and the temperature.

rates of reaction, in mol dm^{-3} s^{-1}, are found by measuring the rate of formation of a product or the rate of removal of a reactant. The usual procedure for finding rates is to measure some property of the reaction mixture, such as its volume, and to see how this property varies with time.

$$\text{Rate} = \frac{\text{change in the measured property}}{\text{time}}$$

Rates are measured in practical units such as "cm per second" and then converted to mol s^{-1} if necessary.

Methods for studying rates include:

- collecting and measuring the volume of a gas formed
- removing measured samples of the mixture, stopping the reaction and then determining the concentration of one reactant or product by *titration*
- using a *colorimeter* to follow the formation of a colored product or the removal of a colored reactant
- using a conductivity cell and meter to measure the changes in electrical conductivity of the reaction mixture and the number or nature of the ion changes.

Factors that affect reaction rates are:

- the *concentration* of reactants in solution – in general the higher the concentration, the faster the reaction (see also *collision theory*)
- the *pressure* of gaseous reactants – high pressures compress gases and increase their concentration
- the surface area of solids – breaking a solid into smaller pieces increases the surface area in contact with a liquid or gas
- the temperature – raising the temperature increases the proportion of atoms, molecules or ions with enough energy to react when they collide

- catalysts – adding a *homogeneous catalyst* or *heterogeneous catalyst* provides an alternative reaction mechanism with lower *activation energy*
- radiation – *electromagnetic radiation* can initiate *free-radical reactions* and the more intense the radiation, the faster the reaction goes.

raw materials: see *chemical industry*.

reacting masses: the masses of elements and compounds that take part in a chemical reaction. Chemists determine *empirical formulas* and *balanced equations* by measuring the masses of reactants and products. They use equations to calculate how much of each chemical they need for a chemical process and the theoretical yield of the products (see *yield calculations*).

Worked example:

Carbon monoxide reduces iron(III) oxide to iron in a blast furnace. What mass of carbon monoxide is required to reduce 20 tonnes of the oxide?

Notes on the method

Start by writing the balanced equation for the reaction.

Work out the *molar masses*, M, of the reactants in g mol^{-1}.

The reacting masses are in the same ratio whether measured in grams or in tonnes.

Answer

$Fe_2O_3(s) + 3CO(g) \longrightarrow 2Fe(s) + 3CO_2(g)$

1 mol $Fe_2O_3(s)$ reacts with 3 mol $CO(g)$.

$M(Fe_2O_3) = (2 \times 56 \text{ g mol}^{-1}) + (3 \times 16 \text{ g mol}^{-1}) = 160 \text{ g mol}^{-1}$

$M(CO) = (12 + 16) \text{ g mol}^{-1} = 28 \text{ g mol}^{-1}$

So (1 mol × 160 g mol^{-1}) = 160 g iron reacts with (3 mol × 28 g mol^{-1}) = 84 g carbon monoxide,

or 160 tonnes iron reacts with 84 tonnes carbon monoxide.

Hence mass of CO needed to react with 20 tonnes iron = $\dfrac{20}{160} \times 84$ tonnes

= 10.5 tonnes

---

reacting volumes of gases: see *gas volume calculations*.

reaction kinetics: the study of the factors that affect the *rates of reactions*. Rates are followed either by measuring the rate of formation of one of the products or the rate of removal of one of the reactants. The results of these studies are summed up in *rate equations* for reactions. *Collision theory* is one model that helps to explain the factors affecting rates. Studying the kinetics for a change can help to elucidate a mechanism for the reaction.

reaction mechanisms: see *mechanism of a reaction*.

reactors are reaction vessels used by the chemical industry for *synthesis*. There are two main types of reactor:

- batch reactors – for *batch processes* in which all the reactants are mixed in a vessel where they are heated or cooled until the process is complete
- continuous reactors – for *continuous processes* in which the reactants are fed continuously into a stirred tank or tube and products drawn out at an equal flow rate.

reagent: any pure chemical, mixture or solution supplied for chemical analysis or synthesis.

"Reagent grade" chemicals match the minimum standards specified for normal laboratory use.

Analytical reagents (AR) are chemicals that are much purer than standard laboratory-grade reagents. They are intended for accurate analytical work where impurities in the reagents would affect the results.

real gases are gases that deviate to a greater or lesser extent from *ideal gas* behavior as predicted by the ideal gas equation. In practice, many gases at room temperature follow the gas laws sufficiently closely for it to be reasonable to treat them as ideal gases.

The assumptions of *kinetic theory* explain why real gases tend to deviate from ideal behavior at:

- low temperatures and moderate pressures – when gases are not far above their boiling points so that they are close to condensing because of *intermolecular forces*
- very high pressures – when the volume of the gas is so small that the volume of the molecules cannot be ignored and the gases are less compressible than the gas laws predict.

rearrangement reaction: a reaction that rearranges the atoms in a molecule to convert one structural *isomer* to another.

One example of a rearrangement reaction is the isomerization of alkanes to make branched compounds to increase the octane number of *gasoline*.

$$CH_3 - CH_2 - CH_2 - CH_2 - CH_3 \longrightarrow CH_3 - \underset{\underset{CH_3}{|}}{CH} - CH_2 - CH_3$$

pentane　　　　　　　　2-methylbutane

Isomerization rearranges the atoms in pentane to make 2-methylbutane, which has a higher octane number.

recrystallization is a procedure often used to purify solid products of *organic preparations*. The procedure is based on a *solvent* that dissolves the product when hot but not when cold. The choice of solvent is usually made by trial and error. Use of a *Buchner flask and funnel* speeds filtering and makes it easier to recover the purified solid from the filter paper.

The procedure is as follows:

1 warm the impure solid with the hot solvent
2 if the solution is not clear, filter the hot solution though a heated funnel to remove insoluble impurities
3 cool the solution so that the product recrystallizes, leaving the smaller amounts of soluble impurities in solution
4 filter to recover the purified product
5 wash the solid with small amounts of pure solvent to wash away the solution of impurities still clinging to the solid
6 allow the solvent to evaporate in a stream of air and then in a *desiccator*.

redox potential: see *standard electrode potentials.*

redox reactions: reactions that involve **red**uction and **ox**idation. In every redox reaction an atom, molecule or ion is reduced while another atom, molecule or ion is oxidized. Reduction and oxidation always go together.

Redox reactions involve the transfer of electrons from the *reducing agent* to the *oxidizing agent.* Writing *half-equations* for redox reactions helps to show electron transfer.

Oxidation numbers help to identify redox reactions. In any redox reaction the oxidation number of one element becomes more positive (or less negative) while the oxidation number of the other element becomes less positive (or more negative).

Equations for redox reactions, like other balanced equations, show the amounts (in moles) of reactants and products involved. Oxidation numbers help to balance redox equations because the total decrease in oxidation number for the element reduced must equal the total increase in oxidation number for the element oxidized. This is illustrated here by the oxidation of iron(II) ions by manganate(VII) ions in acid solutions.

Step 1 – Write down the formulas for the atoms, molecules and ions involved in the reaction:

$$MnO_4^- + H^+ + Fe^{2+} \longrightarrow Mn^{2+} + H_2O + Fe^{3+}$$

Step 2 – Identify the elements that change in oxidation number and the extent of change:

change of –5

$$MnO_4^- + H^+ + Fe^{2+} \longrightarrow Mn^{2+} + H_2O + Fe^{3+}$$

change of +1

Step 3 – Balance so that the decrease in oxidation number of one element equals the total increase of the other element.

In this example the decrease of –5 in the oxidation number of manganese is balanced by five iron(II) ions, which each increase their oxidation number by +1.

$$MnO_4^- + H^+ + 5Fe^{2+} \longrightarrow Mn^{2+} + H_2O + 5Fe^{3+}$$

Step 4 – Balance for oxygen and hydrogen.

In this example the four oxygens from the manganate ion join with eight hydrogen ions to form four water molecules:

$$MnO_4^- + 8H^+ + 5Fe^{2+} \longrightarrow Mn^{2+} + 4H_2O + 5Fe^{3+}$$

Step 5 – In an *ionic equation*, check that the positive and negative charges balance and add state symbols.

The net charge on the left is now 17+, which is the same as the net charge on the right.

$$MnO_4^-(aq) + 8H^+(aq) + 5Fe^{2+}(aq) \longrightarrow Mn^{2+}(aq) + 4H_2O(l) + 5Fe^{3+}(aq)$$

redox titration: a practical technique used to determine the *concentration of a solution* of an *oxidizing agent* or a *reducing agent*. A *titration* measures the volume of a *standard solution* of oxidizing or reducing agent needed to react exactly with a measured volume of the unknown solution. The procedure only gives accurate results if the reaction is rapid and is exactly as described by the chemical equation.

The procedure and method of calculating results is similar to those for other titrations, for example *iodine–thiosulfate titrations* and *potassium manganate(VII) titrations*.

reducing agents: chemical reagents that can reduce other atoms, molecules or ions by giving electrons to them. Common reducing agents are metals such as zinc, iron and tin, often with acid; other common reducing agents are sulfur dioxide, iron(II) ions and iodide ions.

Iodide ions acting as a reducing agent by giving electrons to iron(III) ions. A reducing agent is itself oxidized when it reacts. Reduction and oxidation always go together in redox reactions.

reduction

$$2Fe^{3+}(aq) + 2e^- \longrightarrow 2Fe^{2+}(aq)$$

$$2I^-(aq) \longrightarrow I_2(aq) + 2e^-$$

oxidation

Some reagents change color when they are reduced, which makes them useful for detecting reducing agents.

Test	Observations	Explanation
Add a solution of potassium manganate(VII) acidified with dilute sulfuric acid	Purple solution turns colorless	Purple MnO_4^- ions are reduced to very pale pink Mn^{2+} ions
Add potassium dichromate(VI) solution acidified with dilute sulfuric acid	Orange solution turns green	Orange $Cr_2O_7^{2-}$ ions are reduced to green Cr^{3+} ions

reducing sugars: *sugars* such as glucose and fructose that give a positive result with *Fehling's solution* or *Benedict's solution*. These sugars reduce the blue copper(II) complex in the test solution to an orange-red precipitate of copper(I) oxide.

All monosaccharides and many disaccharides are reducing sugars (see *carbohydrates*), but the disaccharide sucrose is not a reducing sugar.

reductant: an alternative term to *reducing agent* that is convenient when describing *half-equations* for *redox reactions* and *standard electrode potentials*. By convention, when electrode potential values are assigned, the half-equation takes the form:

oxidant + ne⁻ $\rightleftharpoons$ reductant

Every half-equation involves an oxidant and a reductant.

reduction: originally this meant removal of oxygen or the addition of hydrogen but the term now covers all reactions in which atoms, molecules or ions gain electrons. The definition is further extended to cover molecules, as well as ions, by defining oxidation as a change that makes the *oxidation number* of an element more negative or less positive.

$$2Br^- + 2H^+ + H_2SO_4 \longrightarrow Br_2 + SO_2 + 2H_2O$$

Bromide ions reducing concentrated sulfuric acid to sulfur dioxide

Oxidation and reduction always go together in *redox reactions*.

Oxidation number rules apply in principle in organic chemistry but it is often easier to use the older definitions. Reduction is either removal of oxygen or the addition of hydrogen to a molecule.

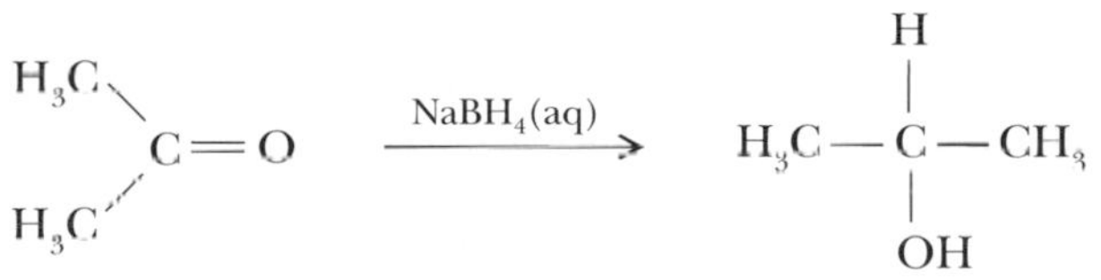

Reduction of ketone to an alcohol by addition of hydrogen

reference electrodes: electrodes used to measure electrode potentials in place of the standard *hydrogen electrode*. A hydrogen electrode is difficult to use so it is much easier to use a secondary standard such as a silver/silver chloride electrode or a calomel electrode. These electrodes are available commercially and are reliable to use. They have been calibrated against a standard hydrogen electrode. (Calomel is an old-fashioned name for mercury(I) chloride.)

$$Hg_2Cl_2(s) + 2e^- \rightleftharpoons 2Hg(l) + 2Cl^-(aq) \qquad E^{\ominus} = +0.27 \text{ V}$$

refining: the processes that separate, convert and purify chemicals in *crude oil* in an oil refinery, or the removal of impurities from metals (see *copper refining*).

reflux condenser: a condenser fitted to a chemical apparatus to prevent vapor escaping while heating a liquid. Vapor from a boiling reaction mixture condenses and flows back into the flask.

reforming: a process in oil refining that converts *alkanes* to *arenes* such as benzene and methylbenzene. This helps to raise the octane number of mixtures used in *gasoline*.

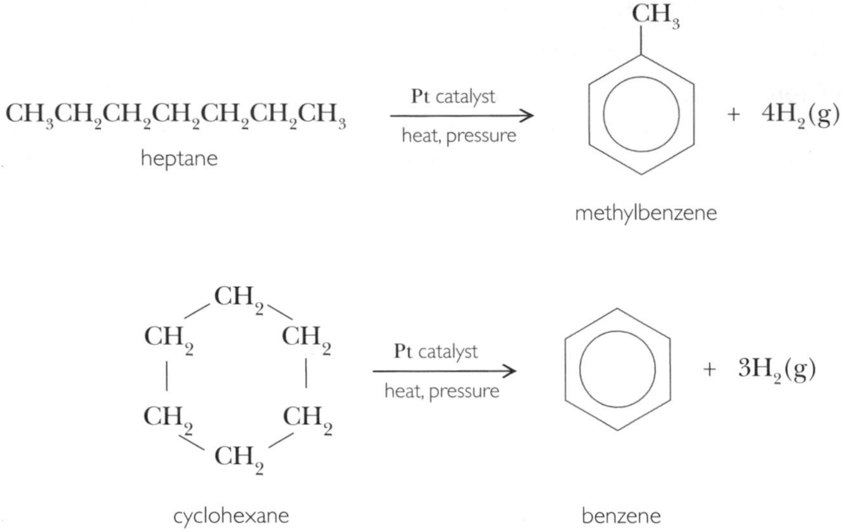

$$CH_3CH_2CH_2CH_2CH_2CH_2CH_3 \xrightarrow[\text{heat, pressure}]{\text{Pt catalyst}}$$

heptane

methylbenzene

$+ \ 4H_2(g)$

$$\text{cyclohexane} \xrightarrow[\text{heat, pressure}]{\text{Pt catalyst}} \text{benzene} \ + \ 3H_2(g)$$

cyclohexane

benzene

Examples of reforming

refractive index: a *physical property* of chemicals and materials that can help to identify unknown samples.

Forensic scientists use an oil immersion method to find the reactive index of fragments of glass from the scene of an accident or crime. The procedure is to immerse a crushed fragment in silicone oil on a slide. The slide is slowly heated, making the refractive index of the oil change as the temperature rises. The fragments of glass seem to disappear when their refractive index exactly matches that of the oil, then reappear when the oil is heated beyond the point where the refractive indices match. The technique is extremely accurate. Repeat measurements lie within a range of $\pm 0.000\ 05$ units.

refractories: materials with very high melting points used to line furnaces and make crucibles. *Ceramics* are refractory materials.

Fireclay is the raw material for making refractory bricks. Some industries need more specialized refractories. Molten *glass* and the *slags* formed during smelting are very corrosive when molten and would quickly destroy ordinary refractory bricks made of fireclay. These industries use refractories such as pure silicon dioxide (an *acidic oxide*) or pure magnesium oxide (a *basic oxide*).

relative atomic mass, A_r: the mean mass of the atoms of an element relative to the mass of atoms of the isotope carbon-12, for which A_r is defined as exactly 12. The values are relative so they do not have units.

Mass spectrometry is the technique for determining accurate relative atomic masses.

Amount of substance in chemistry is defined in such a way that the *molar mass* of an element is numerically equal to its relative atomic mass (but the latter is a ratio and has no units).

Relative atomic masses often do not have whole-number values because elements have *isotopes*. Relative atomic masses are average values for the mixture of isotopes found naturally (see *isotopic abundance*).

relative formula mass, M_r: a term used for the relative mass of ionic compounds or ions to avoid the suggestion that their formulas represent molecules. The scale is the same as for relative atomic and relative molecular masses, that is, $^{12}C = 12$.

The relative formula mass of an ionic compound or ion is the sum of the *relative atomic masses* for the atoms in the formula.

For anhydrous magnesium nitrate, $M_r[Mg(NO_3)_2]$
$$= 24 + (2 \times 14) + (6 \times 16) = 148$$

$\uparrow$ $\qquad$ $\uparrow$ $\qquad$ $\uparrow$

$A_r(Mg)$ $\quad$ $A_r(N)$ $\quad$ $A_r(O)$

Amount of substance in chemistry is defined in such a way that the *molar mass* of an ionic compound or an ion is numerically equal to its relative formula mass (but the relative mass has no units).

relative molecular mass, M_r: the relative mass of the molecules of an element or compound on the scale $^{12}C = 12$.

The relative molecular mass of the molecules of an element or compound is the sum of the *relative atomic masses* for the atoms in the *molecular formula*.

For ethanol, $M_r(CH_3CH_2OH) = (2 \times 12) + (6 \times 1) + 16 = 46$

$\uparrow$ $\qquad$ $\uparrow$ $\qquad$ $\uparrow$

$A_r(C)$ $\qquad$ $A_r(H)$ $\;$ $A_r(O)$

Amount of substance in chemistry is defined in such a way that the *molar mass* of the molecules of an element or compound is numerically equal to its relative molecular mass but as with other relative masses, the relative value has no units.

reserves and resources: the quantities of *minerals* and *fossil fuels* available in the Earth's crust. Estimates of reserves and resources include some that are proven because they have been identified and evaluated and others that seem likely to exist by a mixture of inference and guesswork.

The proven reserves of a mineral have been identified and evaluated so that it is known that it is economical to extract and process them at the current market price of the product. The resources of a mineral include all the possible sources, including those that it is not economical to extract at the time.

Judgments about changes in technology, in the demand for materials and in the economy can all shift the balance of reserves and resources. Figures for reserves have to be interpreted with care because commercial companies do not find it economic to establish reserves for more than about 25 years ahead.

residues: materials left over at the end of a chemical process. The term sometimes refers to a solid caught in a filter paper. Laboratories that use large quantities of valuable chemicals may have a "residues bottle" to collect wastes for recovery of the expensive substances. Residues worth collecting include silver compounds, iodine compounds and solvents.

resins: originally these were natural materials from the sap of trees or from insects. Examples are the rosin used for violin bows, shellac used in varnishes and myrrh, which is added to perfumes. These gummy materials consist of long-chain molecules and on warming they soften before they melt.

Now the term resin refers to synthetic materials made by *polymerization. Thermosetting polymers*, for example, are produced in two stages. The first stage produces a polymer resin. Compressing this resin in a hot mold shapes it and at the same time creates *cross-links* between the polymer chains so that the material sets to a hard plastic.

Similarly, one component of an *epoxy resin* adhesive is a polymer resin that sets on mixing with a hardener to start the chemical changes that cross-link the chains.

Synthetic *ion-exchange* resins consist of polymer beads that have been treated chemically so that they can hold cations or anions.

respiration: biochemical processes in cells that provide living organisms with the energy for growth, movement and warmth.

Aerobic respiration is respiration with oxygen. In the process glucose is oxidized to carbon dioxide and water. Overall:

$$C_6H_{12}O_6(aq) + O_2(g) \longrightarrow 6CO_2(g) + 6H_2O(l) \quad \Delta H = -2816 \text{ kJ mol}^{-1}$$

This is not a one-step reaction; it takes place in a complex series of biochemical reactions that harness the energy from the oxidation process to produce *ATP*.

Anaerobic respiration is respiration without oxygen. Anaerobic respiration in yeast converts *sugars* to carbon dioxide and ethanol. This is the process of *fermentation* used in baking, brewing and winemaking. Anaerobic respiration in animal cells produces lactate ions (the anions of lactic acid). Anaerobic respiration produces much less ATP than aerobic respiration and so is a much less efficient source of energy for processes.

retention time: see *gas–liquid chromatography.*

reverse osmosis: see *osmotic pressure.*

reversible changes are processes that can be reversed by altering the conditions.

Melting is an example of a reversible change of state. Changing the temperature alters the direction of change. Ice melts above 0°C. Water freezes below 0°C. Water and ice are in equilibrium at 0°C. This is an example of *dynamic equilibrium.*

$$H_2O(s) \rightleftharpoons H_2O(l)$$

Many chemical reactions are reversible, including the reactions used in *ammonia manufacture* and *sulfuric acid manufacture. Acid–base reactions* and *redox reactions* are generally reversible too. There are many important reversible processes in living things. Hemoglobin, for example, picks up oxygen from the air in the lungs and then releases the oxygen for *respiration* in body tissues.

The direction and extent of change for a reversible process may vary with the temperature or the concentration of chemicals. *Pressure* is an important variable affecting reactions of gases.

Chemists predict the direction and extent of change for reversible processes when they consider *feasibility*.

rhodium is one of the *platinum* metals that is largely used as a catalyst in the platinum–rhodium alloys found in *catalytic converters* and in chemical plants for *nitric acid manufacture*.

risk, in chemistry, is an estimate of the chance that a hazardous substance or process will cause harm.

There are three questions to consider when assessing the risk of a chemical process:

- what are the hazards?
- what is the likelihood that someone will come to harm because of the hazards?
- what can be done to control and reduce the risks?

When a chemical investigation is being planned the possibilities for controlling risks include the following:

- choosing a nonpractical approach using secondary sources, models and simulations
- adopting an alternative safer procedure with less hazardous chemicals
- modifying the experimental design with different apparatus or a different method of heating
- creating a barrier between the apparatus and people, using safety screens or a fume cupboard
- wearing personal protection such as eye protection and gloves.

RNA: a type of *nucleic acid* in which the five-carbon sugar is ribose and the four nitrogenous bases are *adenine, cytosine,* guanine and uracil. Two types of RNA are important in *protein* synthesis:

- messenger RNA (m-RNA), which takes the genetic code from *DNA* molecules in the nucleus to the sites of protein synthesis in the cell
- transfer RNA (t-RNA), which helps to assemble *amino acids* in the right order during the translation of the genetic code into protein molecules.

In some viruses, such as HIV, the genetic material is RNA rather than DNA.

roasting converts sulfides to oxides during *metal extraction*. Oxides are much easier to reduce to metals than sulfides. Roasting is exothermic so once the reaction has begun it needs little fuel to keep the process going. Roasting produces hot metal oxides, which may be fed directly to a furnace for reduction to the metal.

$$2PbS(s) + 3O_2(g) \longrightarrow 2PbO(s) + SO_2(g)$$

In the past roasting sulfide ores was a major cause of air pollution. The sulfur dioxide was simply released into the air where it caused acid rain. Now the sulfur dioxide is recovered and used for *sulfuric acid manufacture*. (See also *zinc extraction*.)

rotation about covalent bonds is rotation of one part of a molecule relative to another around a single covalent bond. This allow molecules to take up different *conformations*.

Double bonding stops free rotation and this accounts for the existence of *geometric isomers*.

rubber: an elastic material that is easily stretched or bent but which tends to spring back to its original shape when the force is removed.

Rubbers are **elastic polymers** often called *elastomers*.

Elastomer molecules tend to coil up in such a way that they can uncoil as they stretch and coil up again when unstretched. The molecules are *cross-linked* by strong covalent bonds so that they cannot permanently slide past each other unless pulled much harder.

Natural rubber comes from the sap of the rubber tree. This white latex coagulates to a very soft material. Vulcanizing converts natural rubber into a useful elastomer by cross-linking the polymer chains with sulfur atoms. This was the process discovered by Charles Goodyear in 1839.

Structure of natural rubber after vulcanizing. Sulfur atoms cross-link the chains, which are polymers of cis-isoprene (2-methylbuta-1,3-diene).

The science of *polymer chemistry* has helped to develop a range of alternatives to natural rubber suited for specific purposes. Examples are:

- neoprene – used for rubber dinghies
- styrene-butadiene rubber – used for motor vehicle tires
- *polyurethanes* – used for furniture foams and stretch fabrics.

Tires are black because the rubber is mixed with carbon *filler* that makes the material more resistant to wear. Carbon also absorbs *ultraviolet radiation*, helping to slow down the rate at which rubber degrades in sunlight.

rusting is the *corrosion* of iron.

rutile structure: a crystal structure of compounds with formulas MX_2. This is the structure of the mineral rutile, which consists of titanium(IV) oxide, TiO_2.

Examples of other compounds with this structure are the oxides SnO_2, PbO_2, MnO_2 and the halides MgF_2, $CrCl_2$, CuF_2.

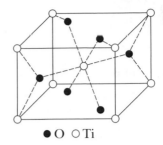

The rutile structure. Each metal ion has 6 nearest neighbors and each nonmetal ion has 3 nearest neighbors. This is 6:3 coordination.

● O   ○ Ti

R_f values: ratios that measure how far a particular chemical moves during *paper chromatography* and *thin-layer chromatography* (tlc).

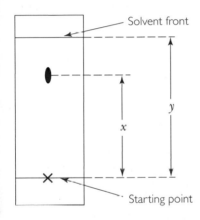

$$R_f = \frac{\text{distance moved by solute}}{\text{distance moved by solvent}}$$

$$= \frac{x}{y}$$

The R_f value is the ratio of the distance moved by the chemical in the mixture to the distance moved by the solvent front.

R_f values can help to identify components of mixtures so long as conditions are carefully controlled. The values vary with the type of paper or tlc plate and the nature of the solvent.

S

sacrificial protection: see *cathodic protection.*

salt bridge: the ionic connection between the solutions of the two *half-cells* that make up an *electrochemical cell.* A salt bridge makes an electrical connection between the two halves of the cell by allowing ions to flow while preventing the two solutions from mixing. At its simplest a salt bridge consists of a strip of filter paper soaked in potassium nitrate solution. Potassium salts and nitrates are soluble so the salt bridge does not react with the ions in the half-cells.

In commercial *reference electrodes* the salt bridge is often a small plug of porous glass.

salt hydrates: see *hydration.*

salting-out effect: this consists of making a chemical much less soluble in water by adding a high concentration of a salt. Adding common salt (sodium chloride) helps to separate *soap* from water after *hydrolysis* of fats or oils.

salts are ionic compounds formed when an *acid* reacts with a *base.* Salts therefore have two "parents." Salts are related to a parent acid and to a parent base.

Acid	Salts
hydrochloric acid, HCl	sodium chloride, NaCl
	calcium chloride, $CaCl_2$
	ammonium chloride, NH_4Cl
sulfuric acid, H_2SO_4	sodium sulfate, Na_2SO_4
	calcium sulfate, $CaSO_4$
	ammonium sulfate, $(NH_4)_2SO_4$
ethanoic acid, CH_3CO_2H	sodium ethanoate, CH_3CO_2Na
	calcium ethanoate, $(CH_3CO_2)_2Ca$
	ammonium ethanoate, $CH_3CO_2NH_4$

Base	Salts
sodium hydroxide, NaOH	sodium chloride, NaCl
	sodium sulfate, Na_2SO_4
	sodium ethanoate, CH_3CO_2Na
calcium oxide, $Ca(OH)_2$	calcium chloride, $CaCl_2$
	calcium sulfate, $CaSO_4$
	calcium ethanoate, $(CH_3CO_2)_2Ca$
ammonia, NH_3	ammonium chloride, NH_4Cl
	ammonium sulfate, $(NH_4)_2SO_4$
	ammonium ethanoate, $CH_3CO_2NH_4$

Neutralization is not the only way to make a salt. Some metal chlorides, for example, are made by heating metals in a stream of chlorine. This is useful for making anhydrous chlorides, such as *aluminum chloride* or iron(III) chloride, both of which are hydrolyzed by water so cannot be dehydrated by heating.

Insoluble salts are conveniently prepared by *ionic precipitation.*

salts of strong and weak acids: see *hydrolysis of salts* and *neutralization.*

sampling for analysis is a vital first step in any analysis because it is important to make sure that the sample is representative of the whole specimen. This is easy when analyzing solutions that are well mixed. It is more difficult when sampling an *ore* made up of lumps of rock each with variable but small amounts of a precious mineral. In these circumstances an analyst has the difficult task of preparing a sample with a mass of about 1 g from a batch of ore with a mass of several tonnes.

Analysts generally prepare multiple samples from the same specimen and work through the analysis with all of them to check on the uncertainty of the results.

saturated compounds are compounds containing only single bonds between the atoms in their molecules. Examples of saturated *hydrocarbons* are the *alkanes.*

The term "saturated" is also used for compounds with saturated hydrocarbon chains such as the saturated *fats* and *fatty acids,* even though these compounds include $C = O$ bonds. Saturated compounds do not undergo *addition reactions.*

saturated solutions are solutions that contain as much of the dissolved substance as possible at a particular temperature. A saturated solution is in equilibrium with undissolved excess of the substance in solution. The concentration of a saturated solution is the *solubility* of the substance at that particular temperature.

saturated vapor pressure: see *vapor pressure.*

s-block elements: the elements in groups 1 and 2 in the *periodic table.* For these elements the last electron added to the atomic structure goes into the *s*-orbital in the outer shell. All the elements in the *s*-block are reactive metals. (See also *atomic orbitals.*)

scaling-up processes: converting a small-scale synthesis in a laboratory or pilot plant to a process that can operate successfully and safely on a commercial scale (see table on page 306).

second law of thermodynamics: see *thermodynamics (laws of).*

second-order reaction: a reaction is second order with respect to a reactant if the rate of reaction is proportional to the concentration of that reactant squared. The concentration term for this reactant is raised to the power two in the *rate equation.* At its simplest the rate equation for a second-order reaction is:

$$\text{Rate} = k[X]^2$$

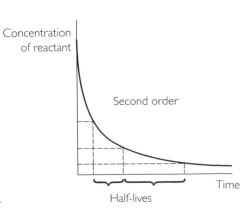

Variation of concentration of a reactant plotted against time for a second-order reaction. The half-life for a second-order reaction is not constant. The time for the concentration to fall from c to c/2 is half the time for the concentration to fall from c/2 to c/4. The half-life is inversely proportional to the starting concentration.

Concentration of reactant

Second order

Time

Half-lives

On a small scale	On a big scale
• Laboratory preparations are normally *batch processes*.	• In industry, manufacturers use *continuous processes* where there is a steady demand for the product.
• A chemist in a laboratory stores chemicals in bottles and transfers them to a reaction vessel with a spatula or by pouring through a funnel.	• In industry, pumps and pipes transfer liquids to reactors. Solids may be handled by the bagful or ingot.
• Manual mixing or shaking is adequate in the laboratory.	• A large reactor typically has a stirrer driven by an electric motor to ensure thorough mixing.
• A laboratory synthesis may happen in a beaker or flask easily heated with a Bunsen flame or cooled by dipping in water.	• It is not to easy to heat or cool large quantities of material. Reactors often have pipes running through them to carry steam for heating or cold water for cooling. Energy from exothermic reactions can raise steam to generate electricity.
• To separate the product, laboratory apparatus can be rearranged for distillation or tipped to pour the products into a filter funnel.	• Solids can be separated as pumps force a liquid through large cloth filters.
• Chemists can pour products from one container to another, perhaps using hand-held tap funnels to extract impurities. *Distillation* or *recrystallization* help to produce a pure product.	• One large-scale approach to crystallization and drying is to spray a solution into a stream of hot air.
• The product can be dried in a *desiccator* or small oven.	

Scaling-up processes

The rate of reaction of 1-bromopropane with hydroxide ions is overall second order. It is *first order* with respect to the halogenoalkane and first order with respect to hydroxide ions. The overall order is the sum of the powers in the rate equation.

$$\text{Rate } = k[CH_3CH_2CH_2Br][OH^-]$$

secondary organic compounds: see *primary, secondary and tertiary organic compounds*.

seed crystal: a crystal added to a *supersaturated solution* to encourage it to crystallize. *Recrystallization* of an organic product sometimes produces a solution that is reluctant to crystallize. Scratching the sides of the container with a glass rod can encourage crystals to form. If this fails, adding a minute crystal of the product may be enough to start rapid crystallization.

selectively permeable membrane: a membrane that allows solvent molecules and perhaps some other small molecules or ions to pass through but is impermeable to larger molecules and other ions. *Osmosis* and *dialysis* both depend on selectively permeable membranes. So does the manufacture of chlorine by *electrolysis of brine* in a membrane cell.

semiconductors are not *electrical insulators* but they do not conduct electricity as well as metals. Examples are elements such as *silicon* and *germanium* and compounds such as gallium arsenide. Semiconductors consist of covalent *giant structures* in which a few of the bonding electrons can break free and become *delocalized* in the structure. The conductivity of semiconductors is enhanced by "doping" with traces of impurity atoms. Doping silicon (in group 4) with an element such as arsenic (group 5) increases the number of conducting electrons. An arsenic atom has one more electron in its outer shell than is needed for bonding in the giant structure.

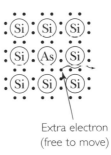

Silicon with an impurity atom from a group 5 element

Extra electron
(free to move)

separating funnel: a tap funnel used to separate liquids that do not mix (*immiscible liquids*). Separating funnels are used to:

- separate an organic product by *solvent extraction* with a solvent such as ether (ethoxyethane) – the product is more soluble in the organic solvent but the ionic reagents and ionic by-products remain in the water
- purify an impure organic product by "washing" it with aqueous reagents (such as dilute acids or alkalis) that dissolve impurities.

Pressure can build up in a separating funnel when a mixture is being shaken if one liquid is very volatile or if a reaction produces a gas. Hence the technique of inverting the funnel while holding in the stopper and releasing excess gas or vapor through the tap.

sequestering agent: a *ligand* that forms such stable complexes with metal ions that it effectively makes them chemically inactive. Examples of sequestering agents are:

- *edta* used to treat people suffering from metal poisoning
- tripolyphosphates added to detergents to complex with calcium or magnesium ions in hard water so a scale or scum precipitate is not formed.

shapes of complex ions depend on the number of ligands around the central metal ion. There is no simple rule for predicting the shapes of complexes from their formulas. Typically complexes with:

- eight ligands are octahedral, e.g. $[Fe(CN)_6]^{3-}$
- four ligands are usually tetrahedral, $[CuCl_4]^{2-}$, but may be planar, $[Pt(NH_3)_4]^{2+}$
- two ligands are linear, e.g. $[Ag(NH_3)_2]^+$.

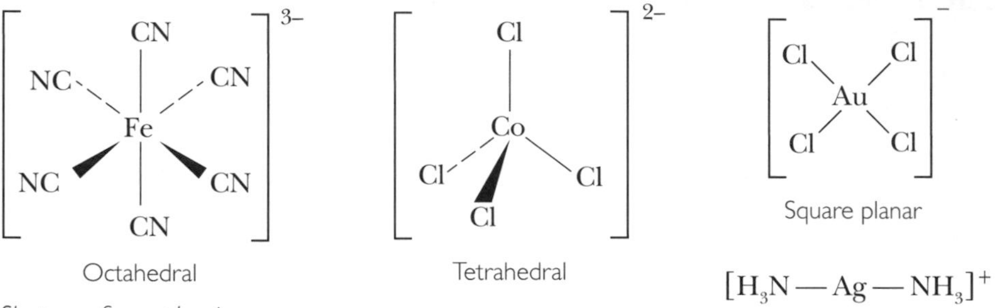

Octahedral

Tetrahedral

Square planar

$[H_3N - Ag - NH_3]^+$
Linear

Shapes of complex ions

shapes of molecules can be predicted by examining the number of bonding and nonbonding *lone pairs of electrons* in the outer shell of the central atom. The expected shape for a molecule is the one that minimizes the repulsion between electron pairs by keeping them as far apart as possible in three dimensions.

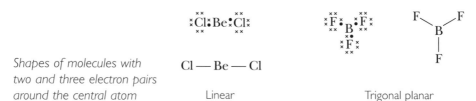

Shapes of molecules with two and three electron pairs around the central atom

Cl — Be — Cl

Linear

Trigonal planar

Nonbonding lone pairs are held closer to the central atom. The result is that the order of repulsion between electron pairs is:

lone pair–lone pair > lone pair–bond pair > bond pair–bond pair

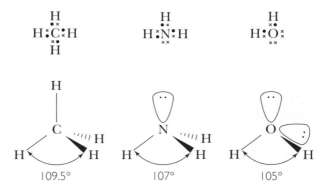

109.5°   107°   105°

Bond angles in molecules with four electron pairs around the central atom. The greater repulsion between lone pairs, and between lone pairs and bonding pairs, means that the angles between the covalent bonds decrease as the number of lone pairs increases.

A molecule with six electrons pairs around the central atom is octahedral. An octahedron has eight faces but six corners.

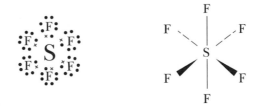

An octahedral molecule

The two electron pairs in a double bond count as one when it comes to predicting molecular shapes.

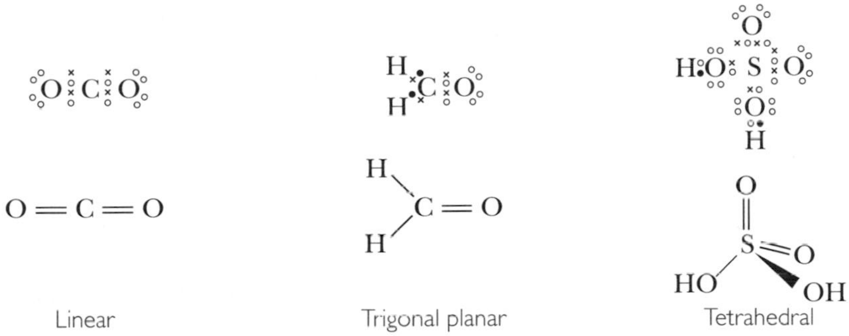

$$O = C = O$$

Linear

$$\underset{H}{\overset{H}{>}} C = O$$

Trigonal planar

$$\underset{HO}{\overset{O}{\parallel}} \underset{OH}{\overset{\parallel}{S{=}O}}$$

Tetrahedral

Shapes of molecules with double bonds

shells are the main *energy levels* in atoms and are numbered 1, 2, 3. These numbers are the principal *quantum numbers*.

shielding is an effect of inner electrons that reduces the pull of the nucleus on the electrons in the outer shell of an atom. Thanks to shielding, the electrons in the outer shell are attracted by an "effective nuclear charge" that is less than the full charge on the nucleus.

Shielding accounts for the fall in the first *ionization energy* for the elements down a group in the *periodic table*.

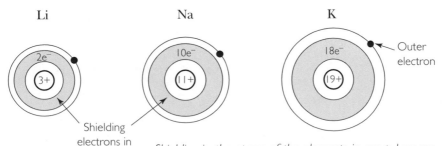

Shielding electrons in inner full shells

Shielding in the atoms of the elements in group I means that the "effective nuclear charge" is 1+. Down the group the outer electron is held less strongly, being further from the same effective nuclear charge.

SI units are the internationally agreed units for measurement in science. There are seven base units in the system. All other units are derived from the base units.

Every physical quantity in the system has a symbol. A physical quantity has a value and a unit. In calculations it is good practice to substitute both the value and the unit in formulas as shown in the worked examples in this book. The six units in this table are the base units used in chemistry. Note that in print the symbols of physical quantities appear in italics but the units do not.

Physical quantity	Symbol	Unit	Unit symbol
length	l	meter	m
mass	m	kilogram	kg
time	t	second	s
electric current	I	ampere	A
temperature	T	kelvin	K
amount of substance A	n_A	mole	mol

side reactions are unwanted reactions that reduce the yield of the product being formed by the main reaction. Side reactions create *by-products*, which are usually wasteful because they have no use.

sievert (symbol Sv) is the unit that measures the biological effect of radiation. Some types of radiation are more damaging to living cells than others. Some parts of the body are more at risk than others. This is allowed for by calculating an effective radiation dose measured in sieverts.

One sievert is a large dose, so effective doses are often quoted in millisieverts (mSv) or microsieverts (μSv). The dose for an individual depends on where they live, how they travel and whether or not they have certain medical treatments. One dental X-ray may involve a dose of about 20 μSv. Radiotherapy can involve very large doses such as 40 Sv.

sigma (σ) bond: a single *covalent bond* formed by a pair of electrons in a *molecular orbital* with the electron density concentrated between the two nuclei. Free rotation is possible about single bonds but not about *pi bonds*.

Sigma bonds can form by overlap of two *s*-orbitals, an *s*-orbital and a *p*-orbital or two *p*-orbitals (see *atomic orbitals*).

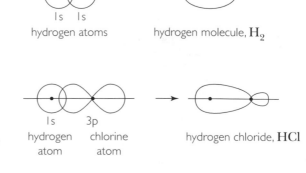

1s 1s
hydrogen atoms

hydrogen molecule, H_2

1s 3p
hydrogen atom / chlorine atom

hydrogen chloride, HCl

Examples of sigma bonds in molecules

silica (SiO₂): also known as silicon dioxide, this is the oxide of silicon that is abundant in rocks as quartz. Silica has a very high melting point at 1710°C, turning to a viscous liquid. On cooling the liquid becomes a *glass*.

Giant structure of quartz. Each Si atom is at the center of a tetrahedron of oxygen atoms. The arrangement of silicon atoms is the same as the arrangement of carbon atoms in diamond but there is an oxygen atom between each silicon atom.

Amethyst is crystalline quartz colored purple due to the presence of iron(III) ions. Sandstone and sand consist mainly of silica. Flint is a noncrystalline form of silica.

silica gel: a noncrystalline, hydrated form of *silica*. Heating silica gel produces hard granules that absorb water strongly, so silica gel is used as a drying agent. Self-indicating silica gel contains enough of an anhydrous cobalt(II) salt to color the granules blue. After the gel has absorbed a certain quantity of moisture the cobalt ions become hydrated and turn pink as a warning that the gel is no longer as effective as a drying agent. Heating drives off the water so that the gel can be used again. Silica gel is also used as the stationary phase in *chromatography*.

silicates are the minerals that make up most of the Earth's crust. The basic building block for silicates is a SiO_4^{4-} tetrahedron. Zircon ($ZrSiO_4$) is an example of a simple silicate mineral with metal ions and silicate ions.

Silicate tetrahedra can join up in chains or strands as in *asbestos*. They can also join up in sheets as in mica, talc or *clay minerals*. In these minerals the negative charges on the silicate part are balanced by positive charges from metal ions such as Na^+, Ca^{2+}, Mg^{2+} or Al^{3+}.

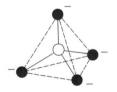

A single SiO_4^{4-} tetrahedron

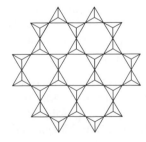

A fragment of a sheet of silicate tetrahedra

In *zeolites* the silicate tetrahedra are built up into three-dimensional networks.

A very wide range of silicate minerals is possible because some of the silicon atoms in the tetrahedra can be replaced by aluminum, boron or beryllium atoms.

silicon (Si) is the second most abundant element in the Earth's crust. Combined with oxygen it forms many minerals including *silica* (SiO_2) and *silicates*. Silicon is the second element in *group 4* of the periodic table. Its *electron configuration* is $[Ne]2s^22p^2$.

Solid silicon has a diamond structure. It is a shiny gray material made by reducing silicon dioxide with carbon in an electric furnace. The silicon formed in this way is not pure enough for use in electronics as a *semiconductor*. The element is purified in several steps ending with *zone refining*.

Silicon compounds are typical of the compounds of a *nonmetal*:

- the oxide SiO_2 is an *acidic oxide* though relatively unreactive because it has a *giant structure*
- the chloride ($SiCl_4$) is a molecular liquid that is rapidly hydrolyzed by water to hydrated silica and hydrogen chloride
- the hydrides, such as SiH_4 and Si_2H_6, are molecular gases (silanes).

silicones are *polymers* based on chains of alternating silicon and oxygen atoms. They are made by hydrolysis of compounds such as dimethylchlorosilane.

$$
\begin{array}{ccccccc}
CH_3 & & CH_3 & & CH_3 & & CH_3 \\
| & & | & & | & & | \\
-Si & -O- & Si & -O- & Si & -O- & Si- \\
| & & | & & | & & | \\
CH_3 & & CH_3 & & CH_3 & & CH_3
\end{array}
$$

A silicone polymer

By controlling the chain length and degree of *cross-linking* it is possible to make a range of silicones for use as oils, greases and rubbery materials. Silicones are water repellent and can be more safely used at higher temperatures than polymers based on carbon atoms. They are electrical insulators and other materials do not stick to them. Silicones are colorless, have no smell and are inert.

Silicones are used:

- to waterproof fabrics
- as an ingredient of polishes
- to coat nonstick surfaces such as the paper backing for self-adhesive labels
- as *lubricants*, especially at high temperatures.

silver halides are insoluble silver salts made by mixing solutions of silver nitrate and a soluble chloride, bromide or iodide. Silver halides are light sensitive and the basis for black and white and color *photography*.

$$Ag^+(aq) + X^-(aq) \longrightarrow AgX(s) \text{ where X = Cl, Br or I}$$

This precipitation reaction is used as a test for halide ions (see *anion tests*). The three silver compounds can be distinguished by their color and the ease with which they redissolve in ammonia solution. The values for the *solubility product constants* show the trend in solubility. Silver chloride is the most soluble.

Silver halide	Color	Effect of adding ammonia solution to a precipitate of the compound	Solubility/ mol dm^{-3}	K_{sp}/mol^2 dm^{-6}
silver chloride, AgCl	white	redissolves readily in ammonia solution forming an *ammine* complex	1.4×10^{-5}	2×10^{-10}
silver bromide, AgBr	cream	redissolves but only in concentrated ammonia	5.5×10^{-7}	3×10^{-13}
silver iodide, AgI	yellow	does not redissolve in ammonia solution	2.8×10^{-9}	8×10^{-18}

sizes of atoms and ions: see *atomic radius, covalent radius, ionic radius* and *van der Waals radius*.

skeletal formulas: outline formulas for carbon compounds that are a useful short-hand for complex molecules such as many natural products. The formulas need careful study because they represent only the hydrocarbon part of the molecule with lines for the bonds between carbon atoms, leaving out the symbols for the carbon and hydrogen atoms. *Functional groups* are included.

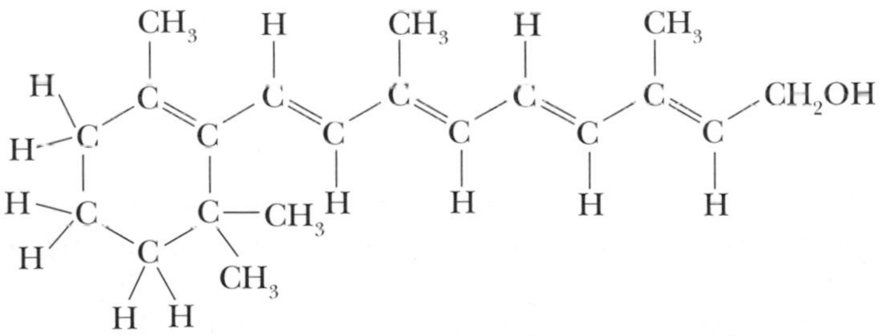

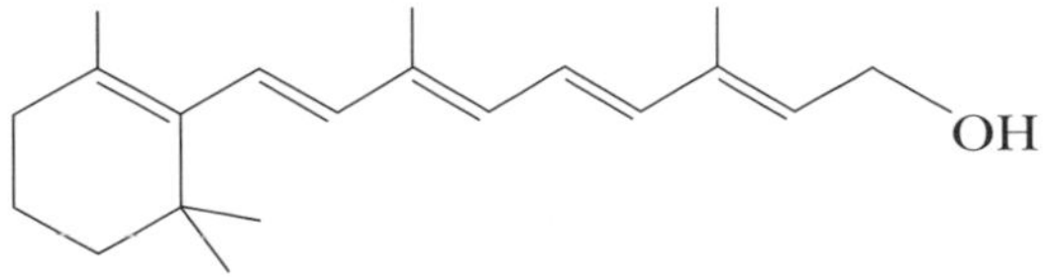

Skeletal formula for vitamin A compared to its full structural formula

slag: the unwanted waste material from *metal extraction* at high temperature (pyrometallurgy). Slag is tapped from a furnace, such as a *blast furnace*. The slag solidifies as it cools and can be dumped or crushed for use in construction or road building.

smelting is a process of *metal extraction* at high temperature (pyrometallurgy). Smelting involves melting the concentrates from metal ores to remove impurities and to reduce metal compounds to metals. Examples of smelting include the extraction of iron in a *blast furnace* and *aluminum extraction* by electrolysis of a melt.

smog: a smoky fog caused by air pollution. Burning coal in homes and industry created the dense city smogs of the nineteenth and first half of the twentieth centuries. The damaging components of these smogs were sulfur dioxide and soot. Many people affected by these acidic smogs died of lung disease. Smokeless zones and the shift of fuels from coal to oil and natural gas have largely eliminated this type of smog.

Today cities are affected by another type of smog caused by motor traffic. This is *photochemical smog*.

smoke: a *colloid* with specks of solid dispersed in a gas. Smokes are examples of *aerosols*.

SN1 and SN2 reactions: see *nucleophilic substitution in halogenoalkanes*.

soaps are made by the *hydrolysis* of *fats* or *vegetable oils* with alkali. Soaps are the sodium or potassium salts of *fatty acids*.

glycerol   sodium stearate (soap)

Saponification: the hydrolysis of a fat or vegetable oil (triglyceride) with alkali to make soap

Soaps are *surfactants* that help to remove greasy dirt because they have an ionic (water-loving) head and a long (water-hating) hydrocarbon tail.

Most household soaps are made from a mixture of animal fat and coconut palm oil. Soaps from animal fat are less soluble and longer lasting. Soaps from palm oils are more soluble so that they lather quickly but wash away more quickly. A bar of soap also contains a dye and perfume together with an antioxidant to stop the soap and air combining to make irritant chemicals.

sodium (Na) is a soft, shiny metal that rapidly tarnishes in moist air. It is the second member of *group 1* with the *electron configuration* $[Ne]4s^1$.

Like other group 1 metals, sodium:

- is stored in oil
- floats on water, melts and reacts violently, forming hydrogen, which catches fire, and NaOH, which is soluble and strongly alkaline
- forms an ionic, crystalline chloride, Na^+Cl^-.

Sodium produces a mixture of the oxide, Na_2O, and peroxide, Na_2O_2, when it burns in air.

Electrolysis of molten sodium chloride is the process used to manufacture sodium. The electrolyte also contains some calcium chloride to lower the melting point. Sodium forms at steel cathodes while chlorine bubbles off the graphite anodes. The cells are designed to keep these two reactive elements apart.

Sodium is a powerful reducing agent used for *titanium extraction* and the extraction of some other metals such as zirconium. Molten sodium is also the fluid that circulates through *heat exchangers* to transfer energy and raise steam in some nuclear power stations and other processes. Sodium is used in streetlights.

sodium chloride structure: the cubic crystal structure of the ionic compound sodium chloride, NaCl. Each positive ion is surrounded by six nearest neighbors and each negative ion is surrounded by six positive ions, so the *coordination numbers* are 6 and 6.

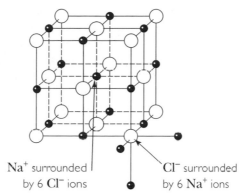

Na⁺ surrounded by 6 Cl⁻ ions

Cl⁻ surrounded by 6 Na⁺ ions

Structure of sodium chloride showing 6:6 coordination. The structure consists of a face-centered cubic array of negative ions with all the octahedral holes filled by positive ions. (See wurtzite structure for a diagram showing octahedral holes in a structure.)

Many other compounds have this structure, including: the chlorides, bromides and iodides of Li, Na and K; the oxides and sulfides of Mg, Ca, Sr, Ba, as well as the fluoride, chloride and bromide of Ag.

sodium hydroxide is a white, translucent solid supplied as flakes or pellets. It is *deliquescent*. Sodium hydroxide is a *strong base*; it dissolves in water to form a highly alkaline solution. It is fully ionized both in the solid and in solution. Note that the solution is alkaline because of the hydroxide ions (not because of the sodium ions).

Sodium hydroxide is a useful test reagent (see *anion tests, cation tests* and *organic analysis*).

The traditional name for the alkali is caustic soda, which is a reminder that it is highly corrosive. Sodium hydroxide is more hazardous to the skin and eyes than many acids.

Sodium hydroxide is manufactured by the *electrolysis of brine*. Sodium hydroxide is widely used for manufacturing other chemicals including *soaps* and *detergents*, rayon *fibers* as well as *aluminum*, sodium cyanide and sodium peroxide.

sodium tetrahydridoborate(III) (NaBH₄) is a *reducing agent* used in organic chemistry. It is a milder reducing agent than *lithium tetrahydridoaluminate(III)* and has the advantage that it can be used in aqueous solution. NaBH₄ reduces *aldehydes* and *ketones* to alcohols.

sodium thiosulfate (Na₂S₂O₃) is used in *iodine–thiosulfate titrations*. In *photography* it is the fixer that removes unexposed silver salts after developing the image (see also *thio compounds*).

A milky precipitate of sulfur forms on adding dilute acid to sodium thiosulfate. This is an example of a *disproportionation reaction*.

$$S_2O_3^{2-}(aq) + 2H^+(aq) \longrightarrow SO_2(aq) + S(s) + H_2O(l)$$

solid: one of the *states of matter*. (See also *crystal structures of ionic compounds, crystal structures of nonmetals, crystal structures of metals, ceramics, glasses, metals* and *polymers*.)

solubility: the mass (g) or amount (mol) of a substance that will dissolve in 100 g water.

As a general rule, "like dissolves like." *Polar solvents*, such as water, dissolve polar or ionic compounds. *Nonpolar solvents*, such as hexane, dissolve other hydrocarbons and nonpolar elements or compounds. Solids generally become more soluble in water as the temperature rises. Gases become less soluble as the temperature rises. Boiling water, for example, removes gases dissolved from the air. Bubbles of gas appear around the edge of a cooking pan before the water boils. The bubbles contain air coming out of solution as the gases become less soluble with the rise in temperature. Gases become more soluble as their pressure rises (see *Henry's law*).

No chemical is completely soluble and none is completely insoluble (see *solubility product constants*). Even so, chemists find it useful to use a rough classification of solubility based on what they see on shaking a little of the solid with water in a test tube:

- **very soluble**, like potassium nitrate; plenty of the solid quickly dissolves
- **soluble**, like copper(II) sulfate; crystals visibly dissolve to a significant extent
- **sparingly or slightly soluble**, like calcium hydroxide; little solid seems to dissolve but the solution becomes quite strongly alkaline
- **insoluble**, like iron(III) oxide; there is no sign that any of the material dissolves.

A similar rough classification applies to gases dissolving in water. Ammonia and hydrogen chloride are very soluble. Sulfur dioxide is soluble. Carbon dioxide is slightly soluble. Nitrogen is insoluble.

Some generalizations about solubilities help to interpret observations during qualitative analysis (see table). The generalizations in the table apply to solutions in water at room temperature. Adding acid or alkali changes the patterns of solubility.

solubility product constants: equilibrium constants for almost insoluble salts in equilibrium with solutions of their own ions. Even salts that are insoluble for practical purposes do dissolve to a very slight extent. There is an equilibrium between the solid and its ions in solution.

$$AgCl(s) \rightleftharpoons Ag^+(aq) + Cl^-(aq)$$

The *equilibrium law* applies. As with other *heterogeneous equilibria*, the concentration of the solid silver chloride is constant and does not appear in the equilibrium law equation. In this context the equilibrium constant, K_{sp}, is the solubility product constant.

$$K_{sp} = [Ag^+(aq)][Cl^-(aq)] = 2 \times 10^{-10} \, mol^2 \, dm^{-6}$$ for equilibrium concentrations

K_{sp} values can be used to predict whether or not a precipitate will form on mixing two solutions.

	Soluble in water	Insoluble in water
Acids	All common *acids* are soluble	
Bases	*Alkalis*: the hydroxides of sodium and potassium (calcium hydroxide is slightly soluble), ammonia, plus the carbonates of sodium and potassium	All other metal oxides, hydroxides and carbonates
Salts	All nitrates	
	All chlorides ...	*except* silver and lead chlorides
	All sulfates ...	*except* barium sulfate, lead sulfate, and calcium sulfate, which is slightly soluble
	All sodium and potassium salts	All other carbonates, chromates, sulfides and phosphates

Solubility

solute: a substance that dissolves in a *solvent* to make a *solution*. In a sugar solution the solvent is water and the solute is sucrose.

solutions are formed when solids, liquids or gases dissolve in a *solvent*. Water is so abundant on Earth that solutions in water (*aqueous solutions*) are particularly important to the natural environment, to life and to chemistry in laboratories and in industry.

Most solutions are solids, liquids or gases dissolved in a liquid but there are also "solid solutions." Nickel–copper *alloys* are examples of solid solutions. In a solid solution atoms of one metal replace atoms of the other metal in the crystal lattice.

solvation takes places when solvent molecules bond to ions or molecules as they dissolve. The bonding may be through weak intermolecular forces, attraction between ions and polar molecules or via covalent bonds. *Hydration* describes solvation when the solvent is water.

Solvay process: a process for manufacturing sodium carbonate from salt and limestone.

solvent: a liquid used to dissolve things. Chemists find it helpful to quote the rule "like dissolves like." What this means is that *nonpolar solvents* dissolve nonpolar substances while *polar solvents* dissolve ionic and polar compounds.

Water is the commonest solvent. It is a polar solvent and dissolves many ionic compounds. Water molecules also dissolve compounds with which they can form *hydrogen bonds*, such as glucose molecules.

Turpentine is a nonpolar solvent consisting of a mixture of *hydrocarbons*. It dissolves oily and greasy materials, including oil paints.

solvent extraction: a technique for separating and purifying substances with a *solvent* that dissolves the product required but leaves all other compounds dissolved in the original solvent. The solvents must not mix so that the two liquids separate after being shaken up together.

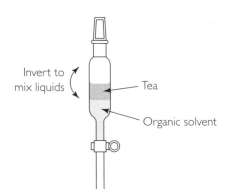

Invert to
mix liquids

Tea

Organic solvent

Use of a tap funnel for solvent extraction. Caffeine is more soluble in dichloromethane than in water. The other chemicals in tea are much more soluble in water. After solvent extraction the caffeine is recovered by distilling off the dichloromethane.

The substance being extracted *partitions* itself between the two solvents until the two solutions are in equilibrium. From the *equilibrium law* it is possible to show that it is more efficient to extract with two or three smaller volumes of solvent than to add all the solvent at once in a single extraction.

Solvent extraction is used in the *perfume* industry to extract fragrant oils from chopped up plant blossom. Solvent extraction is also used to decaffeinate coffee. In both these processes it helps to use a liquefied gas as the solvent. One possibility is carbon dioxide under pressure. After the extraction the solvent is easily removed by lowering the pressure. The solvent turns back to a gas at a low temperature. This allows the use of a nontoxic solvent. It also means that there is no need for heating to distill off the solvent. Heating can easily destroy organic compounds.

s-orbitals: see *atomic orbitals*.

space-filling models: atomic models that show the space taken up by atoms in molecules or crystals. They show the sizes of atoms, molecules or ions and how they pack together. They do not show the bond angles or the numbers of bonds between atoms in molecules as clearly as *ball and stick models*.

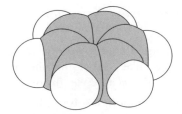

A space-filling model of benzene, C_6H_6

species: a useful collective noun used by chemists to refer generally to the atoms, molecules or ions taking part in a chemical process. A pure chemical species is a collection of identical chemical *entities*.

specific heat capacity: the energy transferred per unit mass when the temperature of a material changes by one kelvin. The SI unit is $J\,kg^{-1}\,K^{-1}$. When working on a small scale in a *calorimeter* chemists often work with values in $J\,g^{-1}\,K^{-1}$.

$$\begin{array}{ccccc} \text{energy transfer} & = & \text{specific heat capacity} & \times & \text{mass} & \times & \text{temperature change} \\ \text{(J)} & & \text{(J g}^{-1}\text{ K}^{-1}\text{)} & & \text{(g)} & & \text{(K)} \end{array}$$

spectator ions: ions in a solution during a reaction that do not take part in the chemical change. For clarity, chemists omit spectator ions from *ionic equations*. Adding silver nitrate to a solution of potassium chloride produces a precipitate of insoluble silver chloride. Both silver nitrate and potassium chloride are ionized in solution.

$$Ag^+(aq) + NO_3^-(aq) + K^+(aq) + Cl^-(aq) \longrightarrow AgCl(s) + NO_3^-(aq) + K^+(aq)$$

The potassium and nitrate ions remain in solution unchanged. They are the spectator ions left out of the ionic equation:

$$Ag^+(aq) + Cl^-(aq) \longrightarrow AgCl(s)$$

spectroscopy: a range of practical techniques for studying the composition, structure and bonding of elements and compounds. These instrumental techniques have been developed in the last 75 years and continue to become more powerful. Spectroscopic techniques are now the essential "eyes" of chemistry.

The instruments used are variously called spectroscopes (emphasizing the uses of the techniques for making observations) or spectrometers (emphasizing the importance of measurements).

Spectroscopy uses the full range of the electromagnetic spectrum to study atoms, molecules, ions and the bonding between them:

- **radio waves** in *nuclear magnetic resonance spectroscopy*
- **microwaves** to study the rotations of polar molecules
- **infrared radiation** in *infrared spectroscopy*
- **visible and UV radiation** in *atomic absorption spectroscopy, atomic emission spectroscopy* and *ultraviolet spectroscopy*
- **X-ray** spectroscopy to study electron jumps between the electron shells in atoms.

spin: the property of electrons that accounts for their behavior in a magnetic field. Electrons behave like tiny magnets. In a magnetic field electrons either line up with the field or against the field.

An *atomic orbital* can hold only two electrons and they must have opposite spins. Arrows pointing up or down represent electrons in *energy level diagrams*.

If all the electrons in molecules or ions are paired with opposite spins the substance is diamagnetic. Elements and compounds with unpaired electrons are *paramagnetic*.

spontaneous reaction: a reaction that tends to proceed naturally. In thermochemistry, spontaneity has the same meaning as a *feasibility*. So strictly speaking any reaction that naturally tends to happen is spontaneous even if it is very slow.

The control of spontaneous reactions is of vital importance in *metabolism*. The hydrolysis of *ATP* is spontaneous. However, if all the ATP in cells were to react rapidly with water, the energy from respiration would be wasted and life would cease. Hydrolysis happens only with *enzymes* to speed up the reaction. With enzymes the energy from hydrolysis can be harnessed to growth and movement.

In practice chemists sometimes use the word spontaneous in its everyday sense to describe reactions that not only tend to take place but also go fast when the reactants are mixed at room temperature. Here is a typical example:

> The hydrides of silicon catch fire spontaneously in air, unlike methane, which has an ignition temperature of about 500°C.

The reaction of methane with oxygen is also spontaneous in the thermodynamic sense, even at room temperature. However, the *activation energy* for the reaction is so high that nothing happens until the gas is heated with a flame. A mixture of methane and oxygen at room temperature is kinetically inert (see *inert chemicals*).

stability of benzene is due to *delocalized electrons.* Benzene is more stable than expected for a compound that is often shown with three double bonds as in the *Kekulé formula.*

A measure of the greater stability of benzene comes from a comparison of the experimental *enthalpy change* on adding three moles of hydrogen to benzene (*hydrogenation*) with three times the enthalpy change on adding a mole hydrogen to cyclohexene.

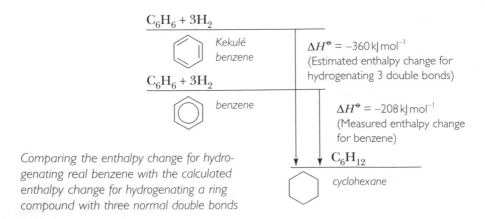

benzene + 3H$_2$ → $\Delta H^\ominus = -208$ kJ mol^{-1}

cyclohexene + H$_2$ → $\Delta H^\ominus = -120$ kJ mol^{-1}

Enthalpy changes for hydrogenating benzene and cyclohexene

Real benzene is more stable than might be expected by about 150 kJ mol^{-1}.

$C_6H_6 + 3H_2$

Kekulé benzene

$C_6H_6 + 3H_2$

benzene

$\Delta H^\ominus = -360$ kJ mol^{-1}
(Estimated enthalpy change for hydrogenating 3 double bonds)

$\Delta H^\ominus = -208$ kJ mol^{-1}
(Measured enthalpy change for benzene)

C_6H_{12}

cyclohexane

Comparing the enthalpy change for hydrogenating real benzene with the calculated enthalpy change for hydrogenating a ring compound with three normal double bonds

stability of compounds: compounds are stable if they do not tend to decompose into their elements or into other compounds. A compound that is stable at room temperature and pressure may become more or less stable as conditions change.

Chemists often use standard *enthalpy changes* as an indicator of stability. Strictly they should use standard *free energy change*, $\Delta G_f^{\ominus}$, values but in many cases $\Delta G_f^{\ominus} \approx \Delta H_f^{\ominus}$.

When discussing the stability of a compound it is important to specify the decomposition reaction. At a high enough temperature, for example, *calcium carbonate* becomes unstable relative to decomposition into calcium oxide and carbon dioxide. The *nitrogen oxides*, however, are unstable relative to decomposition into the elements.

A compound such as the gas N_2O is themodynamically unstable; the compound tends to decompose into its elements. The expressions ΔH_f (= + 82 kJ mol^{-1}) and ΔG_f (= + 104 kJ mol^{-1}) are both positive. The decomposition reaction is exothermic but the rate is very slow under normal conditions. Chemists sometimes say that N_2O is kinetically "stable." It is better to use a different word and to refer to the kinetic inertness of N_2O. (See also *inert chemicals* and *thermal decomposition*.)

ΔG	Activation energy	Change observed	
positive	high	no reaction	reactants stable relative to products
negative	high	no reaction	reactants unstable relative to products but kinetically inert
positive	low	no reaction	reactants stable relative to products
negative	low	fast reaction	reactants unstable relative to products

stability constants, K_{stab}: equilibrium constants that are a measure of the stability of *complex ions*. The greater the value of the stability constant, the more stable the complex. The values for stability constants show that *chelate* complexes formed by bidentate and hexadentate *ligands* are more stable than complexes formed by monodentate ligands.

Complex	$K_{stab}/(\text{mol dm}^{-3})^{-n}$ where n = the number of ligands
$[Ag(NH_3)_2]^+$	1.6×10^7
$[Cu(NH_3)_4]^{2+}$	1×10^{12}
$[Ni\ en_3]^{2+}$ where en is the bidentate ligand 1,2-diaminoethane	2×10^{18}
CuY^{2-} where Y is the hexadentate ligand *edta*	6×10^{18}

Stability constants show the position of equilibrium when a new ligand replaces water molecules in the hydrated ions.

$$[Co(H_2O)_6]^{2+}(aq) + 6NH_3(aq) \rightleftharpoons [Co(NH_3)_6]^{2+} + 6H_2O(aq)$$

For simplicity this is often written as:

$$Co^{2+}(aq) + 6NH_3(aq) \rightleftharpoons [Co(NH_3)_6]^{2+}(aq)$$

The usual rules for writing an equilibrium constant and its units apply.

$$K_{\text{stab}} = \frac{[[Co(NH_3)_6]^{2+}]}{[Co^{2+}][NH_3]^6} = 1 \times 10^5 \text{ mol}^{-6} \text{ dm}^{-18}$$

standard conditions: the conditions used in *thermochemistry* to define standard enthalpy and free energy changes. These conditions are the temperature 298 K and a *pressure* of 100 000 N m^{-2} = 10^5 Pa (1 bar).

When *standard electrode potentials* are being measured the standard conditions are the temperature 298 K, solutions at a concentration of 1.0 mol dm^{-3} and a pressure of 10^5 Pa if gases are involved.

standard electrode potentials are the basis of the *electrochemical series* for predicting the direction of *redox reactions*. They are also used to calculate the emfs of *electrochemical cells*. The standard electrode potential for a *half-cell* is measured relative to a standard *hydrogen electrode* under *standard conditions*.

$$Pt[H_2(g)] \mid 2H^+(aq) \mid\mid Cu^{2+}(aq) \mid Cu(s)$$

The emf of this cell under standard conditions is, by definition, the standard electrode potential of the $Cu^{2+}(aq)$ $Cu(aq)$ electrode.

standard enthalpy changes: see *enthalpy change*.

standard form: the form that mathematicians and scientists use to write very large or very small numbers. Standard form is based on powers of 10.

10^{-9} = 0.000 000 001	10^1 = 10
10^{-6} = 0.000 001	10^2 = 100
10^{-3} = 0.001	10^3 = 1 000
10^{-2} = 0.01	10^4 = 10 000
10^{-1} = 0.1	10^6 = 1 000 000
10^0 = 1	10^9 = 1 000 000 000

Worked example:

The dissociation constant for ethanoic acid, K_a = 0.000 017 mol dm^{-3}

$\qquad\qquad\qquad\qquad$ = 1.7 × 0.000 01 mol dm^{-3}

$\qquad\qquad\qquad\qquad$ = 1.7 × 10^{-5} mol dm^{-3},

$\qquad\qquad\qquad\qquad\qquad$ which is standard form.

Worked example:

The *Faraday constant* = 9 6480 C mol^{-1} = 9.648 × 10 000 C mol^{-1}

$\qquad\qquad\qquad\qquad$ = 9.648 × 10^4 C mol^{-1}, which is standard form.

---

standard free energy changes: see *free energy change*.

standard hydrogen electrode: see *hydrogen electrode*.

standard molar entropy, $S^{\ominus}$: the *entropy* per mole for a substance under *standard conditions*. Chemists use values for standard molar entropies to calculate entropy changes and so predict the direction and extent of chemical change.

The units for standard molar entropy are joules per kelvin per mole ($J\ K^{-1}\ mol^{-1}$).

solids	$S^{\ominus}/J\ K^{-1}\ mol^{-1}$	liquids	$S^{\ominus}/J\ K^{-1}\ mol^{-1}$	gases	$S^{\ominus}/J\ K^{-1}\ mol^{-1}$
carbon(diamond)	2.4	mercury	76.0	hydrogen	130.6
magnesium oxide	26.9	water	69.9	carbon dioxide	213.6
copper	33.2	ethanol	160.7	propane	269.9

The table shows standard molar entropies at 298 K. Gases have higher standard molar entropies than solids. The number of ways of distributing particles and energy in a system of gas molecules is much higher than in an ordered crystalline solid. The more rigid and regular a crystal, the lower its entropy.

Liquids have intermediate values of standard molar entropies. The more atoms in the molecules, the greater the opportunities for vibration and rotation so the higher the entropy values.

standard solution: a solution with an accurately known concentration. The direct method for preparing a standard solution is to dissolve a weighed sample of a *primary standard* in water and to make the solution up to a definite volume in a graduated flask.

Standard solutions are used in *titrations* to determine the concentrations of other solutions. They are also needed for the *calibration* of instruments such as colorimeters.

standard state: the stable state of an element or compound under the *standard conditions* that apply in thermochemistry. *Standard enthalpy changes* and *free energy changes* are defined for substances in their standard states.

When an element such as carbon has two *allotropes*, diamond and graphite, the standard state of carbon is graphite because it is the more stable form.

Standard states normally refer to substances in their stable physical states under standard conditions. Carbon dioxide and methane are gases but water is a liquid.

starch is a *carbohydrate* that consists of long chains of glucose units. It is a polysaccharide. Starch is insoluble in cold water. In hot water, starch gelatinizes, forming a colloidal dispersion. Starch solution gives an intense blue-black color with iodine. The solution is used as an indicator to detect the end point in *iodine–thiosulfate titrations*.

state functions: measurable properties that depend only on the state of a system, not on how the system got to that state. Examples are *pressure, volume* and temperature, as are thermochemical quantities such as enthalpy, *entropy* and *free energy*.

Changes in state functions depend only on the initial and final states of the system and not on the pathway from one state to the other. This is the basis of *Hess's law*.

Equations of state show the mathematical connections between state functions. An important example is the *ideal gas* equation, which relates the pressure, volume and temperature of an amount of a gas.

states of matter: the solid, liquid and gaseous states (see *changes of state*) as well as intermediate states such as *liquid crystals* and mixtures, including aqueous solutions and the colloidal state (see *colloids*).

State symbols in equations indicate the states of the chemicals: (s) solid, (l) liquid, (g) gas, (aq) aqueous (dissolved in water).

stationary phase: see *chromatography.*

steady-state systems: systems in which the concentrations of chemicals stay constant because they are being supplied or formed as fast as they are removed or destroyed. The temperature is constant too because energy is transferred to the system as fast as it is lost to the surroundings.

The blue flame of the Bunsen burner is a steady-state system. There is a constant supply of gas and oxygen, which burn to release energy. The products of burning and energy are constantly lost to the surroundings.

Steady-state systems are important in *environmental chemistry.* The *atmosphere* approximates to a steady state, with gases such as oxygen being added to the air by photosynthesis but removed by respiration and burning.

Problems arise when human activity on a large scale upsets one or more of the processes in a steady-state system. *Ozone,* for example is naturally formed and destroyed in the stratosphere:

rate of formation of ozone = rate of destruction of ozone

The release of chlorine compounds such as *CFCs* has increased the rate of destruction of ozone, upsetting the steady state and lowering the ozone concentration, especially over the poles, hence the "hole" in the ozone layer.

steam cracking breaks up bigger *hydrocarbon* molecules into smaller molecules by heating them with steam at a high temperature. The process is especially useful for converting the *naphtha* fraction from crude oil distillation into starting materials for synthesis in the petrochemical industry.

Steam cracking converts ethane to *ethene,* which is a very important starting compound for chemical synthesis in industry. Steam cracking is thermal cracking, as opposed to *catalytic cracking.*

steam distillation is a useful technique for separating oils from plant materials such as rose petals, cloves, lavender, thyme or fennel. It is an important technique in the *perfume* industry. Steam distillation makes it possible to separate compounds that decompose if heated at their boiling points. The technique works only for compounds that do not mix with water.

Steam distillation is also sometimes used to separate products of organic preparations, leaving behind reagents and products that are soluble in water.

Steam distillation works because the *vapor pressure* of a mixture of *immiscible liquids* is the sum of the separate vapor pressures when they are shaken up together. The mixture boils when the total vapor pressure equals atmospheric pressure. So the mixture of steam and oily product distills at a little below the boiling point of water and well below the boiling point of the oil.

steam reforming is the reaction of steam with methane (or other hydrocarbon) in the presence of a nickel oxide *catalyst* at 800°C under pressure.

$$CH_4(g) + H_2O(g) \rightleftharpoons 3H_2(g) + CO(g)$$

It is followed by further reaction with excess steam. This "shift reaction" converts the CO into CO_2. The reaction happens in the presence of an iron(III) oxide catalyst at 400°C.

$$H_2O(g) + CO(g) \rightleftharpoons H_2(g) + CO_2(g)$$

This mixture of hydrogen and carbon dioxide can be converted directly to methanol (see *carbon*). Alternatively, absorbing the carbon dioxide in alkali provides hydrogen for *ammonia manufacture*.

steels are *alloys* of iron with carbon and often other metals.

Mild steel contains about 0.2% carbon as iron carbide. Crystals of iron carbide in the metal structure make the steel strong and yet it is still *malleable*. Mild steel is used for auto bodies. As the carbon content increases the steel becomes stronger and harder so that it is suitable for rail lines.

Steel is made by the basic oxygen steelmaking process, which removes impurities from *iron extraction* in a blast furnace. During the process a blast of oxygen converts impurities in the liquid metal, such as carbon, silicon and phosphorus, into their oxides. Carbon dioxide escapes as a gas. The oxides of the nonmetals silicon and phosphorus are *acidic oxides*. They are converted to a molten *slag* by adding the *basic oxides* of calcium and magnesium. The slag floats on the surface of the liquid steel and can be poured off separately.

$$SiO_2 + CaO \longrightarrow CaSiO_3(l)$$

Alloy steels consist of iron with small amounts of carbon together with up to 50% of one or more of these metals: aluminum, chromium, cobalt, manganese, molybdenum, nickel, titanium, tungsten and vanadium. The presence of other metals distinguishes alloy steels from carbon steels. Examples of alloys steels are:

- stainless steels, which include chromium and nickel
- tool steels with tungsten or manganese, which make the alloy harder, tougher and keep their properties at higher temperatures so that they are suitable for drill bits and cutting tools.

stereochemistry is the study of molecular shapes and the effect of shape on chemical properties. Stereochemistry is especially concerned with the study of the contrasting properties of *stereoisomers*.

Smell and taste seem to depend on molecular shape. One mirror-image form of limonene smells of oranges while the other form smells of lemons.

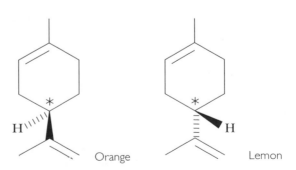

The enantiomers of limonene and their smells. Asterisks mark the chiral centers.

Orange

Lemon

Molecular shape can also subtly alter the physiological effects of drugs, as tragically illustrated by the two enantiomers of thalidomide (see *chiral compounds*).

The *antibiotic* penicillin destroys bacteria by disrupting their cell walls. Penicillin molecules resemble the shapes of molecules used to make the membrane around bacterial cells. The resemblance is enough for enzymes to build penicillin molecules into the structure. But penicillin lacks the part of the natural molecules that *cross-links* the structure. The walls are fatally weakened so that the bacterial cells break open and die.

Molecular shape affects the *physical properties* of materials such as polymers. This is illustrated by the differences between poly(propene) as an *isotactic polymer* and as an *atactic polymer*.

Steric factors can also affect the mechanisms of reactions and the rates of chemical change.

stereoisomers are distinct compounds with the same molecular and structural formulas but with different three-dimensional shapes. There are two kinds of stereoisomerism: *geometrical isomerism* and *optical isomerism*.

stereoregular polymer: a polymer with a regular three-dimensional shape. Poly(propene) can be an *isotactic polymer*. This is the useful stereoregular form. Or it can be an *atactic polymer*, which is irregular and does not have useful properties.

stereospecific reactions are reactions that involve one of the *optical isomers* of a *chiral compound* but not the other. All the biochemical processes involving *amino acids* are stereospecific. The enzymes involved can act on the L-amino acids but not on the mirror-image D-forms.

Enzymes act only on molecules that fit their *active sites*. They are so selective that they can pick out from a *racemic mixture* those molecules that are either left-handed or right-handed.

Since the thalidomide tragedy, the pharmaceutical industry has become much more aware of the importance of chirality and the need to test mirror-image forms of chiral compounds separately. This has encouraged chemists to develop stereospecific reactions to produce particular optical isomers.

steroids are *lipids* with molecules that do not contain *fatty acids*. An important steroid is *cholesterol*. Cholesterol can be converted to biologically active steroids such as the sex hormones estrogen and progesterone.

stiffness is the opposite of flexibility. It is a very important property of materials. Materials scientists seek to develop materials that are both stiff and strong while not being too dense.

Stiffness is measured by the Young modulus for the material.

stoichiometry: a stoichiometric equation is the *balanced equation* for a reaction. It shows the amounts, in moles, of the substances involved in a reaction.

A stoichiometric compound has a composition that corresponds exactly to its formula. A stoichiometric reaction is one that uses up reactants and produces products in amounts exactly as predicted by the balanced equation.

The word stoichiometry sounds mysterious but is simply based on Greek words meaning "element-measure." Stoichiometry is the basis of *quantitative analysis* where amounts are measured in moles.

stp (standard temperature and pressure): the standard conditions for describing the properties of gases. The standard temperature is 273 K (0°C) and the standard *pressure* is 101.3 kPa (1 atmosphere).

The molar volume of an ideal gas at stp is 22 400 cm³ (22.4 dm³).

Note the distinction between these values and the values for defining *standard states* in thermochemistry.

strength is measured by the stress needed to deform and break a material in tension or compression. Stress is the force per unit area of the cross section and is measured in N m⁻². Defining stress in this way allows for the fact that it is easier to stretch a thin sample than a thick one.

Metals such as steel have high tensile strength. Ceramics are weak in tension but have high strength in compression.

For many applications engineers look for materials that combine high strength with high *stiffness.*

strong acids are *acids* that are fully ionized when they dissolve in water. Examples are *hydrochloric acid, nitric acid* and *sulfuric acid.*

strong bases are *bases* that are fully ionized when they dissolve in water. Examples are the hydroxides of *sodium* and *potassium.*

structural formulas show the arrangements of atoms and *functional groups* in molecules.

Sometimes it is enough to show structures in a condensed form such as $CH_3CH_2CH_2CO_2H$ for butanoic acid. Often it is clearer to write the full structural formula showing all the atoms and all the bonds. This type of formula is also called a *displayed formula.*

Examples of structural formulas. Drawn like this the formulas do not show the true shape in three dimensions.

structural isomers: see *isomers*.

sublimation is the change of a solid directly to a gas on heating. Heating iodine crystals makes them sublime to a purple vapor that condenses to shiny crystals on a cold surface. This process is used to purify iodine.

Another substance that sublimes is solid carbon dioxide ("dry ice") because it turns to gas at minus 78°C without melting.

substitution reactions are reactions that replace an atom or group of atoms by another atom or group of atoms. An example is the reaction of butan-1-ol with hydrogen bromide (from sodium bromide and concentrated sulfuric acid).

$$CH_3CH_2CH_2CH_2OH + HBr \longrightarrow CH_3CH_2CH_2CH_2Br + H_2O$$

In organic chemistry, substitution reactions are characteristic of *halogenoalkanes* (see *nucleophilic substitution*) and *arenes* (see *electrophilic substitution*).

The ligand exchange reactions of inorganic complex ions are also substitution reactions (see *ligands*).

substrates, in biochemistry, are the molecules on which *enzymes* act as they catalyze change. An enzyme is specific because it acts only on the substrate that fits into its *active site*.

Literally the word "substrate" means a lower layer on which something else can form or grow. One way of creating a large surface area for an expensive *catalyst* is to spread it over the surface of an inert substrate. This helps to keep down the cost of *catalytic converters* in automobile exhausts.

sugars are water-soluble *carbohydrates*. Sugars vary in their *sweetness*. Sugar molecules have many — OH groups and can *hydrogen bond* with each other and with water. This means that they are solid at room temperature and very soluble in water. (See also *reducing sugars*.)

Ribose and deoxyribose sugars are important in the formation of nucleic acids such as *DNA* and *RNA*.

sulfates are salts of *sulfuric acid*. Soluble sulfates such as blue copper(II) sulfate and green iron(II) sulfate are familiar laboratory reagents.

Some insoluble sulfates are natural minerals, including calcium sulfate, which exists in a hydrated form as gypsum and in an anhydrous form called anhydrite. Heating gypsum produces *plaster of Paris*. Barite is barium sulfate, called "heavy spar" because of its density. (See also *solubilities of salts* and *anion tests*.)

sulfides of metals are salts of hydrogen sulfide, H_2S. Some valuable metals occur as sulfide ores, including copper, silver, mercury and iron. Sodium sulfide is soluble in water but most metal sulfides are insoluble.

sulfites are salts of sulfurous acid that form when sulfur dioxide dissolves in water. Sulfurous acid is unstable and exists only in solution.

$$SO_2(g) + H_2O(l) \longrightarrow H_2SO_3(aq)$$

The most important sulfite is sodium sulfite (Na_2SO_3), made by dissolving sulfur dioxide in sodium hydroxide solution.

Sulfur dioxide and the sulfite ion are *reducing agents*. They reduce chlorine, iron(III) ions, dichromate(VI) ions and manganate(VII) ions.

Sulfur dioxide and sulfites are used as preservatives. They are antioxidants used in foods such as lemon juice. They inhibit the growth of bacteria. (See also *anion tests*.)

sulfonamide drugs: see *chemotherapy*.

sulfonation of benzene is an *electrophilic substitution* reaction that takes place in the presence of fuming sulfuric acid – a solution of sulfur trioxide in concentrated sulfuric acid. The product is benzene sulfonic acid.

The *electrophile* is sulfur trioxide. A sulfur atom attached to three more *electronegative* oxygen atoms is electrophilic.

Sulfonation of benzene

Sulfonation of arenes is important because it helps to produce a range of useful products including *surfactants, ion-exchange resins, dyes* and sulfonamide drugs.

sulfur (S) is a yellow crystalline solid that normally consists of S_8 molecules. Sulfur is a *nonmetal*, coming below oxygen in group 6 of the *periodic table*. Its *electron configuration* is $[Ne]3s^23p^4$.

Sulfur has two solid *allotropes* (see *enantiotropy*). Heating sulfur crystals produces a runny, pale-yellow liquid that darkens as the temperature rises, producing a highly *viscous liquid*. The S_8 rings break and form long tangled chains of sulfur atoms. Further heating below the boiling point (445°C) makes the liquid more fluid because the chains start to break into shorter lengths. Pouring this dark red liquid into cold water produces an elastic, noncrystalline mass of plastic sulfur. In time, plastic sulfur hardens as the sulfur chains gradually reform S_8 rings and produce rhombic sulfur again.

Sulfur is a reactive element but it is a less powerful *oxidizing agent* than oxygen. It combines with most other elements with the exception of nitrogen, iodine, the noble gases and some of the less reactive metals such as gold.

Hydrogen sulfide (H_2S) is a toxic, foul-smelling compound. Despite having a higher relative molecular mass than water, hydrogen sulfide is a gas, because sulfur is not sufficiently electronegative for *hydrogen bonding* between H_2S molecules.

Sulfur forms two *acidic oxides* SO_2 and SO_3, which are both important in the process of *sulfuric acid manufacture*. Sulfur dioxide is a *reducing agent*, as are sulfurous acid and its salts, the *sulfites*.

Bonding in the oxides of sulfur.
Note that the rules for predicting
the shapes of molecules apply.

The reactions of *halide ions* with concentrated sulfuric acid illustrate the range of oxidation states of sulfur.

sulfur extraction: processes that obtain sulfur from underground deposits of the element or from crude oil and *natural gas.*

The Frasch process is an ingenious process for extracting sulfur from underground deposits. Sulfur is a nonmetal with a molecular structure. It melts at 113°C. Superheated steam at 165°C passes down a pipe into the sulfur deposits. The steam melts the sulfur. Compressed air pumped down a second pipe forces the liquid up a third pipe to the surface where it cools and solidifies. The process was developed by Herman Frasch around 1900 to recover sulfur from 30 m thick deposits about 150 m underground along the gulf coast of the USA. The process still operates and supplies about 10% of the sulfur required for industry in the USA. A modified version of the process operates in Poland, which supplies sulfur for the UK chemical industry.

Natural gas and crude oil often contain unwanted sulfur compounds that must be removed before the gas and oil are used as fuels or in the chemical industry. The hydrocarbons are mixed with hydrogen under pressure and passed over a *catalyst.* This converts the sulfur to hydrogen sulfide. The hydrogen sulfide is separated from the hydrocarbons and converted to a mixture of sulfur and sulfur dioxide.

Ninety percent of sulfur is used to make sulfuric acid.

sulfuric acid (H_2SO_4) is a highly corrosive but important chemical reagent because it can act as a *strong acid,* a *dehydrating agent,* an *oxidizing agent* and as a sulfonating agent. Pure sulfuric acid is a colorless *viscous liquid.* The molecules of this *oxoacid* are attracted to each other by *hydrogen bonding.*

Structure of sulfuric acid molecules showing hydrogen bonding

In its different roles sulfuric acid acts as:

- **a strong acid** – sulfuric acid ionizes fully as it dissolves in water
  $$H_2SO_4(l) + H_2O(l) \rightarrow H_3O^+(aq) + HSO_4^-(aq)$$
  Dilute sulfuric acid neutralizes bases. It forms two series of soluble salts called *sulfates* and hydrogensulfates. Hydrogensulfates are *acid salts.*
- **a powerful dehydrating agent** – concentrated sulfuric acid can:
  - remove the elements of water from *sugars* and other *carbohydrates* so that they char and turn to black charcoal

- dehydrate *alcohols*, turning them into *alkenes*
- act as a drying agent to remove water from moist gases
- **an oxidizing agent** – it reacts with *halide ions*, especially bromide and iodide ions
- **a sulfonating agent** – it is used for the *sulfonation of benzene* and other *arenes*.

sulfuric acid manufacture: the contact process for making sulfuric acid from sulfur, which produces over 150 million tonnes of the acid in the world each year.

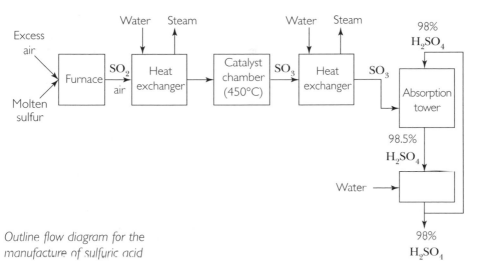

Outline flow diagram for the manufacture of sulfuric acid

The process operates in three main stages:

Stage 1: Burning sulfur to make sulfur dioxide

$$S(s) + O_2(g) \longrightarrow SO_2(g)$$

This is a highly exothermic reaction. The hot gas is cooled in *heat exchangers*, which produce steam used to generate electricity. Sulfuric acid plants do not have electricity bills. Electricity and steam exported from the process help to make sulfuric acid economic.

Stage 2: Conversion of sulfur dioxide to sulfur trioxide

$$2SO_2(g) + O_2(g) \rightleftharpoons 2SO_3(g) \qquad \Delta H = -297 \text{ kJ mol}^{-1}$$

This is an exothermic, reversible reaction that takes place on the surface of a vanadium(V) oxide *catalyst*. The *temperature effect on equilibrium* means that raising the temperature lowers the percentage conversion to SO_3 but the temperature must be high enough to make the reaction go fast enough. The catalyst is not active below 380°C and works best at a higher temperature.

Increasing the pressure would increase the conversion to sulfur dioxide but the extra cost is not usually justified.

Typically the gas mixture passes through four catalyst beds. Between each bed the gas mixture is cooled in a heat exchanger and cold air with more oxygen is added to the mixture. After the third bed the level of conversion is 98%. To ensure conversion of the remaining SO_2, sulfur trioxide is absorbed from the gas stream and more air is added before the gases flow through the fourth catalyst bed. So three factors contribute to converting as much of the sulfur dioxide as possible to sulfur trioxide: cooling, adding more of one of the reactants and removing the product.

Stage 3: Absorption

$$H_2O(l) + SO_3(g) \longrightarrow H_2SO_4(l)$$

Sulfur trioxide cannot be dissolved in water directly because the violent reaction produces a hazardous mist of acid. Instead the gas is absorbed in 98% sulfuric acid. Sulfur trioxide passes up a tower packed with pieces of ceramic, down which the concentrated acid trickles. The circulating acid is kept at the same strength by drawing off product while adding water.

Environmental legislation requires very low emissions of acid gases into the air. A modern plant converts 99.7% of the sulfur dioxide into sulfuric acid in stages 2 and 3.

Sulfuric acid is needed on a large scale to make many other chemicals, including phosphate *fertilizers, paints* and pigments, *detergents, plastics, fibers* and *dyes*.

sunscreens protect the skin from harmful ultraviolet radiation from the Sun. Suntan lotions include chemicals such as 4-aminobenzoic acid, which absorbs UV radiation.

Sunblocks are heavily pigmented so that they form a barrier to sunlight by reflecting and scattering light. The white pigments are zinc oxide and *titanium(IV) oxide*.

superoxides: compounds with oxygen containing the O_2^- ion (see *potassium*).

supersaturated solution: a solution that contains more dissolved solute than a saturated solution. A supersaturated solution is unstable. Crystals form rapidly when the edge of the container is scratched or a tiny seed crystal is added.

The way to make a supersaturated solution is to cool a hot, saturated solution of a salt such as sodium thiosulfate or sodium ethanoate. Sometimes an unwanted supersaturated solution forms when a solid product is purified by *recrystallization*.

Some "instant hand warmers" consist of a supersaturated solution of sodium ethanoate in a plastic bag. Flexing a metal disk in the side of the bag starts crystallization that is exothermic and heats the bag to about 60°C. The hand warmer can be reused after heating in boiling water to redissolve the salt and then allowing it to cool to room temperature so that the solution is once more supersaturated.

surface tension: the tendency of surfaces to contract to the minimum surface area. Surface tension accounts for the spherical shape of soap bubbles.

Surface tension arises because of *intermolecular forces*. Molecules inside the liquid are pulled in all directions by surrounding molecules. Molecules near the surface experience a net pull inward. This means that as many molecules as possible leave the surface, which tends to shrink.

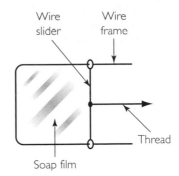

Wire slider

Wire frame

Thread

Soap film

The surface tension of the soap film makes the slider move to the left unless balanced by a pull on the thread.

Intermolecular attraction

Molecule

Intermolecular forces acting on molecules inside the liquid and at the surface

The surface tension of many organic liquids is in the range 15 to 30 mN m^{-1}. The surface tension of water is higher because of strong *hydrogen bonding*. For water the value is about 73 mN m^{-1}. *Surfactants* lower the surface tension of water so that it can wet greasy surfaces (see *wetting*).

surfactants are surface-active agents. They are chemicals with molecules that seek out the boundary surface between two liquids or between a liquid and a gas. One of the important effects of surfactants is that they change the *surface tension* of liquids.

A surfactant molecule has an ionic or polar group attached to a hydrocarbon chain. The polar group is water-loving (hydrophilic). The hydrocarbon chain is water-hating (hydrophobic).

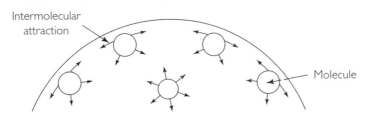

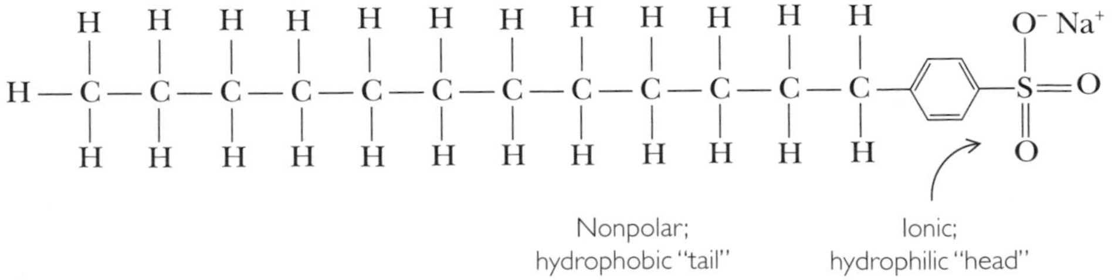

Nonpolar; hydrophobic "tail"

Ionic; hydrophilic "head"

Structure of a surfactant molecule

The hydrophobic chains of surfactant molecules tend to escape from water by moving to the surface or by forming *micelles*. Surfactant molecules at the surface lower the surface tension of the water so that it wets surfaces more effectively. Surfactant molecules adsorbed at the boundary between air and water stabilize bubbles of foam by stopping all the water draining away.

Surfactants help to separate greasy dirt from surfaces. They keep dirt dispersed in water so that it rinses away. They also help to prevent dirt reattaching itself to the surface of fabrics.

Surfactants come in three kinds based on the type of hydrophilic group:

- anionic surfactants such as *soap*, $CH_3(CH_2)_{16}CO_2^-Na^+$
- nonionic surfactants made from *epoxyethane*, $CH_3(CH_2)_{11}(OCH_2CH_2)_6OH$
- cationic surfactants such as *quaternary ammonium salts*, $CH_3(CH_2)_{11}N^+(CH_3)_3Br^-$.

Synthetic anionic surfactants are widely used. They are included in bath foam and shampoos. They make stable foams with water.

Nonionic surfactants are used in many household cleaners because they allow smooth drainage and leave no deposit even when they are not fully rinsed away. Nonionic surfactants also make less stable foams so they are included in washing powders for dishwashers and washing machines.

Cationic surfactants are used in fabric softeners and hair conditioners.

surroundings: see *system*.

suspension: particles of a solid suspended by shaking or stirring in a liquid or gas. In time the particles of a suspension settle out, unlike the smaller particles in *colloids*.

sweetness: a taste sensation on the tip of the tongue produced by *sugars* and a number of synthetic chemicals such as saccharin, cyclamate and aspartame. Sugars vary in their sweetness. Fructose is sweeter than sucrose, which is sweeter than glucose.

Most synthetic sweeteners have been discovered when chemists have accidentally tasted chemicals made for other purposes. Synthetic sweeteners are taken in small amounts especially by people trying to cut the quantity of energy foods in their diet.

Chemical formulas of two sweeteners. Saccharin is 300 times sweeter than sucrose when equal quantities are compared.

saccharin

cyclamate

Cyclamates are banned in the US and UK because some people metabolize the sweetener to another chemical that causes bladder cancer if fed in large doses to rats.

Aspartame is an artificial sweetener that is about 200 times sweeter than *sucrose*. It consists of the methyl *ester* of a dipeptide consisting of two *amino acids* linked by a *peptide* bond.

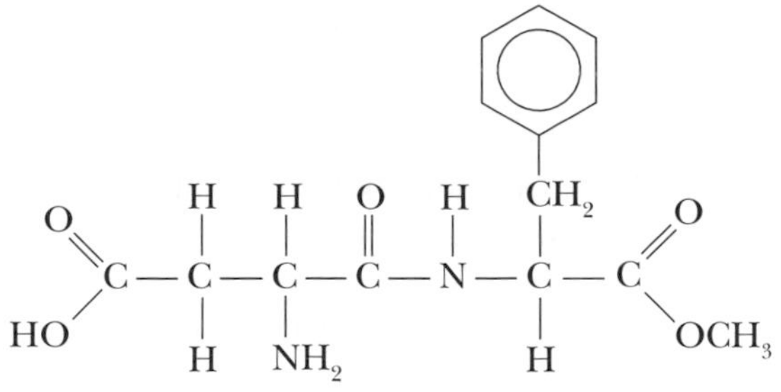

Structure of aspartame

aspartame

Aspartame has no aftertaste but cannot be used in cooking because *hydrolysis* on heating destroys its sweetness. There is a warning on the labels of soft drinks and other foods sweetened with aspartame that they contain a source of phenylalanine. This can harm some people with a genetic disorder. Hydrolysis of aspartame produces phenylalanine.

synthesis: a process of making compounds from simpler starting materials. Synthesis puts things together. It is the opposite of analysis, which takes things apart to see what they are made of.

The Haber process is an example of synthesis: two elements (nitrogen and hydrogen) combine to make a compound (ammonia). This is the method of *ammonia manufacture* on a large scale in industry.

Synthesis of more complex molecules often takes several reaction steps.

system: a term used in *thermochemistry* to describe the material or mixture of chemicals being studied. Everything around "the system" is "the surroundings," which includes the apparatus with maybe a waterbath, the air in the laboratory – in theory everything else in the universe.

An open system can exchange energy and matter with its surrounding. Most chemical reactions in laboratories take place in open systems.

An isolated, or closed, system cannot exchange energy or matter with its surroundings. A mixture of chemicals in a vacuum flask with a stopper comes close to being an isolated system.

temperature effect on equilibria: the shift in the position of equilibrium that happens when the temperature changes. The effect depends on the *enthalpy change* for the reaction. *Le Chatelier's principle* predicts that raising the temperature makes the equilibrium shift in the direction that is endothermic. In *sulfuric acid manufacture*, for example, raising the temperature lowers the percentage of sulfur dioxide at equilibrium.

$$2SO_2(g) + O_2(g) \rightleftharpoons 2SO_3(g) \qquad \Delta H = -98 \text{ kJ mol}^{-1}$$

The equilibrium shifts to the left as the temperature rises because this is the direction in which the reaction is endothermic.

These shifts happen because equilibrium constants vary with temperature.

$$K_p = \frac{p_{SO_3}^{2}}{p_{SO_2}^{2} p_{O_2}}$$

At 500 K, $K_p = 2.5 \times 10^{10}$ atm^{-1}, but at 700 K, $K_p = 3.0 \times 10^4$ atm^{-1}. The value of the equilibrium constant falls as the temperature rises. With a smaller value of K_p the proportion of $SO_3(g)$ falls while the proportions of $SO_2(g)$ and $O_2(g)$ rise at equilibrium.

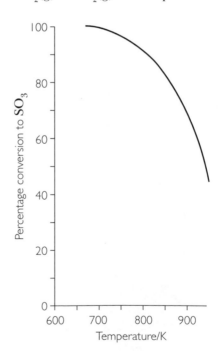

Effect of rising temperature on the equilibrium between SO_2, O_2 and SO_3

temperature effects on reaction rates: see *activation energy* and *Arrhenius equation*.

teratogens: substances that may cause harm to an unborn child if inhaled, swallowed or absorbed through the skin of the mother.

termination: a step in a *free-radical chain reaction* that tends to stop the process by removing free radicals. In a termination step two free radicals combine to form a molecule.

tertiary organic compounds: see *primary, secondary and tertiary organic compounds.*

theoretical yield: see *yield calculations.*

thermal decomposition is a reaction in which a compound decomposes on heating. An important example for industry and agriculture is the thermal decomposition of *calcium carbonate* (limestone):

$$CaCO_3(s) \longrightarrow CaO(s) + CO_2(g)$$

Sometimes heating causes decomposition because a compound is stable at room temperature but becomes unstable at a higher temperature. This is the case with the calcium carbonate and the other carbonates of *group 2* metals.

Sometimes heating causes decomposition of a compound that is unstable at room temperature but does not decompose because the rate of reaction is so slow. This is true of the *nitrogen oxides*, which, at room temperature, are examples of unstable but *inert chemicals*. They all tend to decompose into nitrogen and oxygen but they do so only on heating.

thermal dissociation: a reversible process that splits a compound into fragments as the temperature rises, but re-forms the starting material on cooling.

The brown gas that forms on heating some metal *nitrates* contains an equilibrium mixture of N_2O_4 and NO_2.

$$N_2O_4 \rightleftharpoons 2NO_2$$
colorless   brown

The mixture darkens on heating as more colorless N_2O_4 dissociates into NO_2, which is brown. The color fades on cooling as N_2O_4 reforms.

thermit reaction: a highly *exothermic reaction* use for welding rails and in some incendiary devices. The reaction is similar to the process for chromium extraction but operates on a smaller scale. A magnesium fuse heats and sets off the reaction in a mixture of iron(III) oxide and aluminum. The aluminum reduces the oxide to a glowing mass of molten iron.

$$Fe_2O_3(s) + 2Al(s) \longrightarrow 2Fe(s) + Al_2O_3(s)$$

thermochemistry is the study of energy changes during chemical reactions, including *enthalpy changes, free energy changes* and *entropy* changes. It is a major part of chemical thermodynamics. Thermochemistry is important for theory because it helps chemists to explain the *stability of compounds* and to predict the likely direction of chemical change. With the help of thermochemistry, chemists can decide on the *feasibility* of reactions.

Practically, thermochemistry is important because of the significance of:

- calculating the energy from burning fuels
- keeping large-scale reactions under control in the *chemical industry*
- estimating the impact of energy changes in the environment.

Thermochemistry was developed mainly in the nineteenth and early twentieth centuries.

Antoine Lavoisier (1743–1794): the French chemist who not only pioneered the oxygen theory of burning but also used *calorimeters* to measure energy changes on burning.

Germain Hess (1802–1850): the chemist who was born in Switzerland but moved with his parents to Russia. He studied the heating effect of chemical reactions and demonstrated the importance of the law that is named after him (see *Hess's law*).

Marcellin Berthelot (1827–1907): the French chemist who studied the heating effect of reactions. He concluded that reactions tend to go in the direction that is exothermic. Chemists today still use this idea though they know that it is not always the case (see *feasibility* of reactions).

Josiah Gibbs (1839–1903): the US chemist who devised the quantity *free energy* as a means for predicting the feasibility of reactions.

Ludwig Boltzman (1844–1906): the Austrian physicist who was the first person to explain the laws of thermodynamics in terms of the behavior of atoms and molecules in motion *(kinetic theory)*. He showed how to calculate the distribution of energies for the molecules in a gas molecule (the *Maxwell–Boltzman distribution*). He also showed that the *entropy* of a *system* is determined by the number of ways the particles can be arranged and share the energy of the system.

$$S = k \ln W$$

where S is the entropy of the system, k the Boltzman constant and $\ln W$ the natural logarithm of the number of ways of arranging the particles and energy in the system.

Henri Le Chatelier (1850–1936): the French chemist who proposed *Le Chatelier's principle*, which describes how equilibrium systems shift in response to temperature (and pressure) changes.

Walther Nernst (1864–1941): the German chemist who proposed the third law of thermodynamics, which states that the entropy of perfectly ordered crystals is zero at absolute zero.

thermodynamic control operates where there is a choice of possible products and the main product is the one that is most stable (according to thermodynamics). This contrasts with *kinetic control*, which operates when the main product is the one that forms fastest.

thermodynamics: see *thermodynamics (laws of)* and *thermochemistry*.

thermodynamics (laws of): the laws that govern energy transfers and the direction of change. The laws originally grew out of the study of heating, mechanical working and steam engines. They have now been given a molecular interpretation that makes them applicable to chemical systems.

The first law of thermodynamics says that the total quantity of energy for a system and its surroundings is the same before and after any change. In other words, energy cannot be created or destroyed. This is the law of conservation of energy. Chemists are interested in energy transfers:

- by heating, as energy flows from a higher to a lower temperature
- by working, as a system expands or contracts against atmospheric pressure
- by the flow of an electric current
- by the absorption or emission of radiation.

The value of the first law of thermodynamics is that it provides a check that all energy transfers have been accounted for.

The second law of thermodynamics shows which changes can take place (see *feasibility*). The law states that a change tends to happen if the total entropy of the system plus the surroundings increases. The *entropy* change, ΔS_{total}, is positive. Chemists often find it more convenient to work with *free energy changes*. The rule is that a process tends to happen if the free energy change, ΔG, is negative.

Thermodynamics indicate the possible direction of change but say nothing about the rate of change. A reaction that tends to happen may in practice be so slow that it is kinetically inert.

thermoplastic polymers are solid when cold but they soften and become *plastic* on warming so that they can be molded. Most *addition polymers* are thermoplastics. They consist of long-chain molecules with no cross-linking.

Thermoplastics such as polythene, polypropene and PVC are supplied by the chemical industry as small chips or as powders that can be melted and forced under pressure into closed molds. Plastic buckets, crates, combs and many other articles are made by this process of injection molding.

Thermoplastics can also be extruded by squeezing the heat-softened material through a die to create a continuous strip with a constant cross section. This is the technique for making auto trim, draft seal, curtain track and pipes.

Extrusion through the fine holes of a spinneret converts a thermoplastic such as nylon into *fibers*. Cold-drawing the fibers by stretching them when they are cold lines up the molecules and increases the tensile *strength*.

thermosetting polymers are *resins* that set to strong, stiff material once they have been heated in a mold. Heating *cross-links* the polymer chains with strong covalent bonds. Once formed, a thermosetting *plastic* cannot be melted again.

Bakelite is a cross-linked thermoset made from phenol and methanal (formaldehyde).

Cooking pan handles and electrical fittings are made from thermosets because these plastics do not melt on heating and are electrical insulators.

thin-layer chromatography (tlc) is a type of *chromatography* in which the stationary phase is a thin layer of a solid supported on a glass or plastic plate while the mobile phase is a liquid. The rate at which a sample moves up a tlc plate depends on the *equilibrium* between *adsorption* on the solid and solution in the solvent. The position of equilibrium varies from one compound to another so the components of a mixture separate.

Thin-layer chromatography is quick and cheap. Only a very small sample is needed. The technique is widely used both in research laboratories and in industry. It can be used quickly to check that a chemical reaction is going as expected and making the required product. After an attempt has been made to purify a chemical, tlc can show whether or not all the impurities have been removed.

Colored compounds are easy to see on a tlc plate. However, the technique is often used with colorless compounds as well. A quick way of finding the position of colorless organic spots is to stand the plate in a covered beaker with iodine crystals. The iodine vapor stains the spots.

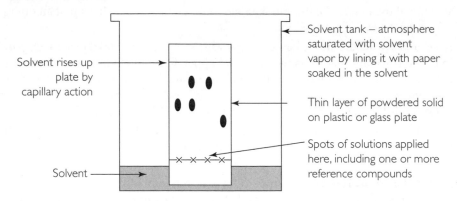

Solvent rises up plate by capillary action

Solvent tank – atmosphere saturated with solvent vapor by lining it with paper soaked in the solvent

Thin layer of powdered solid on plastic or glass plate

Spots of solutions applied here, including one or more reference compounds

Solvent

Apparatus for thin-layer chromatography

An alternative is to use a tlc plate impregnated with a fluorescent chemical. Under a UV lamp the whole plate glows, except in the areas where organic compounds absorb radiation, so that they show up as dark spots.

R_f values can be used to record the distances moved by chemicals in a mixture relative to the distance moved by the solvent.

thio compounds: sulfur compounds with similar formulas and structures to equivalent oxygen compounds. The thiosulfate ion, $S_2O_3^{2-}$, for example, can be thought of as a sulfate ion, SO_4^{2-}, with one oxygen atom replaced by a sulfur atom.

$$S_2O_3^{2-}$$

thiosulfate

$$\begin{array}{c} H_2N \\ \\ H_2N \end{array}\!\!\!\!C\!=\!S$$

thiourea

$$C_2H_5SH$$

ethanthiol

Examples of thio compounds with their oxygen equivalents

$$SO_4^{2-}$$

sulfate

$$\begin{array}{c} H_2N \\ \\ H_2N \end{array}\!\!\!\!C\!=\!O$$

urea

$$C_2H_5OH$$

ethanol

Oxygen and sulfur are in the same group of the *periodic table* with the same number of electrons in the outer shells of their atoms. They therefore form compounds with similar formulas and structures.

tin (Sn) is a shiny metal with a long history. Tin was valued as an ingredient of a range of *alloys* including pewter (with antimony), solder (with lead) and *bronze* (with copper). The main use of tin today is for coating the steel for tin cans. The layer of tin stops the iron corroding. Tin's Sn^{2+} ions are not toxic. Small traces of dissolved tin contribute to the characteristic taste of some tinned foods such as canned fruit and tomatoes.

At room temperature tin has a metallic structure but below the *transition temperature* 13.2°C the stable form is gray tin, which has the diamond structure.

above 13.2°C

gray tin $\rightleftharpoons$ metallic tin

below 13.2°C

It takes a long time for atoms in a solid to rearrange themselves. So metallic tin has to stay cold for a long time before it shows the symptoms of "tin plague" as it gradually alters to the crumbly, brittle, gray form.

Tin, with the *electron configuration* $[Kr]4d^{10}5s^25p^2$, comes below germanium but above lead in *group 4* of the periodic table.

titanium (Ti) is a very strong metal that is much less dense than steel. It melts at the very high temperature of 1675°C. It does not corrode because, like *aluminum*, it is protected by a thin layer of oxide on the surface of the metal. The difficulties of titanium extraction mean that the metal is not as widely used as might be expected considering its properties.

Titanium is a *d-block element* with the *electron configuration* $[Ar]3d^24s^2$. Titanium forms compounds in the +2, +3 and +4 states but only the +4 state is common. Titanium(IV) chloride is a colorless liquid formed as an intermediate in *titanium extraction* and in the manufacture of *titanium(IV) oxide*.

Smoke grenades produce dense clouds of titanium(IV) oxide by the rapid *hydrolysis* of titanium(IV) chloride.

titanium extraction: a process for extracting the metal from its ores, which are rutile (TiO_2) and ilmenite ($FeTiO_3$). Titanium is the fourth most abundant metal in the Earth's crust and it would be more widely used if the methods of extraction were less difficult and expensive. In theory it should be possible to extract titanium from its oxide with carbon but in practice some of the titanium reacts with carbon forming carbides, which make the metal brittle.

After the ore has been purified it is heated with carbon in a stream of chlorine gas at about 1100 K.

$$2TiO_2 + 2Cl_2 + 2C \longrightarrow TiCl_4 + 2CO_2$$

The titanium(IV) chloride condenses as a liquid that can be purified by *fractional distillation*.

In most countries, the preferred *reducing agent* for producing titanium from its chloride is magnesium. In the UK, sodium is the reducing agent. Either way, the production is a *batch process*.

In the UK method, titanium chloride passes into a reactor containing molten sodium at 800 K in an inert argon atmosphere. Exactly the right amount of the chloride is added to react with all the sodium. The reaction is exothermic and so the temperature rises.

$$TiCl_4 + 4Na \longrightarrow Ti + 4NaCl$$

The reactor is kept hot for about two days then it is removed from the furnace and allowed to cool. The solid product is crushed and *leached* with dilute hydrochloric acid, which dissolves the sodium chloride, leaving the titanium metal that is then washed and dried.

Titanium is used mainly to make aircraft engines and airframes. Other major uses are the production components of chemical plants such as *heat exchangers*.

titanium(IV) oxide is a brilliant white pigment. It has two crystalline forms: anatase and rutile (see *rutile structure*). Millions of tonnes of titanium(IV) oxide are made each year. The main use of the pigment is in *paint* but it is also a surface coating for paper, a filler in plastics and an ingredient of cosmetics and toothpaste. The oxide makes a good white pigment because it has a very high refractive index but absorbs almost no light in the visible part of the spectrum. When ground to a fine powder it is both intensely white and very opaque so as a pigment it has excellent covering power. The oxide is also inert and nontoxic, which is why it has replaced lead oxide in many applications.

There are two processes for producing titanium(IV) oxide from ilmenite: the long established sulfate process and the newer chloride process.

titration: an analytical technique for finding the concentrations of solutions and to investigate the amounts of chemicals involved in reactions. Titrations are widely used because they are quick, convenient, accurate and easy to automate.

The procedure only gives accurate results if the reaction is rapid and is exactly as described by the chemical equation. So long as these conditions apply, titrations can be used to study *acid–base*, *redox*, *precipitation* and *complex-forming* reactions.

The measured volume of the unknown is transferred to a flask with a *pipette*, then the standard solution is added carefully from a *burette*. The *end point* is determined by adding a few drops of an indicator or by using an instrument such as a pH meter, a *colorimeter* or a conductivity meter.

Sometimes no indicator is needed because the excess reagent itself produces a permanent color change at the end point. This happens in *potassium manganate(VII)* titrations.

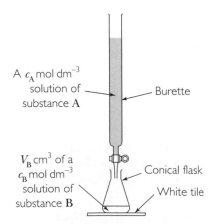

A c_A mol dm^{-3} solution of substance A — Burette

V_B cm^3 of a c_B mol dm^{-3} solution of substance B — Conical flask — White tile

Apparatus for a titration

The diagram shows the apparatus for a titration involving a solution A that reacts with solution B. Suppose the equation for the reaction takes the form:

$$n_A A + n_B B \longrightarrow \text{products}$$

which means that n_A moles of A reacts with n_B moles of B.

In the laboratory volumes of solutions are normally measured in cm^3 but they should be converted to dm^3 in calculations so that they are consistent with the units used to measure concentrations. (1 dm^3 = 1000 cm^3)

The concentration of B in the flask is c_B mol dm^{-3} and its volume is V_B dm^3.

The concentration of A in the burette is c_A mol dm^{-3}. V_A dm^3 of the solution A are added until the indicator shows that the end point has been reached.

The amount of B in the flask at the start = $V_B \times c_B$ mol

The amount of A added from the burette = $V_A \times c_A$ mol

The ratio of these amounts must be the same as the ratio of the amounts shown in the equation:

$$\frac{V_A \times c_A}{V_B \times c_B} = \frac{n_A}{n_B}$$

In any titration, all but one of the values in this formula are known. The one unknown is determined from the results.

(See *acid–base titrations* and *iodine–thiosulfate titrations* and *complex-forming titrations* for worked examples.)

Tollens reagent is a test reagent used to distinguish *aldehydes* from *ketones*. Warming Tollens reagent with an aldehyde produces a precipitate of silver, which coats clean glass with a shiny layer of silver so that it acts like a mirror.

The reagent consists of an alkaline solution of diamminesilver(I) ions, $[Ag(NH_3)_2]^+$. Aldehydes reduce the silver ions to metallic silver. Ketones do not react.

toughness: a property of materials that measures how much energy is needed to break them. Tough materials are hard to break. Metals and polymers are tough. Ceramics and glass are not tough – they are brittle.

toxic substances are labeled with the skull and cross-bones hazard warning sign because they can lead to serious, acute or chronic health risks or even death. Toxic substances can cause harm if inhaled, swallowed or absorbed through skin.

Toxic substances include poisons, *carcinogens*, *mutagens* and *teratogens*.

trace elements: the micronutrients that plants need in small amounts from the soil. Examples are cobalt (Co^{2+}), copper (Cu^{2+}), iron (Fe^{2+} or Fe^{3+}), manganese (Mn^{2+}) and zinc (Zn^{2+}). Plants need these nutrients in much smaller amounts than the nitrogen, phosphorus and potassium supplied by NPK *fertilizers*.

tracers: chemicals used to keep track of chemicals in the environment, in living organisms, in a chemical process or in many other circumstances where chemicals are on the move. The tracer is chosen so that it does not interfere with the changes to be studied. For this reason radioactive isotopes are often chosen as tracers because they are chemically identical with the substances being tracked but easily detected from the alpha, beta or gamma particles emitted during radioactive decay. Examples of radioactive tracers include the use of:

- iodine-131 to study the behavior of the thyroid gland
- hydrogen-3 (*tritium*) to investigate the metabolism of drugs in the human body

- phosphorus-32 to explore the uptake of phosphate fertilizers from the soil by plants.

transition metals are *d-block elements* that have partially filled *d*-energy levels in one or more of their *oxidation states*. In the *d*-block series from scandium to zinc this definition includes all of the metals except for the first and the last. Scandium, $[Ar]3d^14s^2$, is excluded because it only forms compounds in the +3 state and it loses all its three outer electrons when it forms a 3+ ion. *Zinc*, $[Ar]3d^{10}4s^2$, is excluded because all its compounds are in the +2 state. Losing two electrons gives an ion Zn^{2+} with the electron configuration $[Ar]3d^{10}$ in which all the *d*-energy levels are full.

Transition metals share a number of common features. They:

- are *metals* with useful mechanical properties and high melting points
- form compounds in more than one oxidation state
- form *colored compounds*
- form a variety of *complex ions*
- act as *catalysts* either as metals or as compounds.

Many transition metal salts are *paramagnetic* because of the presence of unpaired electrons in the partially filled inner *d*-energy levels.

				+7					
			+6						
		+5							
	+4	+4		+4					
+3	+3	+3	+3		+3	+3			
				+2	+2	+2	+2	+2	+2
								+1	
Sc	Ti	V	Cr	Mn	Fe	Co	Ni	Cu	Zn

Main oxidation states of the elements Sc to Zn. Note that scandium and zinc form ions only in one state.

The chemistries of *titanium, vanadium, chromium, manganese, cobalt, iron* and *copper* provide many examples of these features.

transition state: the state of the reacting atoms, molecules or ions when they are at the top of the *activation energy* barrier for a reaction step. Transition states exist for such a brief moment that they cannot be detected or isolated, unlike the *intermediates in reactions* formed between two steps.

The combination of reacting atoms, molecules or ions in a transition state is sometimes called an *activated complex* (see figure).

transition temperature: the temperature at which two *allotropes* of an element are in equilibrium. One form is stable below this temperature, the other is stable above the transition temperature. (See *tin* and *enantiotropy.*)

transmittance measures the extent to which a sample in a spectrometer absorbs radiation at a particular wavelength. Printouts from some spectrometers show transmittance on one axis.

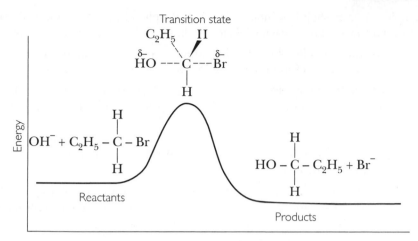

Transition state

Transition state: *energy changes during a reaction with a one-step mechanism showing the transition state*

Transmittance, *T*, is defined as the ratio of the intensity of the radiation leaving the sample, *I*, to the intensity of the radiation entering the sample, I_0.

$$T = \frac{I}{I_0}$$

For a particular wavelength of radiation, transmittance is low when a sample absorbs strongly. It is 100% if the sample does not absorb at all.

Transmittance is a useful term but not so useful as *absorbance.* The advantage of absorbance is that it is proportional to the concentration of a sample in solution.

triglycerides are *esters* of *fatty acids* with glycerol (propan-1,2,3-triol), which is an alcohol with three hydroxyl groups. Animal *fats* and *vegetable oils* are examples of triglycerides. Hydrolysis of triglycerides produces *soap.*

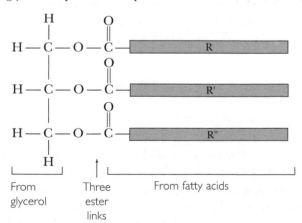

General structure of a triglyceride. In natural fats and vegetable oils, R, R′ and R″ may all be the same or they may be different.

From glycerol

Three ester links

From fatty acids

tri-iodide ion: the ion that forms when *iodine* dissolves in aqueous potassium iodide.

$$I_2(s) + I^-(aq) \rightleftharpoons I_3^-(aq)$$

Iodine is only very slightly soluble in water. It dissolves in potassium iodide solution because it forms $I_3^-(aq)$. A reagent labeled "iodine solution" is normally $I_2(s)$ in $KI(aq)$.

The $I_3^-(aq)$ ion is a yellow-brown color, which explains why aqueous iodine looks quite different from a solution of iodine in a *nonpolar solvent* such as hexane.

tri-iodomethane reaction: a reaction that produces tri-iodomethane (iodoform) from a compound containing either a CH_3C— group or a CH_3C— group.

The reaction conditions are to warm a drop of the compound with a solution of iodine in sodium hydroxide.

The tri-iodomethane reaction is used as a test for the presence of a methyl group next to a hydroxyl group, or a carbonyl group, in an organic molecule. If the result of the test is positive, iodoform appears as a pale yellow precipitate.

The reaction takes place in three steps for an alcohol or two steps for a carbonyl compound. The first step, oxidation to a carbonyl group, is not necessary for a carbonyl compound.

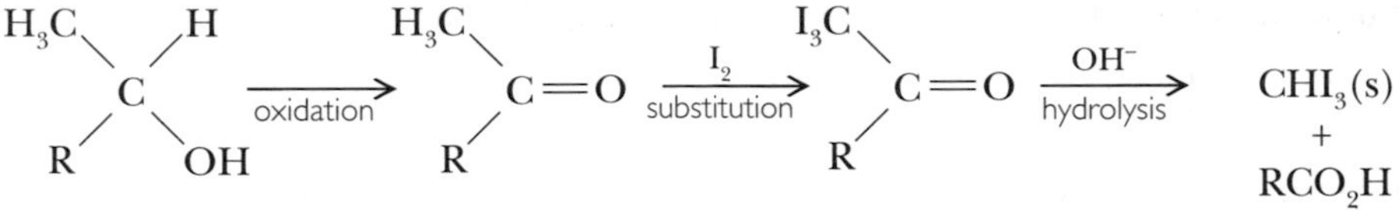

Equations for the tri-iodomethane reaction

Chlorine and bromine in alkali react in a similar way to produce trichloromethane (chloroform) and tribromomethane (bromoform).

trioxygen is the systematic name for *ozone*.

triple bond: three covalent bonds between two atoms as in *nitrogen, alkynes* and the cyanide ion. With three electron pairs involved in the bonding there is a region of high electron density between two atoms joined by a triple bond.

Examples of molecules with triple bonds

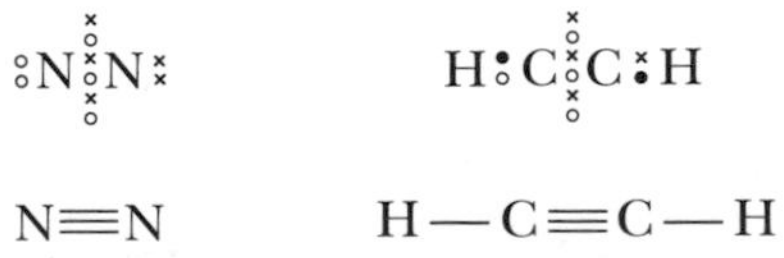

$$N \equiv N \qquad H-C \equiv C-H$$

The molecular orbital model for a triple bond shows that one of the bonds is a normal *sigma bond* while the other two bonds are *pi bonds*.

triple point: the unique combination of temperature and pressure at which the solid, liquid and gaseous forms of a substance are at equilibrium. The triple point of water is at 611 N m^{-2} (0.006 atmospheres) and 273.16 K (0.01°C).

Three lines meet at the triple point on a *phase* diagram for a pure substance.

tritium is the *isotope* of hydrogen, $_1^3H$. It is radioactive and emits beta particles with a *half-life* of 12.3 years.

ultraviolet radiation, UV, is *electromagnetic radiation* with shorter *wavelengths* (and so higher frequencies) than the violet end of the visible spectrum. The energy of UV photons is high enough to excite the electrons in covalent bonds to higher energy levels. Excited molecules may then split into atoms (dissociate). Thus UV light can start chemical reactions by forming *free radicals*.

Ozone forms in the upper *atmosphere* (the stratosphere) where UV light from the Sun shines on oxygen molecules, splitting them into oxygen atoms, which then combine with other oxygen molecules to make ozone. In the laboratory, UV light can start the reaction of chlorine with alkanes by splitting chlorine molecules into chlorine atoms. This is an example of a *free-radical chain reaction*.

ultraviolet (UV) spectroscopy is particularly useful for studying colorless organic molecules with unsaturated *functional groups* such as $C = C$ and $C = O$. The molecules absorb UV radiation at frequencies that excite shared electrons in double bonds. A UV spectrometer records the extent to which samples absorb UV radiation across a range of *wavelengths*.

UV spectrometers make it possible to extend the techniques of *colorimetry* to colorless compounds. In the *pharmaceutical industry*, for example, scientists use UV spectroscopy to check that medicines contain the correct amounts of drugs and that the products do not deteriorate in storage.

unit cell: the smallest unit of a crystal structure which, when piled up in three dimensions, gives a whole crystal.

The unit cell of a cubic crystal is a minute cube. An atom or ion inside the unit cell belongs entirely to that cell. An atom or ion at a corner is shared between the eight unit cells that meet in three dimensions at a corner.

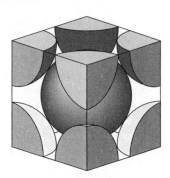

Unit cell for the cesium chloride structure

The unit cell for cesium chloride consists of one cesium ion and $8 \times \frac{1}{8}$ of a chloride ion. So the composition of the unit cell still corresponds to the empirical formula CsCl. (See *cesium chloride structure*.)

universal indicator is a mixture of several *acid–base indicators* that changes color through the colors of the spectrum from red to indigo as the *pH* rises from 1 to 11. Narrower range indicators are also available that cover a smaller range of pH.

unleaded gasoline is *gasoline* formulated for modern motor vehicles by adding chemicals other than tetraethyl lead to raise the octane number.

There are two main objections to adding lead compounds to gasoline. The first is that lead compounds are *toxic* and harmful, especially to young children, when released into the air from vehicle exhausts. The second is that lead compounds "poison" the catalysts in *catalytic converters*.

Instead of lead compounds, gasoline is blended with oxygen compounds that may be *alcohols* or *ethers*. The commonly used additive is MTBE (initials based on the traditional name of the compound, methyl tertiary-butyl ether).

unsaturated compounds are compounds containing one or more double or triple bonds between atoms in their molecules. The term is often applied to the *hydrocarbons alkenes* and *alkynes*, which typically undergo addition reactions. The term is also commonly used to describe unsaturated *fats* and *fatty acids*, which have double $C = C$ bonds in their hydrocarbon side chains.

urea is a white crystalline solid. It is an end product of the metabolism of proteins, and excreted as a waste product in urine.

Structure of urea. Urea is a diamide of carbonic acid so it has the alternative name carbamide.

Urea slowly hydrolyzes, releasing ammonia, making it a useful nitrogen *fertilizer*. It is manufactured by the reverse process of heating ammonia and carbon dioxide under pressure.

Urea and methanal (formaldehyde) are used to manufacture a range of *thermosetting polymers* that are used as adhesives in chipboard, for producing electric outlets and plugs.

urease is an *enzyme* (found in plant materials such as water melon seeds) that catalyzes the breakdown of *urea* to ammonia by *hydrolysis*.

Urease illustrates that enzymes are very specific. They will act only on particular molecules. Urease breaks down urea but has little or no effect on molecules with similar structures, such as *N*-methylurea, ethanamide or thiourea.

N-methylurea   ethanamide   thiourea

Molecules not affected by urease

vacuum distillation: distillation under reduced pressure that makes it possible to distill liquids with very high boiling points below the temperatures at which they start to decompose. Lowering the pressure lowers the temperature at which liquids boil.

The process is used in oil refineries to separate the *hydrocarbons* in the residue from fractional distillation at atmospheric pressure. Vacuum distillation separates lubricating oils and waxes from other hydrocarbons fed to the plant for *catalytic cracking*.

Vacuum distillation is also used on a small scale to separate products of synthesis that would decompose if heated to their boiling points at atmospheric pressure.

vacuum filtration: see *Buchner flask and funnel*.

valence theory covers all the theories of chemical bonding. The outer electrons of an atom are its valence electrons, which take part in chemical bonding. Electron transfer leads to *ionic bonding* or electrovalence. Electron sharing leads to *covalent bonding*.

Chemists use a variety of ways of describing or predicting the number of bonds formed by the atoms of an element. These include:

- the pattern of charges on the ions in a group of elements – *group 2* metals, for example, form 2+ ions
- the number of covalent bonds that atoms normally form in molecules – carbon, 4; hydrogen, 1; oxygen, 2; nitrogen, 3; and the halogens, 1
- the *coordination numbers* in crystals and *complex ions* – giving the numbers of nearest neighbors bonded to an atom
- *oxidation numbers* – which provide a formal code for keeping track of the numbers of electrons taking part in bonding.

None of these are rigid guidelines and there are exceptions to all the rules.

Some writers refer to the VSEPR theory, which is short for the "valence shell electron pair repulsion theory." This theory helps to predict the *shapes of molecules* from the number of bonding pairs of electrons and lone pairs of electrons in the outer (valence) shell of the central atoms in a molecule.

van der Waals forces are weak *intermolecular forces*. Chemists disagree about the meaning of the term. All agree to include *dispersion forces* in the definition; these are the weakest attractions between nonpolar molecules.

Differences arise about the attractions between permanent dipoles, and dipole-induced dipole attractions. Some people include them as van der Waals forces but others do not.

Hydrogen bonding, the strongest kind of intermolecular attraction, is generally excluded from the definition of van der Waals forces.

Johannes van der Waals (1837–1923) was a Dutch scientist who studied *real gases* and their deviations from *ideal gas* behavior. He devised a modified gas equation for real gases. His equation includes two correction factors based on *kinetic theory* – one to allow for the existence of intermolecular forces and the other to allow for the fact that gas molecules have a definite volume.

van der Waals radius: the effective radius of an atom when held in contact with another atom by weak *intermolecular forces.*

Atoms do not have a definite size. The apparent size of an atom depends on the way it is bonded to a neighboring atom, so the *ionic radius* and the *covalent radius* of an atom are not the same. Generally, the stronger the bonding, the smaller the effective radius. Intermolecular forces are much weaker than covalent bonds, so van der Waals radii are relatively large.

van der Waals radii determine the effective size of a molecule as it bumps into other molecules in a liquid or gas, and when it packs together with other molecules in a solid.

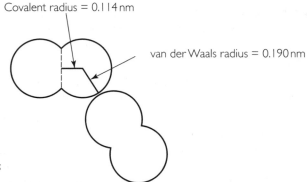

Covalent radius = 0.114 nm

van der Waals radius = 0.190 nm

Covalent and van der Waals
radii for bromine

vanadium (V) is a *d-block* metal with the *electron configuration* $[Ar]3d^34s^1$. The metal is used to make alloy *steels* that are strong and *tough*, making them suitable for machine tools and parts of engines. Vanadium is a typical *transition metal*: it forms colored compounds in several *oxidation states*, it forms *complex ions* and has compounds that can be used as *catalysts* such as vanadium(V) oxide in *sulfuric acid manufacture.*

In solution, vanadium forms ions in the +2, +3, +4 and +5 oxidation states. The +5 state is available as the yellow solid ammonium vanadate(V).

+5 ⌐	VO_2^+ (aq)	yellow
+4 ⊣	VO^{2+} (aq)	blue
+3 ⊣	V^{3+} (aq)	green
+2 ⊣	V^{2+} (aq)	violet
+1 ⊣		
0 ⌐	V	

Oxidation states of vanadium showing the
colors of the ions

Standard electrode potentials help to identify reducing agents to reduce vanadium(V) to the succession of lower states. (See *electrochemical series*.)

Iodide ions, for example, reduce vanadium(V) to vanadium(IV).

$$E^{\ominus}/V$$

$$I_2(aq) + 2e^- \rightleftharpoons 2I^- \qquad\qquad +0.54$$

$$VO_2^+(aq) + 2H^+(aq) + e^- \rightleftharpoons VO^{2+}(aq) + H_2O(l) \qquad +1.00$$

Half-equations and electrode potentials for the reduction of vanadium(V) to vanadium(IV)

Zinc in acid will reduce vanadium(V) all the way to vanadium(II). The $V^{2+}(aq)$ ion is a strong *reducing agent*.

vapor pressure is the pressure of a vapor in a closed container with its own liquid. The full term is either:

- **equilibrium vapor pressure** – a reminder that in a closed container a liquid and vapor reach a state of dynamic equilibrium; or
- **saturated vapor pressure** – a reminder that the atmosphere above the liquid holds as much vapor as it can at equilibrium at a particular temperature.

The vapor pressure of a liquid rises as the temperature rises. A liquid starts *boiling* when its vapor pressure equals the external pressure.

A solution of an involatile substance in a liquid has a lower vapor pressure than the pure solvent. This follows from *Raoult's law*. Because of this effect the solution has to be hotter before it starts to boil at a given pressure. Dissolving an involatile salt in water raises its boiling point slightly.

The lowering of vapor pressure depends on the mole fraction of dissolved particles. It does not depend on the chemical nature of the particles. (So the lowering of vapor pressure is an example of a *colligative property*.)

vapors are gases formed by evaporation of substances that are usually liquids or solids at room temperature. So chemists talk about oxygen gas but water vapor.

Vapors are easily condensed by cooling or increasing the pressure because of relatively strong *intermolecular forces*. Vapors therefore tend to deviate markedly from *ideal gas* behavior.

Physicists sometimes broaden the definition of a vapor to include gases such as butane, ammonia and carbon dioxide, which can be liquefied at room temperature by increasing the pressure. (These are gases below their *critical temperature*.)

vat dyes: *dyes* such as indigo that are insoluble in water but can be converted to a soluble form to dye cloth. Chemical reduction converts indigo to an almost colorless, water-soluble dye that soaks into cloth such as denim for jeans. Oxidation converts indigo back to the insoluble blue form, which precipitates in the fibers.

vegetable oils are liquids extracted from plants that are esters of fatty acids with propan-1,2,3-triol. They are *triglycerides* that belong to the broad class of *lipids*. The *fatty acids* in vegetable oils contain a higher proportion of *unsaturated* fatty acids than animal *fats*. Examples of vegetable oils are olive oil, sunflower oil and palm oil.

Triglycerides with unsaturated fatty acids have a less regular structure than saturated fats. The molecules do not pack together so easily to make solids, so they have lower melting points and have to be cooler before they solidify.

Hydrogenation is used industrially to add hydrogen to double bonds in oils. This produces saturated fats that are solid at room temperature. The process is sometimes called "hardening," and the *catalyst* used is finely divided nickel. Nondairy spreads are a blend of vegetable oils with a high enough proportion of partly hardened fats to make the product a spreadable solid.

vibration of bonds: the springlike vibration of covalent bonds as they bend and stretch. A vibrating *polar covalent bond* is an oscillating *dipole* that can interact with infrared radiation. Like other energy changes involving atoms and electrons, energy is gained or lost in fixed amounts (quanta). According to *quantum theory*, $E = h\nu$. It turns out that the sizes of the energy jumps for vibrating bonds correspond to frequencies in the infrared region of the spectrum. Each type of bond has a particular value for the energy jumps so it absorbs at a characteristic frequency. This is the basis of *infrared spectroscopy*.

viscous liquids are thick and sticky liquids such as syrups and treacle. Some liquids are viscous because they consist of a tangled mass of long-chain molecules. Lubricants from crude oil consist of *hydrocarbons* with chains of over 25 carbon atoms in the molecules.

Other liquids are viscous because of extensive *hydrogen bonding*. Propan-1,2,3-triol (glycerol) is a sticky liquid for this reason. It flows much more slowly than propan-1-ol. Hydrogen bonding also contributes to the high viscosity of concentrated solutions of sugars in water.

On an atomic scale toffee and *glass* have disordered structures like liquids. They are, however, so viscous and flow so slowly that they are effectively solids.

visible radiation is *electromagnetic radiation* with *wavelengths* between 400 nm and 700 nm. This band of radiation is visible because it can bring about reversible chemical changes in cells of the retina. These chemical changes lead to electrical impulses in the nerve cells of the eye, interpreted in the brain as colors. (See figure.)

vitamins are a group of chemically unrelated organic compounds that are needed in very small amounts in the diet for healthy growth and body functions. The B vitamins and vitamin C are soluble in water. The other vitamins are fat soluble.

The B vitamins are essential for the activity of some *enzymes*. Lack of vitamin B_{12} leads to a form of anemia. One of the triumphs of twentieth-century organic chemistry has been the analysis and total synthesis of vitamin B_{12}. Vitamin C is *ascorbic acid*.

volatile substances are solids or liquids that evaporate easily. A volatile substance easily turns into a *vapor*. *Iodine* is an example of a volatile solid. Most familiar volatile compounds are molecular liquids at room temperature. Examples are water, hexane, ethanol and *propanone*.

Visible radiation: the chemical starting point for vision. A photon of light is absorbed by electrons in a double bond of retinal. Exciting the electron allows rotation about the bond converting the cis isomer to the trans isomer. The resulting chemical changes set off an electrical signal in a nerve cell of the retina.

The equilibrium *vapor pressure* of a substance is a measure of its volatility at a particular temperature.

Makers of *perfumes* take advantage of differences in volatility.

voltmeters measure the potential difference between two points in a circuit in volts. Chemists use voltmeters to measure the *emfs* of electrochemical cells.

The value needed when determining *standard electrode potentials* is the emf when no current is flowing between the electrodes. These values are measured with an accurate voltmeter with a very high internal resistance.

volume is the amount of space taken up by a sample. The *SI unit* of volume is the cubic meter (m^3). Gas volumes are converted to m^3 before substituting values into the *ideal gas* equation.

Chemists generally measure volumes in cubic decimeters (dm^3, formerly in *liters*) or cubic centimeters (cm^3).

Measuring volumes of gases and solutions is an essential part of quantitative chemistry. (See *gas volume calculations, molar volume* and *volumetric analysis.*)

volumetric analysis is a very important aspect of quantitative analysis because volumetric methods can be very accurate. An analyst can measure the volume of the liquid from a burette to the nearest $0.01\ cm^3$. If the total volume is $25\ cm^3$, this represents an uncertainty of only 1 part in 2500. Most of the methods recommended for measuring amounts of drugs and medicines are based on volumetric techniques (see *titration*).

wastes are unwanted solids, liquids and gases discarded from homes, commerce, industry, agriculture and the public services. Chemists have a role to play in the management of waste by:

- **reduction** – the chemical industry has an extensive program of research and development to introduce new processes to give higher yields and create less waste so that the disposal problem is cut
- **reuse** – this depends on solvents and detergents that help to clean products or containers so that they can be used again
- **recycling** – a variety of physical and chemical processes recover metals, polymers and other materials so that they can be added to the raw materials used to make new products; in some industries, such as the steel industry, recycling is well established
- **recovery** – this includes the recovery of the energy resources tied up in materials; incineration not only disposes of the waste but provides energy to generate electricity. However, incineration can be hazardous if not carried out at a high enough temperature to ensure that harmful chemicals do not escape into the air.

It is also important to understand the chemistry of the changes that happen when waste is dumped in landfill sites. Anaerobic processes lead to the formation of biogas, which is hazardous unless collected and burnt as a fuel. Water percolating through rotting landfill can dissolve harmful chemicals such as the ions of toxic metals, which can be recovered from the liquids by ion exchange if waste disposal is managed correctly.

water (H_2O) is a familiar liquid with remarkable properties. Despite the small size of its molecules, water is a liquid at room temperature because of *hydrogen bonding*. The O—H bonds in water molecules are highly polar because oxygen is so *electronegative*. Water molecules too are polar because they are not linear, owing to the two *lone pairs of electrons* that help to determine the *shape of the molecule*.

As a *polar solvent*, water can hydrate ions and dissolve salts. Water can also dissolve some organic compounds because it can form hydrogen bonds with hydroxyl groups in alcohols, sugars or carboxylic acids and with — NH_2 groups in amines.

Water plays an important part in many reactions:

- **hydration reactions** – water forms aquo *complex ions* with metal ions
- **acid–base reactions** – water acts as both an acid and as a base because it is an *amphoteric compound*
- **redox reactions** – reactive metals such as *group 1* elements reduce the hydrogen in water to hydrogen gas
- **hydrolysis reactions** – this includes the hydrolysis of *nonmetal* chlorides and of *organic compounds* such as esters (*acid catalysis* or *base catalysis*).

water cycle: the cycling of water in the environment between the oceans, the atmosphere and the crust of the Earth.

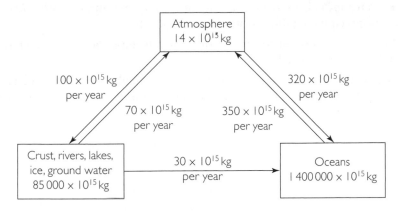

The water cycle, showing the amounts of water in each of the three main reservoirs and the flows between them

The specific latent heat of vaporization of water is relatively large so huge amounts of energy are transferred by the water cycle. Energy from the Sun evaporates water in the tropics. Winds carry the warm moist air to higher latitudes where the energy is released as the water condenses and falls as rain.

water of crystallization: water molecules that make up part of the crystal structure of a compound. There are five molecules of water of crystallization for each $CuSO_4$ unit in blue copper(II) sulfate crystals, $CuSO_4.5H_2O$. The full systematic name for copper sulfate is tetraaquocopper(II) tetraoxosulfate(VI)-1-water, which shows that four of the water molecules hydrate the copper ions; the fifth water molecule forms *hydrogen bonds* with sulfate ions.

Heating hydrated crystals drives off the water as steam, leaving the anhydrous salt. Stronger heating may then lead to other changes (see *nitrates*, for example). Other salts with water of crystallization include:

- hydrated sodium carbonate (sal soda crystals) – $Na_2CO_3.10H_2O$
- hydrated magnesium sulfate (Epsom salts) – $MgSO_4.7H_2O$.

water treatment provides water for drinking, water for industry and water for medical uses.

Some of the chemical processes used to provide water for homes include:

- **coagulation** – the addition of aluminum(III) or iron(III) salts to add positive ions that help to coagulate negatively charged *colloid* particles so that finely divided solids clump together and settle out
- **adsorption** – removing organic chemicals on the surface of activated *charcoal*
- **disinfection** – use of chemicals such as *chlorine* to kill microorganisms that might otherwise cause disease; increasingly *ozone* or *ultraviolet radiation* are being used in place of chlorine because they are less hazardous and do not react with organic impurities to produce chlorinated hydrocarbons, which may be harmful

- **water softening** – removing calcium and magnesium ions from *hard water* by precipitating them as insoluble carbonates.

Ion exchange can remove all the ions from water to give very pure water needed industrially and commercially.

wavelength: the distance between the peaks (or troughs) of a wave. Wavelengths of *electromagnetic radiation* vary from about 1000 m for radio waves down to about 10^{-3} nm for gamma rays.

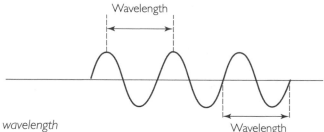

A waveform showing the wavelength

Light in the visible region of the spectrum has wavelengths from about 400 nm at the blue end to 700 nm at the red end.

All electromagnetic radiation travels at the same speed, c, in a vacuum. The *frequency*, ν, wavelength, λ, and speed are related by $c = \nu\lambda$.

waxes are materials that can be molded when warm but are hard and brittle when cold. They are insoluble in water and water repellent. Waxes are ingredients of polishes and are used to waterproof cloth and leather. Natural waxes such as beeswax from honeycombs and lanolin from wool are esters of *fatty acids* with alcohols with only one hydroxyl group. This distinguishes them from *fats* and *vegetable oils*. The formula of beeswax is $C_{15}H_{31}CO_2C_{30}H_{61}$. Carnauba wax, an ingredient of polishes, varnishes and lipstick, comes from the leaves of a palm tree that grows in Brazil.

Hydrocarbon wax, such as the kerosene wax used for candles, is one of the products from the *vacuum distillation* of the residue from the *fractional distillation* of crude oil.

The chemical industry makes synthetic waxes by polymerizing *epoxyethane*.

weak acids are only slightly ionized when they dissolve in water. In a 0.1 mol dm^{-3} solution of ethanoic acid, for example, only about one in a hundred molecules reacts with water to form *oxonium ions*. The more dilute the solution, the greater the degree of ionization. The *acid dissociation constant*, K_a, measures the strength of an *acid*.

Note the important distinction between strength and concentration. Strength is the extent of ionization. *Concentration* is the amount of acid present in mol dm^{-3}. Note that it takes as much sodium hydroxide to neutralize 25 cm^3 of 0.1 mol dm^{-3} of a weak acid (such as ethanoic acid) as it does to neutralize 25 cm^3 of 0.1 mol dm^{-3} of a strong acid such a hydrochloric acid.

Measuring the *pH* of a solution of acid is not enough to show whether or not the acid is strong or weak. A solution of an acid with pH 4 might be a very dilute solution of a strong acid or a concentrated solution of a weak acid.

The salts made from weak acids and strong bases are alkaline in solution (see *hydrolysis of salts*).

weak bases are only slightly ionized when they dissolve in water. In a 0.1 mol dm^{-3} solution of *ammonia*, for example, only about one in a hundred molecules reacts with water to form ammonium ions. The *base dissociation constant, K_b,* measures the strength of a *base*.

As with *weak acids*, it is important to distinguish between strength and concentration.

The salts made from weak bases and strong acids are acidic in solution (see *hydrolysis of salts*).

weathering is a process that breaks down rocks physically and chemically. Physical weathering cracks rocks into smaller fragments, increasing the surface area exposed to chemical attack. During chemical weathering rocks react with water, oxygen and carbon dioxide. The types of reaction involved are *hydrolysis* and *oxidation*. Weathering releases soluble ions that plants need for growth. It also forms insoluble *clay minerals*.

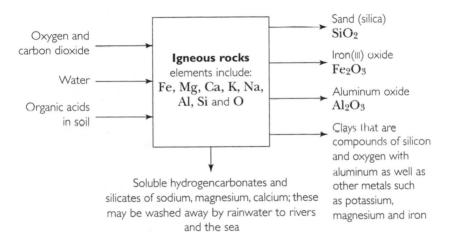

Products of weathering igneous rocks

weight, measured in newtons (N), is the pull of the Earth's gravity on an object. A laboratory balance responds to weight but is calibrated to give readings in grams or kilograms that measure the mass of the sample. On the surface of the Earth the pull of the Earth is proportional to mass.

weight $=$ mass $\times g$ where the constant $g = 9.8 \text{ N kg}^{-1}$

So chemists use "weighing" to determine the mass of a sample. This accounts for the continuing use of concentration units such as weight/volume percent (w/v), which should strictly be the mass/volume percent.

wetting happens when water spreads out and covers the surface of a solid. Water wets clean glassware but breaks up into separate droplets on greasy glassware. This makes it easy to see if pipettes and burettes are clean.

Wetting is an important step in getting materials clean but water does not wet fabrics that are contaminated with greasy dirt. One of the functions of *surfactants* in *detergents* is to lower the *surface tension* of water so that it will wet dirty surfaces.

Surfactants are added to pesticides so that when sprayed onto plants the solution spreads over the leaves and is absorbed. With no surfactant the solution would break up into tiny droplets on the surface of the leaves.

word equation: an equation that describes a chemical change in words instead of symbols. Writing word equations identifies the reactants and products, so it is a useful first step toward *balanced equations* with symbols. For example:

> sodium + water $\longrightarrow$ sodium hydroxide + hydrogen

Word equations are useful as ways of summarizing general patterns of behavior. For example:

> acidic oxide + water $\longrightarrow$ oxoacid
>
> carboxylic acid + alcohol $\longrightarrow$ ester + water

wurtzite structure: the structure of one of the crystalline forms of zinc sulfide (ZnS, which can also crystallize with the *zinc blende structure*). In the wurtzite structure the sulfide ions are in a hexagonal *close-packed* array with zinc ions in half the tetrahedral holes.

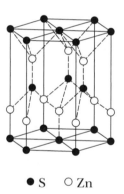

Tetrahedral holes are spaces in a close-packed structure enclosed by four atoms. Octahedral holes are spaces enclosed by six atoms (the centers of these atoms are at the corners of a regular octahedron).

● S   ○ Zn

Each zinc ion is surrounded tetrahedrally by four sulfide ions. Similarly, each sulfide ion has four zinc ions as nearest neighbors. So the *coordination number* for both elements is 4.

Other compounds with this structure are ZnO, AlN, BeO and SiC.

X-ray crystallography is a technique used to determine *crystal structures* by interpreting the diffraction patterns formed when *X-rays* are scattered by the electrons of atoms in crystalline solids. Interference between the scattered X-rays produces patterns recorded on photographic film. Crystallographers have developed techniques for interpreting the patterns so that they can determine:

- the arrangements of atoms, molecules or ions in crystals
- the sizes of atoms and ions
- the *shapes of molecules.*

Since X-rays are scattered by electrons it is possible to draw up *electron density maps* from the diffraction patterns showing the positions of atoms. Small atoms such as hydrogen with few electrons do not show up well, so their position can be hard to determine.

The use of X-ray crystallography to determine the structures of crystals was pioneered by Lawrence Bragg (1890–1971), who developed the theory, and his father William Bragg (1862–1942), who designed the instruments.

Among the great successes of X-ray crystallography were the determination of the structures of:

- the protein α-helix by Linus Pauling in 1951
- myoglobin and hemoglobin by John Kendrew and Max Perutz in the 1950s
- DNA by Rosalind Franklin, Maurice Wilkins, Francis Crick and James Watson in 1953
- vitamin B_{12} by Dorothy Hodgkin in 1956.

X-rays are electromagnetic radiation with very short wavelengths in the region 1×10^{-9} m (1 nm). X-rays have wavelengths of the same order of magnitude as the lengths of atomic bonds. As a result it is possible to use X-ray diffraction to investigate *crystal structures* and the *shapes of molecules* including long-chain molecules such as *proteins* and *nucleic acids.*

xenon (Xe) is a noble gas that makes up less than 0.1% of the atmosphere. Xenon is separated from liquid air by *fractional distillation.* For a long time chemists thought that the noble gas elements of *group 8* were completely unreactive so they called them the "inert gases." This changed in 1962 when the British-born Canadian chemist Neil Bartlett was working on the properties of platinum fluorides. Based on the accidental discovery that platinum(VI) hexafluoride could combine with oxygen molecules, he used values for *ionization energies* to predict the formation of a compound between platinum(VI) hexafluoride and xenon and produced the yellow solid $Xe^+PtF_6^-$. Since then chemists have produced a range of xenon compounds but only with the most reactive elements oxygen and fluorine. Examples are XeF_2, XeF_4 and XeF_6.

yield calculations are used to assess the efficiency of a chemical synthesis. A perfectly efficient reaction would convert all of the starting material to the desired product. This would give a 100% yield.

Few reactions are completely efficient and most reactions, especially organic reactions, give lower yields. There are several reasons why the overall yield may be low:

- the reaction may be incomplete (perhaps because it is slow or because it reaches an equilibrium state) so that a proportion of the starting chemicals fails to react
- there may be side reactions producing by-products instead of the required chemical
- recovery of all the product from the reaction mixture is usually impossible
- some of the product is usually lost during transfer of the chemicals from one container to another when the product is separated and purified.

The theoretical yield is the mass of product assuming that the reaction goes according to the chemical equation and the synthesis is 100% efficient.

The actual yield is the mass of product obtained.

The percentage yield is given by this relationship:

$$\text{percentage yield} = \frac{\text{actual yield}}{\text{theoretical yield}} \times 100\%$$

Worked example:

What is the theoretical yield of aspirin when 15.5 g 2-hydroxybenzoic acid reacts with excess ethanoic anhydride? What is the percentage yield if the actual yield of aspirin is 7.25 g?

Notes on the method

Start by writing the equation for the reaction. This need not be the full balanced equation so long as the equation includes the *limiting reactant* and the product.

Since the ethanoic anhydride is in excess the limiting reactant is the 2-hydroxybenzoic acid. This means that the ethanoic anhydride can be ignored during the calculation.

Answer

The equation:

$$\underset{\text{ethanoic}}{\overset{\text{anhydride}}{\longrightarrow}}$$

The molar mass of 2-hydroxybenzoic acid, $C_7H_6O_3 = 138$ g mol^{-1}

The amount of 2-hydroxybenzoic acid at the start of the synthesis

$$= \frac{15.5 \text{ g}}{138 \text{ g}} = 0.112 \text{ mol}$$

1 mol of the acid produces 1 mol of aspirin.

The molar mass of aspirin, $C_9H_8O_4 = 180 \text{ g mol}^{-1}$

The theoretical yield of aspirin $= 0.112 \text{ mol} \times 180 \text{ g mol}^{-1} = 20.2 \text{ g}$

Percentage yield $= \frac{7.25 \text{ g}}{20.2 \text{ g}} \times 100\% = 35.9\%$

Z

zeolites are sodium aluminum *silicates* in which the three-dimensional structures of the silicon and oxygen atoms form tunnels and cavities into which ions and small molecules and ions can fit.

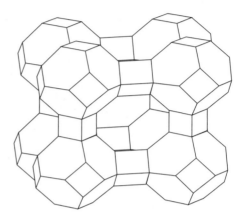

Model of a zeolite crystal structure

Synthetic zeolites can make excellent *catalysts* because they can be developed with active sites to favor the required reactions by acting on molecules with particular shapes and sizes.

Natural and synthetic zeolites are *ion exchangers*. Permutit is a synthetic zeolite used to soften water by swapping the calcium ions in *hard water* with sodium ions. For this reason many washing powders contain up to 25% of zeolites.

Zeolites can be very good drying agents; they can absorb water molecules selectively because the water molecules fit into the holes in their crystal structure.

Similarly, zeolites can acts as "molecular sieves," sorting out molecules by size. Some zeolites will absorb nitrogen from the air while letting oxygen pass through. This is one of the methods used to separate *oxygen* from the *air* on a large scale. Once the zeolite is saturated with nitrogen it can easily be regenerated by lowering the pressure and releasing the waste nitrogen back into the air.

zero-order reaction: a reaction is zero order with respect to a reactant if the rate of reaction is unaffected by changes in the concentration of that reactant. The concentration term for this reactant is raised to the power zero in the *rate equation*.

$$\text{Rate} = k[X]^0 = k \text{ (a constant)} \quad \text{since } [X]^0 = 1$$

(Any term raised to the power zero equals 1.)

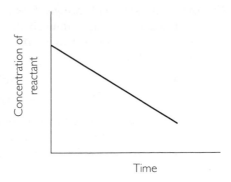

Variation of concentration of a reactant plotted against time for a zero-order reaction. The gradient of this graph measures the rate of reaction. The gradient is a constant so the rate stays the same even though the concentration of the reactant is falling.

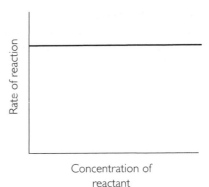

Variation of reaction rate with concentration for a zero-order reaction

The rate of reaction of iodine with propanone in the presence of acid is zero order with respect to iodine.

Rate = k[propanone]^1[hydrogen ion]^1[iodine]^0

Ziegler–Natta catalysts speed up the polymerization of *alkenes* such as ethene and propene, making it possible to produce *addition polymers* at relatively low temperatures and pressures. Ziegler–Natta catalysts are made from titanium(IV) chloride and aluminum alkyls (such as triethyl aluminum) in a hydrocarbon solvent.

There is little chain branching in the polymers, so the poly(ethene) chains formed by this method can pack closely together, forming the high-density form of poly(ethene). Poly(propene) made with a Ziegler–Natta catalyst has a regular arrangement of the methyl side chains. The molecular structure is *isotactic*. The long chains can pack together more closely because of this regularity, allowing stronger *intermolecular forces* between the chains and a strong polymer with the ability to form useful fibers.

zinc (Zn) is a metallic element; the last in the *d-block* series of the fourth row of the periodic table. Zinc is not normally regarded as a *transition metal* because both its atoms, [Ar]$3d^{10}4s^2$ and its Zn^{2+} ions, [Ar]$3d^{10}$, have full *d*-subshells.

Zinc and its compounds show few of the typical properties of transition metals. The metal has lower melting and boiling points than transition elements. It forms only one series of compounds in the +2 oxidation state and these compounds are colorless. Examples are zinc oxide (ZnO), zinc chloride ($ZnCl_2$) and zinc sulfate ($ZnSO_4$).

Zinc oxide and hydroxide are *amphoteric,* which means that they will dissolve in both acids and alkalis. Adding sodium hydroxide to a solution of zinc ions produces a white precipitate of the hydroxide that will redissolve either on adding acid or on adding excess alkali.

$$Zn(OH)_2(s) + 2H^+(aq) \longrightarrow Zn^{2+}(aq) + 2H_2O(l)$$

$$Zn(OH)_2(s) + 2OH^-(aq) \longrightarrow [Zn(OH)_4]^{2-}(aq)$$

Zinc resembles transition elements by forming *complex ions* such as $[Zn(NH_3)_4]^{2+}(aq)$. Adding ammonia solution to a solution of zinc ions produces a white precipitate of the hydroxide that redissolves in excess ammonia solution as the *ammine* complex forms.

$$Zn(OH)_2(s) + 4NH_3(aq) \longrightarrow [Zn(NH_3)_4]^{2+}(aq) + 2OH^-(aq)$$

zinc blende structure: the structure of one of the crystalline forms of zinc sulfide (ZnS), which can also crystallize with the *wurtzite structure.* In the zinc blende structure each zinc ion is surrounded tetrahedrally by four sulfide ions. Similarly each sulfide ion has four zinc ions as nearest neighbors. So the *coordination number* for both elements is 4.

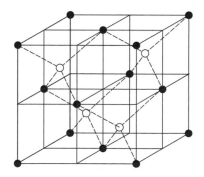

A representation of the zinc blende structure showing the cubic unit cell with sulfide ions in a face-centered cubic arrangement

Other compounds with this structure are BeS, MnS, SiC.

zinc extraction produces the metal from one of its sulfide ores. The most abundant ore is sphalerite (zinc blende), consisting of zinc sulfide (ZnS). *Froth flotation* is commonly used to concentrate the ore, which is then roasted by heating in air to convert the sulfide to zinc oxide.

$$2ZnS(s) + 3O_2(g) \longrightarrow 2ZnO(s) + 2SO_2(g)$$

A neighboring plant converts the sulfur dioxide into sulfuric acid for making fertilizers.

Most zinc (around 80%) is obtained from the oxide by *electrolysis* of zinc sulfate solution made by dissolving the zinc oxide in sulfuric acid. The electrolysis cells have lead *anodes* and aluminum *cathodes.* Zinc forms at the cathodes.

$$Zn^{2+}(aq) + 2e^- \longrightarrow Zn(s)$$

At regular intervals the zinc is stripped from the anodes, melted and cast into ingots with metal at least 99.96% pure.

Oxygen bubbles off from the anodes where sulfuric acid reforms. Recycled acid is reused to dissolve more zinc oxide.

The main use for zinc is for protective coatings such as the layer on galvanized steel. It is also used to make *alloys*.

zone refining is a method of purifying crystals of *semiconductors* such as *silicon*. The process makes very high purity silicon suitable for the electronics industry.

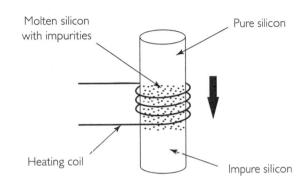

Molten silicon with impurities

Pure silicon

Heating coil

Impure silicon

Zone refining to purify a crystal of silicon. The impurities are more soluble in the molten silicon. The moving heater carries the impurities to one end as the molten zone moves along the rod.

zwitterions are ions with both a positive and a negative charge. *Amino acids* form zwitterions when the amino groups accept protons and the acid groups give away protons.

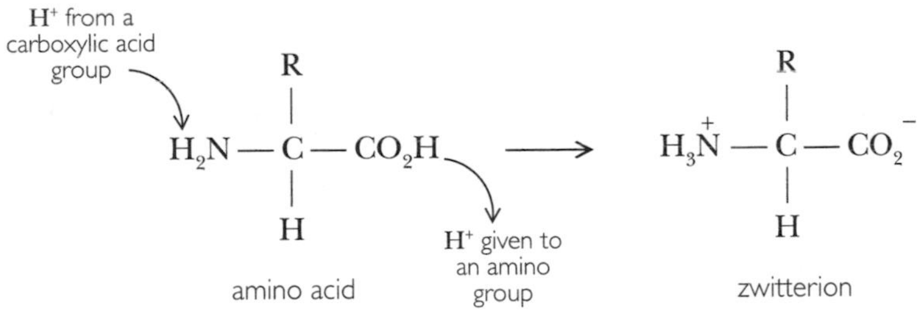

H^+ from a carboxylic acid group

$$H_2N - \underset{\underset{H}{|}}{\overset{\overset{R}{|}}{C}} - CO_2H \longrightarrow H_3\overset{+}{N} - \underset{\underset{H}{|}}{\overset{\overset{R}{|}}{C}} - CO_2^-$$

amino acid

H^+ given to an amino group

zwitterion

An amino acid forming a zwitterion

In crystals and in aqueous solution, amino acids exist largely as zwitterions.

zymase is a group of *enzymes* in yeast that catalyze the *fermentation* of glucose *sugar* to carbon dioxide and the alcohol, ethanol.